Handbook of
FRAUDS, SCAMS, and
SWINDLES

Failures of Ethics in Leadership

Handbook of
FRAUDS, SCAMS, and SWINDLES

Failures of Ethics in Leadership

Edited by
Serge Matulich, Ph.D., CPA
David M. Currie, Ph.D.

CRC Press
Taylor & Francis Group
Boca Raton   London   New York

CRC Press is an imprint of the
Taylor & Francis Group, an **informa** business

CRC Press
Taylor & Francis Group
6000 Broken Sound Parkway NW, Suite 300
Boca Raton, FL 33487-2742

© 2009 by Taylor & Francis Group, LLC
CRC Press is an imprint of Taylor & Francis Group, an Informa business

Library of Congress Cataloging-in-Publication Data

Handbook of frauds, scams, and swindles : failures of ethics in leadership / editors, Serge Matulich and David M. Currie.
   p. cm.
Includes bibliographical references and index.
ISBN 978-1-4200-7285-3 (alk. paper)
   1. Fraud--United States--Case studies. 2. Swindlers and swindling--United States--Case studies. I. Matulich, Serge. II. Currie, David M., 1946- III. Series.

HV6695.H28 2008
364.16'30973--dc22   2008013344

Visit the Taylor & Francis Web site at
http://www.taylorandfrancis.com

and the CRC Press Web site at
http://www.crcpress.com

Dedication

For Anna, Ashley, Andrew, and Sarah

David M. Currie

Contents

Section III   SCIENTIFIC CHEATING

Section IV   SLIMY BEHAVIOR

Preface

This book results from two forces: our careers-long interest in scams and frauds and our desire to create a collection of articles that could be understood by the lay reader. Serge Matulich's interest in scams began while he was a graduate student at the University of California, Berkeley, and continued throughout his academic career as a professor of accounting. As an undergraduate at the University of Florida, David Currie's interest was stimulated when a professor assigned Norman C. Miller's classic, *The Great Salad Oil Swindle*. Once they became colleagues at the Crummer Graduate School of Business at Rollins College in Winter Park, Florida, Matulich and Currie exchanged stories of famous frauds such as Billy Sol Estes, the Mississippi Bubble, and Charles Ponzi. Of course, the field became much more fertile during the 1990s as scandal after scandal rocked not only the United States but also countries throughout the world.

The second force resulted from the overwhelming number of books that have been written about some of the more famous frauds of the distant and more recent past. Although the books almost always are well written, they frequently require technical knowledge that the average reader probably does not possess. We think it is possible to understand what transpired without getting into the mind-numbing arcane language of finance, accounting, law, or other disciplines. Therefore, we asked contributors to write stories in a narrative format rather than a format suitable for an academic journal; this turned out to be a challenge for professors.

We also found that creating a more readable text allows us to note similarities internationally, across disciplines, and through the years. People of one generation frequently think that a scam affecting them is original. In fact, scams have occurred throughout history, throughout the world, and in many fields other than business. That is why this book contains chapters from authors around the world and from a variety of fields.

We are grateful to many people who participated in creating the book. William Bostock, Paul Esqueda, Christopher Ferguson, Richard Fern, James Johnson, Mathew Lee, Fannie Malone, Ashley Mattison, Erika Matulich, Roger Mayer, Robert McMurrian, Philip Murray, Stuart Omans, Jamie Pleasant, James Rovira, Nancy Shelton, Kevin Sisemore, Bahram Soltani, Lindsey Steding, and Nayelah Sultan reviewed the chapters. We are also grateful to Dean Craig McAllaster and Susan Bach, both of the Crummer

Graduate School of Business, for generous financial support. Lynda Boyce of the Crummer School provided valuable technical support. Of course, the book would not have been possible without the contributions of the authors whose stories are included.

Additional material is available from the CRC Web site, www.crcpress. com, on *Handbook of Frauds, Scams, and Swindles: Failures of Ethics in Leadership*. You can also go directly to the Web download site, which is www.crcpress.com/e_products/downloads/default.asp. Teaching notes are available for qualified adopters through CRC academic sales representatives.

The Editors

David M. Currie is professor of finance and economics at the Roy E. Crummer Graduate School of Business, Rollins College, in Winter Park, Florida. He has won awards from national organizations for teaching innovations and from students for the quality of the educational experience. After receiving an undergraduate degree from the University of Florida, Dr. Currie attended the University of Southern California, where he received a PhD. He has published articles and cases in the fields of finance, international education, business management, and ethics. He has been a visiting professor at Groupe HEC in France and a Fulbright scholar in Croatia. Dr. Currie has been an elected official, co-owner of a chain of retail perfume stores, and an examiner for the Georgia Oglethorpe Award process.

Serge Matulich is professor emeritus of accounting at the Roy E. Crummer Graduate School of Business, Rollins College, in Winter Park, Florida. He earned a BS with honors from California State University at Sacramento and his PhD from the University of California at Berkeley. Matulich previously served on the faculties of California State University at Hayward, Indiana University, and Texas Christian University. He also held visiting positions at the University of California at Berkeley and the University of North Texas at Denton. He was a Fulbright fellow at the University of Pula in Croatia and is a certified public accountant.

Dr. Matulich has authored books on financial accounting, managerial accounting, and cost accounting, as well as numerous study guides, technical papers, practice sets, and research papers in academic journals. He has won awards for teaching excellence and for outstanding service. He has extensive business and consulting experience and has served as a director on the boards of several corporations.

Contributors

Brian Ballou
Farmer School of Business
Miami University
Oxford, Ohio

Arnold I. Barkman
Neeley School of Business
Texas Christian University
Fort Worth, Texas

Paul Barnes
Nottingham Business School
Nottingham Trent University
Nottingham, United Kingdom

Jonica L. Burke
Shawnee State University
Portsmouth, Ohio

James Cashell
Farmer School of Business
Miami University
Oxford, Ohio

Dwight V. Denison
Martin School of Public Policy and
  Administration
University of Kentucky
Lexington, Kentucky

Andrew J. Felo
Great Valley School of Graduate
  Professional Studies
The Pennsylvania State University
Philadelphia, Pennsylvania

Christopher J. Ferguson
Texas A&M International University
Laredo, Texas

Richard H. Fern
Eastern Kentucky University
Richmond, Kentucky

Jeannine A. Gailey
Texas Christian University
Fort Worth, Texas

Stephen F. Hallam
College of Business Administration
University of Akron
Akron, Ohio

Dan L. Heitger
Farmer School of Business
Miami University
Oxford, Ohio

Joan Hodowanitz
Signals Intelligence and Electronic Warfare
United States Army, retired

Trish Isaacs
Berea College
Berea, Kentucky

Kevin T. Jackson
Fordham University
New York, New York

Christie W. Johnson
College of Business
Montana State University
Bozeman, Montana

James P. Johnson
Rollins College
Winter Park, Florida

Roland E. Kidwell
Department of Management and Marketing
College of Business
University of Wyoming
Laramie, Wyoming

Patrick Kuhse
Speaker and Business Ethics Consultant

Matthew T. Lee
Center for Conflict Management
University of Akron
Akron, Ohio

Linda M. Leinicke
Illinois State University
Normal, Illinois

Daniel Levy
Bar-Ilan University
Ramat Gan, Israel

Fannie L. Malone
Jesse H. Jones School of Business
Texas Southern University
Houston, Texas

Roger C. Mayer
College of Business Administration
University of Akron
Akron, Ohio

Philip R. Murray
Webber International University
Babson Park, Florida

Joyce A. Ostrosky
Illinois State University
Normal, Illinois

Bonita K. Peterson Kramer
College of Business
Montana State University
Bozeman, Montana

Richard Pitre
Jesse H. Jones School of Business
Texas Southern University
Houston, Texas

Steven Pressman
Monmouth University
West Long Branch, New Jersey

W. Max Rexroad
Illinois State University
Normal, Illinois

Nancy M. Shelton
Valencia Community College
Orlando, Florida

Kevin L. Sisemore
Health Sciences Center
University of Colorado
Denver, Colorado

Steven A. Solieri
Long Island University
Brooklyn, New York *and*
Solieri & Solieri, CPAs, PLLC
New Hyde Park, New York

Bahram Soltani
University of Paris 1-Panthéon Sorbonne
Paris, France

Flora Soltani
Researcher and Consultant

Judith W. Spain
Eastern Kentucky University
Richmond, Kentucky

About the Contributors

Brian Ballou, PhD, is professor of accounting and a codirector of the Center for Governance, Risk Management, and Reporting at the Farmer School of Business at Miami University in Oxford, Ohio. His teaching and research emphasize the areas of governance, risk management, and reporting.

Arnold I. Barkman, PhD, CMA, CPA, is associate professor of accounting at the Neeley School of Business at Texas Christian University in Fort Worth, Texas.

Paul Barnes is professor of fraud risk management and director of the International Fraud Prevention Research Center at Nottingham Business School, which is part of Nottingham Trent University in the United Kingdom.

Jonica L. Burke is a PhD candidate in public administration at the University of Kentucky. She currently serves as university registrar at Shawnee State University in Portsmouth, Ohio.

James Cashell, PhD, is the C. Rollin Niswonger Professor of Accounting at the Farmer School of Business at Miami University in Oxford, Ohio. His teaching and research emphasize the areas of auditing and fraud.

Dwight V. Denison, PhD, is associate professor of public and nonprofit finance at the Martin School of Public Policy and Administration at the University of Kentucky. His research and teaching interests include cash management, tax administration, bond finance, and not-for-profit finance.

Andrew J. Felo, CMA, CFM, is associate professor of accounting at The Pennsylvania State University Great Valley School of Graduate Professional Studies. His work has been published in *Accounting and the Public Interest, Journal of Forensic Accounting, Research on Accounting Ethics, Journal of Business Ethics, Strategic Finance,* and *Decision Support Systems.*

Christopher J. Ferguson, PhD, is assistant professor of clinical and forensic psychology at Texas A&M International University. His research focuses mainly on violent criminal behavior as well as positive and negative effects of playing violent video games.

Richard H. Fern, DBA, CPA, is professor of accounting at Eastern Kentucky University, Richmond, Kentucky. He has published a variety of research articles and case studies related to financial accounting and reporting.

Jeannine A. Gailey, PhD, is assistant professor of criminal justice at Texas Christian University in Fort Worth, Texas. Her research addresses the areas of deviance, masculinities, and public perceptions of organizational wrongdoing.

Stephen F. Hallam is the former dean and currently professor of management at the College of Business Administration at the University of Akron in Akron, Ohio. He is coauthor of a recent book on making a difference in one's life and is a frequent speaker on the topic of business ethics.

Dan L. Heitger, PhD, is associate professor of accounting and a codirector of the Center for Governance, Risk Management, and Reporting at the Farmer School of Business at Miami University in Oxford, Ohio. His teaching and research emphasize the areas of governance, risk management, and reporting.

Joan Hodowanitz, MBA, retired from the United States Army in 1998 after a 23-year career in signals intelligence and electronic warfare. She is a life member of the Veterans of Foreign Wars, Disabled American Veterans, and several other military and nonmilitary organizations.

Trish Isaacs, PhD, CPA, is W. George Matton Professor of Business at Berea College in Berea, Kentucky, where she teaches accounting. She also serves as chair of the Department of Economics and Business.

Kevin T. Jackson, JD, PhD, is professor of legal and ethical studies at Fordham University in New York City. He is the author of *Building Reputational Capital: Strategies for Integrity and Fair Play That Improve the Bottom Line* (Oxford University Press, 2004) and has published numerous articles in academic journals. He frequently gives analyses of legal and ethical issues for the media and has presented seminars on business integrity and leadership for executives, dignitaries, and financial services organizations.

Christie W. Johnson, CPA, MBA, is associate professor of accounting in the College of Business at Montana State University, Bozeman, Montana. She has auditing experience with Haskins & Sells (now Deloitte) in Nebraska and small business consulting experience in Utah and Montana.

James P. Johnson, PhD, is professor of international business at Rollins College, Winter Park, Florida. He has lived and worked in Spain, England, Finland, Yugoslavia, and Mexico.

Roland E. Kidwell, PhD, is associate professor of management in the Department of Management and Marketing in the College of Business at the University of Wyoming. His research interests include family business, franchising, and deviant behavior in the workplace.

Patrick Kuhse is a speaker and consultant on business ethics.

Matthew T. Lee, PhD, is associate professor of sociology and fellow at the Center for Conflict Management at the University of Akron in Akron, Ohio. His book, *Crime on the Border: Immigration and Homicide in Urban Communities,* was published by LFB Scholarly in 2003 and his research focuses on organizational deviance, immigration and crime, and altruism.

Linda M. Leinicke, PhD, CPA, is professor of accounting and director of accounting graduate programs at Illinois State University in Normal, Illinois.

Daniel Levy, PhD, is professor of economics and the director of the Aharon Meir Center for Banking at Bar-Ilan University (Israel) and an adjunct professor of economics at Emory University in Atlanta. He is on the editorial board of *Managerial and Decision Economics* and is a member of the academic advisory committees of Israel's Central Bureau of Statistics and Israel's Ministry of Industry, Trade, and Labor.

Fannie L. Malone, PhD, CPA, is professor of accounting at the Jesse H. Jones School of Business at Texas Southern University in Houston, Texas. She has published and presented in the field of ethics for 15 years.

Roger C. Mayer is professor of management at the University of Akron in Akron, Ohio. He earned his PhD from Purdue University, is a member of the editorial review board of *Academy of Management Journal,* and is considered one of the world's leading scholars on the topic of organizational trust.

Philip R. Murray, PhD, teaches economics at Webber International University in Babson Park, Florida.

Joyce A. Ostrosky, PhD, CPA, is professor of accounting at Illinois State University in Normal, Illinois.

Bonita K. Peterson Kramer, PhD, CPA, CMA, CIA, is professor of accounting in the College of Business at Montana State University, Bozeman, Montana. She has auditing experience with KPMG in Texas and the Montana office of the legislative auditor.

Richard Pitre, PhD, CPA, is professor of accounting at the Jesse H. Jones School of Business at Texas Southern University in Houston, Texas. He teaches contemporary ethics for accountants and is an instructor for one of the Texas State Board of Public Accountancy-approved ethics courses.

Steven Pressman, PhD, is professor of economics and finance at Monmouth University in West Long Branch, New Jersey. He serves as coeditor of the *Review of Political Economy* and as associate editor and book review editor of the *Eastern Economic Journal.* He has published more than 100 articles in refereed journals and as book chapters, and has authored or edited 12 books, including *A New Guide to Post Keynesian Economics* (Routledge, 2001) and the second edition of *50 Major Economists* (Routledge, 2006).

W. Max Rexroad, PhD, CPA, is emeritus professor of accounting at Illinois State University, Normal, Illinois.

Nancy M. Shelton, MS, MBA, graduated from the master of liberal studies program at Rollins College and the master of business administration program at the Roy E. Crummer Graduate School of Business. Originally from Detroit, Michigan, she currently teaches humanities at Valencia Community College in Orlando, Florida.

Kevin L. Sisemore, CFE, teaches fraud examination at the University of Colorado at Denver and at the Health Sciences Center in Denver, Colorado.

Steven A. Solieri, CPA, CMA, CIA, CISA, is assistant professor of accounting and information systems at Long Island University, Brooklyn, New York. He is a member in the CPA firm of Solieri & Solieri, CPAs, PLLC, in New Hyde Park, New York, and Solieri & Solieri, CPAs, PC, in Lake Ariel, Pennsylvania.

Bahram Soltani, PhD, is associate professor of accounting and finance at the University of Paris 1-Panthéon Sorbonne. He has written several books and articles published in English and French. He is the author of *Auditing: An International Approach* (Pearson-Education-Prentice-Hall, 2007) and *Affecting Corporate Governance and Audit Committees in Selected Countries* (The Institute of Internal Auditors Research Foundation, U.S.A., 2005).

Flora Soltani has a PhD in management studies. She is a researcher and consultant and has written several books on organization.

Judith W. Spain, JD, is the MBA director and a professor of business law and ethics at Eastern Kentucky University, Richmond, Kentucky. She has written extensively in the areas of employment law and ethics.

Introduction

Scams and frauds make for enticing plots in movies, books, and TV shows. Reports about them sell newspapers and attract viewers to television newscasts. Often, the focus of these stories is the dollar value of the deception and the lavish lifestyle of the perpetrator. However, attempts to convey the devastation to individuals, businesses, and organizations affected by the treachery of someone's conniving and plotting often fall short.

It is difficult to describe the devastation experienced by a business or organization and its employees, as well as by individuals whose life's work and future plans disappear through the cunning of a scammer. These losses are not only material but also deeply psychological and emotional, leaving lives in ruin. Organizations involved in fraud, either as the victim or the perpetrator, are often destroyed beyond the point of being salvageable.

The chapters of Matulich and Currie's book unfold intriguing stories detailing crafty minds applying what we can only presume are skill and cunning to outwitting others. The editors have engaged numerous authors to share stories of leaders and followers who chose to participate in scams and frauds. The stories are fascinating. I encourage you as readers to find the common threads that connect the stories to see how scams and frauds are repeated under new guises.

Scammers and individuals who engage in fraud often display characteristics commonly attributed to good leaders. These include setting a vision, communicating it clearly, and motivating and developing others to want to follow the person leading. But what if there is a clear vision, but it is devoid of ethical principles? What happens if the motivation is self-aggrandizement or is misguided and ignores moral values and ethical principles? Without ethics—generally referred to as practicing a system of moral values based on principles of good and correct behaviors—leadership is hollow. When leaders appear to have the requisite skills but operate without an ethical foundation, the outcome is likely to create havoc and destruction.

Some academicians may debate whether leadership and ethics can be taught. Others believe that leadership and ethical principles not only must be developed throughout the educational process, but also addressed in all the major institutions in our society. These should be taught in concert, for only through this partnered approach can society expect to develop leaders who do the right things for the right reasons and followers who question leadership devoid of ethical principles.

Susan A. Bach
Executive Director, Center for Leadership Development
Roy E. Crummer Graduate School of Business

Survival of the Fittest and Smartest

I

Scams have been around as long as there have been people to be fooled, and they have occurred throughout the world. A famous nineteenth-century American made a career out of scamming by creating extraordinarily fictitious stories about people (Tom Thumb, Jenny Lind), animals (Jumbo, the elephant), and outright hoaxes (the "Feejee Mermaid"). Scams of this sort were considered normal and frequently were popular.

Sometimes circumstances create an opportunity, if not a necessity, for untruthfulness. Oppressive governments make it unwise or even dangerous to be truthful. One way for a courageous individual to speak out against the government is to create a fictitious person or situation to illustrate a point. This section contains two chapters exploring situations where cheating, plagiarism, or other potentially unethical behavior might be justified.

In "Nature of Honesty," the author explores literary hoaxes, including a hoax perpetrated by one of America's founding fathers. The examples raise the intriguing question of whether a hoax perpetrated in the name of a noble cause can be justified.

People who live in a corrupt society where every aspect of life is under government control sometimes have to adopt unusual methods to survive under the watchful eyes of corrupt politicians. In "Price Adjustments under the Table," you will see that what may be viewed as unethical in one society is considered not only normal but also necessary and a matter of survival in another.

The Nature of Honesty: Exploring Examples of the Literary Hoax in America

1

NANCY M. SHELTON

Contents

Dr. Franklin's Famous Filler

Despite the nation's adamant insistence on honesty in reporting as a direct product of First Amendment protection of freedom of the press, the literary hoax enjoys a long history in American journalism. Possibly the first such case was perpetrated in April 1747 by none other than the revered statesman Dr. Benjamin Franklin, then editor-in-chief of the *Pennsylvania Gazette*.

Merely a few years after a youthful George Washington stood, ax in tremulous hand, regarding the fallen family cherry tree and contemplating the nature of honesty, some combination of social conscience and mischievousness impelled the 41-year-old Franklin to devise what remains one of the most famous American literary shams. He concocted a courtroom speech allegedly delivered by one Polly Baker, the fictional mother of five illegitimate children. In the discourse, supposedly given by a poverty-stricken Polly forced to represent herself before the bench, the defendant admitted to breaking the law against bearing children out of wedlock. As a result, she had twice suffered the penalties of heavy fines and public whipping. However, she said,

> I have brought five fine Children into the World, at the Risque of my Life; I have maintain'd them well by my own Industry, without burthening the Township, & would have done it better, if it had not been for the heavy Charges and Fines I have paid. Can it be a Crime (in the Nature of Things I mean) to add to the King's Subjects, in a new Country, that really wants People? I own

it, I should think it rather a praise-worthy than a punishable Action. (Franklin 1971 [1747], 5)

Polly continued, maintaining that she had never consorted with another woman's husband or young son. She dearly wished to marry, but had received only one proposal and this when she had been a trusting virgin. In her innocence, she not only had lost her virtue, but also had become pregnant. The father had promptly abandoned her and gone on to fame as a magistrate, while she had suffered the particular infamy reserved for fallen women. If, Polly reasoned, her offense was essentially religious in nature, why not leave it to heaven to mete out its eventual retribution? After all, custom forbade a woman to solicit a husband for herself and the law provided none for a woman in Polly's circumstances. When the first duty of nature was to increase and multiply, which Polly had followed without regard to the consequent loss of her own good reputation, she asserted that she deserved not temporal punishment, but rather a statue erected in her honor (Hall 1960, 5–7).

Polly's courtroom saga was published extensively in Great Britain before returning only a few months later to the frontier nation Franklin called home. Surfacing in the *Boston Weekly Post-Boy* on July 20, 1747, the piece traveled from paper to paper, enjoying a life of its own in America. Another 30 years would pass before Franklin confessed to writing Polly's disparaging attack on society's treatment of "ruined women"; the only extant proof of his admission appears in *The Writings of Thomas Jefferson*. In a letter dated 1818, Jefferson quotes an anecdote related by Franklin about a conversation the doctor said had occurred in Paris among the historian Abbé Raynal, Silas Deane of Connecticut, and Franklin at the end of 1777 or the beginning of 1778:

> Raynal provided a meticulous account of Mary Baker's trial in a Connecticut courtroom, for having produced a gaggle of illegitimate offspring. So eloquently did the hapless defendant argue her case that one of her judges rose to the rescue and married her. The story had appeared earlier in Diderot as well, but its inclusion in Raynal's text clinched its validity. Evidently Silas Deane questioned Mary's own legitimacy at dinner one day with the abbé, who briskly defended himself. Deane was mistaken. The story was authentic, protested the gravel-voiced sage. He had documentary evidence. Franklin listened to the debate for some time, silently shaking with laughter, before setting Raynal straight. He had invented Mary himself as filler for his paper in 1746. She was then Polly Baker. At last the ex-Jesuit relented, conceding that he preferred Dr. Franklin's mistruths to anyone else's truths, a statement that fairly summed up Paris's attitude toward the muted propagandist in 1777. From Polly's triumphant European tour Franklin elicited his own moral. What a slippery thing was history! Thirty years had suffered to transform fiction into fact. (Schiff 2005, 83)

Franklin went on to tell Jefferson that he wrote the Polly piece to "fill up vacant columns" in his newspaper; however, over the subsequent years, numerous exhaustive searches of the paper have not been able to confirm that the speech was actually printed in the *Pennsylvania Gazette* (Hall 1960, 80–83). Nevertheless, an unassailable history does exist of the doctor's propensity to use the literary hoax in any number of documented examples. "As a 16-year-old apprentice, he pretended to be a prudish widow named Silence Dogood, and he made a subsequent career of enlightening readers with similar hoaxes such as 'The Trial of Polly Baker' and 'An Edict from the King of Prussia'" (Isaacson 2003, 466).

Jefferson's account of Franklin's confession to the authorship of Polly's speech is accepted as authentic by scholars. There exists no explanation of why the great man perpetrated the scam. However, using this indirect methodology to bring to light the collective plight of the many unfortunate real women on whom Polly was based bears some resemblance in its obliqueness to Franklin's technique of listing the virtues he believed should guide behavior in the area of ethics.

After shunning his father's brand of Christianity, a highly elitist Calvinism, the young Franklin took up Deism. He more or less espoused this philosophy for the rest of his life, but always felt obliged to point out the creed's inadequacies as a code of ethics. According to Tolson,

> Franklin knew that a highly cerebral acknowledgment of the distant, clockmaker God of Deism was no more conducive to ethical behavior than were some of his own deepest instincts. So what did he do? He constructed a rigid—and now famous—system of behavioral self-accounting that would make him not only successful but also a better person. "I made a little Book in which I allotted a Page for each of the Virtues," he wrote in his autobiography. "I rul'd each Page with red Ink, so as to have seven Columns, marking each Column with a Letter for the Day." And for any of the 13 virtues he deemed himself insufficient on any given day—including temperance, industry, and humility—Franklin would ink in a "little black Spot" (2003, 35).

Had Franklin decided, in similar fashion, that his evolving young country, which in 1747 had yet to extricate itself from the grip of British colonialism but was moving inexorably in the direction of independence, possessed a set of laws that, although by and large sufficient, was in need of certain enhancements? He may have thought that a declaration against the unnatural and restrictive legislation regarding procreation outside the accepted state of matrimony, a law that had come straight from the throne of England, at the very least deserved to be examined in the public forum. If so, creating Polly certainly accomplished that aim.

More than two centuries after Franklin's escapade with Polly, a pair of American journalists kept their literary secrets neither as successfully nor as long. In the early 1980s, Janet Cooke of the *Washington Post* and, 15 years later, the *New Republic*'s Stephen Glass found themselves exposed and professionally ruined comparatively soon after publishing fallacious accounts of current affairs.

Janet Cooke Creates "Jimmy's World"

Janet Cooke, who had successfully passed herself off as a magna cum laude Vassar graduate, was working as a reporter for the *Washington Post* when she submitted "Jimmy's World" to her editors in 1981. The attractive young African-American woman's writing had earned glowing appraisals up to this point. The new and ostensibly factual article about an 8-year-old heroin addict interspersed narrative describing Washington D.C. neighborhoods where drug addiction truly was rampant, discourse from sources such as the U.S. Drug Enforcement Agency, and vignettes of what was eventually revealed to be fictional exposition about "Jimmy's" home life. Opportunely timed, concerned with a critical societal issue, and well written, "Jimmy's World" would be awarded a Pulitzer Prize. Early in Cooke's account, the reader learns that

> Jimmy's is a world of hard drugs, fast money and the good life he believes both can bring. Every day, junkies casually buy heroin from Ron, his mother's live-in lover, in the dining room of Jimmy's home. They "cook" it in the kitchen and "fire up" in the bedrooms. And every day, Ron or someone else fires up Jimmy, plunging a needle into his bony arm, sending the fourth grader into a hypnotic nod. (Cooke 1980, A1)

Craftsmanship aside, details that felt a little too patent to the professional discrimination of many of Cooke's colleagues on the *Post* triggered suspicions about the article's authenticity almost immediately.

> Jimmy's mother Andrea accepts her son's habit as a fact of life, although she will not inject the child herself and does not like to see others do it. "I don't really like to see him fire up," she says. "But, you know, I think he would have got into it one day, anyway. Everybody does. When you live in the ghetto, it's all a matter of survival. If he wants to get away from it when he's older, then that's his thing. But right now, things are better for us than they've ever been....Drugs and black folk been together for a very long time. (Cooke 1980, A1)

Later in Cooke's story, she writes:

A fat woman wearing a white uniform and blond wig with a needle jabbed in it like a hatpin totters down the staircase announcing that she is "feeling fine." A teen-age couple drifts through the front door, the girl proudly pulling a syringe of the type used by diabetics from the hip pocket of her Gloria Vanderbilt jeans. "Got me a new one," she says to no one in particular as she and her boyfriend wander off into the kitchen to cook their smack and shoot each other up. (Cooke 1980, A1)

Cooke had inspired an odd mixture of support and resentment among her co-workers since signing on as a reporter at the *Post* in January 1980. Her first byline appeared 2 weeks after she was hired and her first big article, about Washington's crime-infested riot corridor, came out on February 21. By the time "Jimmy's World" was published seven months later, 52 of her stories had made it to print—more than ample justification for descriptions of her as a "self-starter" who "produced" and was a "conspicuous member of the newsroom staff" (Green 1981, A12–15). One colleague described her as "striking, smartly dressed, articulate" and even the *Post*'s executive editor Ben Bradlee said, "She has a dramatic flair." Remarks from Elsa Walsh, who had briefly roomed with Cooke, were less flattering:

"Janet was hard to live with, very high-strung," Walsh recalled. "She bought clothes lavishly. Every day she talked about her ambitions. She had no sense of the past or even the present, except for its consequences for the future. She always looked to the future, and she didn't care about the people she left behind" (Green 1981, A12–15).

Assigned to "District Weekly," Cooke worked under Vivian Aplin-Brownlee, who said of her new reporter: "She was consumed by blind and raw ambition. It was obvious, but it doesn't deny the talent" (Green 1981, A12–15). When Aplin-Brownlee examined Cooke's background material (2 hours of taped interviews and 145 pages of handwritten notes) for a heroin story that she had been assigned, the seasoned journalist immediately saw its potential to become a "Metro" piece. At the time, the "Metro" editor was Bob Woodward, famous as half of the team that broke the Watergate story in 1972.

Cooke's 13½-page rough draft of the story contains exhaustive detail. Although it raised no eyebrows with editors lower in the *Post* hierarchy, "Woodward was to say later that if he had seen the first draft he might have asked questions about the long and seemingly perfect quotations. Woodward never looked at the first rough draft until Cooke's Pulitzer was in question" (Green 1981, A12–15). Woodward did call Cooke in for an interview before the story ran. "He simply wanted to hear her story. 'She was a terrific actress, terrific,' he said. 'She related it all in the most disarming way. It was so personal, so dramatic, so hard in her tummy'" (Green 1981, A12–15).

Held for Sunday publication, "Jimmy's World" ran on September 28 and "the story struck at Washington's heart. The paper had no sooner reached the streets than the *Washington Post*'s telephone switchboard lit up like a space launch control room" (Green 1981, A12–15). Cooke had likely sealed her own fate by appealing so unflinchingly to the sympathy of readers:

> Addicts who have been feeding their habits for 35 years or more are not uncommon in Jimmy's world, and although medical experts say that there is an extremely high risk of his death from an overdose, it is not inconceivable that he will live to reach adulthood. "He might already be close to getting a lethal dose," Dr. Dorynne Czechowisz of the National Institute on Drug Abuse says. "Much of this depends on the amount he's getting and the frequency with which he's getting it. But I would hate to say that his early death is inevitable. If he were to get treatment, it probably isn't too late to help him. And assuming he doesn't OD before then, he could certainly grow into an addicted adult." At the end of the evening of strange questions about his life, Jimmy slowly changes into a different child. The calm and self-assured little man recedes. The jittery and ill-behaved boy takes over as he begins going into withdrawal. He is twisting uncomfortably in his chair one minute, irritatingly raising and lowering a vinyl window blind the next. (Cooke 1980, A1)

By the next day, the chief of Washington's police had launched a city-wide search. "Mayor Marion Barry was incensed. All schools, social services and police contacts were to be asked for 'Jimmy's' whereabouts. The word went out on the streets that big reward money was available" (Green 1981, A12–15). After the story went both national and international, with the *Los Angeles Times–Washington Post* news service moving it out to over 300 clients, "Police were receiving letters from all over the country, including one signed by 30 students in a Richmond school, pleading that they find 'Jimmy'" (Green).

The story prompted doubts right away. Dr. Alyce Gullattee, director of Howard University's Institute for Substance Abuse and Addiction, one of the people Cooke interviewed when she was gathering her original material, said that she "didn't believe any of those people 'fired up' in front of Cooke. 'Junkies,' she said, 'just don't trust reporters like that'" (Green 1981, A12–15). The persistence of this kind of skepticism caused editors at the *Post* to ask the author for substantiation of her material. City editor Milton Coleman requested that she arrange a meeting with the subject, "mainly to protect Cooke from more staff jealousies and to establish once and for all the soundness of her reporting. Cooke kept arranging times and places for such a meeting, but canceled them all before they could occur.

In spite of the somewhat ominous uncertainties, the *Post* entered "Jimmy's World" as a nominee for a Pulitzer Prize in local news reporting in December 1980. On April 3, 1981, ten days before the official announcement, Cooke learned that she had won. Almost as soon as the award winners' names were made public, trouble began:

> The *Post* learned that irregularities might exist in Cooke's autobiographical submission to the Pulitzer board early Tuesday afternoon, when officials at Vassar College called Bradlee and told him that Cooke had not graduated magna cum laude, but in fact had only attended the school for her freshman year. At the same time, the Associated Press called *Post* Managing Editor Howard Simons to report that AP staffers in Ohio were being told that Cooke had not received a master's degree from the University of Toledo. (Maraniss 1981, A1)

In a matter of days, Cooke was disgraced, forced to relinquish the Pulitzer Prize, fired by the paper, and required to make a humiliating public apology for her transgression.

> In longhand, she wrote: "'Jimmy's World' was in essence a fabrication. I never encountered or interviewed an 8-year-old heroin addict. The September 28, 1980, article in *The Washington Post* was a serious misrepresentation which I deeply regret. I apologize to my newspaper, my profession, the Pulitzer board and all seekers of the truth. Today, in facing up to the truth, I have submitted my resignation. Janet Cooke" (Green 1981, A12).

Cooke's mother flew to Washington from the family home in Toledo, Ohio, on April 12 and her father arrived two days later. In a united front, they removed their daughter from the public eye. After a year had passed, Janet Cooke appeared on television on the *Phil Donahue Show* and offered her version of the incident. She blamed her behavior on the high-pressure environment of the *Post*. She "briefly reemerged in 1996 to tell her story to the magazine *GQ*" (Museum of Hoaxes Online, 2005). Thereafter, she quickly and, it seems, permanently fell out of sight.

The last words of Ben Bradlee, the famed executive editor who presided over the *Washington Post* during Cooke's tenure, on the "Jimmy's World" debacle read, fittingly, like an epitaph:

> "It is a tragedy that someone as talented and promising as Janet Cooke, with everything going for her, felt that she had to falsify the facts," said Benjamin C. Bradlee, executive editor of *The Washington Post*. "The credibility of a newspaper is its most precious asset, and it depends almost entirely on the integrity of its reporters. When that integrity is questioned and found wanting, the wounds are grievous" (Maraniss 1981, A1).

Stephen Glass: A "Spectacular Crash"

In contrast to Cooke's single, albeit monumental, display of literary malfeasance, Stephen Glass, a "white hot rising star" reporter for the *New Republic,* one of the most respected of the glossies, prolonged his hoaxing over a "two-and-a-half-year period between December 1995 and May 1998." With his work appearing in a glittering array of popular magazines, from John F. Kennedy, Jr.'s *George* to *Rolling Stone* to *Policy Review* and *Harper's,* for a time Glass pulled off "a breathtaking web of deception that emerged as the most sustained fraud in modern journalism" (Bissinger 1998). Disclosure took longer than it had for Cooke, but after getting away with his sham for more than two years, Glass, whose stories had regularly provoked outraged responses, began to receive closer scrutiny from interested parties. Alarmed, his editor at the *New Republic* began to investigate on his own, and the reporter's elaborate tapestry of lies rapidly unraveled. He admitted to making up elements of dozens of high-profile articles. In a *60 Minutes* television interview aired in May 2003, Glass told correspondent Steve Kroft that he routinely invented people, places, events, organizations, and quotations.

The editor of his college newspaper at the University of Pennsylvania, Glass joined the *New Republic* as an editorial assistant in 1995. Assigned to a minor story on a little known piece of Washington legislation, he decided that it would benefit from embellishment. Before long, his inventive narratives became a trademark. "Everything around him turned out to be incredibly vivid or zany or in some other way memorable," says Leon Wieseltier, the *New Republic*'s literary editor. "And at the meetings, we used to wait for Steve's turn, so that he could report on his next caper. We got really suckered" (Kroft 2003). Glass wrote a piece about a political memorabilia convention featuring Monica Lewinsky condoms. He got away with inventing an evangelical religion whose adherents worshiped George Herbert Walker Bush.

Glass's first full-length effort for the *New Republic*, a piece about the Center for Science in the Public Interest (CSPI), was written under the editorship of Michael Kelly, a well-respected former columnist for the *New Yorker*. The article elicited a stinging rejoinder from the chairperson of the board of CSPI, who wrote: "The sheer quantity of errors in the article not only calls into question whether minimum standards of objective journalism were consciously disregarded, but makes an adequate response in limited space impossible" (Bissinger 1998, 180). Kelly defended his reporter, however, even writing vehemently supportive private letters to CSPI's director and the editor of *Extra!* magazine, who had also questioned the veracity of Glass's story.

From an affluent North Shore suburb of Chicago, Glass had attended its namesake Highland Park High School, where 5 percent of the school's seniors routinely qualified as National Merit scholars. Parents unapologetically pushed their children to succeed. A site of research for Sara Lawrence-Light-foot's 1983 book, *The Good High School: Portraits of Character and Culture,* Highland Park High received mixed reviews. The author "was impressed with the school's stunning academic programs, but noted that values such as character and morality were sometimes little more than brushstrokes against the relentlessness of achievement" (Bissinger 1998, 178). Having attended a high school with a theatrical tradition that had spawned the creators of *The Revenge of the Nerds* movies as well as the director of *Beethoven* and *The Flintstones,* by 1998 Glass could boast of some celebrity himself. He wrote for most of the respected popular news magazines, earned a six-figure annual salary, appeared occasionally on television, and enjoyed a reputation as an inspired spinner of tales, which he described with some relish in his *60 Minutes* interview:

> "I would tell a story, and there would be fact A, which maybe was true. And then there would be fact B, which was sort of partially true and partially fabricated. And there would be fact C which was more fabricated and almost not true," says Glass. "And there would be fact D, which was a complete whopper. And totally not true. And so people would be with me on these stories through fact A and through fact B. And so they would believe me to C. And then at D they were still believing me through the story" (Kroft 2003).

Remaining for a time unscathed by challenges to the veracity of his articles, the glib reporter glossed over complaints, which were frequent. The *New Republic* maintained a policy of assigning fact checkers to vet stories for inaccuracies, but Glass had worked as a fact checker when he had started at the magazine and he knew how to subvert the process. He knew to insert fake errors into his stories so that the checkers would discover the erroneous material, believe that they had accomplished their investigative task, and leave it at that:

> "I knew how the system worked. And I made it so that my stories could get through. I invented fake notes. I later would invent a series of voice mailboxes and business cards. I invented newsletters. I invented a Web site," says Glass. "For every lie I told in the magazine, there was a series of lies behind that lie that I told—in order to get it to be published" (Kroft 2003).

The storyteller's luck would not hold out forever. Michael Kelly left the *New Republic* in September 1997, and not long afterward his successor, Charles Lane, found himself faced with a relentlessly growing body of evidence pointing to Glass's deceitfulness. Executive editor of the *New Republic* from late 1997 until 1999, Lane would go on to become a reporter for the *Washington Post.* He later asserted that no one in his 15 years of journalistic experience had affected him like the ingratiating young scam artist. According to *60 Minutes*' Kroft (2003):

> Glass might still be duping editors, if it weren't for an online version of *Forbes* magazine, which was trying to do a follow-up on an article Glass had written about a convention of computer hackers in Bethesda, Maryland—specifically, a 15-year-old who had hacked into a company called Jukt Micronics and then extorted tens of thousands of dollars not to do it again. The *Forbes* editors told Lane they were having trouble confirming a single fact.

Glass fit the classic model of the criminal mind, which interprets getting away with one misdeed as an invitation, even a mandate, to embark on another. At times he made up entire articles, enhanced with whatever details he deemed were required to deceive his editors and interest his readers.

> "My life was one very long process of lying and lying again, to figure out how to cover those other lies," says Glass. "Like a stock graph, there's going to be exceptions in this. But the general trend of the stories is that they started out with a few made-up details and quotes. And granted a few too many, of course. But a few. And then they progressed into stories that were completely fabricated. Just completely made up out of whole cloth" (Kroft 2003).

His lies did not stop there. He admits that he continued to deceive his colleagues long after questions about his journalistic integrity surfaced. He lied to his co-workers, some of them supporters, right up to the bitter end, never expressing regret over his behavior to any of them:

> "This is the very beginning of a very, very long process of apologies. I didn't apologize to people because I was so ashamed." Certainly Glass could forgive them for perhaps being a little bit cynical about this apology, since he's doing it on national television and not in person. "I don't think that's right though, saying because I'm doing it on national television," says Glass, even though he has a book out now about his life and hasn't been in touch with these people for five years. "I didn't want to give an apology when I didn't yet understand why I had done what I had done wrong," says Glass. "And so I've spent five years coming to understand why I have behaved so terribly" (Kroft 2003).

Glass lost any friends he might have had on the *New Republic*'s staff. The magazine fired him in full disgrace with all the disdain it could muster; yet, he still proved more resilient than Janet Cooke (not to mention more firmly entrenched in the social infrastructure as an upper middle class white male with authentic educational credentials from the University of Pennsylvania). He converted ignominy to a kind of shamefaced glamour as the subject of a 1998 *Vanity Fair* article by *Friday Night Lights* author Buzz Bissinger. "Shattered Glass" went on to become a critically and financially successful film.

Glass also went on. He earned a law degree from Georgetown University and passed the bar exam, although questions persist concerning his character and fitness to practice law. Glass did endure the requisite penance of forfeiting his journalism career, but on a bookseller's Web site promoting his autobiographical novel, *The Fabulist* (for which he received a six-figure advance in 2002), the self-confessed serial liar boasts, "A spectacular crash, I've learned, is the quickest way to incredible accomplishment."

The scorned Cooke would surely disagree, in the unlikely event that she would be invited to offer her opinion on the subject. A drama loosely based on her story, written by rising playwright Tracey Scott Wilson and produced in 2003 at the Public Theater, featured Philicia Rashad, famous for her role as Cliff Huxtable's television wife on *The Cosby Show,* playing the Cooke character. Although the play earned critical acclaim, its success failed to raise the prospects of the disgraced newspaperwoman (McKinley 2003). Her beauty, vivacity, and acknowledged journalistic talent notwithstanding, Janet Cooke vanished from the public eye.

Conclusion

Compared to the exploits of his literary descendants, Benjamin Franklin's invention of Polly Baker seems innocuous, especially considering that he did not indulge in the hoax to increase his own celebrity or treasure, but rather to draw public attention to an inequitable and, in some ways, cruel state of social affairs. In contrast, both Cooke and Glass, relying on their clever frauds' abilities to accelerate the acquisition of money and fame, took the low road out of a queer combination of selfishness, ego, greed, laziness, and even, some would say, a sort of professional malice. Observers usually described both reporters' trajectories to success as meteorically swift; yet, they were impatient. They wanted more acclaim and more riches and they wanted them right away.

Regarded as common con artists, these two appear to be little more than curious examples of the lengths to which some people will resort to achieve their goals—lengths that sometimes seem to have required more effort than it would have taken to conscientiously perform their jobs. Considered in a larger context, their stories may be seen as examples of the widely misguided understanding and exercise of ethics in present-day America.

While Cooke and Glass reaped justifiably bitter harvests of denunciation, the public indignation over their misconduct smacks of hypocrisy. These writers would not have engaged in literary hoaxing had they not been confident that their dishonesty would go undetected. This self-assurance is the reason they both pursued their devious methods right up to the time they realized they were on the brink of exposure. Both journalists believed their deceptions would continue to succeed until the moment they failed. In this respect, the shamed reporters represent everyone, because all of us have faltered at times when it comes to ethical decision making. If we were held to strict standards of honesty, we would be forced to admit that many of our decisions are guided by our estimation of the likelihood that we will get away with making the circumstantially more attractive choice—the one we know in our hearts to be unethical. To quote Bob Dylan: "People don't do what they believe in; they just do what's most convenient and then they repent" (Dylan and Shepard 1986).

In the Gospel of John, the apostle tells the story of Jesus and the cleansing of the temple. He paints a graphic picture of Christ as disciplinarian: wielding a whip of cords; forcing the oxen and sheep, the greedy lenders, and their hapless victims out of the holy place; upending the money changers' tables; and sending golden arcs of coins through the air. John goes on to explain that, because of the acts they witnessed Jesus performing that day, many people in Jerusalem came to believe in Christ's divinity. These new converts decided that they wished to be his friends after all. But, John says, "Jesus did not trust himself to them because he knew them all, and did not need anyone to testify to him about human nature. He himself understood it well" (John 2: 24–25).

It is prudent to interpret John's concluding observation with care. Its misanthropic tone may represent the author's bias rather than that of his protagonist. While Jesus certainly was a realist, he was no cynic. Fully comprehending humanity's weaknesses may have kept him from indulging in fair-weather friendships, but it did not prevent him from loving mankind.

Finally, the stories of Cooke and Glass provide evidence of the wisdom of imitating Christ's ways. When we free our own thinking from the seduction of cynicism and its convenient conclusions, we come to see that working to understand and accept human nature in all of its flawed complexity is a necessary step in our personal struggle to rise above it.

References

Bissinger, Buzz. "Shattered Glass," *Vanity Fair,* September 1998, 176–184.

Cooke, Janet. "Jimmy's World," *Washington Post,* September 28, 1980, A1.

Dylan, Bob, and Sam Shepard. "Brownsville Girl." New York: Special Ryder Music, 1986.

Franklin, Benjamin. *The Facetious Letters of Benjamin Franklin—1898,* 5–58. St. Petersburg, Florida: The Sandstone Press, 1971.

Green, Bill. "The Story," *Washington Post,* April 19, 1981, A12–A15.

Hall, Max. *Benjamin Franklin & Polly Baker.* Chapel Hill: University of North Carolina Press, 1960.

Isaacson, Walter. *Benjamin Franklin: An American Life,* 120–121; 466. New York: Simon & Schuster, 2003.

Kroft, Steve. "Stephen Glass: I Lied for Esteem." CBS News Online. http://www.cbsnews.com/stories/2003/05/07/60minutes/printable552819.shtml (accessed January 16, 2006).

Maraniss, David A. "*Post* Reporter's Pulitzer Prize Is Withdrawn," *Washington Post,* April 16, 1981, A1.

McKinley, Jesse. "Finding Her Own Way to Get the Story Right," *New York Times,* December 7, 2003, B7.

Museum of Hoaxes Online. "Janet Cooke and 'Jimmy's World.'" http://www.museumofhoaxes.com/ (accessed October 25, 2005).

Schiff, Stacey. *A Great Improvisation: Franklin, France, and the Birth of America,* 81–84. New York: Henry Holt & Company, 2005.

Tolson, Jay. "The Many Faces of Benjamin Franklin," *U.S. News & World Report,* June 23, 2003.

Bibliography

Bailyn, Bernard. *To Begin the World Anew: The Genius and Ambiguities of American Founders,* 3–36; 64–69. New York: Alfred A. Knopf, 2003.

Bradlee, Ben. *The Good Life: Newspapering and Other Adventures,* 435–452. New York: Simon & Schuster, 1995.

Brendon, Piers. "It Wasn't Just Watergate," *Columbia Journalism Review,* November/December 1995.

The New American Bible, gen. ed. New York: Catholic Book Publishing Company, 1970.

Price Adjustments under the Table*

2

DANIEL LEVY

Contents

Based on first-hand accounts, this chapter offers evidence on corrupt price setting and price adjustment mechanisms that were illegally employed under the
Soviet planning and rationing regime. The evidence is anecdotal, and is based
on personal experience during the years 1960–1971 in the Republic of Georgia.[1] I offer explicit evidence on the economic corruption of Georgia's markets
and institutions by providing a detailed account of various kinds of illegal economic transactions and activities my siblings were engaged in. While these
transactions usually included common types of corrupt economic activities
such as bribe payments, embezzlement, and fraud, unfortunately sometimes
dishonest acts of cheating, scams, rip offs, etc. also took place.

Georgia, like the rest of the 14 republics in the former Soviet Union, did
not have a free market economy. Rather, the Georgian economy was a centrally planned command economy. That is, government officials and bureaucrats and the members of the Communist Party and its functionaries made
the decisions regarding the products and services to be produced, how much
would be produced, and for whom it would be produced. In Western style
free market economies, in contrast, market forces, along with the flexible
price system, are the mechanisms that determine the answers to these key
questions. Given that market forces in Georgia were not allowed to function
freely, decision-makers such as firms, families, and individuals had to find
ways around the restrictions imposed by the centrally planned totalitarian
economic structure and its inefficient price system in order to overcome the
problems and limitations caused by these inflexibilities.

I was born and raised in Tskhakaya (when Georgia regained its independence from Russia, the town's name was changed to Senaki), a small town
in the western part of Georgia, close to Kutaisi—the regional capital. Three

* Reprinted from Levy, Daniel. "Price Adjustment under the Table: Evidence on Efficiency-
Enhancing Corruption." *European Journal of Political Economy,* 23 (2007): 423–447.
With permission from Elsevier.

of my brothers worked at government stores, selling various types of clothing, shoes, fabrics, etc. The stores were all located in the local market, called *bazari* in Georgian. The bazari was physically set up as a big circle. In the center were the fruits and vegetables market, where local farmers from the outskirts of Tskhakaya would sell their wares. Around the circle, along the bazari's walls, various kinds of stores were scattered, such as hardware stores, clothing stores, barber shops, and book shops, as well as a few restaurants. In addition, there were designated areas for selling milk products, flour and related products, chicken and other meat products, etc.

The stores were all government owned and operated in a similar fashion. No private ownership was allowed or recognized. All goods and services were produced by government-owned factories and manufacturing plants or imported to Georgia by government import agencies. The prices of the goods and services were set by government officials. For example, the prices the barbers charged were set by government directives. Similarly, the prices of shirts, trousers, shoes, and other goods sold at these stores were also set by government officials. The proceeds from sales were forwarded to the government office. The employees of the shops were paid on a monthly basis by the local government salary payment offices.

One main problem with the system was the inadequate level of the salaries. Therefore, the workers had to find some source of supplementary income, and everyone found some way of doing it. For example, the Kolkhoz farmers would sell some of their produce at the bazari at the "free market" price, rather than sending it all to government storage facilities, which paid them a low fixed price, regardless of the quality of the produce. The market price typically was much higher than what the government regulators assessed. Therefore, the farmers who sold their produce at the bazari would pocket nice profits.[2]

Although the bazari's existence was legal and authorized, the individuals who came to sell their wares there had to bribe various officials because otherwise, given the lack of another market, they could be denied entrance to the market or just be harassed by nosy market officials and policemen. Thus, the bazari authorities would happily allow people to bring to the market any legal, borderline legal, or even illegal (e.g., counterfeit) merchandise, as long as they were properly compensated for it. The bribe payments could take various forms, but typically they would include a side payment (in addition to the official nominal fee) to the person at the entrance to the market, who exerted much power because he could deny entrance to the merchants or he could report them to the police. Also, there was a limit to the quantity of merchandise the sellers could bring to the market, and bribing the person at the gate was the only way of eliminating that barrier. Various bazari officials and controllers and often the policemen as well would go around the merchant tables scattered in the bazari and collect their bribe payments, sometimes in cash but quite often in kind.

The employees at these shops and stores used various methods to supplement their miserable government-paid salaries, but most often they would inflate the prices of almost everything they were selling, often by as much as 200–300 percent above the official price. However, they could not pocket all the profit. Instead, they shared it with the store manager, who shared it with his supervisor, who shared it with the local police station staff, etc. This way, everybody in the "food chain" received his or her share with the implicit understanding that as long as everyone played according to the rules, there was no reason to disrupt this remarkably efficient method of income redistribution.

To obtain satisfactory medical care, bribes and other types of under-the-table payments in cash or in kind were necessary. For example, when I was about 11 years old, my older brother and I were sent to Tbilisi, the capital of Georgia, to undergo a tonsillectomy, a surgical procedure that was routinely done in those days to every child. When we visited the doctor's office at the hospital, the first thing my brother did was to discreetly hand him an envelope, saying, "Our parents have asked us to give this envelope to you." The envelope contained 300 rubles. Georgian doctors never refused to accept these kinds of gifts.[3] Naturally, some part of these gifts likely ended up in the hands of the hospitals' chief doctors and administrators.

Similarly, to enter an institute of higher education, payments to the "right people" were absolutely necessary.[4] Incredibly perhaps, bribing teachers was common even after entering the university. For example, students taking written exams would often put in their examination notebooks some amount (20–30 rubles perhaps) before handing in their exam notebooks. One of my brothers was able to improve his grades in his high school diploma after haggling with his teacher on the price. It turns out that the teacher was asking for 4 rubles for each extra point while my brother was only offering 2 rubles. In the end, they settled on 3 rubles per point. Thus, for example, improving a grade from 3 to 5 on a scale of 2 ("fail") to 5 ("excellent") cost my brother a mere 6 rubles.[5] My family members were not unique. As far as we knew, everybody was doing this. In fact, through word of mouth communication, people would often share with one another information about the market bribe rate (i.e., how much money a particular public official was taking).

Under-reporting and/or inflating the official prices and pocketing the extra income was the standard as well as the norm among the stores' and shops' managers and employees. Much of the merchandise these stores sold was produced by Georgian or Russian government manufacturing plants, although some proportion of the merchandise was often imported, typically from Poland, Czechoslovakia, Romania, Bulgaria, and other East European countries. Government officials, who typically were appointed directly by the local or the regional (e.g., district level) Central Committees of the Soviet Communist Party, were in charge of setting the prices of the merchandise. They would set the prices without having any clue about the demand conditions in the market or about the costs of production or importation. In fact, the merchandise was almost always underpriced, giving the store employees powerful incentives to inflate the official prices and pocket the profits.

My siblings faced these kinds of situations on a regular basis. For example, a line of work shirts would arrive with the price tags attached to the shirt buttons. In addition to the price information, these tags would also contain information on the manufacturing date and place, washing and ironing instructions, etc. Now, with a price tag of 4 rubles per shirt, these shirts were grossly underpriced. Therefore, my brothers would order new price tags from a local government printing shop. The new price tags would be identical to the original price tags, with only one difference: Instead of 4 rubles, the tags would indicate a price of 10 or even 12 rubles. Then I, along with my younger brother, Joseph, would remove the original tags and replace them with the new tags. We used to inflate the official prices this way dozens of times each year with the delivery of almost every new shipment of merchandise.

Now, formally, the government printing presses were prohibited from printing any nonofficial government document, and certainly from printing *fake* price tags for *illegally* selling *illegally* manufactured products at *inflated* prices. Naturally, my brothers had to bribe the printing press managers—and especially their director—to secure their full cooperation.

The method of illegally obtaining goods and services in exchange for bribes functioned because everybody that was a part of the group or the circle received his or her share of the profits. The profit-sharing mechanism was designed in such a way that all participants had an incentive to play the game according to the rules. It worked precisely because everybody benefited and thus nobody had an incentive to disrupt its smooth functioning. High-ranking government officials, the police, and the managers at the store level were engaged in enriching themselves by dividing the surplus generated.

In the particular case of my family, following the unwritten profit-sharing rules, my brothers would share the 200–300 percent "profit" with all "club members." For example, if, on a 4-ruble shirt my brother made 8 rubles' profit, then he would keep 1 ruble and give 7 rubles to the store manager, who would pocket 1 ruble, and 6 rubles would go to the director of the bazari. The director and his office employees would keep 2–3 rubles, and the rest would go to the local police station chief, who would share it further with his fellow policemen as well as with his supervisors in the regional capital.[6]

Often, the decision by how much to inflate the price was left for the last moment. I took an active role in this kind of instantaneous price adjustment, which was done under the table, literally. I was about seven or eight years old at the time. On Sundays, which were the busiest market days, I would go to help my brothers because the market was full of shoppers, as families—many of them from the surrounding villages—came with their children to shop.

My brothers worked outside their stores, behind big table counters. These tables—perhaps about 3.5 meters long and 1.5 meters wide—were enclosed and thus were used for storing merchandise. The table counters were covered with merchandise for sale: piles of shirts, pants, socks, etc. Shoes would be scattered among these piles.

My job was to sit underneath the table (which was quite easy for me as I was skinny and small) and help my brothers make on-the-spot instantaneous adjustments of shoe prices. I was equipped with a simple metallic device with rotating sharp heads with numeric stamps that I could use to mark any price on the bottom of the shoe.

A customer would come and look at the shoes displayed on the table, which typically would be quite large or really small in size and would have no prices on them. The customer would ask if we had the shoes in size 43, for example. My brother would at first say, "No, we are out of them." Given the constant shortage of goods and services, Georgians were used to this kind of answer.

However, most of the customers would also know that at this point, if you truly want the merchandise, you must insist that the seller recheck his inventory, since perhaps there is "one last pair" of size 43 shoes left. Based on how strong and how persistent the customer was in his or her request, my brother would guess the price the customer would be willing to pay (i.e., he would intuitively try to assess the customer's price elasticity—the customer's price sensitivity). Finally, my brother would bend and "start looking" for the appropriately sized shoes under the table. I already had the shoes ready as I could hear the entire conversation, and my brother would whisper to me the price that he wanted me to mark on the shoes. Within a few seconds, he would be done searching for the shoes and, luckily, he would find "one last pair" of the requested size.[7]

My brothers were also engaged in buying and selling of counterfeit merchandise. The merchandise would be illegally produced by the same government production facilities that produced the "official" merchandise. However, unlike most of the counterfeit merchandise that one may purchase, for example, at the New York's "counterfeit alley" along Broadway in midtown Manhattan, the quality of our counterfeit merchandise was identical to the quality of the original.[8] For any practical purpose, therefore, the officially manufactured merchandise and the counterfeit merchandise were identical. The only difference was that the production of the counterfeit merchandise would never be reported and thus, as far as government officials were concerned, they had no knowledge of its production.

My brothers would purchase the merchandise from the manufacturing plant employees at a low cost. For example, an exact duplicate of officially produced shirts with an official consumer price tag of 3 rubles could be purchased illegally for 0.50–1.50 rubles, depending on the quantity purchased, and could be sold for as much as 8–10 rubles. For the manufacturing plant employees, these were very profitable transactions, as they pocketed all the revenue they obtained from these transactions but incurred no cost, essentially stealing from the government-owned factories. Obviously, they had to incur the overhead cost of bribing the higher level management and government officials.

Thus, my brothers' store would receive an official delivery of 50 shirts, for example. If these shirts were popular, then my brothers would purchase and sell as many as 500–1,500 counterfeit copies of the shirts within 2–3 weeks, while the official merchandise would remain on store shelves, most of it unsold.

To inflate the official prices more easily, my brothers would often create artificial shortages. The creation of artificial shortages was typically limited to products that were especially popular, such as imported clothing (e.g., shirts, pants, shoes, etc. from Czechoslovakia, Poland, and Hungary), imported food (e.g., Hungarian- and Bulgarian-made canned food), and some domestically produced products that were in constant shortage.[9]

Galoshes are a good example of a domestically produced product for which demand was always high and that was constantly in a short supply. Galoshes are overshoes made of rubber and were popular during rainy winter days, especially among the peasants and villagers, who would often use them as ordinary shoes for working in the field or for walking on the unpaved roads of their villages because they were unable to afford real shoes.

Supplies of galoshes would arrive at the store two to three times a year, and there was always a huge demand for them. People would hurry to stores asking for galoshes but on my brothers' table counters they would find only a single left shoe or only a single right shoe, and when they would ask whether there were galoshes of size 3 or 4 or 5, they would receive a very typical answer: "No, we are out of them."

If they insisted, however, then my brother would give them a hint: "Well, I do not have any galoshes left, but I can send my little brother to another store, and he might be able to obtain a pair of galoshes of the size you want, but the price will probably be 8–10 rubles. Also, you will have to give the boy 2–3 rubles as a gift." They would always agree to the terms of this deal. Of course, I would always manage to obtain for them the right size galoshes in 5 minutes, often with a profit of as much as 400–500 percent. The buyers were happy to receive the galoshes, even at the higher price.

Taking advantage of human temptations was a norm in Georgia. For example, when the store received a delivery of cheap plastic wallets, my brother would put just one wallet on the edge of his merchandise table, making it appear as if it had been left there by accident by one of the shoppers. Customers approaching the table counter would notice the wallet and indeed assume that it was left accidentally by one of the shoppers. My brother would pretend that he had not noticed the wallet. In this type of situation, many customers would pretend that they were looking at the merchandise, quietly pick up the wallet, and put it in a purse or in a pocket. At that point my brother would politely inform them: "Sir/Madam, the wallet you just took costs 6 rubles." Most of the customers would pretend that they intended to buy it and pay the outrageously high price, as otherwise they would be admitting that they were thieves.

The profit-sharing arrangement my brothers had with the government authorities was in some sense a form of tax payment, where my brothers paid tax on a regular basis on the profits earned on every item sold.[10] This was a variable tax in the sense that the tax payments were linked to the quantity sold: the greater the quantity sold at the inflated price was, the higher the tax payments were.

There was another taxation mechanism that was quite popular in Tskhakaya, which was more like a fixed tax. This tax collection mechanism was implemented by the local police force in the form of periodic raids they would conduct on shops, stores, and other businesses. The police would come and, given their knowledge of the illegal activities that were taking place at these establishments, they would look for a "smoking gun." For example, they would look for items with inflated prices. When these raids occurred, the store manager would quickly organize with the store employees and they would instantly collect money to bribe the visiting police officers. The sums would range between 600 and 800 rubles.

There was another mechanism that was often used with the same goal in mind. A policeman would pick a customer whom my brothers would not suspect. The customer would be sent to my brother's store (*ducani* in Georgian) to purchase a product for which the price was inflated. The customer would buy such a product and leave, but later he or she would return with the purchased merchandise, accompanied by the policeman. On one such occasion, one of my brothers saw his customer was approaching him holding the blouse she had purchased just minutes before, and she was escorted by a policeman. Instinctively, he ran away and managed to leave the bazari's grounds despite the police's attempts to quickly seal the market and capture him. It turned out that this particular policeman was an honest policeman, a true Communist, an incorruptible policeman (an oxymoron in Georgia!). My brother, therefore, had to go in hiding for several weeks while the police were searching for him. In parallel, my father was trying to influence this policeman through other (corrupt) police officers. These policemen were paid 1,500 rubles (which was considered a very high price) to convince their fellow police officer to stop chasing my brother.

A raid of a similar type took place at an illegal shoe manufacturing facility where one of my brothers was working. The business was located in a residential neighborhood and it was producing men's and women's shoes. The shoe materials were precut somewhere else and at this facility the shoes were manually assembled by about a dozen workers. This was an illegal operation because in the USSR nobody was allowed to engage in private manufacturing.

In 1966, when my brother was 23 years old, the shop was raided by the city's chief investigative policeman. The policeman came to the shop with a large truck and loaded it with all the materials and merchandise that he found in the shop. However, my brother as well as several other employees managed to escape. He went to a friend's house and from there to the train station and there he took a train to my aunt, who lived in Suhumi, the capital of Abkhazia. There he stayed for three days, until he learned that it was safe to return home, which meant that bribes were paid to the right people—in this case to the chief investigative policeman. Upon his return, my brother learned that the raid was the chief policeman's personal initiative, a part of his annual "tax collection tour" for the welfare and well-being of his family.

One of the most remarkable things about Russia, and perhaps about the rest of the USSR, was the unusually high purchasing power of homemade vodka (*chacha* in Georgian). My father, like other Georgians, used to make chacha from the remains of grapes, after making wine from them. The quality of chacha was determined by pouring it on a plate and throwing in a burning match. If it caught fire, then it was of a high quality. In other words, it was a pure alcohol, no different from after-shave.[11]

Now, with such homemade vodka, one could obtain in Russia everything and anything, from domestically grown produce to imported consumer goods to machine guns.[12] We discovered that with homemade vodka we could accomplish a lot, even in Georgia. One of my brothers, for example, paid two bottles of chacha to his school teacher to have his high school diploma grades improved. In 1970, my father used 4 liters of homemade chacha along with 400 rubles to have our home connected to the town's electric grid, which, by the way, was supposed to be done for free.

To have one of my brothers accepted at an evening school, all my father had to do was to pay a late night visit to the school director's home and bring along 2 liters of homemade chacha. We sometimes went to a doctor's office with a bottle of homemade wine, although wine was not as popular as chacha as a means for making bribe payments, and thus its purchasing power was far lower. However, my father's homemade wine was considered pure (he never used any additives) and of a superb quality, and the entire town knew about it.[13] My father's homemade wine, therefore, was capable of helping us in many of our economic transactions. In particular, about 5 liters of it, along with a payment of 1,500 rubles to the Military Commissariat's officers, were sufficient for one of my brothers to obtain an exemption from serving in the Soviet military during a peace-time period. During war time, no amount of money, vodka, or wine would help: Everybody would be mobilized for the Soviet military.

Religious practice was officially outlawed in the former Soviet Union. Instead, in Georgia as in much of the former USSR, Lenin, Marx, and Engels were the gods and their teachings (e.g., the *Communist Manifesto*) were the bible. Nevertheless, the city Jews somehow found a way to have the authorities allow the local Jewish community to build a synagogue. It was quite strange, however: The signs at the entrance to the synagogue indicated that it was prohibited to pray there. It was supposed to be a place for social gathering only.

We, however, practiced our religion and were able to hold regular daily prayer services at the synagogue because the local congregation collected money on a regular basis and arranged a generous bribe payments to the local city and police authorities. Thanks to small extra payments, they even permitted the families to bring along their kids to the Sabbath services.

In 1971 my family left the Republic of Georgia and immigrated to Israel. The process of obtaining the exit visa was full of hurdles and obstacles that, without side payments, would have been impossible to overcome. It began with an "invitation" from the government of Israel. The invitation was necessary for requesting an emigration permit.[14] The invitation was arranged through other emigrants who had left Georgia before us.

When the invitation arrived at the local post office, the post office director saw an opportunity for profit. This was the standard practice: Every time a letter came from overseas, usually from a family in Israel, the postman would come to our house and tell my parents quite directly and explicitly: "I have a letter for you from Israel. How much are you willing to pay for it?" Typically, one or two shots of chacha along with 50 rubles would suffice.

The value of an invitation from the government of Israel, however, was much higher than that of a single family letter. The post office director recognized this and took advantage of this profit opportunity, given his monopoly power over releasing the letter. In the end, it cost the family close to 600 rubles to obtain the document from the post office.[15] This, however, was only the beginning. The employees of the local office that issued birth certificates were unable to locate our birth certificates. However, a bribe payment of 150 rubles per certificate helped them locate the lost certificates.

Then there was a passport office in Tbilisi. There, we were sure that we would be expected to make a substantial contribution towards the happiness and welfare of the passport office head and his family. It turns out, however, that the person in charge was originally from Tskhakaya, a former star in the town's soccer team. He recognized my father and my brothers and told them that he was not going to take any money from his "old comrades."[16] That was a huge saving for the family.

The last encounter we had with Soviet authorities was in the city of Brest, on the border between Belarus and Poland. This was our point of departure from the Soviet Union to Israel. The Soviets did not allow emigrants to take with them many of their possessions. The border police in Brest, however, were more than willing to allow us to stuff the boxes we wanted to ship with anything we wanted, all in exchange for just one bottle of chacha per policeman.

In Georgia a person could only be employed by the government. No private enterprise was allowed. Even if one had a job that in the West would be described as self-employment, in Georgia he or she had to be registered at a government office, called *arteli*, which was considered his official employer. For example, my father and one of my brothers were registered with the local arteli as glazers. In theory this meant that the arteli's officials could tell them what to do. For example, they could keep them busy by sending them to various government construction projects where glazers were needed. In addition, because the arteli was their official employer, they were supposed to receive their monthly salary from it. Officially, they were not supposed to sell their services to private individuals.

All these rules were only in theory, however. That is because, like most of the self-employed people, my dad had also bribed (quite generously) the arteli's key officials, and therefore he was rarely called to government-run projects. In the rare occasions that he was called, he was rewarded by receiving fairly large quantities of uncut glass for his private business use. For example, periodically he would be called to a government construction project to install window glasses. These sites usually would have large supplies of glass, and the construction supervisors would often offer some of the uncut glass to him for private use because they would almost always receive deliveries of construction materials in excess quantities.

But, perhaps more importantly, thanks to the bribe payments, my father was permitted to sell his glazing services to private individuals quite openly. Moreover, he never reported his income to the arteli's officials, despite the strict regulations that required full reporting of all incomes from all private transactions. In fact, each "self-employed" employee of the arteli was required by the Soviet labor and employment laws to hand in all the income he or she has earned from private transactions. That would count as his or her contribution to the benefit of the proletariat. In return, the employee would receive the government prescribed 30–60 rubles, the monthly salary.

Now, as far as we know, nobody ever handed in their privately earned income to the arteli. The entire thing was a big joke. The arteli's apparatus was full of rent-seeking (i.e., profit-seeking) bureaucrats whose chief goal was to reach as many independent, self-employed individuals as possible to extract rents (i.e., bribes). My father, for example, would go to the arteli's offices towards the end of each month and would report and hand in his 30-ruble privately earned income for the previous month. Needless to say, nobody would ever question the accuracy of his reported income, which always was ridiculously low. In exchange, my father would receive his monthly 30-ruble salary from the arteli. Of course, the monthly salary payment from the arteli was quite minor in comparison to the actual income he regularly earned from his private glazing work. By the mid-1960s, my father got tired of these games, and with an additional lump-sum bribe payment, he obtained a permanent exemption from ever reporting to the arteli. Later on, he obtained similar exemptions for my brother and my uncle.

The cases and the events I have described are consistent with similar, although not as detailed, accounts offered by Simes (1975, 42), Simis (1977, 35; 1982), Grossman (1977, 25), Bergson (1984, 1052), and Hillman and Schnytzer (1986, 87). For example, according to Simis' (1982, 155–156) account, in order to have his business survive in Georgia, one Food Store Five's manager had to "*take money from the sales clerks*, to *sell* goods *at inflated prices*, to *cheat the customers*, and, of course, to *bribe* the top people in the municipal administration, and all the store's suppliers" [my emphasis]. This description summarizes quite well the types of activities many Georgians were engaged in, which suggests that the events I have described here were not limited to my immediate family members or to the time period this chapter covers. Indeed, the ways my family used to deal with the restrictions and inefficiencies of the Georgian economy were not unique in the sense that all of our neighbors and friends had to adopt similar methods and techniques to survive. The anecdotal evidence I offer, therefore, is quite typical and generalizes the behavior in Georgia.[18]

In Georgia's centrally planned command economy, the government officials and bureaucrats were the ones who made the decisions of what would be produced, how much would be produced, and for whom it would be produced. Thus, in Georgia, one of the main causes of corruption was state control over the distribution of the basic resources. The control manifested itself in the cumbersome and inefficient state management system, which made it impossible for individuals to obtain any service from the government without paying a visit to dozens of government officials in various offices. The state control over all economic decisions also resulted in constant shortages of goods and services. In the absence of free markets with flexible price and wage systems, Georgian decision makers had to find ways around the restrictions imposed by the centrally planned economic structure and its inefficient price system. In Georgia, therefore, the problems created by central planning were resolved, at least in part, by developing a black market, a parallel market where many goods and services were traded outside the official markets.

Corruption continued to exist in Georgia even after the collapse of the Soviet Union. The Georgian government did not begin taking serious anticorruption measures until President Saakashvili rose to power in 2003.[19] According to Transparency International's corruption perceptions index, as lately as in 2003, Georgia still was one of the most corrupt nations in the world—on a par with Tajikistan and Azerbaijan and outranked only by countries such as Myanmar, Haiti, and Paraguay. The corruption in Georgia seems to have a strong component of historical and social norms, which likely are contributing to the persistence of corruption in today's Georgia despite the recent political and economic reforms. The existence of these norms makes it unlikely that the corruption will disappear any time soon despite the current Georgian government's extraordinary efforts. Existence of these types of social norms, customs, and rules, therefore, suggests that Georgia and other countries like it could be stuck in a "corruption trap" for a while.

Notes

1. Several existing studies explore the nature of corruption in the former Soviet Union and attempt to explain it as well as its economic consequences. See, for example, Simes (1975, 42), Simis (1977, 35; 1982), Grossman (1977, 25), Bergson (1984, 1052), Hillman and Schnytzer (1986, 87), and Levin and Satarov (2000, 113). For an analysis of corruption in the post-transition Russian Federation, see Levin and Satarov (2000, 113), who offer an interesting discussion of the institutional pathologies in the Soviet economy prior to the collapse of the USSR, which contributed significantly to the persistence of corruption in the republics of the former Soviet Union until recently. For a survey of the theoretical literature on corruption, see Aidt (2003, F632), who offers a detailed and thorough analysis of the existing theoretical models of corruption and possible causes of corruption, as well as its possible consequences.

2. Hillman and Schnytzer (1986, 87) and Grossman (1977, 25) also note that this phenomenon existed in the Republic of Georgia.

3. This kind of payment *prior* to the receipt of a medical treatment is perhaps different from the gifts medical doctors often receive (usually in kind but sometimes also in monetary terms) *after* a successful treatment (such as after a successful surgical procedure) as a recognition of a job well done. These types of postmedical treatment gifts are quite common in many countries, and it is unclear whether they should be considered a bribe.

4. The bribe rate for entering the university was in the range of 1,000–1,500 rubles. In addition, often a payment in kind was also necessary. For example, it was well known in our community that to purchase an admission to university, it was necessary to give a gift of *dvoika* (two-piece suit) or preferably *troika* (three-piece suit) to the university rector's wife. My parents often expressed regret and disappointment for

not being able to send my brothers and sisters to the university. The necessary bribe rate was far too high for them.

5. Another brother used *chacha*—Georgian homemade vodka—to improve his high school diploma grades. Although chacha was sometimes used, money was still the primary means of bribe payments.

6. Marjit, Mukherjee, and Mukherjee (2000, 75) suggest that existence of such strategic interactions between law enforcement agents on the one hand and the criminals on the other make standard anticorruption policy prescriptions quite ineffective. See also Klitgaard (1988).

7. At least once I was arrested by the local police. My crime: illegally inflating the government-set prices. My punishment: a few hours of jail time, until my father came to the police station and paid 150 rubles along with 2 l of homemade chacha to the local police chief.

8. See Confessore (2006, 1) for a detailed description of New York City's counterfeit alley.

9. In Georgia, any product would sell at a premium regardless of its quality, as long as it had anything inscribed on it in any foreign language (i.e., in any language other than Georgian or Russian). Imported goods, therefore, were among the most demanded products.

10. These payments do not constitute an ordinary tax, however, as they would never end at the tax revenue office. Instead, they went to individual policemen and government officials for their private use and benefit, not for the benefit of the general public. Hillman and Schnytzer (1986, 87) refer to these types of payments as "overhead expenditures" or "overhead costs."

11. According to a recent report in the Tel-Aviv edition of the *International Herald Tribune*, Iranians, like the Georgians, have been producing, bottling, and selling homemade vodka and wine for centuries. It turns out that despite the increased attempts by the Iranian authorities to enforce the existing laws that prohibit the consumption of alcohol, Iranians apparently are consuming bootleg homemade vodka and wine in increasing quantities. According to the article, some young Iranian entrepreneurs are even engaged in the highly risky business of delivering the outlawed drinks on scooters to their clients' homes, which points to the universality of the laws that govern humans' responses to incentives. See Fathi (2006, 1).

12. A common perception in Georgia was that chacha's purchasing power in Russia was far greater than in Georgia. We discovered in 1971 that this was indeed the case when we were leaving the Soviet Union. On the way from Georgia to Tel-Aviv, we passed through Moscow and later through Brest, and we discovered that we could accomplish so much more in these two cities by using chacha—substantially more than in Georgia. For example, various types of bribes that we had to make in

"chacha units" in Russia were much lower than in Georgia for similar kinds of goods or services. The main reason for this discrepancy in the vodka's purchasing power was the Russians' love for vodka. They valued it far more than Georgians. For Georgians, wine always ranked first. The purchasing power of vodka, therefore, was far lower in Georgia than in Russia.

13. We used to make the wine at home, which was allowed because it was a form of private activity, no different from home cooking. The men and the boys of the house would wash their feet, while the women would wash the grapes. Then, the men and the boys would jump into giant pots and trample the grapes. The resulting grape juice would be kept in jars for 4–5 years, while passing it through a periodic filtering process using simple cheesecloth. After five years, the wine would be ready. During a visit to Tel-Aviv's Museum Haaretz, the tour guide explained how Byzantines used to make wine. The guide was amused to hear that we used to make wine in Georgia "the Byzantine way" as recently as 35 years ago.

14. According to a recent report of Human Rights Watch (www.hrw.org), the former republics of the USSR have almost completely eliminated the need to obtain an invitation from a foreign government to travel abroad or to emigrate.

15. Because the post office director was a monopolist in this case, the "price" we ended up paying for the invitation letter primarily reflected my family's ability to pay.

16. This is similar to the "identifiable victim effect" (Loewenstein, Small, and Strnad 2007; Small and Loewenstein 2003, 5), which predicts that a greater sympathy will be shown towards identifiable than statistical victims. In the case of Georgia, it appears that it was acceptable to cheat or to steal from someone whom you did not know in person. Social norms, however, prohibited acting dishonestly with people whom you knew in person.

17. A reader might have the impression that, given the sophisticated schemes, cheatings, rip offs, etc. in which some of my family members were engaged, our family must have been quite wealthy. The truth, however, is quite the opposite. Most of the income the family earned was spent on food and other necessities and not much was left for anything else. That is primarily because we were a family with 10 children. Consider the following: unlike our neighbors, we did not have running water (which means that we did not have showers, flushing toilets, etc.). Also, unlike our neighbors, we did not have a refrigerator, a washing machine, a gas burner, an electric oven, a telephone, a TV (we often went to our neighbors' houses to watch a soccer game on TV), or any other standard home appliance. In fact, we did not even have electricity until

1970, about a year before we left the Soviet Union. Until then, we were completely dependent on candlelight and kerosene lamps. We rarely purchased new clothes. As far back as I remember, I always wore my older brothers' clothes. They also wore used clothes, which came from various second-hand sources (e.g., wealthy families). We always purchased black bread because it was cheaper. We would eat chicken once a week and beef perhaps once every few weeks. Because rubber boots were too expensive, in cold Georgian winters we often wore galoshes, which were very inefficient when snow accumulated. For many years, we played using a homemade soccer ball because a real soccer ball was too expensive. Soccer shoes, which most of my friends had, were out of the question! None of my siblings attended an institute of higher education in Georgia because my parents could not afford it: The necessary bribe rate was too high. The family had to save all year long for my mother's annual summer trip to various mineral water sources because mineral water was considered good for diabetics. In short, our living standard was quite low, to say the least.

18. A reader might wonder why we behaved as we did. First, we had no choice. There was no other way a family could live and survive in Georgia without being engaged in these types of illegal activities. Second and perhaps not less important, it was the *norm*. Everybody was doing it, and that provided ethical and moral justification for our actions. Therefore, from the point of view of ethics, bribing, mark-up pricing, side payments in cash and in kind, and other similar kinds of black market activities were not considered immoral. To the contrary, they were considered perfectly normal, a part of everyday life in the former Soviet Union. Even worse types of crimes, such as stealing, cheating, rip offs, etc., which would be considered ethically less defensible to most people under normal circumstances, were considered socially acceptable in Georgia as long as the thief had no personal knowledge of the person he was stealing from. Unwritten social rules prohibited stealing from people you knew in person, such as friends, neighbors, co-workers, etc. Georgian President Mikhail Saakashvili has said, "Georgia was a very corrupt country. Sometimes people don't believe that it was corrupt because it was part of culture" (National Public Radio 2004). Marjit et al. (2000, 76) make a similar suggestion: "It [corruption] is so pervasive that citizens in the developing part of the world have accepted it as a social rule." See also Ludwig and Kling (2006).

19. For example, according to the 1998 estimates of the Georgian State Department of Statistics, the informal (or "black market") economy contributes over one third of the country's gross domestic product (Tavartkiladze 1998).

References

Aidt, Toke. "Economic Analysis of Corruption: A Survey," *Economic Journal,* 113 (2003): F632–F652.

Bergson, Abram. "Income Inequality under Soviet Socialism," *Journal of Economic Literature,* 22 (1984): 1052–1099.

Confessore, Nicholas. "No-Name, Brand-Name or Phony: It's All Here," *New York Times,* October 9, 2006, late edition—final, sec. B.

Fathi, N. "It's Hard to Kick a 7,000-Year-Old Habit," *International Herald Tribune,* April 4, 2006, Tel-Aviv edition, news sec.

Grossman, Gregory. "The Second Economy of the USSR," *Problems of Communism,* 26 (1977): 25–40.

Hillman, Arye, and Adi Schnytzer. "Illegal Economic Activities and Purges in a Soviet-Type Economy: A Rent-Seeking Perspective," *International Review of Law and Economics,* 6 (1986): 87–99.

Klitgaard, Robert. *Controlling Corruption.* Berkeley, CA: University of California Press, 1988.

Levin, Mark, and Georgy Satarov. "Corruption and Institutions in Russia," *European Journal of Political Economics,* 16 (2000): 113–132.

Loewenstein, George, Deborah Small, and Jeff Strnad. 2007. "Statistical, Identifiable and Iconic Victims." In *Behavioral Public Finance: Toward a New Agenda,* ed. E. McCaffery and Joel Slemrod, 33–46. New York: Russell Sage Publications.

Ludwig, Jens, and Jeffrey Kling. "Is Crime Contagious?" Industrial Relations Section, Working Paper No. 510, Princeton University, 2006.

Marjit, Sugata, Vivekananda Mukherjee, and Arijit Mukherjee. "Harassment, Corruption and Tax Policy," *European Journal of Political Economics,* 16 (2000): 75–94.

National Public Radio. "Georgian President Visits Atlanta." Georgian President Mikhail Saakashvili's interview with Elina Fuhrman, August 11, 2004, available at the Web site of Georgia's embassy in the United States, http://www.georgiaemb.org/DisplayMedia.asp?id=355.

Simes, Dimitri. "The Soviet Parallel Markets," *Survey,* 21 (1975): 42–52.

Simis, Konstantin. "The Machinery of Corruption in the Soviet Union," *Survey,* 23 (1977): 35–55.

_____. *USSR: Secrets of a Corrupt Society.* London: Dent, 1982.

Small, Deborah, and George Loewenstein. "Helping *a* Victim or Helping *the* Victim: Altruism and Identifiability," *Journal of Risk and Uncertainty,* 26 (2003): 5–16.

Tavartkiladze, Levan. "Georgia Report for GEO Project. Georgia Greens Energy Group," Paris: Helio International Report, 1998.

Greedy Individuals

II

Perhaps the most famous example of a fraudulent scheme is named after its inventor. Chapter 3 tells the story of Charles Ponzi, for whom the Ponzi scheme is named. He is only one of an army of individuals whose greed helped them separate many people from their money. Some of these fraudsters are simply unscrupulous, driven by greed and the need for an extravagant lifestyle.

In this section are several stories about fraudulent individuals during the 1980s and 1990s. Oscar Hartzell (chapter 5) became a swindler only after being victimized by the scheme that he then adopted. In chapter 6, a Texas school district is defrauded of millions of dollars by an unscrupulous contractor. In Kentucky, Erpenbeck was a successful construction company until its owner became greedy and started diverting checks to his personal account instead of delivering them to the rightful payees (chapter 7). In chapter 9, two members of the press use their influence to affect stock prices. Martin Frankel in chapter 10 took insurance companies for $200 million.

Surprisingly, some of these fraudsters paid their debts to society and became productive citizens, putting their criminal backgrounds to good use. Barry Minkow of ZZZZ Best (chapter 8) now consults with law enforcement agencies, helping them fight fraud. Patrick Kuhse, one of the authors of chapter 4, gives speeches about the experiences that led him to prison.

Charles Ponzi

STEVEN PRESSMAN

3

Contents

In the long history of financial frauds, probably no one is as famous or as infamous as Charles Ponzi. He is responsible for the term "Ponzi scheme," a pyramid scheme in which early investors are paid high interest rates or large returns with funds from later investors. Less known is the fact that what ended up as a gigantic pyramid scheme started out as an ostensibly legitimate way to make money via arbitrage in postal coupons. Over the course of a few months in 1920 Ponzi received more than $10 million from investors (around $100 million in 2007 dollars) before his scheme finally collapsed during several weeks of adverse publicity.

Charles Ponzi was born Carlo Ponsi in Lugo, a small town in northern Italy. Ironically, his father was a postman in Lugo; his mother came from an aristocratic Italian family. The Ponzis were a middle-class family, and they tried their best to provide Carlo with a good life, including an excellent education. When Ponzi was just a few months old, the family moved to Rome, but soon returned north and settled in Parma. From the ages of 5–10, Ponzi attended public school in Parma; then, he attended a prestigious private school.

After graduating, Ponzi was accepted in the University of Rome, acknowledged to be the top school in all of Italy. At the university, he hung around with students who came from the wealthiest Italian families, and he emulated their spending habits and their lifestyles. Consequently, he was frequently in debt and frequently involved in schemes to obtain some extra funds. With his friends, Ponzi would go to fashionable night spots in the evenings, stay up late drinking and gambling, and skip classes. Unable to keep up with his studies, Ponzi had to drop out of school (Zuckoff 2005, 21).

It is not entirely clear why Ponzi left Italy for the United States in 1903. According to one story, he came seeking the wealth and riches that would enable him to maintain the lifestyle he enjoyed while attending the University of Rome. But according to other sources, his relatives paid for a one-way trip to America because they grew "weary of paying his fines for gambling, petty theft, and forgery" (Dunn 1975, 9).

Ponzi landed in Boston and took a train to Pittsburgh in order to be with some relatives, who were food wholesalers. Within a year the family business went bankrupt and Ponzi lost his job (Streissguth 1994, 32). Over the next few years, Ponzi traveled around the Northeast, staying briefly in Paterson, New Jersey; Providence, Rhode Island; New Haven, Connecticut; and New York City. He worked at various odd jobs, such as insurance salesman, waiter, dishwasher, sign painter, grocery clerk, and sewing machine repairman (Wolff 1997, 52). He rarely lasted long at any of these jobs.

In July 1907 Ponzi went to Montreal and eventually found a job as a clerk at the Banco Zarossi. This bank was owned by an Italian, Louis Zarossi, and was popular with the thousands of Italians who had immigrated to Canada. They used the bank to deposit their pay and send money to their relatives in Italy. However, the bank itself was in trouble because the risky loans it had made were not being repaid. It desperately needed an influx of cash. At the time it was paying its depositors 2 percent interest, the going rate in Montreal. Banks used these deposits to purchase government securities that were paying 3 percent interest. Foreshadowing to some extent what was to come, Zarossi decided that his bank would offer the full 3 percent interest in an attempt to attract more depositors. He then decided to add a 3 percent bonus. This increased the total interest rate paid on deposits to 6 percent.

Zarossi said that he could pay 6 percent interest because he was not a greedy banker and paid depositors most of the interest they earned on their money. Of course, he could not actually pay 6 percent when he was only earning 3 percent, so Zarossi began dipping into the funds that immigrants were sending back to Italy. As more money became due, as immigrants wanted to know what had happened to the money they sent home, and as authorities began investigating the bank, "Zarossi packed a bag full of cash and fled to Mexico City" (Zuckoff 2005, 28). Eventually his bank collapsed, resulting in large losses for depositors and for the many immigrants who thought they had sent money to relatives in Italy.

While working as a clerk at Banco Zarossi, Ponzi frequently visited firms to collect their cash for deposit into the bank. One time, when left alone at the Canadian Warehouse Company, Ponzi rummaged through the drawers of the office manager and stole a blank check. He filled in the amount of $423.58, made the check out to himself, and forged the signature of the company office manager. He then cashed the check. With his ill-gotten gains Ponzi bought a new set of clothes and prepared to return to the United States. But before he could leave town, the bank questioned the signature on the forged check. A Montreal detective came to visit Ponzi, at which time he admitted his guilt and was arrested (Zuckoff 2005, 29).

Ponzi was convicted of forgery and sentenced to three years in prison at St. Vincent de Paul Penitentiary, where he spent his days pounding rocks into gravel. Released for good behavior after 20 months, he re-entered the

United States on July 30, 1910; however, Ponzi violated U.S. immigration laws by attempting to smuggle five other Italians with him. For this offense he served two years in an Atlanta jail.

Following his second release from prison, Ponzi returned to Boston. In 1918 he married an Italian stenographer named Rose Marie Guecco and bought out her father's wholesale fruit and vegetable business. But due to mismanagement and a poorly conceived expansion plan, the business kept losing money. Eventually, it had to declare bankruptcy (J.B.C. 1937, 18).

Ponzi was again without employment and still searching for a way to get rich in America. One idea he considered was a business selling American magazines abroad. Seeking advice, he wrote to several people in Europe regarding his idea. One letter that he received back from Europe asked for more information and contained an international exchange coupon.

International exchange coupons or postal reply coupons were established in 1906, when the United States and 60 other countries agreed on a mechanism to deal with problems that arose when trying to send mail from one country to another. At the time, many U.S. immigrants had relatives in Europe and wrote to them frequently. Although they wanted to pay postage for their relatives' response, they were unable to purchase foreign stamps in the United States. The postal reply coupon was a solution to this problem; it was a way to send return postage when sending mail from one country to another. Americans would purchase the coupon and enclose it with their letter going abroad. The recipient of a coupon could bring it to a local post office and exchange it for an appropriate stamp to use for posting a letter back to the United States. Also, firms that had to deal with clients in other countries would sometimes want to send return postage with a package. The solution, again, was an international postal coupon that would be valid in every country and equal to the price of a postage stamp. The coupon was in essence a prepayment that could be redeemed for postage.

When this mechanism was set up in 1906, the cost of a postal exchange coupon was fixed in terms of each country's currency. For example, a coupon might cost 1 cent in the United States and 3 pesos in Spain. Initially, the cost of a coupon was set to be similar throughout the world (i.e., 1 cent and 3 pesos could buy the same amount of postage); however, the value of each nation's currency changed over time.

Ponzi quickly realized that in this situation great gains, with little risk, were possible through arbitrage—buying goods wherever the price is low and selling them wherever the price is high. Ponzi discovered that an international coupon could be bought in Spain for the equivalent of around one U.S. penny. When the coupon was sent to the United States, it could be exchanged for around 6 cents worth of stamps. These stamps could then be sold for cash in the United States. By sending U.S. money to Spain, having it exchanged for Spanish money, buying international reply coupons, sending these coupons back to the United States, buying U.S. postage stamps, and then selling the stamps, Ponzi could increase his initial investment by around sixfold. At the age of 37, Ponzi thought he had finally figured out how to get rich in America.

Such a money-making endeavor is neither illegal nor fraudulent. Arbitrage among national currencies in an attempt to make money from undervalued currencies takes place all the time. In the early twenty-first century, tens of billions of dollars worth of foreign currency get traded daily. Even in the early twentieth century there were no laws against such trading in order to make money. Ponzi (2001, 72) himself thought his scheme was "unethical," but noted that "a breach of ethics was not an infraction of the law."

The main problem with his arbitrage plan was that Ponzi did not have enough money to put it into operation. He thus set out to find some investors. Towards this end, Ponzi established the Securities Exchange Company in December 1919. He rented office space in the Niles Building at 27 School Street in Boston. Then he went to Daniels & Wilson, a furniture dealer, and found some used furniture costing $350; for this Ponzi agreed to pay $50 down and $5 per month.

Opening its new office, the Securities Exchange Company offered to pay investors $1.50 in 90 days for every dollar they invested. Initial sales were slow, so Ponzi offered even better returns—50 percent after only 45 days. At this rate, each dollar invested would grow to $27 in 1 year. Consequently, Ponzi was paying investors an annual rate of return of 2600 percent—far more than he could possibly earn through his postal stamp arbitrage plan.

The company accepted investments of any amount between $10 and $10,000. It gave investors notes or IOUs, signed by one of Ponzi's cashiers, in exchange for their deposits. Green notes were used for investments of $100 or less; orange notes were for investments of $101–$1,000, and blue notes were for investments of more than $1,000. When notes came due, Ponzi sent his investors a postcard telling them to come to his office to redeem their investment. There they could either receive a check for the amount they were owed or reinvest their money. Since Ponzi was paying such good rates, most people left their money with his company.

By the end of February 1920, Ponzi had received more than $5,000 from 17 investors. By March, the Securities Exchange Company had taken in more than $30,000 (Streissguth 1994, 37). To obtain even more funds, Ponzi hired sales agents and paid them a ten percent commission on all the new money they brought in. At this point, the business began to take off. In early spring, Ponzi was taking in $2,000 a day; by the end of May it was $200,000 a day (J.B.C. 1937, 18).

As word spread about the high returns, crowds of investors would line up outside Ponzi's Boston office every business day. During the summer of 1920, Ponzi became the talk of Boston and the East Coast. In June he took in $2.5 million from 7,500 investors. By July he was taking in more than $1 million a week. Seeking to expand further, he opened offices in other Massachusetts cities and then in Maine, New Hampshire, Vermont, Connecticut, Rhode Island, and New Jersey. The lines outside his office became so long, and deposits to the Securities Exchange Company became so large, that Ponzi had great difficulty counting and keeping track of all the money that was coming in.

With all this money coming in, Ponzi found himself controlling a great deal of wealth. There are conflicting reports as to whether Ponzi spent large amounts of this money on himself and his wife. Streissguth (1994, 39) claims that Ponzi "bought fancy cars, expensive suits, and a mansion with five acres of lawn." Wolff (1977, 56) notes that Ponzi bought himself expensive clothing and a lavishly decorated mansion in Lexington, Massachusetts. Yet, an article in the *New Yorker* (J.B.C. 1937, 19) claims that Ponzi spent little on himself beyond necessities and that his only indulgence was a $100,000 charitable contribution to a Boston orphanage.

Ponzi was spending so much time taking money in that he had no time to put his arbitrage plan into effect. Instead, he deposited the money he received into commercial banks paying around 4 or 5 percent interest, made unsecured loans to friends, made some real estate investments, and bought a few small companies. For example, he bought the Napoli Macaroni Manufacturing Company, joking that this would ensure he would never run out of spaghetti (Zuckoff 2005, 143).

This created a number of problems for Ponzi. First and most important of all, none of his investments paid sufficient returns to justify what Ponzi was paying out to his investors. Thus, whenever Ponzi accepted deposits, he lost money. It was thus inevitable that at some point, when investors turned in their colored Securities Exchange Company notes for cash, Ponzi would have to pay them off with funds received from later investors. This is how the famous pyramid scheme named after him began. But there were more substantial problems with the scheme in the long run—an ever increasing influx of money was necessary to pay interest to investors. At some point, the growth of new money would not be sufficient to pay off old investors who wanted to withdraw money. Then, the pyramid scheme would collapse.

Ponzi himself realized that he could not continue to pay out such large returns to investors when he earned only a few percentage points on the money entrusted to him; he needed some way to deal with the huge debt that Securities Exchange Company owed to its investors. Little companies making macaroni were just not sufficient. His plan was to transfer the Securities Exchange Company debts to some large legitimate business by merging with that business. Then he was going to sell shares of stock in the new firm. This would provide the cash to pay off the debt incurred by the Securities Exchange Company (Streissguth 1994, 39). If the firm he bought survived, Ponzi thought he could survive.

Ponzi focused on gaining control of two firms: the Hanover Trust Company, a large and prominent Boston bank, and J. R. Poole & Co., an import–export firm where Ponzi had once worked. Most of his efforts focused on acquiring the bank, since banks had large amounts of cash on hand. Ponzi had been making large deposits into Hanover Trust for months. With $2.7 million in the bank, he was the bank's largest depositor. This gave him a great deal of power. At a meeting with the bank president and board of directors, Ponzi said he wanted to buy a large share of the bank's stock. When they refused, Ponzi threatened to withdraw all his deposits from the bank immediately. The bank did not have this money on hand (having lent out a good deal of it) and could not get so much cash so quickly. The directors also knew that their inability to pay Ponzi would lead to a panic and a bank run among its depositors (this was before the advent of federal or state insurance of bank deposits), so they had to relent. They agreed to let Ponzi buy a majority of Hanover Trust shares and effectively control the company.

Another problem was that Ponzi himself fell victim to a good deal of fraud. He was conned by people who forged colored notes or who added zeros to the notes that Ponzi printed up and gave to investors as receipts. Ponzi paid all the notes presented to him in order to keep his investors happy and to thwart any rumors of problems with his company. Also, many investors were writing bad checks to the Securities Exchange Company and Ponzi's salesmen were claiming phony sales in order to receive more money in commission (Streissguth 1994, 42). Ponzi ignored these problems, worsening his precarious financial situation.

More difficult to ignore was the problem of Louis Cassulo, his Montreal cellmate. Cassulo, a long-time con man, had been living in Boston when he recognized Ponzi due to all the news coverage of his firm. At some point Cassulo confronted Ponzi and demanded a piece of the action; Ponzi gave him a job at the Securities Exchange Company, fearing the consequences if it became public knowledge that he had served time in Montreal for forging a check.

Meanwhile, questions were being raised about Ponzi's enterprise. The first difficulty arose during the summer of 1920. Daniels & Wilson, the furniture dealer, sued Ponzi for $1 million, claiming that they carried debt for Ponzi during the first couple months of his company's existence and therefore were entitled to part ownership of his company and part of the company profits. The suit was reported in Boston newspapers, leading depositors to run to the offices of the Securities Exchange Company seeking to withdraw their deposits. Fortunately, Ponzi was awash with cash and let his investors know that he could meet all their demands for cash. He even ordered his managers to redeem all notes at face value, regardless of their maturity date. This restored confidence among the public, and money continued to flow into Ponzi's company.

A further difficulty was that the rapid growth of the Securities Exchange Company attracted the attention of government officials. International officials worried that someone could profit from trading international reply coupons. France, Italy, and Romania temporarily suspended the sales of coupons. Federal, state, and county officials in the United States also suspected something was illegitimate about Ponzi's business, but they could find no evidence of illegality—in large part because Ponzi did little with the money he was given. A July 24, 1920, *Boston Post* article suggesting that public scrutiny of Ponzi was too lax and lenient spurred government regulatory officials to investigate Ponzi more thoroughly. This time a noted accountant, Edwin L. Pride, was hired to examine Ponzi's books. These stories led to runs against the company. As a result of this bad publicity, Ponzi was forced to pay out close to $2 million over the course of a week; yet he somehow managed to make it through the crisis, and soon more money was again coming into the Securities Exchange Company than was being withdrawn.

But things then took a turn for the worse. The *Boston Post* published a series of stories in August 1920 that led to the downfall of Ponzi. An August 2 story by William McMasters, whom Ponzi hired as a publicity man, alleged that Ponzi was a swindler, hopelessly insolvent, and probably crazy. Then a few days later, Clarence Barron, a prestigious financial news editor, reported that Ponzi was putting most of his cash into savings banks that paid only 5 percent interest. He also reported that the U.S. Post Office denied selling large quantities of postal coupons to either Ponzi or the Securities Exchange Company. Moreover, the article noted that the world supply of international postal coupons (around $200,000) was not enough to furnish the returns that Ponzi had promised to all his investors. Hence, there was no way that Ponzi could pay exorbitant returns to his depositors through a postal coupon arbitrage scheme. Ponzi denied the charges reported in these newspaper articles and responded by filing a $5 million lawsuit. But the articles had done their damage. Investors began to redeem their notes at a frenzied pace and Ponzi faced angry mobs lined up in front of his office.

Things got even worse on August 11, 1920, when the *Boston Post* published a front-page story about Ponzi's prior conviction in Montreal. The story included a mug shot of Ponzi taken in Canada, along with a contemporary photo, so that readers could clearly see that this was the same man. The next day Edwin Pride's report established that Ponzi had $7 million in liabilities and $3 million in assets. It also revealed that Ponzi had bought only $30 worth of international reply coupons during the entire time he was taking in tremendous sums of money (Train 1985, 5). The inescapable conclusion was that Ponzi had been perpetrating a pyramid scheme.

Most con artists start with the goal of taking off with all the funds once their scheme reaches its peak. Ponzi never attempted to flee. He continued to believe that he could make millions through trading postal coupons and that he could extricate himself from the difficulties he created by acquiring legitimate firms (Dunn 1975, 3).

Ponzi was arrested and charged with mail fraud on August 12, 1920. He was denied bail, in the fear that he would flee. The Massachusetts attorney general closed down the Securities Exchange Company and forced it to stop paying investors. It also took over the Hanover Trust Bank, but its actions here were too late. The bank went under, shareholders lost everything, and depositors lost all their savings. Many other New England banks where Ponzi deposited large sums of money suffered a similar fate. The 20,000 investors who held Securities Exchange Company notes at the time of the collapse received funds equal to just 37.5 percent of their initial investment (Zuckoff 2005, 298).

A Massachusetts grand jury indicted Ponzi on 68 counts of larceny on September 11, 1920. Too poor to hire a lawyer, Ponzi served as his own defense attorney. His defense argument was that a promise of profit was not larceny, that circumstances had changed, and that adverse circumstances caused the Securities Exchange Company to go under. At his trial, it seemed that Ponzi did not know many details of his own operation. However, on October 23, 1922, he was acquitted on all 68 charges.

A U.S. grand jury also returned a 43-count indictment against Ponzi for mail fraud. Reluctant to go through another trial, Ponzi struck a deal with prosecutors, pleading guilty to a single count on November 1, 1920. He was sentenced to five years in prison, the maximum sentence at the time. In August 1924, after serving close to four years of his term, he was released for good behavior. Shortly after his release from prison, in November 1924, Ponzi was indicted again by the state of Massachusetts and put back on trial. This time he was found guilty; his sentence was 7–9 years in state prison.

Free on appeal, Ponzi fled the state. He took the alias Charles Borelli and moved to Jacksonville, Florida. There he tried to make a fortune by purchasing real estate, subdividing the land, and selling the subplots. True to form, he promised 200 percent returns in 60 days for any money he was given to help carry out this plan. But Ponzi/Borelli was soon convicted of failing to file proper papers and selling certificates of indebtedness without permission. On April 26, 1926, he was sentenced to 1 year of hard labor at the Florida State Penitentiary in Raiford.

Freed on $1,500 bond pending appeal, Ponzi attempted to flee the country. He disguised himself by shaving his head, growing a moustache, and taking the name Andrea Luciana. He also faked his own suicide in Jacksonville by asking friends to place some of his clothing on a beach along with a suicide note (Zuckoff 2005, 306f.). He then boarded a ship bound for Italy. But Ponzi made the mistake of revealing his true identity to a shipmate. Word quickly spread that the world-famous con artist Charles Ponzi was aboard. As a result, authorities became aware of his whereabouts and he was arrested before the ship had left U.S. territorial waters (Knutson 1996).

Ponzi was returned to Boston in February 1927 and began his sentence at Massachusetts State Prison in Charlestown.

Ponzi was released from prison on February 14, 1934. Federal authorities, fed up with him, immediately arrested him as an undesirable alien. Unable to raise bail, he was deported back to Italy in October 1934. For a time he worked in the financial department of the government of Benito Mussolini, where he secretly stole funds (Streissguth 1994, 48). Ponzi also announced that he was going to write an autobiography. To raise money for this endeavor, he offered investors 1,000 $20 shares in the book's profits and guaranteed returns of 100 percent. By this time almost everyone knew about Ponzi and his ill-fated, get-rich-quick schemes, so few people invested in his book project. Ponzi did write the book, but it was not published until 2001, long after his death.

In 1939 Ponzi was offered a position in the Rio de Janeiro office of the Italian airline LATI and moved to Brazil. This job was arranged by his cousin, a colonel in the Italian Air Force. There is a good possibility that, once again, his family wanted Ponzi out of Italy and far away from them.

In Brazil, while working for LATI, Ponzi got involved in a smuggling ring. When it was discovered in 1942, he was fired. During the last years of his life, Ponzi survived by running a boarding house, teaching English to Brazilians, and collecting unemployment benefits. His declining years brought bad health, with paralysis and partial blindness brought on by a brain hemorrhage. Ponzi spent his final days in the charity ward of a Rio de Janeiro hospital, where he died of a blood clot on the brain on January 17, 1949.

References

Dunn, Donald H. *Ponzi! The Boston Swindler.* New York: McGraw–Hill, 1975.

J.B.C. "Where Are They Now? The Rise of Charles Ponzi," *New Yorker,* May 8, 1937, 18–22.

Knutson, Mark C. "The Remarkable Criminal Financial Career of Charles K. Ponzi, the Postal Reply Coupon, and Denouement and Epilogue" (http://www.ozinternet.com/Knutson©1996).

Ponzi, Charles. *The Rise of Mr. Ponzi.* Naples, FL: Inkwell Publishers, 2001 [1937].

Streissguth, Thomas. *Hoaxers & Hustlers.* Minneapolis, MN: Oliver Press, 1994.

Train, John. *Famous Financial Fiascos.* New York: Clarkson N. Potter, 1985.

Wolff, Jay. "Mister Pyramid," *Audacity* (Summer 1997): 50–61.

Zuckoff, Michael. *Ponzi's Scheme: The True Story of a Financial Legend.* New York: Random House, 2005.

Farm-Town Boy to International Fugitive

4

PATRICK KUHSE
JOYCE A. OSTROSKY
LINDA M. LEINICKE
W. MAX REXROAD

Contents

Introduction

Question: How does a farm-town boy from Iowa end up in a Costa Rican prison and later in U.S. federal prisons? *Answer:* He suffered some serious ethical lapses in his business dealings. This chapter will provide an overview of Patrick Kuhse's personal history and present the unethical activities that changed his address from Wall Street to no street in a prison cell.

Iowa Farm-Town Boy

Patrick Kuhse grew up in a small farming town in rural Iowa. Raised by two very loving parents, Patrick, along with his brother and two sisters, had a typical Midwestern upbringing. His life included attending church, hunting and fishing, playing sports in school, and learning the importance of hard work and ethical behavior. Nothing in Patrick's upbringing would indicate that he would someday become an international fugitive.

Arizona State University

At 17, Patrick graduated from high school and decided to attend Arizona State University (ASU). At that time, ASU boasted an attendance of approximately 40,000 students. It also was known as the number-one party school in America. On the ASU campus, Patrick was far outside his comfort zone and intimidated by his surroundings. He wanted to align with a peer group to feel more comfortable, so he chose to join a social fraternity that centered on parties and fun-loving times around the beer keg. He focused on socializing to the detriment of his academic pursuits.

Patrick soon learned that many of his fraternity brothers came from very wealthy families. They exposed Patrick to a lifestyle he had never known—expensive cars, luxurious homes, and other extravagances. Patrick liked what he saw. It was at this point that his values began to shift. Family and home became less and less important, while amassing wealth started to become his number-one obsession.

Patrick wanted to fit in with his wealthy fraternity brothers. He did not have his family and friends close by to tell him that his partying behavior was unacceptable. With no family and friends to ground his value system, Patrick decided that he liked wealth and that he wanted to amass material items. Patrick began to see his parents as old fashioned. He prided himself on being part of the new generation of baby boomers who were following a different set of ethics: that of believing in the mantra that greed is good. He started to equate success with money, power, and influence.

Patrick was so anxious to go out into the world and pursue his fortune that he did not finish his degree at ASU and left after only three years.

Early Career

After a couple of years in retail management, Patrick was recruited by and joined a securities brokerage firm. As part of the hiring process, he took a personality-profile test that indicated he had a type A personality and was compulsive, driven, and willing to do anything and everything to get ahead. He was a perfect fit for the brokerage firm. Patrick began selling various types of securities products, including mutual funds and limited partnerships, and was very successful. Then, a routine sales meeting started Patrick, almost imperceptibly, down the slippery slope of unethical behavior. At this meeting, the top salespeople of the firm were honored. The person in charge of the meeting announced that he was going to step out of the room. During his absence, the top salespeople shared with the others how they had achieved their award-winning sales. When making a sales presentation to a client, each salesperson was supposed to cover the seven key points about the investment. Patrick had always covered these seven key points. Much to his surprise, the top salespeople were only covering two of the seven points. These two points covered the positive aspects of the investment. The risks associated with the investment were not being presented. The message was clear—to maximize your sales, you needed to cut corners and not dwell on the potentially negative aspects of the investment.

Patrick took this message to heart. He observed that the people who got ahead did not feel compelled to follow the rules. He was surrounded by other salespeople who were being rewarded handsomely for not following the rules. This behavior further eroded Patrick's farm-town values. He noted that adhering to his Midwestern values of acting honestly and following all of the rules was not going to get him ahead fast enough. In his pursuit of wealth, Patrick started to rationalize his omitting coverage of the risky aspects of investments when making sales.

Oklahoma City, Oklahoma

After several years with two brokerage firms, Patrick received a promotion and moved to Oklahoma City as a regional manager. While in Oklahoma, he earned his certified financial planner designation. By this time, Patrick had a wife and two young boys. While in Oklahoma, he met a fellow securities representative who would later play an important role in his downfall. She was one of Patrick's employees, and they became good friends. However, a few years after they moved to Oklahoma City, Patrick's wife wanted to move back to her hometown of San Diego and he agreed to move. He left the brokerage firm to start his own financial-planning practice in California.

San Diego, California

In San Diego, Patrick joined a friend and became co-owner and financial principal of a financial-planning firm. He continued to prosper. Patrick provided financial products to independent brokers nationwide and also developed a personal-client base. Many of his clients were extremely wealthy.

Patrick was working almost nonstop at accumulating wealth. His business flourished; it took him all over the country and often away from his family. He prided himself on closely identifying with the status of his wealthy clients. However, his two young boys were not impressed. They would have preferred to spend more quality time with their father. Patrick had provided his family with what he thought was important—a big house, expensive cars, and lots of spending money. Patrick's values had now totally shifted to wealth accumulation and the attainment of power and prestige. Family and home life were no longer primary values in his life. Patrick was so busy being a big shot that he had almost forgotten about his family. He was clearly on the fast track to success.

Enter His Oklahoma Friend

Out of the blue one day, Patrick was contacted by his long-time friend and business associate from Oklahoma City. She told Patrick that one of her friends was running for the office of treasurer of the State of Oklahoma and that she was working in this friend's campaign. If her friend got elected treasurer, she would be given the job of managing Oklahoma's bond portfolio. Patrick's friend had little to no experience in managing bond investments, but she believed she was up to the task. She suggested that Patrick could become one of the brokers who would invest the bond funds for her office, if her friend were elected. Patrick had no experience doing this type of investing either, but he was intrigued, and—what the heck—the election had not taken place yet, so he expressed his interest.

After a successful election, Patrick's friend called him again in California. She wanted to enlist Patrick as one of ten representatives who would execute the purchases and sales of the bonds for the State of Oklahoma. At this point in Patrick's life, due to his business success and wealth accumulation, he had developed an attitude of super optimism. He felt he was smarter than everyone else and that he could do anything. He had a feeling that he was invulnerable. Despite the fact that Patrick had no experience managing bonds, he immediately decided that he could make it work. He rationalized as follows: "How hard can this be? I can get a book and read up on this." He also thought that investing a pot of money would be easier than chasing clients. This was a seemingly unimportant decision to Patrick at the time. He thought managing Oklahoma's bond fund would look great on his resume. Much to his pleasant surprise, he learned that the bond portfolio was worth several billion dollars.

Patrick went to Wall Street to solicit a brokerage firm to help him handle the Oklahoma bond investments. Once he began trading, he earned what he perceived as very little in the way of commissions. He informed his friend of his feelings. She responded that since she approved all bond transactions, Patrick should charge a much higher commission. He did this, and his income from these commissions began to soar. During this time, a plan was hatched for Patrick to "share" his commissions with his friend. Patrick knew these kickbacks were illegal, so he had to rationalize his behavior. He told himself, "If I give my friend some of the money I have earned, so what? She isn't a stranger; I've known her for years." Patrick further rationalized that he was entitled to his excessive commissions because he had a perceived belief that he was maximizing the returns on his portion of Oklahoma's bond investments. Patrick's rationalization was based on the fact that the current bond managers were earning rates of return far in excess of the returns earned by previous bond managers. By now, Patrick was living the high life and was fully absorbed by his own ego and greed. It was Patrick's greed that allowed him to rationalize his behavior and participate in this unethical and illegal kickback scheme. However, his unethical behavior was taking a toll on his health. He began to develop ulcers, migraine headaches, and noticeable hair loss. He was a nervous wreck. Patrick could lie to his head, but his body was telling him the truth.

Shortly after beginning his association with the Oklahoma bond account, Patrick deposited over $1 million in his checking account. His wife was astonished that they had so much money, and she wanted to know where it came from. Patrick realized that it would be very difficult to justify to his wife the balance in their checking account. He became evasive and alluded to the fact that all his hard work was paying off. His wife was skeptical and feared that he was involved in something illegal. When confronted with her questions, Patrick would immediately become defensive. He used the defensive tactic of asking her, "Don't you love me? Don't you trust me? Do you think for one minute I would ever do anything that would endanger our family?" Instead of acknowledging that his wife was absolutely correct, he justified his behavior by questioning his wife's trust in his business dealings. Patrick was always very close to his mother, but the same thing was happening with her. His mother had also questioned the legality of how he was earning a living. Even though his wife and mother had questions, Patrick continued to be in denial about the illegality of his actions. Greed and rationalization were controlling his life. Patrick was now losing the confidence of his two main supporters—his wife and his mother. At this point, he began distancing himself emotionally from both of them.

Because he knew that he was up to no good, Patrick's stress level increased. He decided that he would continue his involvement in the kickback scheme for only a set amount of time or for a fixed dollar amount. Patrick's behavior was typical of fraudsters who often believe they can stop their fraudulent behavior and exit the fraud scheme whenever they want.

Two years went by. Patrick and his Oklahoma friend were raking in lots of money. She, however, was having personnel problems back in Oklahoma and had to fire one of her employees. The fired employee had observed that Patrick's friend was living well beyond her means. The disgruntled employee contacted the Federal Bureau of Investigation (FBI) and blew the whistle on Patrick and his friend.

The Investigation Begins

The kickback scheme had been going smoothly for so long that Patrick had gotten overconfident and lazy. Instead of periodically flying to Oklahoma to give money to his friend, he looked for an easier alternative. To avoid the plane trips, he sent his friend an automated teller machine (ATM) card with his name on it. She used the ATM card frequently.

Early one morning, Patrick was awakened by a knock on the front door of his San Diego home. An FBI agent and an Internal Revenue Service (IRS) criminal fraud investigator, with badges in hand, were standing on his front steps. Patrick looked through the peephole in his front door. He did not open it. The investigation had begun into whether Patrick was "funneling" money to his friend in return for her favorable treatment of him. The investigation went on for over a year. Finally, Patrick flew back to Oklahoma City to consult with attorneys there. The Oklahoma attorneys gave him two options. Option one was that, although no indictments had been handed down yet, he could anticipate that they would be, so he could prepare for trial. Option two was to go to the FBI and tell on his friend in hopes of getting a reduced sentence. Patrick decided he would not tell on his friend. He had never told on anyone in his life. Interestingly, he believed it was unethical to tell on his friend, yet he seemed to have no problem with the kickback scheme. He had rationalized the theft by telling himself, "There are no victims here. This is a victimless crime. In fact, I am doing the State of Oklahoma a favor. I am earning them a far better rate of return on their bond investments than they've earned previously."

Patrick flew back to San Diego to mull over his options of either going to trial or telling on his friend. Upon his return home, he found a message from the American Broadcasting Company (ABC) news magazine *Nightline* on his answering machine. The show wanted to interview him for a story about to air on the Oklahoma bond-trading investigation. He declined to be interviewed. The story aired the day after Thanksgiving 1993. Realizing that the fraud was falling apart, Patrick decided to flee the country. He researched which countries did not have extradition agreements with the United States. Those countries were Afghanistan, Cuba, Iran, Iraq, Libya, and North Korea. Since none of these countries was acceptable to Patrick, he chose to flee to Costa Rica because it did not have an army and was a democracy. He convinced his wife of his innocence. In order to persuade his wife to go to Costa Rica with him, he played the family card. He told his wife that he was the victim of a political witch hunt. He said, "Honey, they're trying to break up our family. We need to leave the country." Prior to any indictments and under the belief that he was still free to do whatever he wanted, he moved his wife and two sons to Costa Rica.

After discovering his departure, the federal government filed 32 felony counts against Patrick, including bribing a government official, money laundering, and conspiracy.

Costa Rica

After living in Costa Rica for several months, once again Patrick heard a knock on the front door. This time it was four heavily armed men from Interpol. Patrick fled out the back door of his Costa Rican home. He told himself, "People like me do not go to prison." He was still self-centered and lacked a sense of accountability.

For the next three years, Patrick was an international fugitive living on the run. He went to small towns and rural areas and passed himself off as a tourist. He never stayed in one area more than a few days. He was always watchful for any police activity, patrol officers, or anyone who looked his way more than casually. The worst part for Patrick was that he could have no direct contact with his family—no phone calls and no mail. He knew the police were watching his family in Costa Rica, so he had to stay away.

After three years of not knowing whether her husband was dead or alive, Patrick's wife decided to take the children back to San Diego. This was a turning point in his life. The loss of his wife and two sons finally made him realize what his pursuit of wealth had cost him. Not long after their departure, Patrick decided to turn himself in. He called the U.S. Embassy in Costa Rica and made an appointment to give himself up. Upon his surrender, much to his shock, Patrick was placed in the infamous San Sebastian Prison in San Jose, Costa Rica. This prison was a classic example of Third World incarceration. Despite horrendous prison conditions, surprisingly, Patrick had never felt better. He had finally done the right thing for the right reasons. When Patrick had $4 million in the bank, he had never felt worse. Yet, in San Sebastian prison, where his immediate future looked very bleak, he had never felt better. Patrick attributed his newfound sense of calm to his decision to turn himself in and face the consequences of his illegal behavior.

After 3 weeks in San Sebastian, Patrick was extradited to the United States. He spent seven months in a county jail cell. Patrick pled guilty and chose not to go to trial. At his sentencing, the judge said, "Mr. Kuhse, I want to sentence you to 20 years. But, you turned yourself in; you didn't go to trial; you did the right thing." Because of Patrick's decisions to do the right thing, his sentence was not as harsh as it might have been. The judge sentenced him to five years and 11 months in prison, $3.89 million of restitution, three years of probation, and 208 hours of community service. Patrick's friend was sentenced to nine years in prison.

The Prison Years

While in prison, Patrick spent a lot of time reflecting on his past behavior. He tried to determine how a smart guy like him had done such dumb things. He observed that other inmates who had committed white-collar crimes had certain common characteristics. For example, many of these individuals were self-centered super optimists with a sense of entitlement. Patrick finally concluded that everything was not all about him and material wealth, and that real happiness comes from relationships, not money.

During his prison years, Patrick completed his college degree through a correspondence course offered by Western Illinois University. His wife divorced him while he was in prison, and he only got to see his sons briefly in a prison visiting room.

In 2001, Patrick was released from prison after serving four years. He was given 30 days to get a job. Part of his sentence was that he could no longer make a living by trading securities. Patrick went to live with his mother and father who were now living in Arizona. The only job he could find was as a truck driver earning $9 per hour. Patrick drove that truck for a year and a half. During this time, he tried to be the best employee he could be. He was grateful for the second chance he had been given. At this same time, in order to satisfy his community service obligation, he began giving talks on his experiences and lessons learned.

Patrick Kuhse's story illustrates that having a loving family background and successful professional career does not protect one from making bad ethical decisions. When a good person starts to rationalize unethical decisions because of greed, that person is in danger of gradually slipping into activities that might lead to a very unpleasant end.

Epilogue

The period after prison was a struggle for Patrick. He had three years of probation ahead of him, $3.89 million of restitution to pay to the government, and 208 hours of community service, and he was banned from the financial services industry where he had made a living most of his professional career. Fortunately, his parents demonstrated unconditional love and support and let him move in with them when he was 45. Patrick found it difficult to get work. His extensive financial background did not appeal to employers due to his felony convictions. He could certainly understand why three out of four men released from prison go back in within three years. The pressures are tremendous.

To earn a living, Patrick drove a delivery truck for minimum wage and started giving talks to satisfy his community service obligation. To his surprise, he found a passion along the way—that of sharing his stories and observations with others. He decided to stay focused on that passion, and he never gave up. Patrick discovered there was a genuine public interest in knowing why smart people could do such dumb things. Between his personal passion for speaking on ethics and the public's interest and concern about the subject, a new career was born. Many would say this is a classic example of how to make lemonade out of lemons. Patrick firmly believed that if you find your passion and embrace it, stay clearly focused on it, pursue it with all your heart, and stay anchored in principled behavior, you will succeed because it will give you the strength to overcome the adversities along the way.

Once Patrick satisfied his community service obligation, he kept on speaking. For the next 2½ years, he gave hundreds of free talks to hone his skills and messages. It was a financial struggle, but his direction was focused. With financial and moral support from his friends, Patrick continued to pursue his passion for speaking.

Bibliography

American Broadcasting Company. *Nightline,* November 26, 1993.

English, Paul. "State Sues Firms over Trading Fees," *Oklahoman,* February 9, 1994.

Parker, John. "Trial Set to Begin in Treasurer Case," *Oklahoman,* March 14, 1995.

_____. "Kickback Scam Leads to Jail for Ex-trader," *Oklahoman,* February 4, 1998.

Queary, Paul. "Trial Set Today for Ex-trader." *Oklahoman,* March 13, 1995.

U.S. District Court for the Western District of Oklahoma. 1998. Case # CR 94144-2-L. February 3.

Oscar Hartzell and the Estate of Sir Francis Drake

5

STEVEN PRESSMAN

Contents

One thing that sustains people in hard times is the hope that a lucky break could make them a good deal of money and reverse their fortunes. People also have a natural inclination to help others in need. These two facts about human nature help explain the popularity of Nigerian money transfer scams in the late twentieth and early twenty-first centuries. They also help explain the success of Oscar Hartzell and his Sir Francis Drake estate scam. Hartzell convinced tens of thousands of investors that, for a relatively small sum of money, they would receive part of or help the rightful heirs receive their share of the fabulous Francis Drake estate.

The Nigerian money transfer fraud, or advance fee fraud, seeks to extract money from people to help transfer money. In return, those helping to transfer the money are promised a share of the funds transferred. This fraud began in Nigeria in the mid-1980s, and has since spread to other African countries. It has become widespread via the internet (see "Advance Fee Fraud").

The Drake estate scam and the Nigerian money transfer fraud both follow a similar pattern. People are asked to give up some money now and are promised "large returns" on their investment. In both cases, the perpetrators of the scam keep the money and the promised returns never materialize.

These scams raise a number of ethical and legal issues. It is clear that the purpose is to dupe investors. But the key question concerns the responsibility of the government to prevent such scams. On the one hand, if people willingly turn their money over to someone (doing no homework), is it a problem if they lose their money? Should people not be held responsible for their bad decisions? On the other hand, if the buyer must always beware and must always suffer the consequences of dishonesty and deceit, will honest investors not have greater difficulty obtaining funds? And will investment and economic growth not suffer as a result?

Sir Francis Drake, the famous British explorer, was born in the early 1540s. In 1572 he led an expedition to Panama, searching for Peruvian treasures that were being transported to Spain. After several failures, Drake formed an alliance with a French captain and attacked a mule train carrying treasures headed for Spain. Their haul was estimated to be 100,000 gold pesos, or 40,000 pounds sterling (Raynor 2002, 10), the equivalent of around $400 million today. Following this success, Drake went on another expedition in 1577, which earned his commercial backers a return of 4700 percent and 100,000 pounds for Queen Elizabeth. This money helped transform England into a great world power.

Drake used his share of the money to buy a large country estate, where he died on January 20, 1596. Within months of his death, rumors circulated in England that Drake left a great fortune to an illegitimate son conceived by Queen Elizabeth during an affair with Drake. Scams in England during the seventeenth and eighteenth centuries promised investors a share of the Drake estate in exchange for their money, which would be used to help the true heir claim the Drake fortune. Many English citizens lost their life savings participating in this endeavor.

In the mid-nineteenth century the Drake estate con made its first appearance in the United States. Over the next 25 years it became so popular that the U.S. ambassador to England felt compelled to issue a public statement that the Drake treasure did not exist and that people selling shares in it were swindlers. As a result of these warnings, the Drake estate scam disappeared in the United States for several decades.

It was the invention of the telephone directory that changed things. In 1900 a group of swindlers sent a wire to all the Drakes they could find in U.S. phone directories stating that they were heirs to the Drake estate. Then they sent a letter from a London law firm confirming this fact. Next came a follow-up letter stating that problems had arisen; the Drake heirs were asked for money to help resolve these problems and claim their share of the Drake fortune.

In the early twentieth century, the Drake swindle reached Oscar Hartzell, who took it to heights never before seen. Hartzell was born in Monmouth, a small town in western Illinois, in 1876. His father worked hard and acquired more than 400 acres of land. Oscar left school at 16 to work on the family farm. At the age of 19, he married Daisy Rees from nearby Gerlaw. The newlyweds first lived with Hartzell's parents, and Oscar continued to work for his father. Soon he began buying and selling farms. He and Daisy wound up in Madison County, 16 miles south of Des Moines. But Oscar was not happy there and was constantly dreaming of prestige and success.

In 1905, Hartzell's father died as a result of a hunting accident. Oscar took his half of the estate (almost $80,000) and used it as a down payment on a 16,000-acre ranch. By the end of 1907, Hartzell claimed the ranch was worth half a million. But in 1908 he lost his cattle to an infectious virus. A fire in one of his barns cost him $20,000, and cholera killed 800 of his hogs.

Hartzell was in deep financial trouble. A legal suit was also filed against him; he won the suit, but it also created more financial distress.

Hartzell then moved to Des Moines and started a realty firm. But the business soon went bankrupt, and Hartzell became a police officer and soon thereafter a deputy sheriff. In 1914 he ran for sheriff, spending $1,500 on his campaign, but lost the election. He considered himself a failure (Raynor 2002, 31).

As Hartzell was making and then losing a fortune, Sudie Whiteaker was traveling through the rural midwest selling shares in the estate of Sir Francis Drake. She went door to door explaining that many Drakes in Madison County were legally entitled to part of the Drake estate, but complaining that English officials were trying to keep this a secret and hold on to the Drake fortune. Whiteaker claimed that she was trying to get the Drake estate distributed to its rightful heirs. Since this action was expensive, she needed financial support. For a small fee of $25, she promised to use this money to fight for the Drake estate heirs and that their $25 fee would yield returns of 100-fold and perhaps 1000-fold.

At some point, Whiteaker realized she needed legal advice and, through a friend, was introduced to a lawyer by the name of Milo Lewis. She told Lewis the story of the Drake estate and that her cousin, George Drake, was the sole heir of the estate. She also told Milo that she was selling shares in the inheritance for $25 apiece. Lewis told Whiteaker that he was in (Raynor 2002, 41).

Traveling through the Midwest, Whiteaker and Lewis stopped at the Hartzell farm in Madison County. Hartzell's mother believed the story of the Drake estate and, dreaming of future riches, she turned her life savings over to the two swindlers—$6,500 that she hid in a small tin box in the attic. In return, the Hartzells were promised a share of the Drake estate, and Whiteaker and Lewis promised to keep them apprised of the case. But Whiteaker and Lewis soon disappeared. Like other farm families in Madison County, the Hartzells discovered that they were victims of a scam. When Oscar talked to other Madison County residents who were bilked by Whitaker and Lewis, he was surprised that they still expected to realize a large return on their investment. At this point, he realized that there was still a large untapped market for the Drake scam (Brannon 1966, 198).

Oscar decided to find Whiteaker and Lewis. He first went to Sioux City, the closest town with a library, and tried to find information about Sir Francis Drake. He also carefully studied the U.S. postal laws. One important thing he learned was that scams should not use the mail system because it was easy to get arrested for mail fraud (Nash 1976, 79f).

Using his police skills and his connections as deputy sheriff, Hartzell then tracked Whiteaker and Lewis. Following various leads, he finally found them in Des Moines. But rather than arresting them or demanding they return his mother's $6,500, he laughed at them and told them they were "rubes." The three formed a partnership, the Sir Francis Drake Association. Hartzell appointed himself manager, with a salary of $1,000 a month. With Whiteaker, Lewis, and other sales agents, he traveled around rural towns in Iowa, Missouri, and Illinois asking for help getting the Drake estate money to its rightful heirs. At first they only contacted people named Drake. But since names could change through marriage and swindling only people named Drake yielded too little money, they decided to accept money from anyone, promising all contributors a share of the Drake fortune.

In 1917, Hartzell decided he had to go to England to meet the heir to the Drake estate. He also increased his pay to $2,500 a week. Hartzell lived a life of affluence in London, renting a luxurious suite of rooms in one of London's most fashionable districts and dining in the city's best restaurants. He adopted a title of nobility, the Duke of Buckland (Streissguth 1994, 78), and had several regular girlfriends. The father of one girl that he got pregnant had to be placated with shares in the Drake estate (Sifakis 1993, 78).

By 1919, government officials were actively trying to shut down the Drake scam. Illinois disbarred Milo Lewis for inducing people to invest in the Drake estate, and Hartzell had to return to the United States to assure his "investors" that the Drake estate was legitimate. His efforts were aided by the fact that the Illinois court said only that the Drake estate *might* be phony.

At this point Hartzell took full control of the scam. He used the court case to claim that Lewis squandered the money he received to get the Drake fortune. Then he blamed Sudie Whiteaker for getting the facts wrong; her cousin was not the heir to the Drake estate. In addition, Hartzell claimed that Sudie had known this since 1916. He also claimed that he was commissioning a genealogy to determine the real heirs.

Hartzell then returned to London, leaving his assistants and sales agents to run the scam. He hired two of his brothers, offering them $10,000 a year (around $100,000 today), and changed the con a bit. Instead of selling shares, they sought "donations," assuring donors that they would receive their money back, plus 6 percent annual interest, plus a bonus of $500 to $1,000 for each dollar donated, when the estate was settled. This provided some legal protection for Hartzell, since he was no longer selling shares in a scam (Raynor 2002, 79).

In western England, Hartzell found a man named Francis Drake, reputed to be the last living English descendant of the great explorer. For £750 he gave Hartzell whatever remaining rights he had in the Drake estate. At the same time, Hartzell claimed that Sir Francis Drake had married a third time, had a son, and that this son was the true heir to the Drake estate. He claimed to have traced the lineage of this son to a Colonel Drexel Drake who was living in London and that Colonel Drake had assigned the rights of the Drake estate to him (Raynor 2002, 83–87).

Hartzell cabled his associates frequently from London (rather than writing to them). The associates called local investors together and then read them cables from Hartzell. Hartzell reported he had met with the real heir to the Drake fortune, and that "the heir had put Hartzell in charge of the good fight and would pay off at the price of $500 to $1 when the estate was settled" (Slocum 1955, 300). Even his sales force came to believe that a settlement would come soon, and they even contributed their own money to Hartzell.

To steer clear of U.S. laws regarding mail fraud, all money collected by Hartzell's agents was sent to his brother in New York. Once a week, his brother would travel to Toronto, Canada, and cable American Express money orders to Hartzell in London.

Hartzell also demanded that "donators" sign a note promising "silence, secrecy, and nondisturbance" (Slocum 1955, 300). Violating this provision meant losing the rights to one's share in the Drake estate. This promise of silence made it hard for state officials, who wanted to indict Hartzell on mail fraud and stop his operation, to find witnesses to testify.

Money flowed to Hartzell. Raynor (2002, 90) examined American Express records in an attempt to track the growth of the Drake estate scam. In April 1924 Hartzell received around $2,250 ($22,500 today) by wire. In June 1925 he received more than $7,000, and in September 1926 he received more than $8,000. All the while, Hartzell's wires to the United States were filled with self-confidence and optimism. He led people to believe that he was dealing with the highest powers in England, and he told investors that the money would be coming soon.

However, by 1927, some Drake estate victims were becoming uneasy. They had given Hartzell everything they owned and many went into debt sending Hartzell money. Hartzell responded by sending even more optimistic cables to the United States. He said a settlement had been reached, but there were problems with turning the money over to him. First, it was a conspiracy between President Hoover and Andrew Mellon to keep billions of dollars out of the United States because of its effect on the economy. In 1929 he said that the stock market crash prevented the money from being disbursed (Nash 1976, 85f).

In 1928, Iowa's secretary of state sought to stop Hartzell. He wrote a letter to newspapers in Iowa and Minnesota claiming the Drake estate was fraudulent. Then he introduced a bill into the Iowa state legislature that would have required a permit whenever soliciting donations. Hartzell responded by getting his supporters to send letters of protest to their state representatives. The bill was defeated, as legislators proclaimed the right of every American to donate money whenever and wherever he or she pleased (Raynor 2002, 114f).

Hartzell even turned the tables on government officials trying to shut him down. He argued that he was legitimate since he was not shut down by Iowa or Illinois or by Washington. He also seized on an article written by economist John Maynard Keynes in the *Saturday Evening Post* in October 1930, mentioning the Drake treasure and how it led to growth in England, as proof of the great returns that would come to the Drake heirs (Raynor 2002, 119f).

The money continued to pour in. While the stock market crash of October 1929 ended many swindles of the 1920s, the Drake scam continued to thrive, and Hartzell became a hero to rural Midwest residents. American Express records show that Hartzell received $6,000 in November 1929, $9,000 in December 1929, and $10,500 in September 1930. From June 1931 to December 1932 he received more than $250,000, or more than $12,000 a month (Raynor 2002, 118).

The more money Hartzell received, the more he spent. He bought expensive cars, clothing, and cigars. He also continued to support his former mistress and his illegitimate son.

In another attempt to shut down the scam, John Sparks, a U.S. postal inspector, went to see Hartzell's relatives and his employees. The employees described what they were doing and insisted that the deal was legitimate. After his investigation, Sparks got the Post Office to hold hearings and got many of Hartzell's agents to testify. Five signed affidavits agreeing to stop soliciting and receiving money. This was reported in the Iowa press, and donations fell. But Hartzell claimed that since there was no order constraining him from getting the Drake estate and there was no attempt to extradite him to the United States, he was legitimate and the Drake estate was legitimate. His agents increased their efforts, and soon Hartzell was receiving $15,000 a month (Raynor 2002, 126–133).

In 1932 some of Hartzell's agents were arrested and charged with postal fraud. The government held that mail fraud laws applied in this case since monies were sent to these agents through the postal system. Responding to these charges, Hartzell started a letter-writing campaign among his "investors." They were told to write Congress, the attorney general, and the president of the United States protesting the indictment of Hartzell's agents. Investors were informed that if they did not write these letters they would lose the rights to their share of the Drake estate.

By January 1933 the U.S. State Department finally had sufficient evidence to extradite Hartzell from England. He was arrested in London on January 9, 1933, and deported to the United States a month later. Upon arriving in New York, Hartzell was arrested and charged with mail fraud. He was sent to Sioux City, Iowa, and imprisoned there. From prison Hartzell wrote to his followers claiming that his deportation from England proved that the British were frightened of him and vowed to continue his fight to have the money tied up in the Drake estate released to him. This letter got Hartzell more than $130,000 for his legal defense (Slocum 1955, 302). After five days in jail he was released on $10,000 bail.

His trial began October 23, 1933. The government argued that Hartzell was not guilty of mail fraud, but had caused mail to be sent through the postal system with the intent of defrauding others. In his research at the Sioux City library many years earlier, Hartzell failed to note not only that it was illegal to send fraudulent materials through the mail, but also that it was illegal to cause others to do so.

The case went to the jury on November 14. The next morning Hartzell was found guilty of mail fraud, sentenced to ten years in prison, and fined $2,000. Bail was set at $25,000 while Hartzell appealed his conviction. A court of appeals upheld the conviction in August 1934. In December 1934, the Supreme Court refused to hear the case; Hartzell was ordered to enter Leavenworth Penitentiary in Kansas.

His followers, however, continued to believe that the British and American governments were conspiring to keep the multibillion dollar Drake estate for themselves. Even while in prison, Hartzell received contributions from people who hoped to receive part of the Drake estate.

Hartzell, too, seemed convinced of his innocence and believed that there was an international conspiracy against him. Gradually he went out of his mind. Psychiatric evaluations said he was mentally incompetent and subject to delusions of grandeur. In December 1936, Hartzell was transferred to a medical center for prison inmates in Springfield, Missouri, where he died on August 27, 1943.

In total, Hartzell conned between 70,000 and 80,000 Americans out of at least $2 million. All were hoping to get rich quickly by purchasing shares in the estate of Sir Francis Drake. They were living in the go-go years of the 1920s, did not trust the stock market, and saw the Drake estate as their ticket to affluence. Word of mouth at Midwestern picnics, socials, and bars led to a sort of herd effect. One person told someone else, who told someone else, and soon everyone wanted to get in on the action. Many farms in Iowa and other Midwestern states went into foreclosure to meet Hartzell's demands during the 15 years he lived a life of luxury in London. For example, W. H. Shepard and his wife, Adna, were made Iowa sales agents for the Sir Francis Drake Association because Adna's maiden name was Drake. Besides collecting money from their neighbors for Hartzell, they also contributed their own money and mortgaged their home to come up with $5,000 for the project (Slocum 1955).

Unfortunately, during the nearly two decades that Hartzell ran his scam, no one asked the simple questions that might have exposed the fraud. For example, even if Sir Francis Drake did have an illegitimate son, after so many centuries would this son have only *one* heir? Also, no one questioned whether the statute of limitations would have run out on a case more than 300 years old.

In their trial against Hartzell, the U.S. government located Sir Francis Drake's will. Drake was childless and left his entire estate to his widow and his brother, Tom. The two heirs had a legal dispute over the will, which was eventually settled in court. According to the settlement, there was little of value in the Drake estate (Slocum 1955, 302). Finally, the English statute of limitation on wills lasts just 30 years; after that the matter was settled (Nash 1976, 89). So, even if the Drake estate had had hundreds of billions of dollars, and even if Drake had had only one heir, his heir would not have been entitled to any of this money in the twentieth century.

There have been many heir scams in U.S. history, where innocent people believed that they would get millions from some long lost relative if only they would "invest" some money now to help with the legal issues involved in the case. None of these, however, has been as destructive or famous as the Drake estate swindle perpetrated by Oscar Hartzell. It preyed on people's naiveté and their desire to get rich quick without working hard.

References

"Advance Fee Fraud" (en.wikipedia.org/wiki/Nigerian_money_transfer_fraud).

Brannon, William T. "The Fabulous Drake Swindle." In *The Fine Art of Swindling,* ed. Walter B. Gibson. New York: Grosset & Dunlop, 1966.

Nash, Jay Robert. *Hustlers and Con Men,* 77–93. New York: M. Evans, 1976.

Raynor, Richard. *Drake's Fortune.* New York: Doubleday, 2002.

Sifakis, Carl. *Hoaxes and Scams,* 77–79. New York: Facts on File.

Slocum, Bill. "The 70,000 Heirs of Sir Francis Drake." In *Grand Deception,* ed. Alexander Klein, 299–303. Philadelphia: J. B. Lippincott, 1955.

Streissguth, Thomas. *Hoaxers & Hustlers,* 73–85. Minneapolis, MN: Oliver Press, 1994.

A Concrete Example of Fraud at the Fort Worth Independent School District

6

ARNOLD I. BARKMAN

Contents

The time is the mid- to late 1990s. Two men are standing alone in a parking lot. One hands the other a brown paper bag. One of the men is Tommy Ingram, the director of maintenance for the Fort Worth Independent School District (FWISD). The other is Ray Brooks, a major FWISD concrete contractor.

Do people learn from the past? Tommy Ingram may have learned the wrong lesson. In 1979 and 1980, he saw an older generation of athletic coaches and administrators caught up in a maintenance kickback scandal. According to Moffeit and Autrey (2002a), 16 district employees and businessmen were indicted in 1980 in connection with kickback schemes and other abuses. One public official went to prison, and a district purchasing agent committed suicide. The buddy system that encouraged self-dealing provided fertile ground for fraud, and a breakdown in the district's financial controls allowed abuses to flourish. Two maintenance people set up a company that would buy materials from a legitimate vendor at a discount, and then sell those same materials to the FWISD at inflated prices. Employees worked on FWISD time on jobs that had no purpose. Maintenance workers moonlighted for administrators and board members. One of the most common practices was breaking single purchases into several invoices so that the costs would fall under the amount at which standard bidding is required.

Today the FWISD is the third largest school district in Texas and serves about 80,000 students, up from about 72,000 in the mid-1990s. Its budget is about $500 million per year. The Fort Worth School Board has nine members, eight of whom are elected from individual districts; the president is elected at large. The school board members are not paid for their time or services. The superintendent's salary at the time of this story was about $285,000.

In 1995, Ingram was assistant athletic director, and he had a huge credit card debt. He saw the chance to get out of that jam when some concrete needed to be poured at a school athletic facility. He suggested to local contractor Brooks that they jack up the price and split the take. Brooks agreed. He would charge the district for more than a job was worth and then split the extra money with Ingram. The competitive bidding process was skirted by breaking more expensive projects down into smaller amounts and diverting the work to Brooks.

Ingram continued to receive kickbacks from Brooks and after Ingram's promotion to director of maintenance in 1998, the scheme expanded. Brooks and Ingram would meet at construction sites across the district, ostensibly to identify needed concrete work. They would agree on how much to inflate the cost of the work and Ingram would sign purchase orders reflecting the make-believe amount. Brooks would issue a matching invoice and the district would issue Brooks a check. The two men would meet again at construction sites where Brooks would hand Ingram his cut in a newspaper or a paper bag. Federal prosecutors said the scheme ended sometime in 2000. By then, the federal investigation had begun, and an internal audit alerted the FWISD to problems with Brooks' billings.

How could this happen? Construction jobs are supposed to be put out for bids, with the lowest bidder receiving the work. Usually, if a large project were involved, such as remodeling an existing facility or building a new one, engineering drawings would be produced and provided to contractors who would competitively bid in an attempt to secure the job.

For routine small projects (minor concrete jobs such as paving sidewalks, resurfacing a parking lot, etc.), as long as the amount involved was less than $25,000 the process was different. The $25,000 limit was set by the FWISD and Texas law. At the start of the year, contractors would bid for unit amounts, such as dollars per square foot of certain depth concrete or dollars per foot of fencing of a certain height. When a job developed that needed concrete, for example, the low unit-price contractor could be given the job without further bidding, as long as the amount involved was less than $25,000. The intent was not only to get a low price, but also to increase efficiency by avoiding the necessity of board approval for the many routine small jobs that occur throughout the year.

Under the unit-pricing system, Ray Brooks emerged as the district's dominant concrete vendor, receiving more than $30.1 million between 1991 and January 2002. Either Ingram or Eldon Ray, associate superintendent for noninstructional matters and Ingram's boss and pal, approved most of Brooks' work. Brooks worked unsupervised on many projects, and architects or engineers did not independently inspect the work performed to see if it corresponded with what should have been done.

What happened was that larger jobs got broken into smaller pieces, often just barely under the $25,000 limit. Should that not have looked suspicious to those receiving a bunch of bills that were slightly under the limit? However, accounting controls at the FWISD were poor. What should have been normal processes for dealing with contractors and paying bills simply did not exist or procedures were not followed.

Every organization, whether large or small, public or private, profit seeking or not for profit, needs internal controls, not only to enhance the likelihood that financial reporting is appropriate, but also to enhance the likelihood that the directives and policies of management are being followed throughout the organization. Proper controls should also minimize the probability that fraud could occur or at least provide a reasonable likelihood of detecting attempts at fraudulent behavior.

Two elements of control are vital. The control environment sets overall tone of the organization and the way in which it operates, and this environment is set by top management. For the FWISD that would be the board of trustees, its president, the superintendent, and the other top administrators. This tone is the most important element of internal control. What top management says and does—and does not say and does not do—sends a powerful message throughout the entire organization.

Another critical element is made up of policies and procedures put into place to ensure that management's directives, such as approvals, authorizations, verifications, reviews, and separation of duties, are carried out. These control activities include what laymen usually think of as accounting internal controls: checks and balances such as approvals of purchase orders prior to work being done, and verifications and independent reconciliations, such as matching purchase orders with invoices with the work actually performed.

For example, before a job is given to a vendor, a supervisor should approve a purchase order. That purchase order should detail exactly what work is supposed to be done. When the job is finished, the work should be inspected to make sure that the work that was supposed to have been done was in fact done, and done properly. When the contractor's invoice is received, someone who had no part in approving the purchase order or inspecting the work should match the invoice against the purchase order and the inspector's report to make sure that the bill agrees in all respects with what was ordered and what was done. Such standard operating procedures, commonly called accounting internal controls, either were not in place or were often circumvented for the sake of expediency. In some instances, when accounts payable personnel questioned invoices that seemed suspicious (for example, dated prior to the supporting purchase order or for amounts just slightly below the $25,000 unit price contract limit), those higher in authority ignored their concerns. In short, the environment was such that collusion between Ingram and Brooks was possible and could remain undetected for quite some time.

Internal controls also include personnel policies. Personnel should have competencies commensurate with their duties. However, at the FWISD promotions were often based not on ability or qualification but rather on personal friendship. Ingram was a high school coach who was subsequently elevated to maintenance superintendent even though he had no background for that job. In September 2001, Thomas Tocco, FWISD superintendent, promoted Ingram to executive director of maintenance even though Tocco knew that the FBI was investigating allegations of wrongdoing in the maintenance department.

Eventually concerns developed within the FWISD regarding the work of contractors, Brooks in particular. From 1999 through year end 2001, Brooks received $22.6 million from the FWISD for concrete; all except seven of his invoices were close to $25,000. During that time period Brooks received 443 checks between $24,000 and $24,999 for a total of $11 million. IBM, which received the second most checks in that category, was issued 45 checks of less than $25,000 each for a total of approximately $1 million (Moffeit and Classen 2002).

In late 1999, anonymous FWISD employees went to the FBI, which began investigating whether Brooks committed fraud and was aided by district employees. An accounts payable supervisor said she found proof as early as 1999 that maintenance supervisors were approving Brooks' work without proper authorization. The district paid Brooks more than $800,000 for work that was not approved until after it had begun.

Steve Fortenberry, the FWISD chief financial officer, started to look more closely at Brooks' invoices. One bill for $24,940—just $60 below the threshold for bidding—caught his attention. Brooks had charged for 1,860 hours of work that April for a concrete curb. Fortenberry attached a note to the paperwork: "1,860 hours? That's an entire work year for 1 person" (Moffeit and Autrey 2002b). The job required only five days. Brooks resubmitted the paperwork, saying he had meant to charge for 186 hours of labor but had mistakenly added a zero. He was paid $8,200.

Fortenberry also was concerned about other Brooks invoices: "They were putting down basically total cost. But they might have been showing it as laying of concrete when really what was actually done was pulling out trees" (Moffeit 2001). Fortenberry asked the district's internal auditors to look at a sample of Brooks' work including parking lots and tennis courts at two middle schools.

In June 2000, Maria Alvarez Phillips, at that time the lead internal auditor for the FWISD, produced a report that found the following: Brooks' invoices did not detail the actual work performed, and management did not review the invoices to ensure that the amount charged reflected the work done. The purchase orders were not consistently processed and approved before the work was performed. In fact, some purchase orders were approved after the work had been completed. District policy that all construction projects

$25,000 or more be competitively bid was not followed. Included in the audit were three of Brooks' jobs that had been broken into 20 separate purchase orders for an average of about $23,086 each.

At a particular school site, it seemed that Brooks had charged for more concrete than Phillips found, so she asked him to justify the amount of his bill. He submitted a revised bill that matched the figure that Phillips had provided to him, and he assured Phillips the revised invoices were correct. However, Phillips inadvertently had given Brooks the wrong amount. Fortenberry said in August 2002, "It gives the appearance he reconstructed the numbers to satisfy the auditor. He reconciled to the penny the erroneous amount" (Moffeit and Autrey 2002b).

Phillips' report went to Fortenberry and Tocco. The FBI also received a copy of her report. Tocco told board president Gary Manny about the audit findings, but neither Tocco nor Manny informed the rest of the school board until October 2001, 16 months later.

Here we see a failure both of leadership and control. Why was the rest of the school board not informed immediately about the internal audit findings? Autrey (2003) reported that trustees and others who knew Tocco's management style described him as hands-on when it came to areas he considered his expertise, such as curriculum or legislation, but disengaged in business operations.

When an internal audit showed that contracting rules had not been followed, Tocco kept the results from the full school board for 16 months, thinking that a few changes would be sufficient. He did not follow up on what should have been reasonable suspicions that the bidding policies had been subverted as part of a broader plan. Later, Tocco's defense was that the operations side was not his forte and that he was focused on raising academic performance. Although student performance had improved on Tocco's watch, that excuse was not enough. Autrey (2003) wrote: "A big-city superintendent takes the job—with its lucrative compensation—knowing that it's a massive, complicated operation that requires him to stay abreast, even in areas outside his expertise."

Tocco later said, "Do I wish we had told the board we have found some irregularities in billing and and fix[ed] the problem? We felt we had done that...It doesn't appear that we were overcharged. But there was a discrepancy in pricing and categorization of charges. We had to tighten up internally. But we were doing nothing illegal" (Moffeit 2001). Fortenberry said he could not remember whether the audit findings prompted him to suspect fraud at the time of the audit.

On August 21, 2000, the FBI took possession of the FWISD's accounts payable and maintenance files for Brooks for fiscal years 1996–2000; the internal audit files for the June 9, 2000, audit report; and computerized summarized records of payments made to Brooks.

After the school district's internal audit in 2000, FWISD payments to Brooks in amounts between $24,000 and $24,999 dropped dramatically. In 2000, those payments were about $2.8 million. In 2001, such payments totaled only $97,770.

Brooks continued to receive FWISD contracts even though he was under FBI investigation because the FWISD's attorneys advised the trustees that Brooks could not be excluded from bidding unless there was a legal reason to do so. In October 2002, Tocco said the district would stop doing business with Brooks because the contractor had failed to finish several projects. He removed Brooks from a list of vendors under consideration for concrete work over the next year.

Phillips' audit was not the only one conducted on FWISD operations. In June 2001, a Texas State Controller's Office routine performance review of the FWISD found that the purchasing department was not monitoring spending by individual campuses and district departments to ensure they followed state and district policies. The state's report condemned the purchasing department's practice of issuing purchase orders after work had begun and also found that the accounting department only superficially monitored purchasing activity.

Alarmed over information from anonymous tips and FBI involvement, Superintendent Tocco and board president Manny called for an outside investigation into FWISD construction practices. School officials removed the financial records from the administration building and sealed them at a secret location. Tocco said that district officials may have been guilty of lax oversight but that he had no reason to believe that criminal wrongdoing had occurred. He did say that a full investigation was important, "since the matter is one which goes to the heart of public trust" (Moffeit and Deller 2001). Tocco and Manny said they believed an audit should explore purchase orders, invoices, unit-price projects, and quantities and quality of work done.

On November 6, 2001, the trustees approved hiring an outside auditor to investigate FWISD construction projects. The rationale was to clear the air and to restore public confidence in FWISD after the public had been reading about alleged abuses in the *Fort Worth Star-Telegram*. The board was also aware of the information from anonymous sources to the FBI and the FBI interest in the situation. The proposed audit would cover construction work done by outside contractors from September 1, 1991, to August 31, 2001. Manny said the audit was expected to include a review of 2,000–3,000 documents, including purchase orders and invoices involving projects contracted between the district's maintenance department and vendors hired to do concrete, fencing, and other work.

In January 2002, the board selected Whitley Penn and Associates to conduct the external audit. Whitley Penn reported to the FWISD board on January 28, 2003. Trustees were told that Brooks Concrete may have overcharged the

FWISD as much as $4.8 million on five construction projects over ten years. That amounted to about 74 percent of Brooks' billings of about $6.7 million that were included in the audit. The FBI received a copy of Whitley Penn's findings.

Tocco did not think any district employees were involved in intentional wrongdoing. He said, "Either our employees were stupid or obtuse or incompetent, or there was something going on. I prefer to think they were stupid, obtuse, or incompetent" (Deller 2003).

Whitley Penn (2003) noted the following items in its audit executive summary. Unqualified personnel (including Ingram) were promoted to positions of authority and oversight within the maintenance department. District personnel and purchase orders failed to define specifically the nature and scope of work to be performed. Brooks defined the details of the nature and scope of his own work. There was intentional disregard of the intended purpose and use of the unit-price method. There was a lack of established internal controls and procedures within the purchasing department to monitor and identify multiple purchase orders issued just below $25,000 for one property and one vendor. Construction documentation on the part of the FWISD was inadequate.

In December 2002, Ingram resigned from the FWISD. He later admitted that he was not qualified for the maintenance job. He had worked only as a teacher and coach at North Side and Southwest High Schools before being named assistant athletic director, a position he held for nine years. Ingram told Whitley Penn (2003) that "concrete-wise, I guess construction-wise, I was certainly in over my head."

The FWISD internal and external audits and government agency investigations led to federal charges being brought against both Brooks and Ingram in March 2004. The U.S. attorney's office calculated that Brooks padded his bills by three times as much as the value of his jobs from May 1995 to July 2000, and that the fraud and kickback scheme cost the FWISD $15.9 million.

Both Brooks and Ingram agreed to plead guilty to one count each of mail fraud. In September 1999, the FWISD sent Brooks a check for $605,672.50. Prosecutors said the check was payment for false, fictitious, and fraudulent materials and concrete work at 12 district sites. Once the U.S. Postal Service delivered the check, mail fraud became a possible charge. Ingram also pled guilty to filing a false income tax return, and Brooks pled guilty to under-reporting business income taxes. Charges of mail fraud and tax fraud are traditional tactics used for combating white-collar crime.

Tommy Ingram signed off on all except one of the invoices. The check covered bills for 32 jobs supposedly done at the 12 sites over three weeks in August. Each of the 32 invoices was for less than $25,000. Fifteen were for amounts from $24,600 to $24,999.65. All except four of the jobs were reportedly started and completed during one seven-day period. An examination of the 28 invoices that Brooks sent the district for that period illustrates that it would have been all but impossible for him and his small contracting company to do everything for which he was paid. From August 25 through August 31, 1999, Brooks claimed that he poured 84,447 square feet of surface concrete, equal to almost one and a half football fields. He said he poured an additional 7,937 feet, almost a mile and a half, of foundation. He said he hauled 37,695 cubic yards of dirt, which would stand almost 18 feet high if piled on a football field including the end zones (Heinzl 2004).

Defrauding the FWISD is not a federal crime, but failing to report the income fraudulently obtained is a federal crime. Ingram submitted a fraudulent joint federal income tax return for 1998. He reported taxable income of $116,000 when it should have been $698,000. Brooks underreported his income on a corporate tax return form for 2000. He failed to report about $2.1 million in funds obtained fraudulently from the school district. He reported taxable income of $5.3 million when he should have reported $7.4 million.

U.S. District Judge John McBryde sentenced Ingram and Brooks to eight years in prison for defrauding the district of $15.9 million. Judge McBryde said he regretted that federal sentencing guidelines precluded him from handing out even tougher sentences in light of the harm that the two men did to Fort Worth schoolchildren (Heinzl and Autrey 2004). In a letter sent to federal court officials, Tocco explained what the FWISD could have done with the embezzled funds. A lack of funds led to cuts in services and programs, such as $7 million to retain the planning and professional development period for all middle and high school teachers, $500,000 for band equipment, $1 million for tutoring, and a combined $1.5 million for art, music, and conversational Spanish instruction at elementary schools.

Assistant U.S. Attorney Ron Eddins, the lead prosecutor, said he hoped that the tough sentences would send a clear message to the community: "We hope that this acts as a deterrent to any future activities like that in the Fort Worth school district involving contractors or employees. That's one of the reasons we prosecute cases like that, because of its deterrent value" (Heinzl and Autrey 2004).

In addition to prison time, Brooks and Ingram were required to jointly pay restitution of $15.9 million. By June 2004, the FWISD had received a little more than $1.3 million in cash from Brooks and more than $300,000 from Ingram. In addition, Brooks agreed to turn over to the district 73 vehicles owned by him or his companies. The vehicles included 12 mixer trucks, eight truck tractors, two dump trailers, a brush-chipping truck, two pneumatic bulk trailers, two Jaguars, two Corvettes, and a Mercedes-Benz SL500 roadster. An auction of the construction vehicles raised $1.2 million for the school district. A separate automobile auction raised another $148,500.

On the witness stand, Ingram described his lifestyle during the height of the fraud. He was swimming in cash. He matter of factly talked about approaching Brooks to overbill the district, about later suggesting a 50–50 split of the profits, about putting the money toward $540,000 in gambling losses, about paying off $50,000 of annual Visa credit card debt, about accumulating up to $700,000 in a lettuce bag in his bedroom closet, and about spending $30,000 on travel and incidentals. Ingram said he stopped cheating the district from June 1996 to April 1998, but began again when he became the district's maintenance director and could personally approve the inflated bills that Brooks submitted.

Ingram said he might not have understood how much cheating went on. He painted a picture of himself as woefully incompetent in his school district job. He said he did not know how to calculate how much Brooks inflated charges on concrete projects, even though it was his responsibility to oversee the jobs. Ingram told the judge, "I didn't figure the job amount—I didn't know how to figure it." The judge asked him, "How long did you hold a job you had no idea how to perform?" and Ingram replied, "From 1998 to 2002"—the entire time he was the maintenance director (Heinzl and Autrey 2004).

As a result of the events presented in this chapter, the FWISD has a new look. There is a new superintendent. On March 23, 2004, the trustees voted seven to one to make revisions to Tocco's contract. He would leave the superintendent's post June 30, but would remain a full-time district consultant until December 31, at which time his contract expired and he would sever all relationships with the FWISD.

There is a new president of the school board. There are new school board members. After the May 2004 school board election, four of the nine board members were not associated with past events, thus offering an opportunity for a new leadership tone at the FWISD.

There are also tighter controls. The unit-price limit is $10,000. There is a new deputy superintendent of operations management, and he has separated responsibilities for maintenance and construction between two other individuals. There is a new chief financial officer. The internal audit function has been strengthened by adding and upgrading positions and having it report directly to the school board instead of the superintendent.

With new leadership, stronger controls, and perhaps an ability to learn from the past, the FWISD might emerge from the scandal reported in this story as a better and more responsible district. Present and future FWISD employees may learn a better lesson from these events than did Ingram. Exchanges of paper bags containing cash may become merely a bad memory.

References

Autrey, J. "District's Reforms Fall by the Wayside," *Fort Worth Star-Telegram*, November 9, 2003, final news, 1A.

Deller, M. "School Bidding Problems Tackled," *Fort Worth Star-Telegram*, January 30, 2003, final metro, 1.

Heinzl, T. "Two Men Convicted of Bilking District," *Fort Worth Star-Telegram,* March 6, 2004, final news, 1A.

Heinzl, T., and J. Autrey. "Pair Gets 8 Years for School Fraud; Brooks, Ingram Sentenced for Construction Scheme; District Cheated Out of $15.9 Million through Inflated Bills," *Fort Worth Star-Telegram,* June 26, 2004, final news, 1a.

Moffeit, M. "Bidding Policies Skirted, Audit Says," *Fort Worth Star-Telegram,* October 19, 2001, final news, 1.

Moffeit, M., and J. Autrey. "1980 Investigation Revealed Rampant Fraud in District," *Fort Worth Star-Telegram,* September 22, 2002(a), final news, 25.

———. "Collapse of Control; Investigation Uncovers Overbilling and Flawed Work by 2 Construction Firms and a Lack of Scrutiny by Fort Worth School District," *Fort Worth Star-Telegram,* September 22, 2002(b), final news, 1.

Moffeit, M., and J. Claassen. "District's Deals with Contractor Examined," *Fort Worth Star-Telegram,* February 17, 2002, final news, 1.

Moffeit, M., and M. Deller. "Tocco Makes Call for Outside Audit," *Fort Worth Star-Telegram,* November 6, 2001, final news, 1.

Whitley Penn. "Report of Professional Services to Fort Worth Independent School District," Fort Worth, TX, January 28, 2003.

Bibliography

Frazier, M. "Taped Board Session Focuses on Lost Trust," *Fort Worth Star-Telegram,* December 15, 2003, northeast edition, metro, 4B.

My (S)old Kentucky Home: The Erpenbeck Homebuilder Case

7

JAMES CASHELL
BRIAN BALLOU
DAN L. HEITGER

Contents

Introduction

In 2001, Bill Erpenbeck's company began construction of the house in Independence, Kentucky, that eventually would be purchased by Charles and Sherry Mitchell. At the time, Erpenbeck was the fourth largest homebuilder in the Greater Cincinnati–Northern Kentucky region. He and his affiliated companies were responsible for building hundreds of new homes and whole condominium projects in many of the region's most prestigious areas.

Bill Erpenbeck built the house in Independence on spec (speculation of eventually finding a buyer). Building spec houses is a common practice among builders. Rather than having a buyer prior to beginning construction, the builder begins construction of the house and speculates that a buyer will eventually be found, possibly after the house is finished.

Whenever a house is built on spec, a typical practice is for the builder to take out a loan, called a construction loan, to finance the construction costs for the spec house. In addition, the builder may also arrange to delay payments to some of the subcontractors and material suppliers until after the house is sold. Bill Erpenbeck used all of these financing strategies for the house being built in Independence, including taking out a $139,489 construction loan from the Kenwood Savings Bank. In return, Kenwood Savings Bank was given a lien on the Independence property.

Construction loans are to be repaid when the spec house is eventually sold. To protect its loan until it is repaid, the construction lender holds a lien on the property. In the event that the construction loan is not repaid, the lien allows the bank to put a claim on the house, and resell it if need be, to recover the amount of the defaulted loan. The property lien is released once the construction loan has been repaid.

In October 2001, Charles and Sherry Mitchell agreed to purchase Erpenbeck's Independence, Kentucky, spec house for $198,000. They were looking for quality and value, and they believed that they had found both in their new home (McNair and Crowley 2002).

Like most homebuyers, the Mitchells needed to borrow much of the $198,000 needed to purchase their new home. They arranged for a mortgage through Citicorp. With a mortgage, the buyer (the Mitchells) borrows money from some financial institution (Citicorp) and promises to repay the mortgage loan by making monthly payments over a period of time (e.g., 15–30 years). Citicorp, the mortgage lender, holds the deed to the house as collateral until the mortgage loan is repaid. If the Mitchells fail to make their mortgage payments, Citicorp could claim the house and sell it to recover its defaulted mortgage loan.

Prior to granting the mortgage loan, Citicorp required the Mitchells to purchase title insurance, which they did through Insured Land Title. This is a common practice. The title insurance guarantees that Citicorp, the mortgage lender, would not incur any losses in the event that it is later discovered that someone else (e.g., Kenwood Savings Bank) also has a lien on the property. As part of the insurance, Insured Land Title conducted a title search on the property to identify all of the liens and lien holders.

Once the title inspection was done and the title insurance was established, the Mitchells scheduled the closing for their new home. At the closing, the homebuyers, with the help of their mortgage company, pay for the house and the seller transfers the property deed to the buyers.

As is typical, a representative from the title insurance company, Insured Land Title, served as the closing agent and presided over the closing of the Mitchell's new home. A few days prior to the closing, the closing agent instructs the buyer's mortgage company to whom to make out checks and the amounts. For the Mitchell's closing, three of the required checks were:

- a check for $139,489 to Kenwood Savings Bank to pay off the construction loan and to release the lien on the property;
- a check to Bill Erpenbeck to cover his profit in the sale of the house (the $198,000 purchase price less the checks needed to pay off all of the construction liens); and
- a check to Insured Land Title to pay for the title insurance.

At the closing, the checks were handed over to the closing agent. The agent was then supposed to distribute the checks to the various recipients. The deed to the property would then be transferred to the new owners and their mortgage company.

Once the checks from the closing are delivered to the lien holders, such as Kenwood Savings Bank, those parties release their liens on the property. After this is done, it is normally expected that the only claim remaining on the property is the one held by the mortgage company. The mortgage company holds the deed and a claim on the property until the mortgage is eventually paid off.

The Mitchell's closing followed the preceding process except for one modification. At the time, it was a fairly common practice in the Greater Cincinnati area for the closing agent to deliver all of the lien-holder checks to the builder—in this case Bill Erpenbeck's representative—rather than directly to lien holders such as Kenwood Savings Bank. This was being done as a convenience to homebuilders. By getting the checks themselves at the closing, the builders were able to pay off their construction loans—and thus get new construction loans to begin new projects—a few days faster than would otherwise occur through the normal closing process (Alltucker, May 26, 2002).

Unfortunately, Erpenbeck took advantage of the modified closing process, wherein all of the checks were given to him rather than directly to the lien holders. At the Mitchell's closing, the $139,489 check that was made out to Kenwood Savings was given to Bill Erpenbeck's representative, who was then supposed to deliver it to Kenwood Savings Bank. Unbeknown to the others at the closing, however, the check was never delivered to Kenwood Savings Bank. Instead, it was deposited into one of Erpenbeck's own accounts at Peoples Bank.

After the closing, Charles and Sherry Mitchell moved into their new home. They had every reason to believe that all of the liens on their new home had been removed and that as long as they made their monthly mortgage payments they could live in their new home and eventually would own it free and clear.

Unfortunately, three months after they moved into their new house, the Mitchells learned that the check at the closing that was made out to Kenwood Savings Bank to pay off the construction loan was never delivered and, accordingly, the lien was never released. Kenwood Savings was now considering exercising its lien on the house in order to recover the $139,489 it was owed.

This discovery created a tricky legal situation for the Mitchells. Instead of just their mortgage company, Citicorp, holding a claim to their new home, they also had to deal with the claim held by Kenwood Savings Bank. To pay off both claims would cost the Mitchells $139,489 more than they originally expected to pay for the house (which was $198,000 plus interest on the mortgage loan). If the Mitchells chose to ignore the Kenwood Savings Bank's claim, the bank could potentially force the sale of the house and recover its loan from the sales proceeds. If this happened, there would not be enough money left over from the forced sale to settle the mortgage with Citicorp. The Mitchells not only would have lost their home, but also would still owe a significant amount to Citicorp to satisfy the mortgage balance on the property. Further, it would be extremely difficult for the Mitchells to sell the house with multiple outstanding liens. Most buyers would not want to put themselves in the middle of that type of situation.

Because of the tricky legal situation they found themselves in, the Mitchells were forced to hire an attorney. In a similar case involving another Erpenbeck home sale, the homeowner's attorney said that resolving such conflicts often takes considerable time and that legal fees can run in the thousands of dollars (Driehaus, May 1, 2002).

How Was Erpenbeck Able to Deposit the Check into His Account?

Anyone familiar with banking might ask how Erpenbeck was able to deposit a check made payable to Kenwood Savings Bank into his own account. Surprisingly, he was able to accomplish these deposits without much difficulty. According to John Yeager, a Peoples Bank board member, bank employees normally inspect the endorsements on the checks being deposited but they often exercise less care if they know the customer (McNair, May 4, 2002). In this case, Erpenbeck conducted much business with Peoples Bank and would have known the bank tellers quite well. In addition, John Yeager also noted that Erpenbeck was careful to conceal these particular deposits, thus reducing the likelihood that they would be detected. Purportedly, the lien-holder checks from the closing were being inserted into a pile of legitimate checks for each deposit. The first few checks in the stack legitimately belonged to Erpenbeck, which reduced the likelihood that the clerk would even look at the remaining checks.

Why Did Title Insurance Not Protect the Homebuyers?

Another question the Mitchells probably asked was why the title insurance they paid for at the home closing did not protect them. As discussed earlier, mortgage holders typically require homeowners to pay for title insurance that indemnifies the insurance holder against any undiscovered liens on the property. That is, the insurance company covers any loss that the insurance holder might incur as a result of undiscovered liens. Citicorp required the Mitchells to do this. The Mitchells purchased the mortgage insurance through Insured Land Title.

But why did the title insurance not protect the homeowners? The answer is simple: Most homeowners do not buy title insurance for themselves; rather, they purchase it for the mortgage lender. In this case, the Mitchells purchased title insurance for Citicorp, not for themselves. Many buyers apparently are not aware that the title insurance does not also cover them. Fewer than one in five homeowners in the Cincinnati area purchased their own title insurance even though they are required to purchase it for the mortgage lender (Alltucker, May 20, 2002).

There is still the argument that Insured Land Title was negligent in this case since it oversaw the closing and did not directly distribute the check to Kenwood Savings Bank, but rather gave it to Erpenbeck with the expectation that he would deliver the check to Kenwood Savings Bank. The title companies countered that they were not negligent in this practice since neither Ohio nor Kentucky had laws regulating the closing process (Alltucker, May 20, 2002). Regardless of who is right in the preceding argument, it does explain why the Mitchells found themselves involved in a costly legal battle.

The Mitchell case had one further twist. At one point after the closing, Insured Land Title suspected that Erpenbeck may have failed to deliver some of the checks to the lien holders. At this point, the company requested evidence that the Kenwood Savings Bank lien had been released. Erpenbeck provided a letter, purportedly from Kenwood Savings Bank, stating that the payment had been received and the lien removed. It was later determined that the letter was a forgery and Kenwood Savings had no knowledge of it (McNair and Crowley 2002).

The Mitchell's Case Was Not an Isolated Incident

More than 200 homebuyers found themselves in similar situations to that of the Mitchells. In all, Erpenbeck was accused of using the previously described scheme to divert checks valued at more than $33 million into his own accounts.

Diverting checks at closings was not Erpenbeck's only money-generating scheme. In all, it has been estimated that Erpenbeck's schemes cost the Cincinnati region in excess of $100 million (Driehaus 2003). In other schemes, condominium owners found themselves living in partially completed complexes and with condominium associations that never received the promised funding to pay for insurance, property maintenance, and other items. Many subcontractors that worked on Erpenbeck construction projects were never paid.

In one of the bigger schemes, Erpenbeck engaged in a bank loan arrangement wherein he was aided by the two top officials at Peoples Bank: John Finnan, president, and Marc Menne, executive VP. Although neither bank official appeared to be involved in the check diversion scheme, they both admitted to other charges. One charge was that they provided a $4 million unsecured loan to Erpenbeck and hid it from the bank's board of directors. The money was used to cover overdrafts on the Erpenbeck account. In another instance, both Finnan and Menne arranged a $24 million loan to Erpenbeck through a consortium of banks. Peoples Bank was unable to lend Erpenbeck the full amount he needed at the time, so Finnan and Menne established a consortium of 24 banks in Kentucky and Indiana to provide the $24 million Erpenbeck needed. Finnan and Menne, however, failed to provide the full information about Erpenbeck's financial problems to these banks (McNair, May 16, 2002). Erpenbeck later defaulted on the loan. While it did not pose a risk to any of the banks' ability to continue operating, it was expected to be costly to them (Driehaus 2005).

Why Did Erpenbeck Do It and How Did He Expect to Get Away with It?

It is not really known why Erpenbeck got involved in so many schemes. The only real conclusion that can be drawn is that he needed the money. It was apparent from the consortium loan scheme that Bill Erpenbeck's enterprises were having financial problems (McNair, May 16, 2002). Why he needed the money though is not clear. It is likely that Erpenbeck was not a very good businessman. He may not have been making as much money on his construction projects as he thought he was. His companies employed several Erpenbeck family members who presumably were paid good wages. His lifestyle might also be partly to blame. His Cincinnati home was valued at $1.3 million and he had a condominium in Florida valued at $270,000 (Crowley 2002). Perhaps he lived a higher lifestyle than his businesses could support.

Given the nature of the schemes, one has to wonder how Erpenbeck thought he could get away with it. He would have had to know that the frauds would quickly be discovered. For example, not paying off a construction lender would quickly result in a filed lien on the property. Normally, people who develop schemes that they know will be quickly discovered get the money and run. Erpenbeck did not run.

Although this is pure speculation, it may be that Erpenbeck really believed he would eventually be able to pay off everyone and make everything right. Many of the schemes, particularly the consortium bank loan, appeared to be entered into to keep the building empire going. It is possible that Erpenbeck viewed his financial problems as temporary, and that the current cash infusion would enable the business eventually to grow out of the problems and provide enough money to repay everyone. Obviously that did not happen. Unless Bill Erpenbeck someday explains his reason and rationale for his activities, they probably will never be known for certain.

The Victims and Aftermath

Homeowners such as the Mitchells were lucky. A class action lawsuit was settled in November 2002 that cleared up the construction liens on their properties. Peoples Bank, along with the various other financial institutions and title insurance companies involved with the Erpenbeck deals, agreed to share responsibility and to resolve the problems without further hurting the unwary homeowners. The homeowners were lucky in that they only had to incur some attorney fees and the inconvenience of having their homes tied up in ownership limbo for approximately one year (Driehaus, November 16, 2002).

The reputation of the Peoples Bank of Northern Kentucky (Peoples Bank) was so badly damaged that the bank was forced to liquidate its assets and cease operations. While the bank could have absorbed the direct losses of Erpenbeck's schemes, it began losing deposits and customers because of its association with Erpenbeck. As a result of its damaged reputation, the Board of Directors determined that the bank could not be sold as an entity and that the only viable option was to sell off the bank's assets. As testament, the Bank of Kentucky refused to buy any of the loans tied to any Erpenbeck-related entity or affiliate. Fortunately, the Bank of Kentucky retained the 54 employees of Peoples Bank (McKinney 2002).

Many subcontractors were also hurt in the Erpenbeck scandal. One in particular, Phil Tromm of Tromm Construction Company, lost almost everything. The checks that were to be paid to him at the closing were deposited into Erpenbeck accounts instead. Tromm depleted his personal savings and even had to sell his power tools to settle some of his bills (McNair, June 22, 2002).

Bill Erpenbeck, president of Erpenbeck Company, was sentenced to prison for his involvement in the check diversion and other real estate schemes. Although Erpenbeck was the apparent ring-leader, he did not act alone. Many others also received prison sentences as a result of their participation in Erpenbeck's schemes. Some of the more notable included:

- Bill Erpenbeck, president of Erpenbeck Co. was sentenced to 30 years for leading his financial schemes.

- Tony Erpenbeck, Bill Erpenbeck's father, was sentenced to six years for obstruction of justice. He was charged with pressuring his daughter, Lori Erpenbeck, into taking the blame for the fraud scheme.
- Lori Erpenbeck was sentenced to 1 year for aiding the financial schemes.
- Michelle Marksberry, a former Erpenbeck closing agent, was sentenced to two years for participating in the closing check diversion scheme.
- John Finnan, an executive with Peoples Bank, was sentenced to more than four years on collusion charges related to the bank loan schemes.
- Marc Menne, another executive with Peoples Bank, was sentenced to more than four years on collusion charges related to the bank loan schemes.

References

Alltucker, Ken. "Erpenbeck Fiasco Making More Weigh Title Insurance," *Cincinnati Enquirer,* May 20, 2002.

_____. "Payment Practice Is Revised," *Cincinnati Enquirer,* April 26, 2002.

Crowley, Patrick. "Erpenbeck Has Fla. Advantage," *The Cincinnati Enquirer,* May 16, 2002.

Driehaus, Bob. "Young Couple in New Home Unsure What's Next," *Cincinnati Post,* May 1, 2002.

_____. "Home Liens Set for Release," *Kentucky Post,* November 16, 2002.

_____. "Erpenbeck Accepts Plea Deal," *Cincinnati Post,* April 9, 2003.

_____. "Two Sentenced in Bank Fraud," *Kentucky Post,* October 25, 2005.

McKinney, Jeff. "Peoples' Decision Was Its Only Choice," *Cincinnati Enquirer,* July 24, 2002.

McNair, James. "3rd-Party Checks Examined in Erpenbeck Probe," *Cincinnati Enquirer,* May 4, 2002.

_____. "Erpenbeck Fall Batters Small Banks," *Cincinnati Enquirer,* May 16, 2002.

_____. "Erpenbeck Fallout: Selling Tools to Pay Bills," *Cincinnati Enquirer,* June 22, 2002.

McNair, James, and Patrick Crowley. "Couple Surprised by Murky Home Title," *Cincinnati Enquirer,* May 7, 2002.

Bibliography

Black, Henry. *Black's Law Dictionary,* 5th ed. St. Paul, MN: West Publishing Co., 1979.

ZZZZ Best: Taking Investors to the Cleaners

8

TRISH ISAACS

Contents

Introduction

Most small businesses fail in their first five years. Hindsight reveals that ZZZZ Best should have been among them. How did Barry Minkow take a small carpet cleaning service, run from his parents' garage, to a multimillion dollar public stock offering by the time he was 21 years old?

Humble Beginnings

In 1981, high school sophomore Barry Minkow began ZZZZ Best (pronounced "zee best"), a small carpet cleaning business, in his family's garage. He learned about carpet cleaning as a child, first from accompanying his mother to work and later working for the carpet cleaning business where his mother was employed. Barry Minkow possessed charm, energy, and intelligence. He instinctively understood personalities and generally made a positive impression on everyone he met. He was not completely polished, but this passed for innocence, which was an important aspect of his mystique. He was young, with little education and no inherited wealth. He worked hard, and by the time he graduated from high school he led a rapidly growing company (Akst 1990).

The business he started at age 15 grew into a public company with a peak market value exceeding $211 million (Akst, July 9, 1987, 1). The phenomenal growth of his company allowed him to move out of his parents' modest home into a condominium when he was 19. Not long afterwards, he bought a 3,600-square-foot Spanish-style house in a gated community (Akst 1990, 76). Minkow's taste was extravagant, and his ego was enormous. He acquired numerous luxury automobiles. His Ferrari had a "ZBest" license plate. He gave extravagant gifts and hosted extravagant parties. He required that everyone in his office, including his mother (who worked for him), call him Mr. Minkow.

Very early on, the company incurred losses and Minkow had trouble meeting payroll. He borrowed first from banks, then from questionable contacts with ties to organized crime. By the time this credit ran out, his debts were so large that only a public stock offering would cover them.

From all appearances, the business grew quickly. Minkow repeatedly vowed to make his company the "General Motors of carpet-cleaning" (Akst 1989, 126). By 1985 the company reported that it was expanding into the building restoration business. During 1985 and 1986, ZZZZ Best reported high profits from several large restoration projects.

A Public Offering

When ZZZZ Best stock was offered to the public, it quickly became one of the hottest stocks on Wall Street. Barry Minkow enjoyed enormous popularity. He was recognized by the Young Entrepreneurs Organization as one of the 100 top entrepreneurs in America. He also received two commendations from Los Angeles Mayor Tom Bradley. The first praised Minkow as a fine entrepreneurial example for obtaining the status of a millionaire at the age of 18; the second, which came later, recognized his philanthropy. Mayor Bradley also declared Saturday, November 8, 1986, Barry Minkow Day (Akst 1990, 10). Minkow was featured in *Newsweek* and in *USA Today*, as well as many other newspapers. He appeared on the *Oprah Winfrey Show* (Akst 1990, 181).

Minkow facilitated his company's public stock offering by merging ZZZZ Best into Morningstar Investments, a public Utah shell corporation that ZZZZ Best would ultimately control. In this way, the company could quickly and cheaply become a public concern "without all the expensive, embarrassing and time-consuming disclosures that would be required if it tried to go public by itself" (Akst 1990, 86–87). However, as Minkow began the process of going public, it was necessary to involve independent auditors and Wall Street attorneys. During the public-offering process, Ernst & Whinney conducted a review of the ZZZZ Best financial statements for the quarter ended

July 31, 1986, with the promise of an audit to come. Thus, Ernst & Whinney's name appeared in the prospectus (Akst 1990, 169). However, audited ZZZZ Best financial statements were never produced.

Minkow convinced auditors and attorneys that his business was legitimate. He produced documentation to support the earnings reported in ZZZZ Best financial statements. Though he never had an accounting class, he understood the importance of documentation in the audit process. Minkow described one of his associates as a master of the copy machine: Mark Morze could make any document; as long as it could be copied, Morze could produce it (Association of Certified Fraud Examiners 1991). Further, the quality of his work was exceptional (Akst 1990, 135). Morze helped Minkow produce fictitious invoices, checks, and restoration contracts. With them, Minkow provided documentation to support fictitious claims that customers owed ZZZZ Best for services. Legitimate accounts receivable would have been collected in a fairly short period of time. Cash that would be collected thus represents a significant asset. The accounts receivable reported by ZZZZ Best, however, did not exist.

One reason that Minkow's scheme worked for a time was that he also understood the auditor's process for verifying accounts receivable. When one of his customers was contacted for confirmation of a receivable, Minkow knew it because the customers were fictitious. He had created numerous front companies as his customers and as his suppliers as well. Correspondence to these companies ultimately came to him. When a confirmation was sent, Minkow complained to the auditors that they were interfering with his business and that they would cause him to lose a large contract. He threatened to take his audit elsewhere, using the competitive environment for accounting and auditing services of the 1980s to his advantage. The auditor did not want to report to his managing partner that he had lost a major audit client or that a client was planning to sue the auditing firm for loss of business.

Minkow further manipulated audit procedures by documenting subsequent payment of the fictitious receivables. Subsequent payment is important in substantiating the validity of accounts receivable. If a customer subsequently pays an account receivable, the payment provides confirmation that the customer did, in fact, owe the company.

However, in the case of ZZZZ Best, the subsequent payments were part of a kiting scheme. Unlike the customer confirmations, Minkow did not object to the auditors' verification of bank account balances. His kiting scheme supported the information found in the bank statements. Kiting is a commonly used method of overstating cash by recording the same cash twice or, in Minkow's case, three or four times. A kiting scheme involves writing, but not recording, a check on one bank account near the end of the period, then depositing the check in another bank account, being sure that the deposit is made late enough in the period so that the check does not clear the first account until after the end of the period. Such a scheme should be revealed by the auditor's tests of interbank transfers (Arens, Elder, and Beasley 2003). For ZZZZ Best, there is no indication that the auditors' tests, which would have revealed the kiting scheme, were conducted. Minkow so often resorted to check kiting to create funds that for his 21st birthday his cronies gave him a giant kite with a blowup of a check on it (Akst 1990, 117).

ZZZZ Best would raise money from investors, banks, or anyone else and then pay the money out to Marbil Marketing, supposedly an employment contractor that hired workers to perform the ZZZZ Best restoration jobs awarded by Interstate Appraisal. Marbil would recycle the money back to ZZZZ Best. Both Marbil and Interstate were private companies and therefore beyond the scrutiny required of a public company. Checks were paid to ZZZZ Best from Interstate Appraisal for restoration work performed. The checks, by design, matched deposit slips; this was part of the scheme to fool the auditors. In 1986, about $10 million moved between Marbil and ZZZZ Best; in the first half of 1987, the amount was $44 million. In this way, Barry and his friends made it appear that his company was generating revenue and receiving payments like a legitimate business (Akst 1990, 106). Purportedly, Interstate Appraisal provided the lucrative refurbishing jobs that accounted for nearly 90 percent of ZZZZ Best revenue, while Marbil Management was serving as a contractor working on restoration jobs on behalf of ZZZZ Best. Examiners later described this scheme as a "monstrous check kite" and a "cash racetrack" (Akst 1990, 222).

Minkow also manipulated the auditors by establishing social contacts with them and their wives. He later said that he had wanted the auditors' wives to see him as a "nice kid" so that if the auditor expressed concern about ZZZZ Best, the wife would come to his defense. He also diverted the auditors' attention by seeking their advice about improving a particular store's performance (Association of Certified Fraud Examiners 1991).

Another tactic Minkow used was to steer auditors to the legitimate part of his business, his carpet cleaning. As long as they focused on his carpet-cleaning business, they dealt with a work force that was not involved in the fraud. Only upper management was part of the fraud team. Minkow tried to shift attention away from the restoration business, which generated 80 percent of the reported income, citing confidentiality agreements with his customers. It was only because of the auditors' insistence that Minkow reluctantly consented to an auditor's visit to a $7 million restoration site in Sacramento. Since there was no restoration project, Minkow dispatched two of his assistants, Tom Padgett and Mark Roddy, to scope out a likely site. Upon arrival in Sacramento, they soon discovered that only one building in the city was large enough to have $7 million damage. They quickly leased the space and created Assured Property Management, complete with office, furniture, phones, and copying privileges. The fictitious firm was supposedly in the business of

looking after the interests of the insured party in restoration jobs, and it provided Roddy the credibility to represent the building's owners, managers, and
insurers, each of whom would prove troublesome if contacted directly by the
auditor. Several props were positioned to make the space appear to be legitimate, including a ZZZZ Best tee shirt, and all was prepared for the visit of
the auditor and an attorney (Akst 1989, 126–127). The independent auditor
agreed in writing "not to disclose the location of the site to anyone, even at
their own firms." The letter also stated that he would "not make any follow-up
telephone calls to any contractors, insurance companies, the building owner,
or other individuals (other than suppliers whose names have been provided
to this firm by the Company) involved in the restoration project" (Akst 1990,
151). The auditor was left with no objective means to verify that actual restoration work was occurring; contact was permitted only for fake companies that
were within the control of Minkow and his fraudulent associates.

The auditor later insisted on visiting another site on which restoration
had purportedly just begun. Padgett and Roddy were again dispatched, this
time to San Diego. A building was located, and the auditor's visit was hastily arranged. When ZZZZ Best reported that the project was nearly done,
the auditor insisted on seeing it again. Minkow and his team went to great
lengths to lease the same building and arrange for a contractor to wire, dry-
wall, paint, carpet, and otherwise complete six floors of office space in ten
days (Askt 1989, 132). The auditor did not notice during this visit that, in
some rooms, the ceilings were dropped so low that closet doors would not
open. Both site visits were arranged for the weekend so that other occupants
of the building would not be around to talk with the auditor.

In addition to visiting these "construction sites," the auditor also visited
two warehouses, one in California and one in Texas. He saw "$168,000 worth
of the cheapest carpet they could get" in California. Later, the auditor saw
carpet in a warehouse in Texas; it was the same carpet he had seen in San
Diego earlier (Akst 1990, 129). Minkow's newly developed building restoration business was reporting contracts that were four times as large as those of
legitimate restoration businesses at the time. They had no payroll records or
OSHA reports. A multimillion dollar restoration contract was a single-page
document. The auditor did not check for a construction permit, talk to the
local public-safety officials, contact the building's owners, or call around in
the restoration business to see if anyone knew of this particular job or if such
large jobs were even plausible (Akst 1990, 170).

Minkow also duped his attorneys. He obtained a registration statement
(part of the process for public offering of his company's stock) from a prestigious Wall Street law firm. The attorney insisted on seeing a restoration
project as the auditor had done, and he actually accompanied the auditor to
the first staged restoration site. Like the auditor, the attorney signed the written statement that he would not follow up with independent verification with

other companies and individuals involved in the restoration project (Akst 1989, 127).

Minkow defrauded numerous banks, borrowing more than $20 million from 15 different banks. In addition, he borrowed large sums of money from several private individuals. Anytime an auditor, an attorney, a banker, or the press raised questions about the legitimacy of his business, Minkow leveraged one against the others. To the auditor, he would point out that the Wall Street law firm, the banks, and the press said he "was gold." If the banker doubted the wherewithal of the company, he pointed him or her to the phenomenal growth of the stock price (Association of Certified Fraud Examiners 1991).

The Scheme Unravels

Minkow's undoing, while inevitable, was hastened by a phone call to the *Los Angeles Times* from a young mother who had been overcharged for flowers she had sent to an ailing friend. Robin Swanson chose a flower shop close to the hospital, Floral Fantasies. She placed the order by phone, using her Bank One Visa card to pay $23.95 for the flowers. When her statement arrived, the charge was $601.11. Mrs. Swanson called Floral Fantasies to complain and was referred to the owner, Barry Minkow. He thanked her for calling and promised that her account would be credited right away. However, when her next bill arrived, the charge was still there, along with an additional $23.95 (the original price for the flowers). After repeated appeals to have the charges removed, first to Minkow and then to the bank, Swanson was enraged. She was also tenacious. She took her cause to the Los Angeles Police, the Los Angeles County District Attorney's Office, and the State Attorney General's Office, all to no avail. Then, on November 17, 1986, she called the *Los Angeles Times* and reached Daniel Akst, a reporter who had just completed a story reporting on Barry Minkow's ties to a notorious gangster and ZZZZ Best's enormous debt and its reliance on a single customer, Interstate Appraisal (Akst 1990, 157–161). After reports that ZZZZ Best and a flower shop owned by a top executive submitted phony credit card billings for many customers and the other investigations that ensued, ZZZZ Best stock prices began their fall from a high of $18.375 to pennies, and trading was suspended by the SEC as the story unfolded (Akst, July 7, 1987, 5).

Minkow's explanation for the overcharges was that unscrupulous former subcontractors, who had been caught and fired, were responsible. This explanation contradicted the company's public offering statement, which indicated that "the company hires no subcontractors for any of its residential or commercial carpet cleaning jobs" (Akst, July 7, 1987, 5). As investigative reporters uncovered more and more instances of overcharges to carpet cleaning customers' credit cards, they soon found also that the company's restoration contracts were largely fictional.

The firm engaged as the company's auditors, Ernst & Whinney, resigned just 2 weeks after the *Los Angeles Times* reported that ZZZZ Best used customers' credit card numbers to run up at least $72,000 in inflated charges. It never completed its initial audit. ZZZZ Best said the resignation was not over accounting differences. After Ernst & Whinney, ZZZZ Best hired another auditing firm, Price Waterhouse & Company. When allegations of fraud and unanswered questions about management integrity surfaced later, Price Waterhouse also resigned.

ZZZZ Best was cited in congressional hearings as proof that "the SEC's system for reporting changes of auditors...must be overhauled completely and replaced with one that gives shareholders and the public real and timely warning when management is perpetrating financial skullduggery" (Kullberg 1988) That reform was subsequently enacted. No reform will eliminate fraud, but as a result of these changes, "auditors can and should plan a more effective role in narrowing the odds that illegal and irregular practices will persist in companies" (Kullberg 1988).

Amid investigations by various law enforcement agencies for alleged offenses ranging from misstating financial results to laundering drug money, the assets of ZZZZ Best, which had been listed in its bankruptcy filing at $4.4 million, sold for $62,000 at auction. These assets included carpet-cleaning machines, office equipment, and computers from the 21 carpet cleaning stores. The company's liabilities were listed at $26.7 million (Jeffrey 1987).

This scam had many victims. ZZZZ Best had 715 shareholders of record when it collapsed. The actual number, however, was substantially higher, since trust companies and others acting as stand-ins for many were counted as one. Also, there were about 3,000 creditors in the company's bankruptcy. The biggest losers among the creditors were banks and investment firms; one bank lost $7 million (Akst 1990, 271).

Minkow and 11 ZZZZ Best insiders were sentenced to prison. Most agreed to a plea bargain. Barry Minkow did not. He seemed to think that he could con the jury as he had conned so many investors. However, this time he was not successful. In December 1988, Minkow was convicted of 57 counts of fraud (Adelson 1988, D13). He was later sentenced to 25 years in federal prison. In his sentencing memorandum, the judge described Barry Minkow as a remorseless liar and a thief; his schemes had cost victims more than $100 million. His sentence was, for many years, the largest on record for white collar crime. He was also ordered to pay $26 million in restitution to victims of the ZZZZ Best fraud scheme. He served 7½ years, including 1 year in solitary confinement, before being released on parole. This is more time behind bars, Minkow notes, than "disgraced junk bond wizard Michael Milken, insider trading kingpin Ivan Boesky, and tax cheat Leona Helmsley combined" (Carey 2004). While in prison, Minkow rose at three o'clock in the morning most days to bake bread and doughnuts, a far cry from his lavish lifestyle before his fall. Also in prison, Minkow completed his bachelor's and master's degrees, and he worked toward completion of a doctorate in theology (Matzer and Linden 1994). Minkow says he was paroled because the judge was convinced that he had changed and was ready to be given a second chance.

How Did It Happen?

The rapid growth of ZZZZ Best was unbelievable, but the idea that a young man with a high school education could pull off such an audacious fraud scheme seemed even more unbelievable. What is so amazing is not that the scheme fell apart, but rather that it lasted as long as it did.

The company's debt load was enormous, and it was completely dependent on a single customer. The company's owner was extremely young and he dealt with a mobster. Serious questions should have been raised in the minds of investors and potential investors. However, Minkow's story was compelling, and Minkow was compelling. The phenomenal growth of ZZZZ Best was simply too good to be true. Minkow did pay phenomenal returns to a lot of investors, but the funding for these returns on their investments came from subsequent investors and from loans. Minkow's scheme was predicated on the idea of perpetuity, of raising more and more money from new investors to pay off the old (Akst 1990).

ZZZZ Best did not clean nearly as many carpets as it claimed, and it did not restore a single building. Actual revenues were 90 percent less than reported. More than 85 percent of ZZZZ Best's cash flow came from undisclosed loans fronted by organized crime in New York City—all booked as revenue for supposed contracts to renovate distressed housing (Zagorin 2005). By one count, Minkow falsified more than 22,000 documents to conceal his fraud. He lied about what he owed, and he lied about what he earned. In all its years of existence, his company never made a legitimate profit. As Minkow later stated, "There was only one problem with the company and me. We were both frauds" (Association of Certified Fraud Examiners 1991).

Analysis of ZZZZ Best financial statements during its time of unbelievable growth should have raised many questions to auditors, bankers, attorneys, analysts, and investors. A legitimate business would be investing in assets. Yet, for all the company's reported growth, it did not report a lot of owned assets. Further, the company was heavily in debt. As Minkow stated from prison, a fraudulent business is always in need of money. Unlike the typical entrepreneur, who can wait to grow the business, a fraudulent entrepreneur has to have the money immediately. He owes it to someone, or he has to use it to hold a scheme together (Association of Certified Fraud Examiners 1991). Use of common tools of financial analysis would not have proved fraud, but they certainly should have provided reason to look further. The falsified financial statements of ZZZZ Best simply did not make sense. As stated by Professor W. Steve Albrecht, "The inescapable logic of the accounting equation ensures that any major overstatement of assets or profits, such as the infamous ZZZZ Best case, will show up over time" (Wells 2001).

Minkow Today

Within three days of his release, Minkow started working for the FBI, training agents how to detect fraud (Palagyi 2005). He now splits his time serving as a fraud consultant, conducting training on catching fraud and helping to catch fraud, and serving as one of the ministers of a church in San Diego. For the last 12 years, Minkow has continued making monthly restitution payments to his victims, even though a judge lifted his restitution order in 2002 (Soukup 2004). Proceeds from sales of his books also go to his victims (www.barryminkow.com). With his level of earnings today, he will never fully repay his victims. Of his time in prison, Minkow says, "I did hard time, and I deserved it because I was wrong" (Dunn 2002, B2).

The name Barry Minkow has been in the headlines for years—first as an extremely successful young entrepreneur, then as a prison inmate, and today as a "fraud buster." Recently, after a 17-month undercover operation by Minkow, a New Zealand man was apprehended and now has pled guilty to scamming 30 investors out of more than $16 million (Tisdale 2005). Minkow's name also appeared in a front-page *Wall Street Journal* article in February 2006. This time, instead of being the perpetrator, he was listed as a key figure in uncovering the scheme (Maremont 2006). According to James Asperger, a former head of the major-fraud section of the U.S. Attorney's Office in Los Angeles who prosecuted the case against Minkow, "Barry has now recovered far more fraud than he ever perpetrated" (Zagorin 2005). Minkow says he plans to be remembered for more than the ZZZZ Best Company fraud. He hopes his current efforts as head of the Fraud Discovery Institute (which, in 2002, was responsible for uncovering six frauds totaling $1.1 billion) and as pastor of a church in San Diego will supersede his activities as CEO of the carpet-cleaning company (Calabro 2005).

Conclusion

Minkow has observed that many investors are more careful in choosing fruit in the produce section of the grocery store than they are in choosing their investments. He lauds the provisions of Sarbox (Sarbanes-Oxley Act of 2002) because it hits "at the common denominator of corporate fraud: bypassing systems of internal controls," the policies and procedures designed to protect assets from waste, fraud, and inefficiency. He says he would not have been able to perpetrate the ZZZZ Best fraud if he had not been able to bypass internal controls. Of internal auditors and the Public Company Accounting Oversight Board, he says, "Unless you're a perpetrator, you don't know how good these moves are" (CFO Staff 2005). Thus, he agrees that the strengthening of internal control provisions is a positive step in preventing fraud. As Minkow speaks to executives, wearing his orange prison jumpsuit for effect, he says, "The best way to stop fraud is to talk people out of perpetrating it in the first place by doing two things: increasing the perception of detection and increasing the perception of prosecution" (CFO Staff 2005). The unsettling truth is that there are a lot of Barry Minkows out there (Association of Certified Fraud Examiners 1991).

References

About Barry. http://www.barryminkow.com/aboutbarry.html

Adelson, Andrea. "Founder of ZZZZ Best Is Convicted," *New York Times,* December 15, 1988, sec. D.

Akst, Daniel. "How ZZZZ Best Alleges $18 Million Fraud in Suit Filed against Founder, 4 Others," *Wall Street Journal,* July 7, 1987, Western edition, sec. A.

_____. "How Whiz-Kid Chief of ZZZZ Best Had, and Lost, It All," *Wall Street Journal,* July 9, 1987, Western edition, sec. A.

_____. "How Barry Minkow Fooled the Auditors," *Forbes,* 144 (1989): 7, 126–132.

_____. *WonderBoy Barry Minkow: The Kid Who Swindled Wall Street.* New York: Charles Scribner's Sons, 1990.

Arens, Alvin A., Randal J. Elder, and Mark S. Beasley. *Auditing and Assurance Services.* Upper Saddle River, NJ: Prentice Hall, 2003.

Association of Certified Fraud Examiners. *Cooking the Books: What Every Accountant Should Know about Fraud.* Association of Certified Fraud Examiners, 1991. http://www.acfe.com/documents/cooking%20the%20books.pdf.

Association of Certified Fraud Examiners. *Cooking the Books: What Every Accountant Should Know about Fraud.* Association of Certified Fraud Examiners, 1991. Videocassette.

Calabro, Lori. "Barry Minkow," *CFO,* 21 (2005): 1, 20.

Carey, Christopher. "Businessman Who Committed Fraud Now Helps Uncover It," *St. Louis Post-Dispatch* (MO), June 15, 2004.

CFO Staff. "Ten Questions for Barry Minkow," *CFO Magazine* (2005). http://www.cfo.com/article.cfm/3516399/c_3516777?f=magazine_alsoinside.

Dunn, Julie. "Barry Minkow: "The Knowledge of the Perpetrator," *New York Times,* March 17, 2002, sec. B.

Jeffrey, Nancy. "ZZZZ Best Name, Inventory, Attract $62,000 Auction Bid," *Wall Street Journal,* July 27, 1987, Western edition, sec. A.

Kullberg, Duane. "Commentary: Duane Kullberg on the Profession," *Accounting Horizons,* 2 (1988): 108–19.

Maremont, Mark. "Web Sites Offering Big Returns for Viewing Ads Face FBI Probe," *Wall Street Journal,* February 10, 2006, sec. A.

Matzer, Maria, and Dana Wechsler Linden. "Faces behind the Figures: Where Are They Now? Barry Minkow," *Forbes,* 154 (1994): 4, 134.

Palagyi, Zsa Zsa. "Barry Minkow: From Con to Christ," Christian Broadcasting Network (2005). http://www.cbn.com/700club/features/Amazing/Barry_Minkow061405.asp?option=print.

Soukup, Elise. "Making Good a *Million* at a *Time*," *Newsweek,* 143 (2004): 13–14.

Tisdale, Ruth L. "Guilty plea in $6 M scam," *Newsday,* August 10, 2005, sec. A.

Wells, Joseph T. "Irrational Ratios," *Journal of Accountancy,* 190 (2001): 80.

Zagorin, Adam. "Scambuster, Inc.," *Time,* 165 (2005): 5, 47–48.

The City Slickers Share Price Scam[*]

9

PAUL BARNES

Contents

Introduction

This case relates to what is known in the United States as a "pump and dump" scheme, technically termed "insider trading" or "market abuse." It involves two journalists and a friend (a former day trader in shares) in the United Kingdom who bought shares, tipped them through a newspaper column, and then sold them.

The "City Slickers" Column

James Hipwell and Anil Bhoyrul were financial journalists employed by the *Daily Mirror*, a national newspaper in the United Kingdom, to write a regular column entitled "City Slickers." The column was devoted to reporting rumors and making recommendations to readers to buy and sell shares based on these rumors. At some point they were joined by Terry Shepherd, who gave them tips and ideas and helped to broadcast these on the Internet.

The *Daily Mirror* is a typical "red top" tabloid. It is read by people with relatively little interest and expertise in investments and the workings of

---

[*] Paul Barnes acted as expert witness for the defense in the case. This case study was prepared using press reports during the trial and does not draw on any information that he may have obtained as an expert witness.

financial markets and relatively little money to invest. Nevertheless, the "City Slickers" column became well known. Its tips were regarded as exceptionally good to such an extent that they were ranked in a survey as second only to the *Financial Times*. Anyone who followed the column regularly would probably have made a substantial profit. Hipwell and Bhoyrul (2000) were also the authors of a book on investment.

Some examples of their tips include a healthcare company called Oxford GlycoSciences. Hipwell, Bhoyrul, and Shepherd all bought shares the day before they tipped it in the column. "City Slickers" stated that the previous day Oxford GlycoSciences had announced a deal with Merck to develop a diabetes vaccine and was close to creating a partnership with Pfizer to begin development of an AIDS vaccine. On the afternoon before the story appeared, Hipwell, using the pseudonym William Corlyon, put out a message on the bulletin board of a private investor Web site, www.iii.co.uk, encouraging investors to buy the stock. Under the heading of "City Slickers—Urgent News," the message read: "Strong rumors that the boys from the *Daily Mirror* are working on a big story re: Oxford GlycoSciences—something about developing an AIDS vaccine—so could be profitable to pile in big time." The three sold their holdings in the healthcare company a few days after the story had appeared but lost money on the deal. The share price rose on the day prior to the tip but remained static for the next few days. A few months later it rose considerably.

Another case involved Leeds Sporting, the holding company of Leeds United Football Club, which was mentioned several times in "City Slickers" in August 1999. Hipwell and Bhoyrul bought shares in the company at about 25 pence a share on August 10, 1999 and then wrote a story a week later suggesting that the broadcaster BSkyB was about to offer 45 pence a share to take a near ten percent stake in the group. "That should push the price up big time," the column said. "Get in very quickly or you'll miss the bonanza." Hipwell and Bhoyrul sold their shares on the day the story was published, when the share price was around 27 pence. The next day they wrote an article saying that it was probably "too late to get a taste of the action." A deal with BSkyB never materialized, although it was generally thought likely at that time and reported in other newspapers.

The most famous case was that of Viglen Technology plc, a computer company, run by Sir Alan Sugar, a high-profile businessman. Sugar was well known to readers of the *Daily Mirror* not only because of having been a "hands-on" chairman of Tottenham Hotspur Football Club but also because Viglen was probably the best known hardware company in the United Kingdom and recognized as highly successful. Sir Alan Sugar is also the star of the U.K. version of the TV program *The Apprentice*.

In January 2000, when excitement in Internet developments was at its peak, "City Slickers" informed its readers under the headline "Sugar to Head

Next Gold Rush" that Viglen was about to set up a company to market its products over the Internet. Almost immediately, the price of Viglen shares virtually doubled. It also emerged that the editor of the *Daily Mirror*, Piers Morgan, had bought £67,000 worth of shares in Viglen the day before the "City Slickers" tip. Hipwell and Bhoyrul were aware of the effect of their tip and made the usual sort of boast about their power. They also wrote that "Sir Alan Sugar made the fastest £100m in City history yesterday because of us." As a result of this, there were rumors that various people at the *Daily Mirror* had taken advantage of the situation and articles and complaints began appearing in the press.

The Regulation of Market Information

The orderly flow of information relating to companies is very important if the market in a company's shares is to work properly and fairly where no one is able to obtain an unfair advantage. In the case of the London Stock Exchange, the Regulatory New Service (RNS) is designed so that this may be achieved. There is an obligation on listed companies (i.e., those whose shares are traded on the stock exchange) to report an event, an expected event, or any new information as soon as possible, if it is likely to affect the share price (known as "price-sensitive" information) and investors should know about it. This is to prevent the occurrence of a false market in the shares.

Most newspapers release the same information and most of it is from the RNS. If a majority of them report a piece of news, it is likely to be true (but not necessarily) and certainly believable. A single source (e.g., a newspaper column) may have an impact on the share price, depending on its and the information's credibility. This may be followed up with similar information coming from other sources later, which would act to confirm it. The share price would respond to their confirmation. If there is no confirmation, this may suggest it is not true. In this case, the share price would adjust back to what it was in the first place. It is therefore very difficult for a newspaper to run a regular column simply based on tips as companies that are affected have an obligation that specific information relating to them is reported to RNS. A column such as "City Slickers" therefore depends on already published information. For unpublished information about a company, it depends on rumor and leaks relating to decisions that may not yet even have been made or finalized and is thus unreliable. It is difficult, therefore, for a journalist to influence the buying or selling of a heavily traded stock and its price. Some readers may, of course, act on the information but it is another matter whether this would have a significant effect on the stock as a whole. A journalist may think he or she has an effect (sometimes journalists have large egos and are financially naive) but reality may be different.

Not all share price changes are caused by the release of new information to the market. The decision of a financial institution to buy or sell a company's shares may directly affect its price because of the size of the transaction. These decisions are made in a different way from those made by an individual and are based on other forms of information. Financial institutions buy and sell in line with their liquidity requirements. As financial institutions may invest in any company listed on the London Stock Exchange, the share price of a relatively small listed company, the trading in whose shares may be rather thin, may be particularly susceptible to the buying and selling of financial institutions. (A "thinly traded" market is one in which there are relatively few regular daily transactions.)

A market that behaves in such an orderly way in regard to the release of new information is described as "informationally efficient" (Fama 1970). The London Stock Exchange, along with most other large stock exchanges throughout the world, is regarded as informationally efficient in the "semistrong" form. This implies that (1) that new information is "impounded" into a share price instantly, and (2) at any one point of time, the share price reflects all publicly available information. Because no one is able to predict the future and a share price already reflects all known information affecting the company, no one is able to predict successfully whether it will rise or fall. As a result, no one is able consistently to earn a significantly higher than average return on his shares. On the other hand, if an investor had price-sensitive information prior to its being made public (that is, "inside information") he would be able to use this to buy and sell shares ahead of price movements and make a much higher return. The principal reason for market abuse legislation is that the market needs to be protected from those who profit from inside information or attempt to manipulate it for their own purposes at the expense of others. The market needs to be, and is seen to be, fair. Otherwise, investors will consider themselves to be disadvantaged and may not invest in stocks. This is not in the public interest.

An Investigation by the Regulators

The interest of the U.K. regulatory authorities was aroused by the very significant rise that the London Stock Exchange had noticed in the shares of Viglen. The exchange alerted the Department of Trade and Industry's (DTI) Companies Investigation Branch, which duly appointed inspectors to ascertain whether there had been a contravention of the insider dealing legislation. As a result of their findings, a criminal investigation was undertaken by investigation officers of the DTI Investigation Officers Section. The investigators discovered that Hipwell, Bhoyrul, and Shepherd regularly bought shares the day before they tipped them in the column and then sold them at a

profit the following day or soon afterwards as the price rose. In the opinion of
the investigators, the tip was a deliberate act of manipulating the market by
inflating (or "ramping") the share price from which they were able to profit.

The *Daily Mirror* sacked Hipwell and Bhoyrul in early 2000 for gross
misconduct. They and Piers Morgan were also criticized by the Press Complaints Commission, the U.K. newspaper industry's self-regulatory agency,
for breaking its code of conduct. Morgan denied Hipwell and Bhoyrul's claim
that Morgan encouraged them to buy the shares they were tipping. According to them, Morgan said that if the *Daily Mirror* was in the business of tipping shares he was happy for its journalists to trade in them. He even used
the analogy along the lines of "you would not learn to drive from somebody
who had never been in a car. You would not learn from a manual."

The Trial

Hipwell, Bhoyrul, and Shepherd were charged with conspiracy to contravene
section 47(2) of the Financial Services Act of 1986, which refers to creating "a misleading impression as to…the value of any investments" by using
the "City Slickers" column in the *Daily Mirror* to tip those investments and
inducing people to acquire them contrary to section 1(1) of the Criminal Law
Act of 1977. The DTI decided not to pursue Morgan.

The 7-week trial began in October 2005 and received widespread press
interest—not least because it was perpetrated by journalists on a national
newspaper and involved its editor, who had a high media profile. The prosecution claimed that Hipwell and Bhoyrul had conspired between August
1999 and February 2000 to buy shares in 44 companies that they later tipped
in their column or on Internet sites. Hipwell made £41,000 ($62,000), Bhoy-
rul £15,000 ($23,000), and Shepherd around £17,000 ($25,000). Hipwell and
Bhoyrul were also accused of writing stories, on more than one occasion,
simply to ramp the value of shares in a particular company "quite irrespective
of the accuracy…of the story." The prosecution claimed that the purchase, tip,
and sale of shares implied there was an intention by Hipwell, Bhoyrul, and
Shepherd to use the "City Slickers" column to manipulate the market adding
that some stories behind the tips were "untrue, inaccurate, or otherwise fairly
misleading." The prosecution also made the point that Hipwell and Bhoyrul did not inform readers that they had already invested in the shares they
had tipped. "The intentional failure by them to disclose what they were really
doing is the most serious aspect of this case," the prosecution said. It was also
claimed that the three used an Internet bulletin board to further ramp the
shares by posting news of the forthcoming tip in the "City Slickers" column.

During the trial, the prosecution described Hipwell and Bhoyrul as
"pretty low-grade financial journalists" with "cynical disregard for accuracy

and truth." The judge said their offense involved "an element of feathering one's own nest, leaving aside any question of dishonesty, by carrying out operations which had no regard to whether others would or would not suffer loss, and which put into severe jeopardy the integrity which people come to expect from the press."

On the other hand, the defense argued that the tips were genuine, they were well researched, and Hipwell and Bhoyrul were simply "doing their job" and doing it so successfully that they were prepared to invest in the companies they tipped. Their wrongdoing merely consisted of failing to inform readers that they also dealt in the tipped shares. While this was contrary to journalists' Code of Conduct, it was not against the law. In other circumstances, say in horse racing, such action would be regarded as acceptable and simply regarded by punters (gamblers) as an indication of a good tipster. The defense also argued that the companies tipped turned out to be particularly good investments. If readers had bought and held the shares, they would have made more money than the defendants, who usually sold their holdings soon after the tip.

The Sentence

All three were found guilty and two were sentenced to jail. Bhoyrul, who had admitted conspiracy before going to trial, was sentenced to 180 hours' community service. Hipwell was jailed for six months and Shepherd for three months. Lawyers for Hipwell later argued the disparity of the two men's sentences was hard to justify. They also said Hipwell suffered from a severe kidney problem. But the appeals court judge told Hipwell he had no right to feel aggrieved that he had been handed a jail term while Bhoyrul had not.

After the trial and when sentencing had been done, the U.K. government's competition minister issued a statement that the "verdict should send out a clear message that the government will take action against those who break the law for their own financial gain. The DTI is committed to establishing and maintaining fair markets."

References

Fama, E. F. 1970. "Efficient Capital Markets: A Review of Theory and Empirical Work," *Journal of Finance*, 25 (1970): 383–417.

Hipwell, J., and A. Bhoyrul. *The City Slickers: Make a Million in Twelve Months.* London: Blake Publishing, 2000.

Bibliography

Chan, T. W., and J. H. Goldthorpe. 2007. "Social Status and Newspaper Readership," *American Journal of Sociology,* 112 (2007): 1095–1134.
Deloitte & Touche. *Wealth and Portfolio Choice.* London, H. M. Treasury Report, 2002.

Martin Frankel

STEVEN PRESSMAN

10

Contents

Martin (Marty) Frankel became world famous in the summer of 1999. After stealing more than $200 million from several insurance companies over a 5-year period, he became an international fugitive, hiding for months in Europe from U.S. and international authorities.

Marty Frankel's father, Leon, was a New York lawyer. After his wife died of leukemia, Leon moved to Toledo, Ohio, to join his brothers' wholesale underwear and hosiery business. A few years later he married Tillie, who became a mother to the two children from his previous marriage. Leon and Tillie had two children of their own; Marty, born in 1954, was the younger (Pollock 2002, 11).

In high school Marty was the typical nerd; he did not fit in with any group, did not care what others thought about him, and was bored most of the time. He attended the University of Toledo after high school, but because he suffered severe anxiety when it came to taking exams or writing term papers, he never graduated.

At an early age Marty became fascinated with astrology. Once he did a chart for a friend and told his parents that the chart looked very gloomy. Shortly thereafter the friend suffered a devastating accident, which reinforced Marty's belief in astrology. He was soon making astrological charts to predict the price of company stock by finding out exactly at what time and date the company was incorporated (Pollock 2002, 14f.).

With his interest in financial markets growing, Marty hung around brokerage firms in the Toledo area. There he met brokers and offered free advice to other investors; frequently his predictions were good. Marty even opened his own trading account and invested small sums of his own money; but he did not do much better than break even. One big problem was his extreme nervousness about making trades with real money.

Eventually Marty received his broker's license and was hired as a broker at Dominick & Dominick in the Toledo area. One of his clients, Ted Bitter, was a close friend of John Schultze, who owned the brokerage firm. Thinking Marty was a brilliant market analyst, Bitter gave Marty his life savings (around $50,000) and asked him to invest it. But Marty feared making a wrong decision and did not trade. Finally, under pressure from Bitter to trade, he invested $20,000 in the futures market. Immediately, he began to worry and decided to sell the investment the following day. This decision turned out to be a good one—Marty made $18,000 for Bitter in one day (Pollock 2002, 20).

Despite this success, Marty and his boss did not get along well. Marty was not bringing much new money into the brokerage firm and was not generating much in commissions through his trading. Schultze also resented the fact that his wife, Sonia, was developing a close personal relationship with Marty. A final problem was that Marty ordered expensive equipment and news services for the office so that he could keep track of what was going on in world financial markets.

In February 1986, Schultze fired Marty, who then set up trading operations at home. Although his only expenses were for up-to-the-minute stock quotes and the Reuters news service, Marty was continually behind on his payments and had to avoid his creditors. To shield himself from personal liability, he set up a corporation, Winthrop Capital, using a phony name (James Spencer) and a mail drop as the company address. He used a discount brokerage in Chicago so that he could make trades and placed an ad in the *Toledo Yellow Pages* promising low commissions.

In late 1986 Marty met Douglas Maxwell, who owned a small brokerage firm. Together they set up the Frankel Fund, a limited partnership, to invest the money coming in to Marty. The fees and legal work to set up the fund were paid for by the investors without their permission, a violation of securities laws (Pollock 2002, 28). However, the big problem was that Marty still had trader's block. He could not buy, and when he did buy stocks he would get nervous and soon sell them.

In an attempt to get over his trader's block and to end the constant fighting with his parents, Marty left for Florida in 1987 accompanied by his sister Amy. Marty's parents supported this arrangement and may have even pushed Amy to accompany Marty and help care for him.

After meeting some wealthy Palm Beach residents and getting them to invest, the Frankel Fund assets grew to over $1 million. Marty lost money trading; more importantly, he was paying personal expenses out of Frankel Fund shareholder accounts, including his $3,000 monthly rent and fees for news and stock-quote services. He also wrote checks from shareholder accounts to his sisters and his mother, and for his own spending money (Pollock 2002, 32).

In January 1988 one investor, John Herlihy, became worried about the $300,000 he had in the Frankel Fund. He was not receiving regular statements, and Marty's West Palm Beach number was disconnected. When he finally reached Marty, Herlihy asked for his money back. Marty persuaded him to change his mind, telling Herlihy he would guarantee any losses and promising at least a ten percent return on his money in the Frankel Fund. He also sent Herlihy a statement saying his account was worth more than $327,000, up $2,000 for the month. In fact, Marty had transferred all the money out of Herlihy's account to cover trading losses in other accounts and his personal expenses (Pollock 2002, 32).

Another Frankel Fund client, John Burns, asked to redeem $500,000 in April 1988 because he too could not reach Marty and was not getting regular statements. Unlike with Herlihy, Marty could not convince Burns to change his mind, so Marty paid off Burns using money from other client accounts.

Worried because there was little money relative to what the Frankel Fund owed its clients, Marty moved all remaining cash into a Florida bank account in his own name. He told Bitter that the Frankel Fund had collapsed, blaming Maxwell, whom he accused of stealing money and making bad trades. Bitter lost his life savings. Marty had to move back home to Toledo. He also hired an attorney, whom he gave the remaining $249,000 in Frankel Fund cash. This money was turned over to the Securities and Exchange Commission (SEC), which began an investigation of Marty and the Frankel Fund.

Marty admitted to the SEC that he lied when he told investors that he had managed accounts holding millions of dollars and that he had averaged yearly returns of over 20 percent. But hearings dragged on for several years. Finally, in 1992, Marty made a deal with the SEC. He paid a fine and gave up his broker's license. Bitter and Herlihy also filed suit against Marty. In August 1992, at a National Association of Security Dealers (NASD) hearing, Herlihy was awarded $622,000 and Bitter $176,632. They were also awarded attorney fees (Pollock 2002, 77).

In the fall of 1989, while the SEC investigation was still ongoing, Marty launched a new fund, Creative Partners, claiming he was in the top rank of money managers in the late 1980s. But because of the SEC investigation, Marty had to distance himself from Creative Partners, so he claimed that the fund was owned by another firm, Rothschild International Investments, and set up a secret Swiss bank account to hold the Creative Partners/Rothschild money. Sonia Schultze, who had decided to divorce her husband, set up a new brokerage firm just 20 minutes away from her husband's office, and her brokers started directing their clients to Creative Partners. Several hundred thousand dollars flowed into the fund.

Marty also set up the Donar Corporation, listing himself as president. The firm paid $70,000 for a home in Toledo across the street from his parents' house. Sonia moved into the house with her kids. Marty set up a swing set in the backyard for Sonia's daughters and also wired more than $300,000 from his Swiss bank account to Sonia's lawyers to help pay for her divorce and child custody battles (Pollock 2002, 52–4).

To keep money coming in to Creative Partners, Marty hired two part-time Chicago brokers in their 20s. He rented them office space and equipment, including expensive stock-quote services. Over the next year and a half, they put 15 clients into Creative Partners, giving Marty access to several hundred thousand dollars more. The brokers received a percentage of the profits reported by Marty on these accounts. But since he was not trading and not making money, these reported profits were all fictitious.

Amazingly, the SEC knew that Marty had started up Creative Partners and that he had a history of fraudulent activity, but took no action. One reason for this is that the SEC was overworked and understaffed in the late 1980s and 1990s. During the Reagan era, the U.S. government sharply cut funding for the SEC, despite the fact that more people were investing and more mutual funds were opening. The Chicago SEC office, responsible for the Toledo area, had around 15 scams to contend with at the time; someone who lived at home with his parents and who controlled little money was just not a top priority (Pollock 2002, 61).

As the SEC investigation continued, Marty realized that he would have to hide his identity and his money, so in 1990 he paid $8,000 for Frisch Investments, an inactive broker and dealer, and changed its name to Liberty National Securities. He made William Kok, a broker who worked for Sonia, its president. In this way, Marty was not connected with Liberty National, although he controlled all its money.

Searching for more money to support himself and his operations, Marty set his sights on financial institutions. First, he looked at community banks, but the regulatory oversight on banks was too strict and he decided that buying an insurance company would be easier. Insurance companies are chartered by individual states and regulated by state insurance commissions. Regulatory laws require insurance companies to put cash aside against claims and to invest conservatively so that they have money to pay out when claims are made.

John Hackney owned a little insurance company, the Franklin American Life Insurance Company, in his home town of Franklin, Tennessee. Franklin American sold burial insurance. Hackney was making very little money in insurance, but Franklin American had a large pool of cash, held as reserves against future claims, since at some point all customers would submit a claim to the firm. Marty put Hackney on a $5,000 per month retainer before he sought to buy Franklin American. After the deal, Hackney was paid a salary of $80,000 a year, plus bonuses for finding more insurance companies that Marty could acquire.

To buy Franklin American, Marty set up a trust fund, which he named Thunor, for the Scandinavian god of thunder and lightning. Hackney, Sonia, and one of his young salesmen in Chicago headed up the fund. In October 1991, Thunor Trust bought Franklin American Life Insurance for $3.7

million. Marty's name did not appear on the change of ownership application. Hackney was made president of the firm, and Thunor told Tennessee regulators that Sonia had put up $2.5 million of her own money and Marty's Creative Partners salesmen had put up $900,000 as capital. This money was supposed to guarantee insurance claims against the company in case the premiums were insufficient.

State insurance commissions did not check the trustees of Thunor to verify their financial condition and their contributions to Thunor. They also did not question why individuals would provide money to Thunor but have no control over it. This highly unusually relationship should have raised questions about who actually controlled Thunor. State regulators also failed to keep track of Thunor's assets to make sure that they were invested conservatively so that insurance claims could be paid. Nor did they question things like the consistently high returns on trading government bonds that Thunor reported (GAO 2000, 16–30).

Once the deal was final, Marty directed Hackney to transfer the $18 million in Franklin American assets to Liberty National Securities. This money went through several banks and then into a Creative Partners Fund bank account in Toledo. Marty could now pay off all Creative Partners investors and close down the only fund with his name on it. This money was also used to pay Frankel Fund losses, including judgments in favor of Herlihy and Bitter from their NASD lawsuits. What remained of the Franklin American assets was now in Thunor, which had no paper connection to Marty even though Marty controlled all its money.

Starting in February 1994 and continuing over five years, Thunor bought six more insurance companies in Mississippi, Oklahoma, Missouri, and Arkansas. Because of his astrology obsession, Marty demanded to know the birthdates of all parties involved in these deals and insisted on closing dates that were "astrologically correct" (Pollock 2002, 79).

To make his operations appear legitimate, Marty fabricated phony account statements showing positive returns on insurance assets. He reported these to the insurance companies, who then reported these results to state insurance commissions (GAO 2000, 12). And to obtain additional money, Marty made reinsurance agreements with other insurers. Reinsurance is when an insurance company takes out insurance. If one insurance company writes a policy for hundreds of millions of dollars, it may not want the risk of having to pay off such a large sum of money. In this case it will make payments to another insurance company, which now takes on part of the risk of a claim being filed. As a reinsurer, Marty was able to collect premiums from other insurance companies, leading to a large inflow of cash.

With plenty of money at his disposal, Marty decided to leave Toledo again. He rented a large mansion in Greenwich, Connecticut, an exclusive suburb of New York City. It became Marty's headquarters in the spring of

1993. The rent was $20,000 a month; the house had five bedrooms and eight baths and sat on 4 acres of land. The living room became Marty's trading room. Sonia moved in with her two children. He introduced himself to neighbors as "Mike King." Eventually, he bought the house for $3 million using Franklin American money. In an attempt to keep his involvement secret, all his companies had mail drops in New York. Marty's trading block remained; he could not invest the cash generated from investors and insurance companies. As a result, Marty had to devote more and more time to preparing phony statements for Liberty National investors showing that they had made a good profit.

Then things got pretty weird. Marty became involved with a sadism and masochism (S&M) organization. He put personal ads in a New York newspaper, the *Village Voice,* and on S&M Web sites describing himself as a rich man seeking a submissive woman wanting to serve a kinky and perverted master. Soon there were numerous strange women living in the Greenwich house. Many did small jobs, like helping with office work and laundering money. Marty gave them blank travelers' checks to pay for expenses. One collected expensive bottles of wine. Besides the growing jealousy among these women, they were beginning to figure out that Marty's operations were phony. This meant that even when Marty sent them away from Greenwich, he still paid their rent and expenses to keep them happy. Marty also hired several security guards, maintenance men, chefs, and maids. The monthly American Express bill was in the hundreds of thousands of dollars. Over time, Marty spent around $9 million on his "support staff" (Pollock 2002, 102–115).

This new obsession with women destroyed his relationship with Sonia, who left the Greenwich residence and soon remarried. However, she did return once a month to help Marty produce phony statements for investors.

Unable to make money from trading, due to his mental block and other distractions, and finding it more difficult to buy small insurance companies, Marty turned to the Catholic Church for help. He started the Saint Francis of Assisi Foundation and hoped that with backing by the Vatican, the foundation would dispel any concerns of state insurance regulators and also insurance executives selling out to Marty. This would allow Marty to keep acquiring insurance companies and raiding their assets.

Introduced to Catholic charity and senior Vatican officials, Marty claimed that he had found religion and wanted to be a great philanthropist. In return for Vatican support of the Assisi Foundation, Marty promised to donate $50 million to a charitable organization run by the head of one of the oldest churches in Florence, Italy. But when it came time to close the deal, there was no $50 million donation and the deal fell through. Then Marty tried another approach—donating $55 million but only giving $5 million to the Catholic charity. The other $50 million would be deposited in a Swiss bank account controlled by Marty. To help sweeten the deal, Marty contributed money to some favorite causes of the Vatican parties involved in the negotiations. He donated $100,000 to fund a church hospital in Tirana, Albania, the favorite project of Cardinal Pio Laghi, a Vatican official who was once the Pope's representative to the United States. Marty also gave cash gifts and cars to church officials working on the deal.

Involving the Catholic Church only made it harder for Marty to buy more insurance companies. Questions were immediately raised about whether the Assisi Foundation was real, whether it really was connected to the Vatican, and why such an organization would want to buy a small insurance company.

Another problem for Marty came from his Greenwich neighbors. They were worried about guards with guns, deliveries at all hours of the night, dozens of cars parked out on the street, and, of course, all the weird women running around the neighborhood. They feared drugs, money laundering, and prostitution, so the neighbors hired a private investigator. The investigator traced an Ohio license plate number to Marty's father; he also learned that people in the compound called Marty "King Marty." A computer search turned up an article from 1993 about John Schultze's quest to win his kids from Sonia. The article noted that Sonia Schultze was living with "former Toledo stockbroker Martin Frankel" (Pollock 2002, 181). Further searches found that Marty had been barred from the securities business by the SEC. The private investigator contacted the SEC.

A final problem for Marty was brewing in Tennessee. Billy Lovelady, a state insurance regulator, figured out that Franklin American assets were being held by Liberty National Security, Marty's brokerage firm. Lovelady ordered Hackney to put the Franklin American assets into a bank and also alerted Mississippi insurance regulators to this problem. Marty immediately wired $69 million to the Prudential Savings Bank in Georgia, but since the money was needed to pay household expenses, it could not stay there for long. Marty secretly moved the money again—first to a Dreyfus account in New York and then to his Swiss bank account (Pollock 2002, 194f). He also tried to find some high-powered lawyers with political connections to get state regulators off his back, but these efforts were to no avail (Pollock 2002, 184f). By early February 1999, it had become clear that neither Tennessee nor Mississippi would let the assets of a state-regulated insurance company be controlled by a tiny out-of-state brokerage firm that they could not monitor.

Lovelady was also concerned about the Wall Street mail drop address for Liberty National and the fact that it had capital of less than $100,000—peanuts for a firm supposedly trading hundreds of millions of dollars. When Lovelady discovered that Marty had removed the $69 million from the Prudential Savings Bank, he forced him to return it. Lovelady called a hearing for April 29, 1999.

Feeling cornered, Marty began to plot his escape. He bought $10 million in diamonds and obtained a phony passport. Fearing his Swiss bank accounts would be frozen, he sought, unsuccessfully, to buy a Jordanian bank. Most of the rest of his money was gone—spent on houses, women, bodyguards, legal and consulting fees, payments to Church officials and various partners, and expensive bottles of wine.

Marty flew to Rome with two of the women from his Greenwich mansion. Before he left, he distributed auto titles to those who drove corporate cars. The staff at the house, sensing that Marty was abandoning ship, stole expensive rugs, computers, and stereos from the Greenwich house.

From Rome, Marty hired a lawyer in Connecticut and instructed two women who remained in the Greenwich house to shred all remaining documents. The women got bored with shredding and tried burning the documents in the fireplace. The house caught fire, and the Greenwich fire department was called. Among the items they found were a Ouija board and a to-do list with "launder money now" at the top of it (Edwards 2004).

During his second week in Rome, Marty tried making deals in order to get his hands on some additional cash. On May 12, he bought an Italian health care firm, Sanità Più, for $28 million, which was pretty much all the money he had left in his Swiss bank account; however, the deal was rescinded when news of Marty became known throughout the world. Four days later a Connecticut judge issued a warrant for Marty's arrest, accusing him of wire fraud and money laundering, based upon what was found in the Greenwich mansion and other evidence against Marty. During the next few weeks, all Marty's insurance companies were put into receivership since their assets had vanished. On May 26 his assets in Switzerland were frozen. Interpol was alerted and there was a global manhunt. Marty hung out in Rome's cyber cafés checking for news about his case. The FBI tried to get Marty to turn himself in by spreading rumors through his Connecticut lawyer that several people were out to kill him.

Marty made plans to go to Munich on June 29 and from there to fly to Cyprus, which had no extradition treaty with the United States. He consulted his astrological calendar and noted that the planned trip to Cyprus on July 1 would be a bad day, so he went to Hamburg instead, where he hid from the people supposedly trying to kill him. He had only $250,000 in cash left, and his diamonds would be hard to convert to cash with law enforcement officials all over the world pursuing him.

Marty was turned in by Cynthia Allison, one of the women from his Greenwich compound that he was traveling with. Tired of running and hiding, she called a lawyer in the United States and told him where they were staying. On September 4, the Hamburg police arrested Marty and Cynthia in their hotel room. Cynthia was released since there was no warrant for her arrest. Marty was imprisoned because he had a phony passport. He whined and complained in jail, but soon became a celebrity and gave out legal advice to the other inmates. Interviewed on the ABC News show *20/20,* he refused to talk about the charges against him and made a case that he should be allowed to stay in Germany. Marty made the same case in German courts in an effort to avoid being tried in the United States for securities fraud. He was tried and sentenced in Germany to three years in jail for failing to pay customs duties on his diamonds and for possessing a phony passport.

Marty fought extradition from Germany as best he could, but in March 2001 he was returned to the United States in handcuffs, accompanied by federal marshals. Many of his accomplices, such as the women living in his Greenwich house who helped Marty launder money, Sonia Schultze Howe, and John Hackney, made deals with federal prosecutors and pleaded guilty to money laundering, participating in a conspiracy to defraud the public, transacting interstate commerce with the intent to commit bribery, and/or making false statements and reports to insurance regulatory agencies. An elderly Vatican official received two suspended 5-year sentences for his role in Marty's scam. Hackney's house in Franklin, Tennessee, was seized and sold for $670,000. Marty's fleet of cars was located, seized, and sold for $750,000. His diamonds were auctioned off by the U.S. Treasury and sold for $9 million (Green 2005).

Setters Life, an insurance company in Virginia, lost $45 million in 1999 when Thunor could not pay its reinsurance claims because its assets were gone (GAO 2000, 13). In an attempt to recover money lost by the residents of his state, Mississippi's insurance commissioner filed suit against the Roman Catholic Church, claiming that Vatican officials violated the federal Racketeer Influenced and Corrupt Organizations (RICO) Act (Edwards 2004).

In jail in Connecticut, Marty was kept on suicide watch. In May 2002, he pleaded guilty in federal court to 24 counts of securities fraud, racketeering, conspiracy, and wire fraud. During sentencing, in December 2004, Marty apologized for the scheme and said he began stealing to help his girlfriend's children. "When Judge Ellen B. Burns questioned why he needed $200 million to help the children, Frankel said things just got out of hand" (Christoffersen 2004). Marty was sentenced to nearly 17 years in jail. He was also sentenced in Tennessee for looting state insurance companies. His 16-year sentence there ran concurrently with his federal sentence, on the condition that he would cooperate with local authorities to help recover the money that he stole. At the end of 2004, Marty petitioned that his prison sentence be reduced to ten years because of his mental state and the harsh prison conditions he had to endure in Germany. On March 23, 2006, a federal judge refused to reduce Marty's sentence (New York Times 2006).

As a result of the Frankel case, there was a rush to figure out where insurance oversight broke down and what could be done to prevent a similar situation in the future. The state comptroller of Tennessee blamed the state insurance department for lacking the money and expertise to oversee

Franklin America. He felt that state insurance regulators took far too long to discover violations of state insurance rules.

References

Christoffersen, John. "Federal Judge Sentences Martin Frankel," Associated Press, December 11, 2004.

Edwards, Lynda. "Suing Vatican Bank, Insurance Officials Charge Racketeering," Associated Press, July 4, 2004.

GAO (U.S. General Accounting Office). Insurance Regulation: Scandal Highlights Need for Strengthened Regulatory Oversight, September, GAO/GDD-00-198, 2000.

Green, Barbara. "Fugitive's Diamond Auctioned, Victims Get $9 Million," *National Jeweler,* 99(2) (2005): 12.

Pollock, Ellen Joan. *The Pretender.* New York: Wall Street Journal Books, 2002.

"17-Year Sentence Affirmed for Investor Who Looted Insurers," *New York Times,* March 23, 2006.

Bibliography

GAO (U.S. General Accounting Office). Insurance Regulation: The NAIC Accreditation Program Can be Improved, August, GAO-01-948, 2001.

Johnson, Joe A., Jr. *Thief: The Bizarre Story of Fugitive Financier Martin Frankel.* New York: Lebhar-Friedman Books, 2000.

Scientific Cheating

Unethical behavior is not restricted to business situations; it can be found in any aspect of human endeavor. It can be particularly reprehensible in areas that normally require the highest level of honesty and integrity. In this part of the book, we present stories of fraud that did not involve monetary greed or financial rewards. Instead, we see government performing experiments on humans without their knowledge or consent. We see scientists causing irreparable harm by forgetting the search for knowledge requires a commitment to absolute truth. The publication of a fake manuscript purportedly written by a religious order was designed specifically to harm those who practice that religion. These actions were not motivated by greed and the pursuit of wealth, but rather involved the twisting of truth with a goal of promoting opinions or ideologies.

Human Experimentation Involving Radiation, Syphilis, and Scurvy

11

MATTHEW T. LEE
JEANNINE A. GAILEY

Contents

Introduction

International law, as well as medical ethics, has long recognized that all participants in research must grant permission before the study begins. This consent must be both "informed" (meaning that risks are identified and understood) and totally "voluntary" (free of coercion). These principles are thought to be timeless and independent of national laws or local customs. Research that violates these principles is both unethical and illegal. For example, German doctors and researchers were convicted by the Allies in 1947 at the war crimes trials in Nuremburg for crimes against humanity, which included conducting harmful experiments on people without obtaining their voluntary, informed consent (for the text of the Nuremburg Code see Hornblum 1998, xi). Some defendants argued that their actions were legal within the framework of German law and ethical according to prevailing norms. They also argued that if the Allies wished to create a new law requiring informed consent that it should not be imposed ex post facto. The Allies asserted that voluntary, informed consent was a fundamental human right that transcended jurisdictional boundaries and that the Nuremburg trials were not establishing new law, but rather reaffirming existing law.

To what extent have researchers in the United States adhered to these timeless legal and ethical standards? An answer to this question is beyond the scope of this chapter, but we do provide three examples that are suggestive: radiation experiments conducted during the Cold War, the Tuskegee syphilis study, and research that induced scurvy in a group of prisoners.

The Cold War Human Radiation Experiments

In May 1945, the same week that Germany surrendered in World War II, a 58-year-old house painter named Albert Stevens arrived at the University of California Hospital in San Francisco. He had moved from Ohio to California in the 1920s to ease his wife's asthma. In the months before entering the hospital, he had suffered terribly from sharp stomach pains. The doctors who examined Stevens at the hospital advised him that he had stomach cancer and probably would not live more than six months. Unfortunately, a gastroscopy recommended by a doctor to confirm the diagnosis was not conducted and Stevens was misdiagnosed. Possibly as a result of his bleak prognosis, medical personnel selected Stevens for inclusion in a research study that examined the effects of plutonium on human beings. Behind this decision were scientists from the Manhattan Project—the top-secret U.S. military research project that developed the atomic bombs used against Japan. Although he entered the hospital seeking treatment, Albert Stevens was injected with a nontherapeutic and highly toxic radioactive material without his knowledge or consent. Scientists who participated in the experiment believed that he had been given a "carcinogenic dose" or a "lethal textbook dose" of plutonium (Welsome 1999, 92, 94).

Plutonium is an important ingredient in the atomic bomb and government scientists were concerned about the potential health effects that might befall those who worked on the bomb. Although scientists knew that radioactive isotopes like plutonium are extremely dangerous to humans and animals, they did not have accurate data on the length of time required for it to be excreted through urine or feces, or how much of it might settle in the body. Because they were not certain whether the plutonium injection would seriously injure or kill a person, scientists attempted to select subjects like Albert Stevens who had a "relatively short life expectancy" (Langham et al. 1980, 1033). Some of the subjects, like Stevens, were misdiagnosed as terminally ill and lived years beyond doctors' expectations. During a surgical procedure designed to remove what doctors assumed to be a large cancerous growth in Albert Stevens's abdomen, half of his liver, his entire spleen, and other parts of organs were removed. Doctors later discovered that he did not have stomach cancer after all, but rather a "benign gastric ulcer with chronic inflammation" (Welsome 1999, 93).

Despite this revelation, doctors did not advise Stevens that he did not have cancer or disclose his unwitting participation in the plutonium injection experiment. The scientists involved in the plutonium injection were troubled by the fact that their subject did not have a short life expectancy after all. Yet none of the researchers ever told Stevens that he had been used as an atomic guinea pig, even though he lived for several decades with a massive amount of plutonium deposited in his bones. While he remained hospitalized, government scientists were able to collect and analyze his urine and feces in order to study the rate at which he excreted plutonium. But when he was discharged from the hospital after a month, researchers were concerned that, in the words of one senior scientist, "the man may sell his house and go to live at some distant point which would, of course, put an end to our most interesting series of experiments" (Welsome 1999, 95).

The scientists had a solution to this problem: The government would pay Stevens to collect his own urine and feces in jars, which hospital staff would retrieve each week from a shed behind his house. A nurse would turn the samples over to government scientists who would then be able to quantify the rate at which he excreted plutonium over the years. According to his son, Stevens believed that collecting his own biological waste was part of his follow-up treatment for stomach cancer. His family did not question this rather unusual activity. They were just grateful that he was able to receive free medical care because he did not have health insurance as a result of being unemployed. They also continued to believe that he was receiving effective treatment for his stomach cancer. Stevens surprised doctors by living two decades longer than expected, despite his exposure to radiation levels that scientists calculated were 858 times greater than what an average person receives from natural sources. It is unclear how the plutonium might have affected his health over this time period, although it is suggestive that he never regained the strength to resume painting houses, he could not gain weight, and he suffered significant bone deterioration in his spine (Welsome 1999).

Another plutonium injection subject whose life span exceeded doctors' expectations was Ebb Cade, a cement mixer from North Carolina. Cade was involved in a serious car accident in April 1945 and suffered multiple factures. He was rushed to the Oak Ridge Army Hospital, where scientists selected him for inclusion in the plutonium experiment. Unlike Albert Stevens, Cade's medical prognosis was not dire at the time that researchers decided to inject him with the radioactive material. Other than broken bones and a "somewhat diminished" kidney function, Cade was in relatively good health. Regardless, Cade received a dose of plutonium that researchers at the time considered five times larger than a harmless amount. According to Joseph Howland, the doctor who administered the plutonium, Cade did not give his consent and was in fact unaware of the procedure. Then a young doctor, Howland stated that he objected to participating, "but in the Army, an order is an order" (Welsome 1999, 85). In the days following the injection, medical personnel would collect Cade's urine, feces, bone samples, 15 teeth, part of his jawbone, and gum tissue for analysis. His bones were slow to heal, prompting one scientist to ask whether this was due to the frequent laboratory work being conducted on him as well as whether he had "received some stuff" (i.e., plutonium) while he was hospitalized (Welsome 1999, 87).

Illustrating the scientific view of human subjects as merely the means to an end, one of the scientists commented that Cade represented the "opportunity we've been waiting for," but when he was discharged unexpectedly the researchers "lost the valuable data that we were expected to get" (Morgan 1995, 21).[1] This researcher was concerned about lost data, not the potential danger to Cade that may have resulted from having been injected with plutonium. No follow-up medical checks were conducted. One month after the injection, another scientist described the Cade case to other researchers in a classified talk about the Manhattan Project. He observed that the experiment deposited "a maximum amount in the bone where it is probably the most damaging." Ebb Cade died of heart failure eight years after he was injected with plutonium. The health effects of the plutonium during the eight years remain unknown or undisclosed.

A few short years after Albert Stevens, Ebb Cade, and dozens of others were unwittingly injected with harmful amounts of radioactive materials by government-funded scientists, thousands of American soldiers and untold numbers of civilians would become de facto research subjects in a series of radiation experiments conducted on a much larger scale. Government officials deliberately exposed perhaps 100,000 soldiers—and civilians living downwind of the test sites (the "downwinders")—to radioactive fallout from the atomic bomb tests conducted in Nevada in the 1950s and early 1960s (Uhl and Ensign 1980; Advisory Committee on Human Radiation Experiments [ACHRE] 1996). The doses varied from test to test, depending on such factors as the intensity and proximity of the explosion and the direction of the prevailing winds. In these tests, soldiers were frequently ordered to kneel in trenches near "ground zero" or march in the direction of the blast, often coming within a few thousand feet of the explosion. In fact, some soldiers were so close to ground zero during the blasts (e.g., 2,000 yards), that their feat has earned them a place in the *Guinness Book of World Records* for being "the closest any known personnel had been since the atomic bombs were dropped on Japan" (Uhl and Ensign 1980, 73). The objectives of the tests varied, but military officials were especially interested in knowing how soldiers would perform on an atomic battlefield and in understanding the fallout patterns of different sizes of bombs.

Norris Bradbury, the director of the Los Alamos National Laboratory in New Mexico, was in charge of running many of the tests. He later explained the government's decision to locate the test site in Nevada:

You had to test somewhere…and the reason for using Nevada, of course, was that [the radioactive material] would fall out, drop out of the atmosphere before it got to civilization. Nevada was as convenient a place as you could get to. We took all the precautions we knew how to take. ("Cover-Up at Ground Zero" 1994, 2)

But the fallout did make it to civilization, landing most prominently in the communities of southern Utah. Although government propaganda films shown to soldiers and civilians in nearby towns repeatedly emphasized that the tests were safe, even using phrases such as "there is no danger" ("Cover-Up at Ground Zero" 1994, 3), the tests were only conducted on days when the wind blew away from Las Vegas, the most populous city near the test site. Other cities downwind of the blast, such as St. George, Utah, often received heavy doses of radioactive fallout. In fact, when classified internal memos prepared by the Atomic Energy Commission (the precursor to the Department of Energy and the agency in charge of overseeing the tests) were later declassified, they revealed that government officials did not know whether the tests were safe ("Cover-Up at Ground Zero" 1994).

The ethics of such government programs as the atomic bomb tests are brought into sharp relief by the actions of Norris Bradbury. At the time that the tests were conducted, Bradbury's son's family lived in St. George, Utah, downwind of the test site in Nevada. Despite the great lengths to which government officials went to assure the downwinders in St. George that the tests posed no danger (i.e., producing a propaganda film using residents of St. George as actors), Bradbury—the director of the program—was concerned about the health of his unborn grandchild. He warned his daughter-in-law that she should not stay in St. George while she was pregnant. When she failed to appreciate the gravity of the situation, Bradbury persisted with his warning, saying, according to his daughter-in-law, "Look, this is a serious situation and this is not a good place to be, and you ought to go somewhere else" ("Cover-Up at Ground Zero" 1994, 5). She suggests that Bradbury "didn't want to have anything go wrong with one of his grandchildren" ("Cover-Up at Ground Zero" 1994, 5). When confronted by a television reporter with her statement, Bradbury at first said that he did not recall giving such a warning, but then admitted, "Maybe I did" ("Cover-Up at Ground Zero" 1994, 5). He also told the reporter that "radiation is not a good thing, but I don't know of any death that's been caused by it" ("Cover-Up at Ground Zero" 1994, 4).

Albert Stevens, Ebb Cade, Joseph Howland, and Norris Bradbury are four of the players in a national drama that has come to be known as the "Cold War human radiation experiments." This phrase has been used by the media, scholars, government officials, and laypersons to categorize thousands of research programs involving radiation that were funded by the U.S. federal government dating from the final months of World War II through the early

1970s (see also Gailey and Lee 2005).[2] Throughout this time period, government directives advised researchers to maintain secrecy on the grounds of national security and more mundane concerns, such as the threat of civil lawsuits. For example, one government memo from 1947 argued against declassifying a report related to the plutonium injection experiment because "the experimenters and the employing agencies, including the U.S. [government would be] laid open to a devastating lawsuit which would, through its attendant publicity, have far reaching results" (Welsome 1999, 195).

The researchers who participated in the Cold War human radiation experiments generally did not raise ethical objections. Joseph Howland represented one exception, but even he went along with the order to inject Ebb Cade. Some scientists seemed to be concerned that the failure to conduct controlled experiments on a small number of research subjects would mean exposing thousands of atomic workers and soldiers on a potentially nuclear battlefield to unknown hazards, thus representing a "vast experiment" on a larger population that would also not be able to grant their informed consent (Welsome 1999, 45). Researchers were wary of repeating the tragic events that unfolded at the United States Radium Corporation in New Jersey, where workers who painted watch dials with radium died from exposure to that radioactive material. Ignorance, born of a lack of empirical data, could do much more damage in the frantic race to build a nuclear arsenal at the end of WWII and into the Cold War. Scientists and government officials feared the national security implications of exposing workers and soldiers to unknown dangers. An accident in 1944, during which a researcher accidentally swallowed a substantial amount of plutonium, increased the sense of urgency felt by scientists to build an empirical understanding of the potential harms posed by the radioactive materials that were being developed by the government.

The radiation experiments conducted in the United States did not result in prosecutions for Nuremburg Code violations. The effectiveness of the attempt to keep the programs secret played an important role in preventing prosecutions. After three decades of secrecy, a report on the plutonium injection experiment was openly published in a scientific journal, except that the potentially lethal doses were fraudulently described as "small tracer amounts" and the identities of the research subjects were not disclosed (Langham et al. 1980, 1033). Scientists use the word "tracer" to describe doses involving trivial, harmless amounts of material, so this was clearly not an accurate description of the injections that Albert Stevens and Ebb Cade received. In fact, one of the scientists referred to plutonium as "fiendishly toxic, even in small amounts" (Welsome 1999, 40). None of the research subjects were ever advised of the potential health effects of their exposure to high levels of radiation and no follow-up medical studies were ever conducted. Similarly, many of the atomic veterans, downwinders, and unwitting research participants did not learn the full extent of their exposure to potentially harmful radiation in their lifetime, although family members did learn some details during the intense media coverage of the experiments in the 1990s.

Although defenders of the Cold War human radiation experiments argue that the studies were conducted to advance national security, this argument is not applicable to many of the ethically problematic research programs that have been conducted in the United States.

The Tuskegee Syphilis Study

Perhaps the most infamous medical study in American history is the Tuskegee syphilis study (for the definitive history, see Jones 1993). This study was conducted by the U.S. Public Health Service (PHS) from 1932 to 1972, thus overlapping the era of the Cold War human radiation experiments. The research setting was Tuskegee, Alabama, and roughly 400 impoverished and generally illiterate African American men infected with syphilis served as subjects. The PHS was interested in studying the course of syphilis and even though this potentially fatal disease was readily treatable with penicillin by 1947, participants in the study were denied treatment. The subjects did not give informed consent and were not even informed that they had syphilis. Instead, researchers lied to them by explaining that they had "bad blood," for which they were ostensibly receiving treatment. The "special treatment" that they were receiving consisted of exams, including dangerous and quite painful spinal taps, to track the progression of the disease. When some subjects had the opportunity to receive penicillin from a national drive to eradicate venereal disease, experimenters actively prevented the subjects' participation due to their scientific interest in following the course of the disease. Estimates of the death toll vary, but at least two dozen subjects are believed to have died as a direct result of syphilis and about one hundred died of related health complications. Many more suffered needlessly from the disease. In addition, a number of the wives and children of the research subjects also became infected with syphilis during the course of the study.

Syphilis is highly contagious and causes severely painful and debilitating symptoms. It leads to tumors and lesions in the skin, bones, and organs. The disease attacks the heart and central nervous system in its late stage and is often fatal. Given the horrific consequences of the illness, the American public had difficulty understanding how doctors and public health officials, sworn to protect health and cure disease, could have participated in such an insidious experiment. To many observers, the most ethically problematic decision was the withholding of penicillin in the 1940s. Dr. John Heller, the director of the Division of Venereal Disease at the PHS during this time, has been identified as the likely decision maker with regard to this critical situation. He has not said much about his role in the study, other than to proclaim,

"There was nothing in the experiment that was unethical or unscientific" (Jones 1993, 8). Heller admitted that he was "horrified" by the Nazi experiments that caused death and injury to subjects and resulted in the Nuremburg prosecutions, but he saw no connection between those experiments and the Tuskegee study (Jones 1993, 179). As for his failure to provide penicillin and thus end the study in the late 1940s, Heller obliquely responded, "The longer the study, the better the ultimate information we would derive" (Jones 1993, 179).

Ironically, the discovery of a safe and effective cure for syphilis seems to have only strengthened the resolve of the PHS to continue the Tuskegee study. Maintaining a control group of untreated subjects was justified on the grounds that it would firmly establish the effectiveness of the new treatment and that the data collected by researchers would, in the words of one PHS report, "never be duplicated since penicillin and other antibiotics are being so widely used...thereby affording a definite treatment for syphilis" (Jones 1993, 179). In other words, syphilis would soon be eradicated and the Tuskegee study provided the final opportunity for data collection. Why these data were so crucial given that a cure had been found was never explained. Other researchers outside the PHS justified the withholding of penicillin on the grounds that it was untested. However, even before penicillin was available, the medical community preferred to risk using the earlier treatments rather than leaving the disease untreated. Critics suggested that once the initial decision was made to deny treatment in the 1930s, the advent of new and better treatments a decade later would not alter that decision. Physicians not involved in the study defended it and the findings of the research had been openly discussed in the research literature for years. One doctor publicly blamed the subjects for their own deaths and defended the scientists. Critics countered that racism was at the heart of study: In the words of one newspaper editor, it "could only happen to blacks" (Jones 1993, 12). Another editorial lamented the "moral astigmatism that saw these black sufferers simply as 'subjects' in a study, not as human beings" (Jones 1993, 14).

Racism was certainly part of the story and the physicians who examined the subjects were often "harsh and condescending" (Jones 1993, 157). But what accounts for the participation of Eunice Rivers, a black nurse with the PHS whose job was to track the participants in the study? She played a key role in preventing doctors from treating the men by saying, "He's under study and not to be treated" (Jones 1993, 6). Although different PHS researchers participated in the study for varying lengths of time, the one constant was Nurse Rivers. The subjects came to see themselves as part of a social club: "Miss Rivers' Lodge" (Jones 1993, 6). Rivers believed that the benefits of participating in the experiment were substantial, such as the burial stipend, which was a "godsend" to poor families who could not afford a funeral (Jones 1993, 154). Additionally, she enjoyed working with the subjects and considered them family, stating, "We had a good time...that was the joy of my life" (Jones 1993, 161). Perhaps most important, Nurse Rivers never gave a second thought to the ethics of the study and she never advocated treating the men. She viewed herself as a good nurse, who "always did what the doctors ordered" (Jones 1993, 163).

She did not believe that she had a personal responsibility to determine the treatment that the subjects received; that was an issue for the doctors. Besides, she reasoned, in the early days the treatment for syphilis was itself potentially harmful. Once penicillin became available, thus providing a safe and effective treatment, not treating the men had become routine for the nurse. In addition, the subjects were receiving health care for other ailments by virtue of their participation in the study. Most similarly situated black men received virtually no such care in their entire lives. On balance, Rivers believed that some care was better than none at all, even if that meant that a potentially fatal disease like syphilis had to remain untreated. The primary ethical issue for her was turning away applicants who came "begging to be admitted to the study" (Jones 1993, 165). Looking back on her participation, Eunice Rivers believed that she had provided a valuable service to the subjects and behaved ethically.

As for the subjects, they were enticed by letters from the PHS promising "special free treatment" for their "bad blood" (Jones 1993, 127). Charles Pollard, one of the subjects, recalled being told by a doctor that he was receiving a "spinal shot" containing medicine, when in fact he had been given a nontherapeutic spinal tap designed to track the progression of the disease. This painful and invasive procedure caused a tremendous amount of fear in the subjects, as well as debilitating side effects such as fainting, severe headaches, and temporary paralysis. Some complained years later that they still had not fully recovered. The men were provided with pink pills that turned out to be aspirin, which did have some therapeutic effects and helped to convince them that they were receiving treatment. For this impoverished population, even aspirin was a luxury that many could not afford.

Charles Pollard and Herman Shaw both remarked on the great trust that they placed in the doctors who were treating them, partly because, in the words of Shaw, "We were unable to do anything for ourselves physically" (Jones 1993, 160). Both men also remember being prevented from receiving treatment for syphilis in clinics in the distant city of Birmingham. Nurse Rivers stopped Pollard from boarding a bus that would have taken him to the clinic, while another nurse actually pulled Shaw out of line at the clinic and sent him back to Macon County. The men had no idea that they were not receiving treatment and even decades later, when the actual purpose of the study was exposed and they were compensated by the government, many still had no idea what they had been put through. Shaw remarked, "I don't know what they used us for. I ain't never understood the study" (Jones 1993, 219).

Scurvy Research on Prisoners

The Tuskegee study was not an ethical aberration. Another example of institutionalized ethical lapses by American medical researchers during the same time as the Cold War human radiation experiments and the Tuskegee study involved prisoners as research subjects in a clinical examination of experimentally induced scurvy that resulted in substantial harm to the participants (see Mitford 1974). Unlike the radiation case, the scurvy study did not involve national security concerns. And, in contrast to the Tuskegee study, the scurvy research was not the product of a racist culture that justified harming subjects who were thought to be less than human. However, the scurvy study was similar to the syphilis research in the use of a dehumanized population—in this case, prisoners. It is no coincidence that the Nazi doctors convicted of crimes against humanity at Nuremburg for participating in harmful medical experiments defended their actions by pointing to American medical research conducted on prisoners (Mitford 1974). Briefly, the Nazis argued that American researchers had infected prisoners with such diseases as plague and malaria in order to study their effects, causing intense suffering and even death. Therefore, the German doctors reasoned, why should they be sentenced to death or imprisonment for crimes against humanity while U.S. doctors who engaged in analogous practices were not even indicted?

We focus on the scurvy research in this section simply to illustrate ethical lapses that were common throughout the thousands of studies conducted on prisoners prior to the mid-1970s, but after the promulgation of the Nuremburg Code in 1947. In many of these studies, prisoners were viewed simply as a means to an end—in this case, advancing medical research (and the careers of the scientists conducting them). Dr. Albert Kligman, a dermatologist who became famous after discovering the enormously popular skin cream Retin-A, epitomized this mindset when he said of prisoners upon his arrival at Philadelphia's Holmesburg Prison: "All I saw before me were acres of skin. It was like a farmer seeing a fertile field for the first time" (Hornblum 1998, xx).

The scurvy study was published in 1971 and involved systematically depriving prisoners of vitamin C in order to "study the metabolism of this vitamin more precisely," as well as the health effects of this deprivation (see Hodges et al. 1971, 432). Dr. Robert Hodges was the principal investigator on this research project. Long a proponent of using prisoners in research studies, Hodges began his relationship with the Iowa prison system in the 1940s, even though he was aware that using prisoners in medical research was not "specifically permitted by law" (Mitford 1974, 159). In fact, the Iowa attorney general determined that the practice was illegal and Hodges was forced to suspend his efforts to recruit subjects for two years. But Hodges did not passively accept defeat. Instead, he worked towards passing a new law to allow recruitment of prisoners and his persistence was ultimately successful. His legal reform efforts paid off handsomely, as over 80 scientific papers were published based on studies of Iowa prisoners.

The benefits to researchers are obvious, but why would prisoners subject themselves to pain and even the possibility of permanent injury by participating? The meager $1 per day that inmates earned by serving as research subjects does not seem like a very effective motivator, and, in fact, there were other, more important benefits. According to Hodges, participation would break up the "monotony and oppressiveness of the prison routine" (Mitford 1974, 160). Hodges saw the prisoners as "companions in medical science and adventure," suggesting that the lure of excitement and new experiences was a powerful draw for inmates. But there was another reason that prisoners might be particularly keen to join scientists on this "adventure": the possibility of a reduced sentence for their involvement in research projects. Hodges wrote a positive letter to the warden for each inmate who participated and he admitted that the letter might have had a favorable effect on the parole board. Although Hodges maintained that inmates gave their voluntary consent to serve as research subjects and that the projects complied with all relevant legal and ethical standards, ethicists have long recognized the inherently coercive situation facing prisoners whose very freedom may depend on agreeing to take part in potentially harmful experiments.

Hodges's study of scurvy was published in the *American Journal of Clinical Nutrition*. The article noted that scurvy was induced in all of the subjects and resulted in more severe symptoms than in a previous attempt, including bleeding in gums, skin, and eyes; joint swelling and pain; nerve damage; hair loss; dental cavities; depression; and other mental abnormalities. One subject lost his ability to walk. After being deprived of vitamin C for 112 days, the prisoners were subjected to a cold climate (50°) for 4-hour periods over the course of four days. Hodges's research article also nonchalantly notes that the mineral supplement that was supposed to be included in the prisoners' formula (administered via a gastric tube due to "unpalatability") was "inadvertently omitted" for 34 days (Hodges et al. 1971, 433). He offers the "interesting clinical observation" that Sjogren's syndrome—a connective tissue disorder—developed to some degree in all of the subjects and that two of them "developed the complete syndrome" (Hodges et al. 1971, 436). The report concludes that "rather small doses of ascorbic acid [vitamin C] can cure scurvy, given sufficient time" (Hodges et al. 1971, 442).

The study has been criticized as a "senseless piece of savage cruelty" (Mitford 1974, 163) because the health effects of scurvy are severe and possibly irreversible (no follow-up examinations were conducted with the subjects). The study was also "pointless," in the words of one doctor, because "the cause and cure of scurvy has been well known in the medical profession for generations" (Mitford 1974, 163). Even if useful knowledge could have been obtained by the study, it is still difficult to justify potential heart damage or "hemorrhage into femoral nerve sheaths" (Mitford 1974, 164), a painful and possibly permanent form of nerve damage. Yet prisoner research of this type was widespread, not just in Iowa, but throughout the United States until the mid-1970s, possibly because, in the words of one scientist, prisoners were "much cheaper than chimpanzees" (Mitford 1974, 152–153).

Conclusion

Despite the seemingly obvious relevance of international laws such as the Nuremburg Code, as well as state laws, none of the individual scientists or organizations who conducted the radiation, syphilis, or scurvy experiments was ever prosecuted for crimes. Jones (1993) points out that a number of state health laws were violated in the Tuskegee study and that Alabama governor George Wallace even announced that his office would look into the possibility of legal charges—unsurprisingly, none was ever filed. The only justice victims or their families ever received came in the form of financial compensation. In the case of the radiation experiments, the federal government settled with 16 of the 18 families of subjects who were used in the plutonium injection study, paying between $160,000 and $400,000 per family (Welsome 1999). In the case of the atomic bomb tests, the National Cancer Institute estimated that between 10,000 and 75,000 extra cases of thyroid cancers were caused by the Nevada bomb detonations in the 1950s. Most of these cancers remain undiagnosed and thus uncompensated (Welsome 1999). As of July 7, 2006, 15,706 downwinders, veterans, and workers have been approved for over $1 billion in financial compensation as part of the federal government's Radiation Exposure Compensation Program (Department of Justice 2006). Only 982 veterans have been approved, with downwinders accounting for most of the approved claims. Most of the veterans who were harmed by the bomb tests died without compensation, while even the downwinder population continues to criticize the compensation program (Bauman 2005).

In the Tuskeegee case, the government agreed to pay $10 million to participants or their families. This resulted in payments of $37,500 for each participant who was still alive and $15,000 to heirs of deceased subjects (Jones 1993). None of the subjects in the scurvy study was ever compensated. All of the experiments have been criticized, not only on ethical grounds, but also as bad science due to flawed methods or as superfluous because they added no new knowledge (Welsome 1999; Jones 1993; Mitford 1974). Even one of the officers of the PHS, the agency that conducted the Tuskegee study, concluded that "nothing learned will prevent, find, or cure a single case of infectious syphilis or bring us closer to our basic mission of controlling venereal disease" (Jones 1993, 202).

The majority of the researchers and functionaries who participated in the studies we have reviewed did not perceive these research efforts as unethical or illegal (Welsome 1999; Jones 1993; Mitford 1974). Many scientists remained unrepentant even decades later after public outcry led to reform of the practice of science. The major reform was the creation of Institutional Review Boards at universities, research centers, and government agencies, to monitor the risks and ethics of research. Virtually none of the researchers involved with the plutonium, syphilis, or scurvy studies decided to "blow the whistle" and expose the ethical failings to a larger audience. The ethical issues became headline news and the subject of public debate only after journalists "discovered" the stories of research subjects who were harmed (or at least wronged) by the studies, decades after the research had been openly debated in the scientific literature. This suggests that the ethical lapses associated with the experiments were part and parcel of an institutionalized ethical astigmatism that afflicted the American biomedical community prior to the mid-1970s. The reforms that have been forced on the research community since that time have improved the situation, but they cannot resolve the ethical dilemmas of medical research for all time. Such dilemmas must be continually examined and debated in open forums involving laypersons as well as scientists and government officials.

Notes

1. Page references to interviews collected by the U.S. Department of Energy and ACHRE refer to the copies held by the first author.

2. The exact number of experiments that should be captured by the umbrella term "Cold War human radiation experiments" is the subject of a great deal of controversy, with some scientists arguing that the term is greatly overused and exaggerates both the connection to the Cold War and their experimental nature (Mann 1994; Goldman 1995). Some clearly involved experimentation to collect data for military purposes, others were primarily therapeutic, and some had combined purposes. The selection of the time period is arbitrary (1940s–1970s) and is also contested by scientists who stress the continuity of practices before and after this period (Gofman 1995). The mid-1970s was selected because the development of institutional review boards in this era is thought to have curbed the worst scientific abuses (but see Pasternak and Cary 1994). President Clinton's Advisory Committee on Human Radiation Experiments used the 1944–1974 time period (ACHRE 1996).

References

Advisory Committee on Human Radiation Experiments (ACHRE). *The Human Radiation Experiments: Final Report of the President's Advisory Committee.* New York: Oxford University Press, 1996.

Bauman, Joe. A fallout over eligibility: Many N-victims don't live in compensation counties. *Deseret Morning News* (Salt Lake City), April 13, 2005. http://deseretnews.com/dn/view/0,1249,600125827,00.html (accessed July 10, 2006).

"Cover-up at ground zero." Transcript of ABC News *Turning Point,* broadcast February 2, 1994. Copy on file with the first author.

Department of Justice. 2006. Radiation Compensation Exposure Program. http://www.usdoj.gov/civil/torts/const/reca/about.htm (accessed July 10, 2006).

Gailey, Jeannine A., and Matthew T. Lee. "The Impact of Roles and Frames on Attributions of Responsibility: The Case of the Cold War Human Radiation Experiments, *Journal of Applied Social Psychology,* 35 (2005): 1067–1088.

Gofman, John W. Human Radiation Studies: Remembering the Early Years—Oral History of Dr. John W. Gofman, M.D., Ph.D. Interview conducted on December 30, 1994; published in June 1995 by the U.S. Department of Energy. Copy on file with the first author.

Goldman, Marvin. Human Radiation Studies: Remembering the Early Years—Oral History of Radiation Biologist Marvin Goldman, Ph.D. Interview conducted on December 22, 1994; published in September 1995 by the U.S. Department of Energy. Copy on file with the first author.

Herken, Greg, and James David. "Doctors of death," *New York Times,* January 13, 1994, sec. A21.

Hodges, Robert E., James Hood, John E. Canham, Howerde E. Sauberlich, and Eugene M. Baker. "Clinical Manifestations of Ascorbic Acid Deficiency in Man," *American Journal of Clinical Nutrition,* 24 (1971): 432–443.

Hornblum, Allen M. *Acres of Skin: Human Experiments at Holmesburg Prison—A True Story of Abuse and Exploitation in the Name of Medical Science.* New York: Routledge, 1998.

Jones, James H. *Bad Blood: The Tuskegee Syphilis Experiment.* New York: Free Press, 1993.

Langham, Wright H., Samuel H. Bassett, Payne S. Harris, and Robert E. Carter. "Distribution and Excretion of Plutonium Administered Intravenously to Man," *Health Physics,* 38 (1980): 1031–1060.

Mann, Charles C. 1994. "Radiation: Balancing the Record," *Science,* 263 (1994): 3–4.

Mitford, Jessica. *Kind and Usual Punishment: The Prison Business.* New York: Vintage Books, 1974.

Morgan, Karl. 1995. "Human Radiation Studies: Remembering the Early Years—Oral History of Karl Z. Morgan, Ph.D." Interview conducted on January 7, 1995; published in June 1995 by the U.S. Department of Energy. Copy on file with the first author.

Pasternak, Douglas, and Peter Cary. Tales from the Crypt: Medical Horror Stories from a Trove of Secret Cold-War Documents, *U.S. News and World Report,* September 18, 1995.

Uhl, Michael, and Tod Ensign. *GI Guinea Pigs: How the Pentagon Exposed Our Troops to Dangers More Deadly Than War.* New York: Wideview Press, 1980.
Welsome, Eileen. *The Plutonium Files: America's Secret Medical Experiments in the Cold War.* New York: Dial Press, 1999.

Doctoring the Data: Ethical Failures in Medical Research

12

KEVIN L. SISEMORE

Contents

As to diseases, make a habit of two things—to help, or at least, to do no harm.

From *Epidemics*, by Hippocrates (Greek physician, 460–377 b.c.)

Introduction

The idea of "do no harm" has been a part of medicine and the ethics of medical professionals for over 2,000 years. It is a part of our collective consciousness and plays a central role in how we perceive and relate to doctors, medicine, and medical research. The overwhelming majority of physicians and researchers honor this ideal and strive to make sure all their actions are meant to help their patients and the public at large. However, the pressure to succeed and the allure of fame have led to ethical lapses by those in a position of medical trust and leadership failures in the institutions that support them. Many of these ethical lapses involve manipulating research to show convenient, though misleading, conclusions and treatment plans. Doctoring the data not only fails to help; it most certainly fails to "do no harm."

A Tale of Three Countries

Ethical challenges in medical research are not unique to any field of study, type of institution, or national boundary. They come with many faces and in many languages.

Appreciating the breadth and scope of these ethical challenges requires a journey around the world. During the course of 2005 and into early 2006, researchers on three different continents found just how much they had in common with one another. All were world-renowned researchers and were held in the highest esteem by their peers and their institutions. All had published in the world's most prestigious journals and had access to millions of dollars in funding. What they most had in common was a history of ethical crossroads where they each faced decisions that tested his commitment to honesty, integrity, and science.

Dr. Eric Poehlman (United States) was an esteemed researcher and a star at his university. He had been conducting research into women's health issues that were being published in the most prestigious medical journals. These published reports showed the beneficial effects of hormone replacement therapy (HRT) on the health of postmenopausal women. Poehlman's results were so dramatic that doctors around the world confidently prescribed HRT to women based on the results of his research. Poehlman also had risen to the top in the field of obesity research with study conclusions that redefined the scope of obesity as a disease. All of his work had been funded with millions of dollars in research grants from U.S. federal government sources.

Dr. Jon Sudbo (Norway) had been studying possible treatments for oral cancer, a disease threatening the lives of people all over the world. The results of Sudbo's research, featured prominently in an article for the journal *Lancet* in October 2005, announced that using nonsteroidal anti-inflammatory drugs (NSAIDS), which were readily available over the counter without prescription, could reduce the incidence of oral cancer.

Dr. Hwang Woo Suk (Republic of Korea) had become the leading expert in cloning and had moved on to the cloning of human embryonic stem cell lines. It has long been a goal of medical research to use stem cells in the development of rejection-resistant tissue that could be used in transplants to treat many "untreatable" diseases. Hwang's work raised the hopes of countless patients with hard-to-treat diseases and medical conditions. Though his work was controversial, there was talk of his being considered for a Nobel Prize.

Dr. Gerald Schatten, a University of Pittsburgh researcher, had closely aligned himself with Hwang. Schatten had been the senior author of one of the Hwang team's stem cell studies published in the journal *Science*. He accepted $40,000 in honoraria from Hwang, as well as $200,000 in private funding for this research.

Dr. Eric Poehlman

Dr. Poehlman spent most of his research career (1987–1993 and 1996–2001) as a professor of medicine, physiology, and nutritional sciences at the University of Vermont (UVM). His research was primarily funded by federal grants that had provided him roughly $2.9 million during his tenure at the University of Vermont College of Medicine and the University of Maryland in Baltimore (1993–1996). Eventually his research and his career took him to the Université de Montréal (2001–2005).

Beginning in August 1997, Poehlman and his colleagues recruited over 100 women between the ages of 40 and 50 to examine their health history as they progressed through menopause, the stage of life when a woman's estrogen hormonal levels drop significantly. Poehlman's idea was that these hormonal drops corresponded to declines in many areas of women's health. To prove this, Poehlman gave his test subjects yearly exams to measure changes in caloric expenditure, body fat distribution, and insulin sensitivity. The exams also measured the daily energy needs of the subjects to provide better nutritional guidelines for women during menopause.

Poehlman reported that his research was interested in measuring the natural menopause transition and how it might contribute to diabetes. He further noted that his study would examine the link between the loss of estrogen and factors that increase heart disease.

The grant that funded this specific study was the fourth in a series of grants to Poehlman and his research team to evaluate women's health issues. The work that came out of this series of grants established both Poehlman and UVM as leaders in women's health research. In December 1996, Poehlman received three more grants from the National Institutes of Health, the Department of Agriculture, and the Department of Defense for studies to investigate a number of related women's health issues: first, whether an "obesity gene" might exist that causes some women to gain weight more easily than others; second, to determine if menopause represents a period of accelerated aging; and third, the evaluation of various exercise routines for women to determine the best options.

The conclusions reached by Poehlman were considered groundbreaking in terms of women's health after menopause. A paper published in the 1995 *Annals of Internal Medicine* claimed that menopause caused numerous health problems, including women's muscle loss and fat gain. The paper suggested that hormone replacement therapy (HRT) could prevent the increase of body fat and declines in energy. Poehlman's work was considered so momentous that it compelled doctors to prescribe HRT for years.

For the eight years in which Poehlman conducted and reported on this government-funded research, his findings astounded the world. From 1992 to 2000, the almost $3 million in federal research funding he received was based on research data that time and again supported his theories and served to make his work appear more promising. Poehlman's research was impacting the medical treatment for perhaps millions of women.

In 2000, Poehlman won the Lilly Scientific Achievement Award given through the pharmaceutical industry's North American Association for the

Study of Obesity. His work changed the future of obesity research priorities and, at the same time, placed millions of Americans into the government's new official "overweight" category. The research community viewed this as an achievement award for Poehlman's groundbreaking work. However, the adjusted criteria for "overweight" sent a new segment of the population out in search of prescription diet drugs and weight loss procedures.

During that same year, Poehlman's research assistant, Walter DeNino, began noticing irregularities in the spreadsheets used to record the data collected in the studies. The data on the spreadsheets showed the energy expenditures and lipid levels of the study subjects over time. Postmenopausal changes in these levels were the key to Poehlman's theories. The problem, at least in DeNino's eyes, was that the raw data did not seem to support the theory. In fact, some subjects appeared to be getting healthier as time went on.

Initially, DeNino did not believe these irregularities were anything serious, but he did believe that they needed to be addressed. He tried to discuss the matter with Poehlman, but the discussions never got very far. At one point, Poehlman took a computer disk of the data home for the weekend. He had told DeNino that he would examine the data for clerical errors and statistical anomalies to alleviate DeNino's concerns. When he returned Monday morning, Poehlman returned the disk to DeNino for reanalysis. The data had transformed into a much darker depiction of postmenopausal health. At first, DeNino assumed he had made the mistake. But when he decided to compare the original data against the data on the disk, DeNino could see that women were getting healthier over time. DeNino concluded that Poehlman had reversed the order of test results, making it seem that their cholesterol levels and blood pressure readings were getting worse, not better. The only reason for this, in DeNino's assessment, was that Poehlman was fabricating the age-related deterioration of menopause to support his original ideas.

DeNino considered confronting Poehlman with his concerns. However, this is not a small matter in a university. Respected researchers are a special class of employee in these institutions and are not easily challenged. But DeNino looked past these concerns and confronted his mentor. Poehlman responded in two separate memos justifying his changes as an effort to correct data entry mistakes. DeNino was not convinced and finally reported Poehlman to university officials. DeNino has since said that at least four other UVM researchers told him privately that they had concerns as well about Poehlman's work, although none had brought his or her concerns to university authorities.

The University of Vermont took DeNino's accusations seriously, but the research community circled around their colleague. Other researchers in Poehlman's lab cast doubts on DeNino's claims and DeNino himself. Poehlman's attorney threatened to sue DeNino if he made any public claims against Poehlman outside the investigation. Ultimately, DeNino told UVM officials that

Poehlman entered false and fabricated data into laboratory spreadsheets for Protocol 678, his longitudinal study of aging. DeNino further told authorities that Poehlman had presented that data as true and accurate for statistical analysis as part of his published reports.

As the UVM investigation continued, Poehlman managed to keep the allegations against him quiet. In 2001, before the investigation was completed, Poehlman resigned his tenured professorship. But this was not a step down; it was actually a step up in the academic research community. He had accepted an endowed chair, one of academia's highest honors and usually reserved for senior professors, at the Université de Montréal. By all accounts, the Université de Montréal had no knowledge of the allegations or the UVM investigation.

Poehlman's departure did not stop UVM's investigation. When completed, the investigation's findings confirmed the worst of DeNino's allegations. Much of the actual data on Poehlman's studies showed that the health of postmenopausal women was not deteriorating the way his reports claimed. In fact, the health of some test subjects actually improved in terms of heart disease risk and energy expenditure after menopause. The results clearly ran counter to Poehlman's ideas, the very ideas that had secured the bulk of his funding.

UVM's administration turned their findings over to the Department of Health and Human Services (HHS), the Office of Inspector General, the Office of Research Integrity, and the United States Attorney's Office. These government investigators came to the same conclusions as UVM: Poehlman made fabricated claims that HRT helped slow weight gain after menopause. Further, those falsified conclusions, based on faked data, helped him win a $542,000 grant from HHS to continue his work. At that point Poehlman stopped the denials and admitted he had faked the test results for all but 3 of the 35 women in a long-term study of the health effects of menopause. The U.S. attorney in Burlington, Vermont, found that Poehlman had destroyed electronic evidence, presented false testimony, presented false documents, and influenced other witnesses to provide false documents.

The Annals of Internal Medicine had to retract Poehlman's findings in 2003, after the University of Vermont reported the evidence of the fraud.

This type of research misconduct does not usually rise to the level of criminal charges. In Poehlman's case it did. By most reports, it became a criminal matter out if its shear size. Poehlman had perpetrated the fraud for so long that normal remediation efforts by UVM could not sufficiently address the problem. It also became a criminal matter because Poehlman had used over $2 million in government grants for his studies. The money was obtained by reporting exaggerated claims based on fabricated data. Poehlman resigned from UVM in September 2001. He had been listed on more than 150 research papers, almost all of which had been supported by grants from government health service agencies. By May 2004, the Université de Montréal had removed Poehlman from his research chair and professorship. He officially resigned on January 22, 2005, when his contract expired.

Poehlman pled guilty on April 5, 2005, to fraudulently obtaining a $542,000 grant from the National Institutes of Health by fabricating data on menopause, aging, and hormone replacement while working as a professor at the University of Vermont's College of Medicine. Federal prosecutors said Poehlman submitted to federal granting agencies 17 grant applications, worth $11.6 million, including false and fabricated research data (Kintisch 2005). Poehlman agreed to pay $180,000 to settle a civil complaint related to numerous false grant applications he filed while at UVM. Most significantly, he was permanently excluded from seeking or receiving funding from any federal agency and from participating in all federal health care programs. As the whistle blower, DeNino received 12 percent of the settlement amount.

In May 2005, Poehlman contacted the editors of the *Annals of Internal Medicine* to acknowledge the appropriateness of their retraction. On June 28, 2006, Dr. Eric Poehlman was sentenced to prison for 1 year and 1 day for fabricating data and making false statements related to his research studies (Silverman 2006). Poehlman is the first researcher to serve prison time as a result of falsifying data in a grant application to the National Institutes of Health.

Dr. Jon Sudbo

The Norwegian Radium Hospital in Oslo, Norway, was proud of Dr. Jon Sudbo. Their researcher had quickly become a worldwide sensation after his groundbreaking paper on a new cancer treatment was published in the journal *Lancet*. His research showed that the use of nonsteroidal anti-inflammatory drugs (NSAIDs), a common over-the-counter medication, could reduce the risk of oral cancer in tobacco users. The paper was based on a study of 908 subjects with histories of significant tobacco use. The paper had the added credibility of citing data obtained from a national health database held by the Norwegian Institute of Public Health.

Sudbo reported that smokers who had taken a daily NSAID for at least six months were 65 percent less likely to develop cancer than smokers who had not. Further, his research showed that as the use of NSAIDs increased, the risk of cancer decreased.

Sudbo had given hope to long-time tobacco users around the world. Tobacco users had long been told that their habit put them at risk of disease and an early death and their only hope was to quit as soon as possible. Now, with Sudbo's extraordinary revelation, they had a new option. If they could not or would not kick their habit, they could simply pop a daily aspirin, ibuprofen, or naproxen and dramatically cut their risk of mouth cancer. Previous studies by other researchers had shown some sign that NSAIDs might be effective in preventing some forms of cancer, and Sudbo's work showed that the same was true for oral malignancies (tumors of the mouth) (Fouche 2006).

In published accounts, Sudbo represented that NSAIDS could cut in half the risk of some smoking-related cancers. His statements offered a hint that his ultimate goal was to extend this research to include lung cancer, the number-one cancer killer of smokers.

Sudbo presented his findings on April 18, 2005, at the annual meeting of the American Association for Cancer Research, in Anaheim, California. His team reported that benefits were not found in long-term users of a non-NSAID pain reliever such as acetaminophen. Their conclusion was that NSAIDs contained a particular property that worked to ward off mouth cancer.

Other prominent cancer researchers not only accepted but also praised these findings. Some said they were not surprised by the findings and noted that earlier data had supported the idea of reductions in risk for gastrointestinal cancer, esophageal, and gastric and colorectal cancer connected to long-term NSAID use. Sudbo was just the first to prove the reduction in cancer risk using actual patient data.

By late 2005, the *Lancet* article had received wide distribution and everything was going extremely well for both Sudbo and the Norwegian Radium Hospital. During that holiday season, Camilla Stoltenberg, who worked at the Norwegian Institute of Public Health, was catching up on her reading. She was especially interested in the work of her countryman, Jon Sudbo. What caught her attention most was his reference to the data he obtained from the national health database held by her institute. What she knew (and what Sudbo apparently did not know) was that the database referenced was not available to researchers at that time and there was no way that he could have accessed it. Stoltenberg contacted both Sudbo and the Norwegian Radium Hospital.

The director of the Division of Epidemiology at the Norwegian Institute of Public Health reacted quickly to Stoltenberg's questions and started asking his own questions about the data. This ultimately led to a full-scale investigation by the hospital's administration. The hospital investigators began hearing rumors that Sudbo not only had lied about accessing the national database but also had completely fabricated the 908 individuals who served as the basis for his paper in the *Lancet*. One of the clues, reported in a Norwegian daily newspaper, was that 250 of the 908 people had the same birthday (Fouche 2006). At the end of the investigation, the hospital's management came to the conclusion that Sudbo had, in fact, fabricated everything.

Faced with the hospital's conclusion, Sudbo finally admitted the fabrications to his superiors and to the public. He confessed that he had faked all 908 of the patients in his study. He had faked everything, including the names, the cancer histories, and patients' gender, weight, and age. The Norwegian Radium Hospital issued a statement expressing its shock at Sudbo's fraud, acknowledging that this was the worst thing that could happen in a research institution. Hospital management contacted the *Lancet* to inform the journal that the work was faked. They discovered that the *Lancet* was conducting its own investigation. Their focus was not just on Dr. Sudbo but on all 13 coauthors on the paper, including several researchers from the United States. The *Lancet* would end up issuing an expression of concern (Mundell 2006). "Basically it means we have very good reason to think the work is unsafe, but not a cast-iron admission," the journal reported. Once the investigation had been completed, a retraction of the original Sudbo paper was issued.

Sudbo has since stated that he regrets his ethical lapses, but has declined to explain why he did it. Since the revelations of his faked NSAID work he has also admitted he made up data for an article in the *New England Journal of Medicine* that appeared in April 2004 and another article that ran in the *Journal of Clinical Oncology* in March 2005 (UPI 2006).

Sudbo's acts prompted the Norwegian government to establish a commission to fight fraud and forgery in research as well as enact a new law under which research fraud can result in jail time. The Norwegian government may have taken such swift and strong action because Sudbo's fraud had such a negative impact on their nation's scientific reputation. Or, possibly, the government took such swift and strong action because the Norwegian prime minister happened to be Camilla Stoltenberg's brother.

Dr. Hwang Woo Suk

In the Republic of South Korea, the government reacted with great pride over the groundbreaking work of their "supreme scientist" Dr. Hwang Woo Suk. Their scientist had stunned the world with the claims of the first cloned human embryos and the successful extraction of stem cells from them. In all, Hwang announced the creation of 11 patient-specific embryonic stem cell lines. Adding to the prestige, the work was being done at South Korea's flagship institution, Seoul National University. All told, Hwang received $33 million in government funding and millions more in private donations. The government awarded him with medals for his scientific advances and even went so far as to issue a postage stamp in honor of the work and the researcher.

Hwang had always dreamed of becoming a scientist. He trained as a veterinarian at Seoul National University, before completing an MSc and then a PhD in theriogenology—the science and practice of animal reproduction. He reported that he cloned a cow in 1999 and a pig in 2002. But this was just the start; Hwang had a bigger goal. He was not trying to clone human embryos to make babies; rather, his goal was to create human embryonic stem cells to replace and repair the human body (Lim 2005). His initial project used 242 donated human eggs and genetic material from patients with a variety of diseases in an effort to create stem cell lines that were replicas of the patients for use in their treatment. This experiment resulted in only one stem cell line and the clones were replicas of the egg donors, not the patients.

Hwang's team tried the experiment again with DNA from skin cells of the volunteer patients and 185 donated human eggs. This time the team removed the original DNA from the donated eggs and replaced it with the samples from the volunteer patients. The new effort resulted in the successful production of 31 embryos and created 11 new stem cell lines. Hwang capped all of this in August 2005, when his team introduced Snuppy, an Afghan hound, as the world's first cloned dog.

Hwang, meanwhile, reported to the world that his stem cells could replace old or dead cells and tissues, a breakthrough that could be used to treat degenerative diseases and physical conditions such as Parkinson's and Alzheimer's diseases. Further, stem cell research showed promise in treating spinal cord injury, burns, diabetes, arthritis, stroke, and even heart disease. Researchers from the United States were intrigued by the prospect of working on such a successful stem cell project. President Bush had recently restricted the study of stem cells in the country, making South Korea the leader in the field. In fact, President Bush had gone so far as to publicly criticize Hwang's work.

At the height of his fame, Hwang received foreign stem cell scientists in his lab for lessons. These scientists had hopes of using stem cells to replace and repair diseased and damaged parts of the body. Notable among them was University of Pittsburgh stem cell researcher Dr. Gerald Schatten, who had been unsuccessfully trying to clone monkey embryos for years. Schatten visited Hwang's lab three times, trying to glean a new technique to revitalize his own work.

Hwang's discoveries were giving patients with life-threatening diseases new reasons for hope. He and Schatten announced the successful creation of embryonic stem-cell lines in a jointly authored article in *Science*. The results became news around the world, making the front page of mainstream papers, not just medical journals. Their techniques were talked about as the first steps in finding effective treatments for many currently incurable medical conditions.

Hwang's collaboration with Schatten was relatively short lived. Schatten ended their work together abruptly, publicly citing concerns over the origins of the donated human eggs used in both experiments. Schatten's statements prompted both the scientific community and the media to scrutinize Hwang's work and his claims of such extraordinary success. The journal *Nature* interviewed one of Hwang's PhD students and reported her claim that she, rather than outside volunteers, donated the eggs used in the experiments. Hwang quickly dismissed the student's claim. He told the journal that none of his students provided the eggs used by the team and that the student's poor English led to a misunderstanding with the reporter.

Hwang's denials did not stop the questions and the allegations that he used unacceptable practices to acquire eggs from human donors. Eventually the South Korean government stepped in. The South Korea Health and Welfare Ministry did its own investigation and confirmed that two of Hwang's students had provided their ova for the team's research. Despite this revelation, the Seoul University Ethics panel took the position that there was nothing illegal or unethical about using the eggs of his staff. Such reassurance did not stop Hwang from resigning all his official posts and issuing a public apology. At the same time, Schatten contacted *Science* to tell them he was no longer working with Hwang.

Perhaps Hwang resigned his official posts in the hope that the controversy would die down. But that was not to be the case. The earlier reports prompted more investigations and more interviews of his team. These subsequent investigations reported that the human eggs used in Hwang's experiments were not provided voluntarily. Some members of his team reported being coerced into undergoing the painful procedure in order to stay on the team and avoid retaliation.

Throughout these revelations, Hwang maintained that while the eggs may not have been obtained from volunteers outside the team, the results of the experiments were not impacted by the source of the eggs. He tried to continue his stem cell research and build on his earlier accomplishments. But the scrutiny continued and Hwang contacted *Science* to report some "errors" in the 2005 paper, none of which he believed affected the paper's conclusions. After that, he asked Seoul National University to open an investigation into his research in an effort to clear his name.

Shortly after Hwang's report to *Science,* Schatten contacted the journal to request a retraction of his coauthorship of the paper because of his "substantial doubts" about the paper's accuracy. Other stem cell researchers around the world publicly called for Hwang to allow them to review the data from his experiments and the stem cell lines to confirm the accuracy of his conclusions. But before this could happen, a member of Hwang's team made a stunning announcement. He told the world that the irregularities extended well beyond coercing female staff members. This research associate was now saying that Hwang had directed his staff to fabricate most of the data reported to the public. The fabricated data included the number of embryos and the number of stem cell lines created. Essentially everything reported in the 2005 paper was a fake. The research assistant was not aware of any cloned stem cell lines and Hwang had confirmed to him that none existed.

When the details of his fabrications came out, Hwang apologized in tears and resigned from his position as head of his lab. Though he apologized for the scandal, he has continued to insist that junior members of his team had deceived him and he truly believed he had made significant discoveries. Unfortunately for Hwang, few were willing to believe him. Seoul National

University, reeling from the impact the scandal was having on its international reputation, terminated Hwang's appointment. Six other professors who worked with him were either suspended or had their salaries cut.

Hwang's fall came as an enormous shock to the people and the government of South Korea. Besides the stamp and the recognition, the South Korean government had provided Hwang with very generous financial support and now was concerned about how its money was actually spent. Hwang could not completely account for his research funds and in early 2006 he was indicted on embezzlement and ethics charges. If convicted, he could face ten years in jail (Sang-Hun 2006).

Back at the University of Pittsburgh, Dr. Gerald Schatten had a dilemma. Though he had ended his professional relationship with Hwang, he had built his current work on their collaboration. "We could have been struggling for decades," Schatten said. "Now our work is taking off fabulously. I think the whole world owes the Republic of Korea a debt of gratitude."

In fact, Schatten's work had taken off to the tune of $16.1 million (Bails 2006). He had applied for and been awarded a grant based on the now-discredited stem-cell findings of Hwang, some of which had appeared in articles that Schatten had coauthored. The dilemma facing Schatten and the University of Pittsburgh was what to do now.

Schatten chose to keep the money. He stated that he would use the money for his own "ambitious" stem-cell research program. University of Pittsburgh officials must have certainly considered whether Schatten should be trusted to lead research projects and receive grants. A panel appointed by the medical school dean had recommended that the university discipline Schatten in connection with a stem-cell article he published in June in the journal *Science*. The panel did not conclude that Schatten had committed research misconduct, but rather "research misbehavior." Of specific concern to the university was that, by coauthoring a paper with Hwang, Schatten conferred his, and the University of Pittsburgh's, credibility to a fraudulent report.

In 2007, a report by researchers at the Children's Hospital Boston and the Harvard Stem Cell Institute concluded that Hwang's research had accidentally created the world's first human embryonic stem cell to be derived by a process called parthenogenesis. This process creates an embryo containing genetic material only from the donor egg and could, conceivably, lead to an "ethical" means of creating stem cells. Hwang had been so focused on fabricating his cloning results that he never realized his work had, in fact, produced groundbreaking results.

References

Bails, Jennifer. "Fake Findings Used to Secure $16M Grant," *Pittsburgh Tribune-Review,* February 22, 2006.

Fouche, Gwladys. "Respected Norwegian Scientist Faked Study on Oral Cancer," *Guardian,* January 16, 2006.

Kintisch, Eli. "Researcher Faces Prison for Fraud in NIH Grant Applications and Papers," *Science,* March 25, 2005.

Lim, Bo-Mi. "South Korea Hwang Woo-Suk Is the King of Cloning," *USAToday,* April 23, 2005.

Mundell, E. J. "Medical Journal Casts Doubt on Oral Cancer Research," *HealthDay,* January 20, 2006.

Sang-Hun, Choe. 2006. "South Korean Scientist Indicted in Cloning Scandal," *International Herald Tribune,* May 31, 2006, health and science sec.

Silverman, Adam. "Former UVM Professor Sentenced to Jail for Fraud," *Burlington Free Press,* June 29, 2006.

UPI (United Press International). "Norwegian Scientist Admits More Cheating," January 23, 2006.

From Fraud to Holocaust: The Protocols of the Elders of Zion

13

CHRISTOPHER J. FERGUSON

Contents

Introduction

Perhaps one of the deadliest frauds and scams of recent history is a largely plagiarized document entitled *The Protocols of the Elders of Zion*. This work comes in the form of an "initiation manual" for new members of a fictitious council of Jewish rabbinical elders, discussing their plans for secret world domination through control of the economy and banking systems. Despite the illogic of a secret society conveniently detailing its plot for world domination in a written form that could be easily disseminated, the *Protocols* have been presented as factual by a number of organizations during the last century. In each case these various groups, contrary to historical evidence regarding the fraudulent nature of the book, have presented the *Protocols* as fact in order to stir religious and cultural hatred toward Jewish people to further their own goals.

The *Protocols* present an extreme case of the misuse of information (in this case fraudulent information) by government entities. This chapter will discuss the history of the *Protocols* and their impact on the history of the twentieth century, as well as discuss implications of this work on the use and misuse of information by governments and businesses today.

Origins of the Protocols

The *Protocols* have their origins in some of the political and philosophical tumults of the nineteenth century. Throughout Europe and elsewhere, persecution of Jews was pervasive and, at times, violent (Carroll 2002). The French monarchy had recently come to a violent and spectacular end and the liberal and revolutionary social elements that looked toward the bloody French revolution for inspiration gave the remaining European monarchies cause for great concern. Liberal, revolutionary, anticlerical (i.e., anti-Catholic), and Marxist agitators, as well as groups such as the Freemasons and Freethinkers, were increasing in influence and activity. There was a feeling in many countries, from the newly united Italy through Germany and Austria to increasingly strife-ridden tsarist Russia, that conservative monarchist powers were under assault from entities that were radical and inherently evil.

Ironically, the major influence for the *Protocols* was an antigovernment pamphlet entitled "Dialogues in Hell between Machiavelli and Montesquieu" by Maurice Joly, whose goal seems to have been a criticism of the French emperor of the time, Napoleon III (Segel and Levy 1995). The pamphlet made no mention of Jewish conspiracies, but its framework of a conspiracy became the influence for a German anti-Semite named Hermann Goedsche. Goedsche was a postal worker suspected of spying for the tsarist secret police against Prussia. He appeared to enjoy Joly's "Dialogues" and plagiarized portions of it in developing his work, "The Jewish Cemetery in Prague and the Council of Representatives of the Twelve Tribes of Israel." This work affirmed that once every hundred years Jewish leaders would meet in a secret location at midnight and discuss their plans for world domination. The alleged discussions reviewed the progress over the previous hundred years and planned for the next hundred years. By fomenting instability in existing governments and seizing control of world economies, the fictitious Jewish conspirators hoped to rule the world. Although the effectiveness (as well as logistical nightmare) of meeting once every hundred years in the hopes of world domination is questionable, the basic thrust of Goedsche's work was that Jewish leaders operate behind the scenes to destabilize and take control of the world's governments.

The late nineteenth century was marked by an increase in the number of groups dedicated to overthrowing established forms of social control in Europe, including monarchical governments and the papacy. Many of these organizations sought to establish new governments based on principles ranging from equality to atheism. During a time when many such radical, liberal, communist, and anticlerical groups were indeed behaving in a manner directed at destabilizing or destroying existing political and religious institutions, it was tempting to consider the possibility that these various groups were, in fact, being guided secretly by the intrigues of a single group (conveniently, a group of individuals culturally and religiously distinct from the European non-Semitic majority).

In the late 1800s and early 1900s, tsarist Russia was becoming an absolute monarchy in decline. Russia, like France in the late 1700s, had stalwartly defied calls for government reform and modernization from its own citizens and from abroad, and it had maintained a cultural and societal division that left the majority of its population poor and disenfranchised. Democratic, Marxist, and anticlerical groups were becoming more active in the country; combined with the stubborn but ineffectual rule of their tsar, Nicholas II, the future for a stable Russia seemed increasingly bleak. The Russian secret police, the Okhrana, were charged with enforcing the status quo and resisting reformist movements. Noting that liberal reformers commonly sympathized with Jewish peoples and that Jews were often involved in social reform movements, Goedsche's anti-Semitic work became a useful tool for the Okhrana in associating the liberals with the Jews. The message was clear: Reform movements are part of a secret Jewish conspiracy to overthrow rightful governments and seize control of the world political and economic stage.

Likely, it was the spiraling out-of-control atmosphere of the last days of tsarist Russia that allowed Goedsche's fraudulent text to gain the power that it did. The *Protocols* in their "modern" form were first published publicly in 1905 following revolution in Russia that same year (Ben-Itto 2005). The revolutionary movement was blamed on Jewish conspiracy and the propaganda helped the Russian secret police turn popular sentiment against the revolutionaries. Revolutionary sentiment continued to simmer through Russia's disastrous performance in World War I. Dissatisfaction with the tsarist government led to the chaotic 1917 Bolshevik Revolution, during which tsarist forces once again used the *Protocols* to incite hatred of both the Bolsheviks and the Jews, who were blamed for inciting the Bolshevik Revolution. Jewish people were often summarily attacked during this period, whether they were actually involved in the revolutionary movements or not. Many Jewish people were actively sought out and killed, one of the many tragedies in the chaos of the Bolshevik Revolution.

The Russian secret police had deliberately used a fraudulent document—the *Protocols*—to take advantage of anti-Semitism within their country to further their own political goals. Cynically, they had proved willing to trade the lives of innocent people in furtherance of these goals. They succeeded only in spreading misery and, ultimately, lost control of their own propaganda. That the Russians failed in their goal of preserving the monarchy and that the *Protocols* were clearly recognized as forgeries soon after their release (the *London Times* published a series of articles to this effect several years after the Bolshevik Revolution) did not prevent their continued use by other groups as political propaganda.

Use of the Protocols in Nazi Germany

Germany was defeated in World War I, but many Germans felt that this was a surprising and unjust end. German people had been assured of imminent victory almost until the November 11 Armistice and thus could not understand how their country lost the war. The German military had performed remarkably during the war, effectively forcing the Russians to sue for peace on the Eastern front and holding superior numbers of Entente (French, British, Italian, American) soldiers at bay on the Western front. The combined efforts of the British naval embargo and the entrance of the United States into the war against the Central Powers (with the United States providing the Entente powers a fresh and far more stable alternative to the loss of Russia) made Central Power defeat all but inevitable. To many German citizens, it seemed that Germany had been deprived of its rightful victory in World War I due to the treachery of some members of its own populace. It was into this atmosphere of suspicion and mistrust that the *Protocols* once again emerged as a means of propaganda that this time resulted in the death of millions of Jews as well as countless non-Jews.

The Nazi regime in Germany was swept into power by capitalizing on the discontent of a nation that felt it had been unjustly deprived of victory in the First World War and subsequently forced to endure financial and social hardships and humiliation. The Nazis were able to argue successfully to the German people that the loss in World War I was due to a "fifth column" of conspirators—mainly Jews and Communists—who had brought about Germany's loss as part of their plan to achieve world domination (Cohn 1996). The Nazis were able to point to other nations where this conspiracy appeared to be active. Indeed, Russia, from whence the *Protocols* had originally emerged linking the Jewish conspiracy with radical movements, had ultimately fallen to a communist revolution, inadvertently supporting concerns raised by the *Protocols* propaganda. Nazi propaganda was also able to note that Communist and other radical sympathizers appeared poised to vie for power in China (where they ultimately succeeded), Spain (where they ultimately failed), and other European nations. Thus, the forces of radicalism were not entirely imagined, and it may have seemed plausible to many that the underlying origin for such radicalism was due to a global conspiracy rather than widespread social and economic unrest due to income disparity or some other cause.

In his infamous memoir, *Mein Kampf,* Adolph Hitler specifically refers to the *Protocols* as authentic evidence of a Jewish plot that swept Germany under its control. Hitler was likely exposed to the *Protocols* by Alfred Rosenberg, the Nazi ideologue responsible for many of the Nazi philosophies such as the supremacy of the Aryan race. Hitler referred to the *Protocols* in several speeches warning of "Jewish-Bolshevik" plans for world dominance. The *Protocols* became a popular book in Germany as well as elsewhere in the world. As the Russian tsarists had attempted to do, the Nazis strengthened support for their own movement (which, ironically, was geared toward European if not world political domination) by using the *Protocols*. The *Protocols* were used by the Nazis as one of many propaganda instruments in turning the German people against their Jewish population. The Nazis justified their rise to power on the *Protocols'* depiction of widespread Jewish conspiracy. Thus, it was largely inevitable that, upon attaining power, the Nazis would turn toward persecution of Jewish people, using the *Protocols* as evidence of their guilt. The *Protocols* were not the cause of anti-Semitism in Nazi Germany, but the book was promoted as evidence in support of the anti-Semitic cause. The result was the death of at least six million Jews, as well as countless other people such as communists, homosexuals, Gypsies, Poles, and Russians (Cohn 1996).

The Nazis' use of propaganda—in this case, fraudulent and misleading information—was initially successful as they achieved power in Germany. The *Protocols* were successfully used to capitalize on preexisting anti-Semitism in Germany to rally the populace to the Nazi cause. During their time in power, the Nazis printed 23 separate editions of the *Protocols*, some of them used in schools as a means of indoctrinating students. Their use of anti-Semitism as a pillar of their own rise to power made it all but inevitable that they would essentially need to wage war against a portion of their own population, diverting resources that could have better served in supporting their war effort in World War II. Their use of information that was both biased and hateful also could have only hurt their credibility in the eyes of other world governments (although this may have been tempered by a culture of anti-Semitism).

After World War II

Since World War II, most political leaders of European and Latin American nations have avoided suggestions that the *Protocols* retained any validity. With the exception of the Soviet Union's anti-Zionist campaign in the late 1960s (Sachar 2005), most Western promotions of the *Protocols* have involved racist groups such as the Ku Klux Klan or Islamic or Palestinian groups within Western countries. Among Middle Eastern countries, belief that the *Protocols* are factual remains common among both militant groups and established governments, particularly as a means of anti-Israeli propaganda.

Jewish immigration to Palestine (the goal of Zionism) occurred in several phases between the late 1800s and 1947 (Bright 2000), often in response to persecution in European or Arabic countries. Following defeat of Turkey in World War I, political responsibility for Palestine shifted to the British.

Migrations of Jews from other countries significantly increased the Jewish population in Palestine, leading to tensions between the Jews and indigenous Arabic peoples. Disappointed in the ability of the British to defend them from Arabic attacks, in the 1920s the Jewish people began forming militia groups such as Haganah, providing the first organizations of Jewish unity in Palestine. During this time the use of terrorist violence (violence directed at civilian targets as a means of instilling fear) began to be used by both Arabic and Jewish groups. Tension and violence between the Jews and Arabs of Palestine contributed to Britain's decision to withdraw from the Palestine mandate in 1947. The 1947 UN Partition Plan was developed to split Palestine more or less equally between Jews and Arabs, with Jerusalem as a "free city" run by the UN. This plan was accepted by the Jews under David Ben-Gurion (the first prime minister of Israel), but was rejected by the Arab League. Increased tensions developed into all out warfare between the Jews (supported by the United States) and several Arabic nations, including Egypt, Syria, Jordan, Iraq, and Lebanon (often supported by the Soviet Union). The 1948 war resulted in a Jewish victory and the creation of the modern Israeli state. The creation of Israel led to mass expulsions of Palestinian Arabs from their homelands, as well as Jews from Arabic countries involved in the 1948 war.

Creation of the modern Israeli state is not the beginning point of tensions between Arabs and Israelis, but the ongoing violence between Israel and Palestinian Arabs has been a source of cultural strife in an area that is strategically important due to the presence of large reserves of oil. Arabic countries found themselves on the losing end of wars against Israel during the 1956 Suez Canal Crisis, the 1967 Six-Day War, and the 1973 Yom Kippur War, as well as numerous smaller conflicts. This frustration at the permanence of the Israeli state and the support that Israel receives from the United States has fueled conspiracy theories in the Arab world regarding Jewish plans for regional or international dominance—theories that are supported by use of the *Protocols* as propaganda.

As such, Arabic nations and militant groups have been largely responsible for resurrecting the *Protocols* as a propaganda tool, attributing its debunking in the Western academic world as simply further evidence of the pernicious plot described in the book. For example, many Saudi Arabian textbooks refer to the *Protocols* as factual in nature and assert that conclusive evidence exists that the *Protocols* are not a forgery. The implication is that the *Protocols* remain a dominant force in Israeli political strategy and that Western nations have already been co-opted by Jewish conspiracies. Often these texts exhort readers about the necessity of eliminating the state of Israel. No less a figure than Saudi King Faisal had been known to present copies of the *Protocols* to state visitors during the 1970s (Rothstein 2006).

Egypt has been officially at peace with Israel since the 1970s, yet discussions of the *Protocols* as factual continue to surface in Egyptian newspapers to the present day. In 2002, Egyptian television ran a miniseries entitled "Horseman without a Horse" that was billed as a "historical drama" based on the *Protocols*. The series documents a Jewish conspiracy to dominate the Middle East, leading to the development of the Israeli state at the expense of Arabic peoples. Despite condemnation by Israel and Western nations, the series ran and proved to be popular on Arabic language television.

Iran is another nation that continually produces "factual" editions of the *Protocols* and uses the *Protocols* as part of its anti-Israeli campaign in newspapers and other media. Such appearances of support for the veracity of the *Protocols* have greatly increased since the 1978 Iranian Revolution, which ushered in a conservative clerical Islamic regime in Iran. In a 2005 appearance at a "World without Zionism" conference, Iranian president Ahmadinejad stated that Islam should have as its goal wiping Israel off the map and reiterated the conspiracy theory of Jewish dominance over Western affairs, particularly in regard to occupation of the Middle East.

Other Middle Eastern nations and militant groups continue to promote the *Protocols* as factual. These include, but are not limited to Syria, where the Ministry of Information recently authorized an edition of the *Protocols;* Lebanon, where the *Protocols* are a best-selling book of "nonfiction" (Karsch 2003); the Palestinian Authority, which had been teaching the *Protocols* as factual in schools until 2005 (Jewish Virtual Library 2005); and Hamas (militant group and current dominant force in Palestinian government), whose charter (Article 32) explicitly refers to the *Protocols* as factual and calls for the elimination of the Israeli state.

Thus, although the *Protocols* continue to maintain influence among anti-Semitic groups worldwide, greatest acceptance of and attention to the *Protocols* seems currently to be focused on the Middle East. As such, the potential for the *Protocols* to be involved in anti-Semitic violence appears highest in nations that promote it as factual to their populace. In many instances the goal may be to distract a nation's own citizens from discontent that otherwise might be directed at the autocratic or theocratic governments of the Middle East. Thus, the anger individual citizens may feel regarding their own restricted freedoms may be directed outward, toward Israel, rather than internally toward a government that is corrupt and mismanaged. The end result increases prejudice and intolerance in a part of the world that remains strategically important and prone to violence.

References

Ben-Itto, Hadassa. *The Lie That Wouldn't Die: The Protocols of the Elders of Zion.* Portland, OR: Vallentine Mitchell, 2005.

Bright, John, *A History of Israel.* Louisville, KY: Westminster John Knox Press, 2000.

Carroll, James. *Constantine's Sword: The Church and the Jews.* New York: Mariner Books, 2002.

Cohn, Norman. *Warrant for Genocide: The Myth of the Jewish World Conspiracy and the* Protocols of the Elders of Zion. Junction City, OR: Serif Publishing, 1996.

Jewish Virtual Library. "Palestinian Authority Promises to Remove Protocols References from Textbooks," 2005. http://www.jewishvirtuallibrary.org/jsource/Peace/patext2.html (accessed 4/21/06).

Karsch, Efriam. *Rethinking the Middle East.* Oxford, England: Routledge, 2003.

Rothstein, E. "The Anti-Semitic Hoax That Refuses to Die," *New York Times,* April 21, 2006. http://www.nytimes.com/2006/04/21/arts/design/21holo.html?_r=1&ex=1146024000&en=d32bbd5d2002bf7c&ei=5087%0A&oref=slogin (accessed 4/25/06).

Sachar, Howard. *A History of the Jews in the Modern World.* New York: Knopf, 2005.

Segel, Benjamin, and Richard Levy. *A Lie and a Libel: The History of the* Protocols of the Elders of Zion. Lincoln, NE: University of Nebraska Press, 1995.

Bibliography

Marsden, V. *The Protocols of the Meetings of the Learned Elders of Zion* (translated). York, SC: Liberty Bell, 2004.

Slimy Behavior   IV

One of the most important commodities in the modern world is oil. Scientists continually find new uses for oil derivatives, disputes over oil sometimes escalate to war, and countries with oil reserves change the political and economic landscape. The market for oil creates opportunities for speculative behavior. Sometimes the speculation is legitimate, but other times the speculation results in unethical or illegal behavior.

This section presents three chapters related to oil in two different guises. Chapters on China Aviation Oil (chapter 14) and SH Oil (chapter 15) concern irregular behavior in the market for petroleum oil. Whether the irregularity was unintentional, as in the China Aviation Oil case, or intentional, as in SH Oil, the result was the same: a breakdown in ethical behavior. The Spanish Cooking Oil incident (chapter 16) concerns a different kind of oil—the edible kind. Although not a scam in the traditional sense, it is a good example of failure in government leadership.

The China Aviation Oil Scandal

14

KEVIN T. JACKSON

Contents

Introduction

On December 2, 2004, barely a decade after Nicholas Leeson brought down Barings Bank, the China Aviation Oil scandal was rocking Singapore. China Aviation Oil (Singapore) Corporation, Ltd. nearly toppled overnight after suffering losses of $550 million. The total losses exceeded the company's registered capital of $549 million. As the shocking news spread, it quickly touched off an international scramble among some big-name financial institutions, deepened doubts about investing in Chinese companies listed overseas, raised questions concerning internal control and risk management of Chinese companies, tainted the reputations of both Singapore and China, and prompted demands for corporate governance reforms.

Company Background

China Aviation Oil (CAO) began in May 1993 as a joint venture of China Aviation Oil Supply Corporation (CAOSC), China Foreign Trade Transportation Corporation, and the Singapore-based Neptune Oriental Lines, Ltd. Within its first two years of operation CAO sustained heavy losses. In February 1995 it became a wholly owned subsidiary of CAOSC after the other two joint venture partners sold their shares back to CAOSC.

During Chen's tenure, with the benefit of government connections, the company enjoyed a virtual monopoly on jet fuel imports to China. Upon his arrival in Singapore from Beijing with limited capital and resources, Chen began shifting the company from ship brokerage to oil trading, emphasizing jet fuel procurement. Oil trading activities took off in 1998 when CAO returned to profitability with a pretax profit of approximately $4.5 million. In acknowledgment of its performance and contribution to the Singapore economy, CAO was awarded approved oil trader (AOT) status by the Singapore government in July 1998. Under the AOT program CAO enjoyed a concessionary tax rate of 10 percent of income from qualifying trading transactions for five years, effective from January 1998. These oil trading activities included trading petroleum or petroleum products, trading oil futures and options contracts, and receiving and making payments under oil swaps. By 2000, CAO had obtained 92 percent market share for the jet fuel imports to China, constituting one third of China's total jet fuel needs. With the near monopoly and concessionary tax rate, profits rose quickly for the next few years. CAO was listed on the main board of the Singapore Exchange in December 2001, the only overseas-listed entity of CAOSC.

At the time of listing in 2001, the company's business was in the procurement and trading of petroleum products. The derivatives CAO was trading at this point were futures and swaps. They were used for either hedging or speculative purposes by CAO. Speculative option trading began at a later date. CAO's aviation oil procurement business depended heavily on its parent firm. In 2000, 98.3 percent of such trades were with the parent company. In 2001 and thereafter, it became nearly 100 percent, accounting for 40 percent of total physical trading revenue in 2002 and 2003. The other 60 percent came from trading in jet fuel, gasoline, fuel oil, and petrochemical products.

After its listing, CAO launched a second stage of transformation. It set up strategic investments to expand its revenue base and ensure growth on a sustainable basis. CAO instituted a three-pillar strategy: jet fuel procurement, international oil trading, and strategic investments in oil and gas-related infrastructure and logistics projects.

As a state-owned enterprise in the People's Republic of China (PRC), China Aviation Oil Holding Company (CAOHC) owns approximately 75 percent of the enlarged share capital of the firm. Under relevant provisions of China's law governing industrial enterprises owned by the whole people, CAOHC's assets are deemed to belong to "the people of the PRC"—that is, the state.

CAO was considered one of the most successful, transparent, and reputable of the more than 60 Chinese-listed firms in Singapore. In 2002, CAO was named Singapore's most transparent company by Singapore's Securities Investors Association. In 2004, the company was honored for having "outstanding risk-management structure and procedures" by the China National Enterprise Federation at its 10th Annual Creative Management Awards.

Evolution of CEO Chen's Leadership

As has been shown, under the leadership of CEO Chen, CAO's growth was meteroric. A series of successful financial deals catapulted the company to an elite firm listed on the Singapore Stock Exchange. Accordingly, Chen was deemed one of the most prominent business executives in both Singapore and China. Pulling down an annual salary of about $4.6 million made Chen the highest paid CEO of Chinese companies in China and one of the best compensated executives in Singapore. In 2003 Geneva's World Economic Forum elected him one of the forty "new Asian leaders."

Born in China's Hubei Province in 1961, Chen spent his childhood in the Cultural Revolution. He attended the prestigious Peking University, earning a BA with a specialization in Vietnamese from the Department of Oriental Languages. He later received a postgraduate diploma in international private law from China University of Political Science and Law in 1996 and an executive MBA from National University of Singapore in 2001.

Though having no formal business training, Chen's natural acumen landed him important positions in the airline companies he joined. He worked as a translator in many important negotiations. Later, he received a law degree from China University of Law and Administration. At the time the scandal emerged, Chen was working part-time on a PhD in law at China's Tsinghua University.

Initially, Chen began working at Air China, the country's largest international airline. In 1993 he joined the parent company of China Aviation Oil in Beijing as chief negotiator and project manager. In 1997, China Aviation Oil Holdings gave him the task of establishing China Aviation Oil in Singapore, appointing him as a general manager. Later he became managing director, and eventually he served as both managing director and CEO until his suspension. His initial capital was $210,000. Backed by strong demand for aviation oil on the Chinese mainland, Chen soon turned his small firm into an influential company. By 2003 China Aviation Oil was worth $326 million. Chen credited the tripling of the firm's market value within three years to his use of "Chinese wisdom"; indeed, the company motto read: "Chinese wisdom, international expertise."

As we shall see, however, he authorized and engaged CAO in a series of risky bets on oil options. Such misconduct not only threatened to collapse the enterprise he had once labored so hard to build, but the misdeeds also earned him a hefty jail sentence.

The Stage Is Set

CAO started option trading in March 2002. As mentioned previously, it had traded futures and swaps for both hedging and speculative purposes before conducting option trading. The early option trading was limited to back-to-back trades with airline companies. The back-to-back option trades involved Chinese airline companies selling options to CAO, which then sold them under similar terms to external counterparties. The rationale for the back-to-back trades was that airline companies often have insufficient credit standing to transact directly with option dealers. Thus, CAO was assuming the counterparty credit risk of the airline companies. Throughout 2003, such option trading was profitable. The company successfully bet on oil prices rising as it bought calls and sold puts.

During the second half of 2003 CAO's traders, under Chen's watch, started speculative option trading in its own account. CAO embarked upon derivative trades in oil options with the simple aim of making profits. Derivatives are securities bearing a contractual relation to some underlying financial asset or rate. They may be listed on exchanges or traded privately over the counter. For example, derivatives may be futures, options, or mortgage-backed securities. An option gives the right, but not the obligation, to undertake a course of action within a specific time period. For example, if one thinks the price of oil will increase over the next three months, one might buy an option to purchase oil at a specified price. When it comes time to purchase the oil, one buys at the market price or the option price, whichever is lower. If the option price is lower, one exercises the option to purchase at the option price. If the market price is lower, one lets the option expire without being exercised. Of course, having an option to do something that might save money is worth something, so options have value. They cost something to purchase. Options are used frequently to protect against an adverse event, so they are a form of hedging. However, they also can be a method of speculation. Making such types of speculative trades was not CAO's core business, but the company had publicly disclosed that speculative trades were part of its strategy to bolster its profile in the marketplace.

The Scandal Unfolds

In the fourth quarter of 2003, CAO took a bearish view of oil prices and began selling calls and buying puts, some of which are compound options, in order to receive more premium or improve strike price. As the oil price did not decrease as the traders anticipated, the option portfolio started losing money.

Chen was betting that the oil price would decline. Therefore, he purchased options on two million barrels of oil. Chen priced his price-put option at $3 a barrel or $22 a ton. He anticipated the oil price would stay below $400 a ton when the future contracts matured. Initially, the market went with the bet. However, as the war in Iraq intensified, oil prices started to rise. When the contract transaction had to be executed, the market oil prices hit $450 and losses began to mount. China Aviation Oil stood to lose $30 for any ton of oil it sold.

Had Chen followed CAO's risk-management procedure, CAO would have had a stop-loss at approximately $5 million. Yet Chen did precisely what Nicholas Leeson had done at Barings Bank: He raised the bet. However, the oil price continued to rise. By the end of June 2004, CAO's option portfolio had even higher negative mark-to-market (MTM) or paper losses than it had had in early 2004. (Mark to market involves assigning a value to a position held in a financial instrument based on the current market price for that instrument, or on a fair valuation based on the current market prices of similar instruments.) CAO saw paper losses of $30 million.

Seeing potential losses, Chen raised his bet yet again, hoping to recoup his losses. To avoid realizing the losses, he restructured a significant proportion of options using the strategy of buying back short-dated options and selling longer dated options, thus increasing CAO's risk exposure even further.

Oil prices continued to increase after June 2004, resulting in substantial margin calls on the options CAO sold in June 2004. CAO managed to meet those margin calls through a third round of zero-cost option rollover restructuring with additional counterparties and deploying yet more options. The goal of the restructuring was to prevent crystallizing the paper loss for the third quarter of 2004. The assumption was that the oil price would eventually trend downwards.

With more and more options sold and oil prices continuing to increase, margin calls were becoming more and more frequent and in higher amounts. Prior to June 2004, CAO met the margin calls through standby letters of credit and afterwards principally through cash. By the end of September 2004, CAO lacked financial capacity to meet the margin calls. In early October 2004, the jump in both oil price and volatility ushered in more significant margin calls. CAO's option portfolio had a negative MTM value of $367 million. By October 2004, CAO had options on 52 million barrels of oil with $180 million in paper losses.

CAO's Singapore trading partners began to demand that it make payments—a so-called margin call, which is a demand upon an investor to put up additional collateral for securities bought on credit. A lender, normally a brokerage firm, makes the call when the equity in the investor's account falls beneath the level set by the brokerage. Here, the margin call on CAO forced the company to close some of its positions. But CAO was unable to meet all of its margin calls. After all, it had already used $26 million of its own cash, $68 million from its jet fuel sales, and yet another $100 million from a loan. And it still faced $80 million in margin calls.

It was at this point, with little cash or banking facilities left to satisfy the margin requirements, that Chen asked the parent company CAOHC in Beijing for assistance. On October 9, 2004, in a letter to CAOHC, Chen revealed that CAO had suffered significant losses and faced liquidation unless the tables could be turned. He also disclosed that CAO had an unrealized loss of $180 million and requested financial support of $130 million. The request included the caveat that the amount could potentially rise to $550 million if oil prices were to reach $61 per barrel. He estimated that if all the positions were closed on October 8, 2004, the company's loss would be $550 million. However, if the company could meet the margin calls in time, the unrealized loss could be reduced or even eliminated when oil prices came down. The letter noted that Singapore law mandated that CAO disclose unrealized loss in the forthcoming quarterly results slated for release in November 2004, which might precipitate the company's liquidation.

During the period from October 10, 2004, to November 2004, CAOHC held no less than 11 emergency meetings to devise a rescue package for CAO. CAOHC provided an emergency loan of $100 million. As oil prices kept rising, the company's losses continued to accumulate. The loan from the parent company quickly proved insufficient. A more adequate rescue proposal would be needed.

Without alerting its shareholders, CAOHC sold a stake of approximately 15 percent to Deutsche Bank in Singapore for $108 million. In turn it lent the proceeds to CAO. Then Deutsche Bank divided the stake into smaller increments and sold them to hedge funds. Hedge funds are little regulated private investment partnerships for large investors. They wager huge sums in global currency, bond, and stock markets.

By November 2004 CAO had booked $3,481 billion in losses from its misadventures in oil options. It faced an additional $246 million in demands from creditors, including roughly $144 million to the Japanese trading company Mitsui, $33 million to the European Fortis Bank, and $26.5 million to the British Barclays Bank, plus another $160 million to a syndicate of banks led by the French bank Societe Generale.

On November 24, CAO's parent blocked its planned purchase of a stake in oil refiner Singapore Petroleum Company, raising doubts about the company's true financial status. On November 25, investors began selling the stock. Its value declined 23 percent in two days. On November 29, CAO suspended its share trading after its stock price had fallen 32 percent during that month, down 49 percent from its peak in March 2004.

With total losses of $5.5 billion, Chen realized the company was being stretched way beyond its means. On December 2, 2004, CAO announced that it would be seeking protection from creditors. On December 7, CAO asked the bankruptcy court for a six-week extension for a debt plan, intending to satisfy creditors' claims within six months. News of the pending collapse immediately touched off a scramble among the company's international creditors. The government of Singapore jumped into action as CAO's collapse was the biggest ever white-collar crime involving a prominent Chinese company. The auditing firm PricewaterhouseCoopers was promptly retained to sift through CAO's records in the hopes of getting to the bottom of what went wrong.

Legal Fallout

The official reaction from China was measured and cautious. Chen was summoned to Beijing on November 30, 2004, by his superiors at CAOHC. The departure sparked indignation from investors, who called for his prompt return to Singapore to aid the investigations by local authorities there. Statements were issued that the entire scandal was the sole responsibility of CAO and that CAOHC had no knowledge whatsoever prior to seeing the news, while promising that CAOHC and CAO would cooperate fully with the Singapore government in the pending investigations.

After his suspension, Chen flew back to Singapore on December 8, 2004, and was immediately apprehended by the Singapore police. The following day he was released on bail after having been questioned by police. Chen stated to Singapore's *Sunday Times*: "If I had committed 1,000 crimes, I would face up to them honestly...I do not blame anyone. I have let the company down...At worst, after a few years, I will go home and grow rice."

In an effort to assure CAO's creditors, CAOHC quickly bought a group of Chinese state-owned enterprises that included China's two biggest oil firms and Air China, in a plan to inject needed capital for the restructuring of CAO.

PricewaterhouseCoopers released a report on March 29, 2005, concluding that CAO had taken "imprudent and unwarranted risks" and cited "incorrect accounting and financial treatment, valuation methodology and consequent errors in financial disclosure by the Company."

After a 2-year jail sentence had been handed down for Peter Lim, CAO's former finance chief, and a hefty fine imposed on three members of the board, Chen pleaded guilty on March 15, 2006, to six criminal charges that were mounted against him. He was sentenced to four years' incarceration for cheating, three months for failure to inform the Singapore Exchange, and four months for insider trading. In addition, Chen was fined $330,000 on two counts of issuing false and misleading statements.

In arguing for leniency in the sentencing phase, Chen's legal counsel stressed that Chen had made significant contributions in leading CAO from a loss-producing subsidiary into an international publicly listed oil trading enterprise that, until its collapse in 2004, had been extremely successful. Chen's attorney also portrayed his client as a basically responsible and competent businessman who was the victim of misfortune with oil prices and a recipient of some bad advice from his colleagues.

In response, the prosecution maintained that Chen's behavior breached accepted norms of accountability and that the case illustrated serious problems in internal controls, disclosure, and corporate governance.

Effect of Internal Risk Controls

According to an independent report issued by PricewaterhouseCoopers and released by CAO on June 3, 2005, failures existed at every level of the company. The report stated that senior managers in CAO on many occasions overrode internal risk controls.

After suffering losses in its derivatives trading in 2000, CAO engaged Ernst & Young to develop a comprehensive risk management system. The system was to be modeled on the best practices from the international oil industry. With the assistance of external auditors, CAO implemented the risk management system in 2002. Using a multilayer approach, the system engages managers from various levels in the risk management process: division heads, independent risk management committee, internal audit division, the audit committee, and the board. Chen himself talked about CAO's risk management system in a Chinese convention. The system even won a major award in China.

Although the risk management system was formally in operation in March 2002, it is doubtful that the board and the audit committee had the time and experience to understand the system fully. The system was approved on a test-run basis by the board. Further, it did not address the issue of option trading. Moreover, the system could not be used for option trading, given that option trading is far more complicated than other types of derivatives such as futures and swaps. No option trading limit was set until the end of 2003 and early 2004, when the paper loss from the option portfolio had exceeded the trading limit. Traders were given stop-loss limits. However, the limits were not strictly enforced by the company since it was bent on avoiding recording losses. Had CAO decided to cease option trading totally instead of restructuring the option portfolio, its loss would likely have been limited and manageable. Yet CAO restructured its option portfolio not once, or twice, but three times and greatly increased its risk exposure each time. In doing so, the senior managers of the company knowingly went for broke and pushed the company to the verge of collapse.

CAO's MTM valuation methodology only took into account the intrinsic value of the options, ignoring the time value component. Accordingly, the impact of volatility, option maturity, interest rates, and so on was not captured in its valuation methodology. Consequently, CAO's own MTM value of its options would differ, sometimes substantially, from those reported by its counterparties on request for margin calls.

Role of Disclosure

According to the PricewaterhouseCoopers report, CAO's options trades had not been properly accounted for. Thus, CAO should have reported a pretax loss for third quarter 2004, instead of a profit, if the options trades were correctly tallied.

Moreover, CAO misled investors, including Temasek Holdings, Ltd., Singapore's government investment company, which owned about 2 percent of CAO shares. As mentioned earlier, following the report of its losses to the parent company in Beijing, CAO engaged Deutsche Bank to place out 15 percent of its stake to institutional investors. Yet CAO failed to disclose its true financial condition and deceived about the real purpose of the proceeds. On October 21, 2004, CAO's company spokesperson represented that cash was needed by the parent company to make an investment. On October 28, 2004, CAO stated that the sale would render the company more transparent due to a greater presence of institutional investors, consequently ensuring best corporate practice from CAO.

In recent years, Singapore has deregulated the financial sector, placing greater emphasis on the role of market discipline in regulating the financial industry. Banks and companies are required to provide accurate disclosure of material information regarding their operations. Investors are encouraged to assess the risk of their investments. While CAO had reported its huge loss to its parent company on October 9, 2004, it did not disclose the financial problem to the general public until the end of November, in violation of Singaporean disclosure requirements.

Conclusion

The near collapse of CAO shocked the business world in Singapore and China. After all, CAO had been regarded as a leading Chinese firm listed in Singapore and was thought to have possessed some of the best corporate governance standards in Asia.

The CAO scandal revealed a failure of internal control at virtually every level of management. Traders used options to speculate on the oil price direction instead of volatility and ignored the impact of volatility and other factors on the mark-to-market value of the option portfolio. The risk management committee did not set any trading limits on option trading. The internal audit division failed to report the internal control deficiencies regularly and correctly to the audit committee. Both CEO Chen and the board overrode internal controls by taking an excessive amount of risk in order to avoid realizing losses.

The debacle reminded investors of the risks of investing in Chinese state companies as a result of limited transparency. The scandal highlights the need to improve corporate governance and internal control in such companies.

Bibliography

Arnold, Wayne. "Failed China Fuel Supplier Waited Too Long for Help," *New York Times*, December 4, 2004, international business sec.

_____. "After Crash, China Aviation Oil Offers Creditors Sweeter Repayment Deal," *International Herald Tribune*, May 13, 2005, business sec.

"Auditor's Report Finds Pattern of Errors, Risky Behavior at China Aviation Oil," *Financial News*, March 29, 2005.

Burton, John, Mure Dickie, Francesco Guerrera, and Joe Leahy. "A Collapse That Waves a 'Big Red Flag' about Business with Beijing," *The Financial Times*, January 21, 2005, comment and analysis sec.

Burton, Katherine, and Lu Wang. "Big Investors Wary of Scandals and Slowing Growth in China," *Vancouver Sun*, December 29, 2004, business sec.

China Aviation Oil 2003 Annual Report.

Corporate Profile, China Aviation Oil, http://caosco.com/profile.html.

"Integrity an End All Firms Must Realize," *Business Daily Update*, March 31, 2006.

Quah, Michelle. 2006. "Defense, Prosecution Paint Conflicting Pictures of Chen," *The Business Times Singapore*, March 17, 2006, top stories sec.

"Singapore Court Fines Three More CAO Board Members," AFX-Asia, March 2, 2006.

"Singapore-Listed CAO Strengthens Corporate Governance," AFX-Asia, February 28, 2006.

The SH Oil and Gas Exploration Scandal

15

PHILIP R. MURRAY

Contents

The Investment

Consider the following investment opportunity circa the 1980s. Stephen L. Smith, a businessman in the small town of Winter Haven, Florida, runs a company called SH Oil and Gas Exploration. The nature of the business is locating oil and gas underground, drilling wells, and selling the gas and oil in the energy market. The returns are remarkable. You show an interest in investing in SH Oil and Smith agrees to meet you in his offices at 505 Avenue A, Northwest.

The office is clean and organized. A framed picture of his wife and a duck decoy decorate the desk. An appointment book is in the center of the desk and a large contour map marked with push pins is on the wall behind. The preppy-looking, 30-something Smith invites you to sit down and begins talking about business. Business is good. Smith owns more than three hundred oil wells. The map shows where he intends to drill next. He is on the cutting edge of energy prospecting. There is a technology, he explains, a "black box" that sits aboard a plane in order to identify underground reservoirs of oil and natural gas. The technology is so reliable that Smith can boast of striking oil in 114 of his last 120 attempts. He shows you checks written by the Amoco Company in the amount of approximately $1 million to pay for purchases of oil and gas (Sills, October 12, 1991; Calonius 1990; Cardinale, June 3, 1989).

There is no stock prospectus outlining SH Oil's assets, liabilities, net income, and risks. Instead, Smith hands you a pamphlet titled "Background of SH Oil and Gas Exploration." According to the pamphlet, Smith has been around the oil industry since 1973. SH Oil has wells where you would expect, in places such as Texas and Oklahoma, and where you might not expect, such as Pennsylvania, New Mexico, and three other states. Smith does not sell stocks or bonds to finance SH Oil. He sells investments in "projects" and a "production pool." Investing in a project involves "the partial assignment of leases to oil or gas wells." Your income from a project flows from the sale of oil or gas from the well. The production pool is "like a small bank." Your income from the production pool is similar to interest. Rates of return on projects range from 60 to almost 100 percent a year. Returns on the less risky production pool are about 20 percent a year. In addition to those impressive returns, there is a possibility of an investment tax credit for what you invest in SH Oil. Actually, Smith does not invite you to become an "investor." He conveys a different mindset. He views you as a "customer." The pamphlet states: "Based on objectivity, the Company will always deal fairly with any and all of its customers" (Calonius 1990; *Winter Haven News Chief,* January 20, 1988; Cuthbertson and Sills, February 4, 1988, January 20, 1988; Sills, October 12, 1991).

There are hundreds of delighted investors in the SH Oil Gas and Exploration company. One describes Smith's character: "He said he works harder than three men." Everyone seems to be making money; losers are unheard of. The only unhappy investors are those Smith rejected. The word around town is positive, which is why you are interested in the first place. But there is another reason to support investing in SH Oil. Barnett Bank of Polk County evidently approves the business plan. According to some investors, representatives of Barnett describe SH Oil as a "squeaky clean" organization. Other investors say that John Dunn, a vice president of Barnett, personally testifies to Smith's business acumen. Dunn reportedly authorized a geological study of SH Oil's properties. Smith took other Barnett officials on a helicopter tour over SH Oil's wells in Pennsylvania. Barnett lends directly to Smith and, in an indirect way, lends to investors who then buy SH Oil securities. One investor says a loan officer at Barnett goes so far as to claim that SH Oil is "better than sliced bread" (Sills, October 12, 1991; Cuthbertson and Sills, January 7, 1988; Cuthbertson, March 9, 1988; Calonius 1990).

It all sounds so good, especially the high rates of return. But those returns are so high and sustained for so many years you wonder if they are too good to be true. You wonder what kind of character Steve Smith really is.

The Profile

Stephen L. Smith is not an outsider who raises one's natural suspicions. He is the third generation of an accomplished Winter Haven family. Smith graduated from Winter Haven High School in 1969. There, he was an honor student, president of the Spanish club, class treasurer, and member of the Interact service club—an organization of future business leaders. Classmate Steve Baker describes Smith: "He was friendly and very courteous; extremely well groomed—Steve was a person who always did everything right." The promising high school graduate earned a bachelor's degree from Stetson University in Deland, Florida, and a master's degree in business administration from the University of Georgia. He worked in Texas, where he became familiar with the oil business and learned the industry jargon. He sold stocks and bonds for Merrill Lynch during the latter half of the 1970s. Smith parlayed what he knew about oil and finance to create the SH Oil and Gas Exploration Company as a sole proprietorship in the late 1970s. One experience from the past is perhaps significant: A Netherlands Antilles company led Smith to believe it was going to lend him $18 million to invest in orange groves and oil wells. Instead, the company bilked him out of $40,000 (Leach 1988; Sills, March 3, 1989; Cuthbertson and Sills, January 6, 1988; Calonius 1990).

The "S" stands for Stephen; the "H" for his wife Heather. Heather was Steve's high school sweetheart, from an "upper middle class" Winter Haven family. The couple's primary residence is a house with pool and tennis court on Lake Hamilton in Winter Haven. They also own real estate in Ocala, Florida; South Carolina; and posh Sea Island, Georgia. Steve collects cars, four Aston Martins among them. He bought a Rolls Royce for Heather. The couple literally lives the jet-set lifestyle, flying up and down the East Coast in their $500,000 Rockwell Saberliner. Although work consumes much of his time, Steve enjoys hunting at his leisure. Heather rides horses and collects jewelry. All this wealth is real and you can see the Smiths living in luxury year after year (Loftus 1991; Sills, January 20, 1988).

Doubts about SH Oil

The SH Oil and Gas Exploration business model appears to work well. The company sells securities in its well-drilling projects, accepts deposits into its production pool, and makes payments to investors on a monthly basis. Barnett Bank officials apparently endorse SH Oil and put the bank's money where its officials' mouths are with loans of its own. Various other banks, including Bankers Trust and Citibank of New York as well as Mellon Bank of Pittsburgh, also lend money to SH Oil's operations. The only nagging suspicion, however, is that even though investors have been earning substantial returns on SH Oil for years, the returns are far above those available on alternative investments. Investors in the stock market, for example, expect to earn about ten percent a year on average, which seems mediocre compared to returns ranging from 20 to 100 percent annually on SH Oil.

Smith tells investors, "If you are the least bit uncomfortable in the way I do business, we'll be happy to refund your capital." Mitchell Kalogridis grew uncomfortable with the way SH Oil did business. He was the brother of Peter Kalogridis, the lawyer for SH Oil. Mitchell traveled to Pennsylvania in order to confirm SH Oil's ownership of assets in that state but was unable to do so. Upon his return he revealed what he learned to Smith who agreed, as he said he would, to refund Mitchell's investment. Other business-minded members of the community voiced their concerns that the emperor might not be wearing clothes. Ron Brown, a certified public accountant, made a similar fact-finding trip to Texas in 1984. He could not verify that Smith owned any oil wells there. When Brown shared his findings (or lack thereof) with Peter Kalogridis, the latter mollified him with the point that Smith listed properties in "nominee names" to protect his privacy. (A "nominee name" is a legal term for agent or trustee.) The Briggs family was a group of wary investors. Sometime during 1985 Dr. Deane Briggs of Winter Haven shared his reservations about SH Oil with his father, Colver Briggs of Connecticut. The father employed a land assessor who reported back that he could not verify the existence of any oil wells in Texas owned by Smith or SH Oil. The land assessor also doubted Smith's success rate in drilling wells and striking oil. He dubbed the business "a very shady deal." Ed Rooney, of Rooney Investments, likewise could not verify that SH Oil owned any wells in Pennsylvania and informed John Dunn of Barnett Bank. In early 1986 businessmen Bill Herndon and Mark Bostick told Larry J. Pitts of Sun First National Bank in Winter Haven that the high rates of return Smith was paying implied that "there must be something either illegal or immoral with his business." Pitts consulted other bankers who rejected Herndon and Bostick's suspicions. Despite these doubts about the veracity of Smith and his ability to pay spectacular rates of return through SH Oil, investor sentiment remained for the most part optimistic (Sills, August 25, 1991, October 12, 1991, January 8, 1992, March 13, 1992; Calonius 1991).

The SH Oil money machine came to an abrupt halt in December 1987 due to "the letter."

The Letter

An anonymous tipster mailed a letter from Lakeland, Florida to the state comptroller's office in August 1987. The letter alleged that the SH Oil and Gas Exploration Company was a Ponzi scheme. In such a scheme, named after conman Charles Ponzi, the perpetrator solicits an initial group of investors, then recruits another group of investors and pays the first group attention-getting returns with funds put up by the second group. The chief characteristic of a Ponzi scheme is that the perpetrator pays the last round of investors with investments made by the next round of investors. In this way the pyramid of investments and payouts grows unless or until investors demand the return of their principal. The whistleblower on SH Oil wrote: "These returns are not being produced by the earnings of the company, but rather, are coming from the capital being invested in the company. The returns are so good that the investors cannot resist reinvesting their earnings with the company." He or she also alleged that "most of the investors have an idea of what is going on, but the returns are too great for them to stop." The public apparently never learned the true identity of the letter's author, who type-signed it "Florida citizen" (Sills, October 12, 1991).

Whoever wrote the letter and prompted the government intervention shook the foundation of the SH Oil pyramid like no one else. The author's skepticism, coupled with a government investigation, finally exposed a fraud that lasted about a decade. The state comptroller began the investigation in October 1987. Lawrence H. Fuchs, a deputy comptroller in Tallahassee, assigned the Orlando office to conduct the investigation along with the Florida Department of Law Enforcement. Three and a half months of investigation were enough to stop Stephen Smith from perpetuating the fraud (Cuthbertson, January 1, 1988; Sills, October 12, 1991).

An investigator doing research at the Polk County courthouse stumbled across an SH Oil "partial assignment of lease" security. Another investigator contacted the owner of the security for information. The owner informed Smith, who then contacted the comptroller's office and agreed to meet with investigators as if he had nothing to hide. Smith and his lawyer, Peter Kalogridis, told investigators of a "secret agreement" between SH Oil and Amoco Corporation. News reports left it to one's imagination *why*, according to Smith and Kalogridis, secrecy was necessary. In a later meeting, Kalogridis attempted to convince investigators of SH Oil's legitimacy by showing them checks written by Amoco in the amount of several million dollars. Representatives of Amoco inspected the checks and concluded that they were forged. Amoco officials also denied the existence of any secret agreement with SH Oil. Shortly thereafter, Polk County Judge Dennis P. Maloney ordered that SH Oil be closed. It was December, 30 1987 (Sills, October 12, 1991).

Investors resisted the idea that their King Midas was a fraud. Nick Pund said, "It's impossible for it to be what they say it is. I believe in Steve Smith." Twila Rhodes said, "Steve just wouldn't do a thing like that. Bless his heart, he just can't be in trouble." "I've known him all my life," claimed Steve Owen, "and I'm confident that what he told me is true." Some investors defended Smith and expressed resentment toward the government's actions. Twila Rhodes said, "The papers are crucifying him...but I still think I'm going to get my money back. It isn't a case of him running away." Nick Pund asked, "If [Smith] was running a scheme that needed money, a 'Ponzi' scheme, then why did he turn down potential investors?" Investor W. N. Scarborough predicted that "if [state authorities] don't stick their noses in it, I think it will all work out." Deputy Comptroller Fuchs offered sobering commentary. He stated, "In cases of this type, a recovery of 10 cents on the dollar would be optimistic." In response to investor Nick Pund's question as to why Smith would reject some investors, Fuchs answered, "That is fairly common in these kinds of schemes. If you make it something exclusive, then people think that, somehow, it is a privilege to get involved" (Cuthbertson and Bygrave 1988; Cuthbertson and Sills, January 7, 1988; Cuthbertson, December 31, 1987; *Winter Haven News Chief,* January 9, 1988).

Judge Maloney's court designated William H. McBride, Jr., as "receiver," responsible for seizing Smith's assets and investigating the financial operation of SH Oil. McBride delivered his first report in late January 1988. He reported that "contrary to the expressed perceptions of those who allege investment interests in the businesses, Smith and SH Oil do not have identifiable, prov-able, or perfected interests in oil and gas projects (except a few limited inter-ests of small value)." By his estimate, 591 investors had put $109.1 million into the "projects" and the "production pool." He documented a "typical pattern" of the financial transactions between Smith and his investors. The following passage illustrates the "meticulous" nature of Smith, which is one way he deceived investors:

> The investor would indicate to Smith that the investor had a desire to par-ticipate in a particular Project. Smith would mail the investor an invoice that listed the Project, the amount of the investor's investment in the Project, and the investor's purported percentage interest in the Project....The inves-tor would mail Smith a check in the amount of the invoice. Smith would then mail the investor an invoice evidencing that the investor had paid in full for the investor's interest in the Project....In addition, Smith would mail the investor two duplicate partial assignments of leases which specified the investor's interest in the Project and lease....The investor would then execute both duplicate partial assignments of leases and return one of the duplicates to Smith. Investors in Projects would receive checks on a monthly basis that listed the amount paid to the investor for the previous month with respect to the various Projects....Investors that deposited monies in the production pool would follow a similar procedure except that Smith would mail the investor duplicate participation agreements rather than duplicate partial assignments of leases....Persons who invested in the production pool received a check each month from Smith which purportedly paid interest on their investments. (*Winter Haven News Chief,* January 20, 1988; Cuthbertson and Sills, January 20, 1988)

McBride noted that "smart, tough business people" fell for the scam. In fact Smith fooled a wide variety of people. One reporter made a list of vic-tims: "elderly widows, small businessmen, entire families, and some of the community's most powerful and influential people." Another reporter made this list: "Smith's grandmother, prominent Winter Haven doctors and lawyers, and a former Winter Haven mayor." A journalist writing for *Fortune* magazine put it this way: "Smith took checks from grandmothers and pensioners; from the people who took him swimming as a child, who double-dated with him at Winter Haven High. He defrauded citrus managers, bankers, small-business executives, wealthy retirees, dentists, lawyers, an Episcopal priest, and an otolaryngologist." This perpetrator, in other words, did not just victimize strangers and unsophisticated investors. He betrayed family members, long-term friends, and educated professionals (Cuthbertson and Sills, January 15, 1988; Sills, March 3, 1989; Cardinale, May 30, 1989; Calonius 1990).

When investigators searched SH Oil offices, they discovered a balance sheet prepared December 31, 1987, and signed by Smith, which listed SH Oil's net worth at $8.5 million and Smith's net worth at $78.2 million. McBride prepared "a rough estimate of the potential assets and liabilities of Smith and SH Oil," which gave a completely different picture than the one Smith portrayed. McBride pegged the assets of Smith and SH Oil at approximately $12 million compared to liabilities of about $116 million. Certain participants in the scheme fared well. McBride determined that a few recovered up to six times the principal they invested. Others lost everything. McBride asked, "Should those investors who profited be treated the same as those who didn't profit?" That question would take years for the courts to decide. McBride also recommended that the authorities pursue "aiders and abettors" who helped Smith build his pyramid (*Winter Haven News Chief*, January 20, 1988; Cuthbertson and Sills, January 20, 1988).

In his next report, released in February 1988, receiver McBride revised his figures to show that there were 717 accounts with investments totaling $138 million in SH Oil. The owners of those accounts collected "refunds, withdrawals, and income distribution" in the amount of $119 million. Recall that some individuals invested in "projects" involving partial assignments of leases. Table 15.1 is the result of a forensic accounting investigation commissioned by the receiver and released to the public in March 1988. It shows investments in projects, payouts to investors in projects, and the difference, which Smith kept for SH Oil and himself, over time. The table illustrates the nature of a Ponzi scheme whereby the perpetrator diverts investments in the company toward the previous group of investors, not toward the purchase of plant or equipment to produce goods and services. The table also illustrates the construction of a financial pyramid. Investments in the projects rose every year to a total of $106,987,866 by the end of 1987. Returns from the projects rose every year to a total of $88,658,124. The overall net gain to SH Oil and Smith from projects amounted to $18,324,842 (Cuthbertson and Sills, February 27, 1988; Sills, October 12, 1991; *Winter Haven News Chief*, March 24, 1988).

Table 15.1   Investments, Investor Returns,
and Net Gains to SH Oil from Projects

Year	Investments in projects	Returns to investors	Net gain to SH Oil
1978	$20,000	$39,354	–$19,354
1979	225,585	111,086	114,499
1980	496,877	172,470	324,407
1981	594,370	365,595	224,775
1982	1,441,366	446,230	995,136
1983	2,831,556	946,397	1,885,159
1984	8,572,104	4,560,009	4,011,195
1985	14,163,653	12,539,689	1,623,964
1986	28,402,480	20,940,760	7,461,720
1987	50,239,875	48,536,534	1,703,341

McBride reported that some investors in projects made money. Specifically, he wrote that "240 accounts received refunds and income distribution in excess of investment, with an average return of 136.82 percent." A larger number of investors in projects, however, lost money. According to McBride, "312 accounts received refunds and income distribution in an amount less than investment, with an average return on investment of 57.65 percent" (*Winter Haven News Chief*, February 27, 1988). One should interpret what the receiver means by "return" with caution. It appears that the receiver's calculation of return is the sum of income and refund divided by investment, which is neither the same as average annual return or cumulative return. A "return" greater than 100 percent, the way the receiver reports it, simply means the investor recovered more than what he put in. A "136.82 percent" return earned over 1 year is impressive, for example, but not so impressive the longer the number of years over which one earned it. A "return" less than 100 percent means the investor recovered less than the principal invested.

Likewise, some investors in the "production pool" made money while more lost. Receiver McBride reported that "66 accounts showed withdrawal and income in excess of deposit, with an average return over investment of 110.77 percent." These individuals recovered more than they put in. But note that if they rolled over their principal for, say, three years and received about 11 percent more than what they put in, that is not so impressive. On the other hand "99 accounts showed withdrawal and income in an amount less than deposit, with an average return of 53.11 percent," implying that these investors got back only 53 percent of the amount they invested.

Perhaps the following account, written with the benefit of some time having passed, is sufficiently accurate: "According to court papers, some investors reaped hefty returns from their investments, receiving up to 130 percent return on their money, while others suffered losses, getting back less than 60 percent of their original investments." Putting it conservatively, over 600 investors put more than $100 million into SH Oil. Some made money but most lost (*Winter Haven News Chief*, February 27, 1988; Cuthbertson and Sills, March 8, 1988, March 14, 1988; Sills, March 2, 1989).

Authorities arrested Smith in February 1988. John Montjoy Trimble, Smith's lawyer, informed the media that Smith would cooperate and appear in person. Trimble added that "he may have to arrive by helicopter to avoid being mugged on the way into town." The lawyer's comment referred to "death threats" against Smith, who did not, as it turned out, fly into town. Authorities charged Smith with grand theft, racketeering, securities violations, and fraud. Prosecutors wanted bail set at $100 million, which would have required Smith to post a $10 million bond. Although a first judge did set the bond at $10 million, the next judge on the case lowered it to $225,000. Smith's parents put up real estate as collateral for the bond. At the bond hearing, Smith claimed to be working on a plan to reimburse investors in SH Oil but he revealed no specifics. While out on bail, Smith maintained a low profile. He communicated to the public at a minimum through his lawyers. The lawyers expressed their frustration at trying to defend a client whose assets had been frozen since the shutdown of SH Oil in late 1987. In the meantime authorities continued to build their case (Cuthbertson and Sills, February 3, 1988, February 8, 1988; Cuthbertson, February 10, 1988; Sills, October 12, 1991).

Smith initially pleaded not guilty as charged in October 1988. He filed for bankruptcy in February 1989, ostensibly because receiver McBride had drained three fourths of a million dollars from the estate during the investigation. Florida Comptroller Gerald Lewis speculated that Smith filed for bankruptcy because the state refused to give Heather Smith more than $500,000 of the assets. Lewis fumed: "The bankruptcy filing by Stephen Smith is absolutely outrageous. After a full year of work by the court appointed receiver, Smith's cavalier action shows his complete disregard for the investors" (Sills, February 25, 1989, March 18, 1989, October 12, 1991; Cardinale, March 3, 1989). Although Lewis suggests that Smith filed for bankruptcy to encumber the compensation due to SH oil investors, the declaration of bankruptcy did enable Smith's creditors to queue up for payment.

Investigators had built a persuasive case against Smith. They showed that SH Oil and Gas Exploration actually owned few claims on royalties from oil wells. Rather than use investors' monies to invest in the oil business, Smith altered papers to fake claims on numerous wells. He lacked licenses for SH Oil, for selling securities, and the securities themselves. Federal officials charged Smith with fabricating accounting statements to apply for bank loans (Sills, March 1, 1989, October 12, 1991; Cuthbertson, January 1, 1988; *Winter Haven News Chief*, March 1, 1989).

Prosecutors brought this case to the brink in early 1989. They plea bargained with Smith. On the verge of a trial in March 1989, Smith pleaded guilty to "organized fraud," "selling unregistered securities," and "selling securities by an unregistered broker." The following month he pleaded guilty to the federal charge of bank fraud by doctoring accounting information to obtain bank loans (Cardinale, March 2, 1989, March 3, 1989; Cardinale, May 30, 1989).

The Sentence

Judge J. Tim Strickland sentenced Smith to 15 years in prison and ten years of parole on state charges in May 1989. The federal charge of bank fraud cost the perpetrator a ten-year sentence in federal prison. Judge Strickland set several requirements for Smith's parole. Among a long list of conditions, he required Smith to compensate investors within a year and a half after his release. He capped the parolee's income and assets and showed a bit of creativity by obligating Smith to talk to students in the state universities of Florida and the public schools in Polk County about business ethics. One of Smith's future lawyers would later complain that Smith's legal representation at the time did not foresee the severity of the parole requirements when they plea bargained. Smith's grandmother, a staunch defender of her grandson, dropped this bombshell: "If I had my way, I'd bag all them guys up and send them all to Russia where they belong." She was referring to "state investigators and prosecutors" (Sills, June 1, 1989; Cardinale, May 30, 1989, June 1, 1989, January 29, 1995).

In early June 1989, Smith appeared in bankruptcy court before creditors and investors. He publicly confessed that the payments he made to investors were not based on revenues earned from oil and gas production. In fact he confessed that he never drilled any oil wells. He admitted there was never any "secret agreement" between SH Oil and Amoco Corporation. Despite these admissions, Smith blamed the collapse of his company and the resulting misfortune of investors on the state comptroller's office. He told investors, "'I want each and every one of you to understand what occurred and the problems that arose from it resulted from the Comptroller's actions.'" The confidence man retained his gall. He explained his "reimbursement plan" to compensate investors, which involved using the $15 million left in his estate to earn interest and repay investors over time. But a federal trustee controlled those $15 million. One lawyer assisting the trustee of the estate dubbed the plan "'Ouija board' economics." The trustee said, "The plan is taking assets and playing investment games with them." In his judgment, investors would have been better off receiving their individual pittances of the $15 million, licking their wounds, and getting on with their lives. One loyal investor "told

Smith he still believed in him. 'We still love you, Steve,' he said" (Cardinale, March 2, 1989, June 3, 1989; Cardinale, May 30, 1989).

Authorities put Smith in Saufley Field federal prison in June 1989 (Cardinale, June 7, 1989).

Parallel Controversies

The fall of SH Oil spawned parallel controversies involving squabbles over his estate, suspicion of "aiders and abettors" who may have helped Smith build his Ponzi scheme, legal battles over responsibility for the losses between Barnett Bank and SH Oil investors, what to do with the profits of "winning" investors in SH Oil, and foreign intrigue.

When Smith filed for bankruptcy in February 1989, the administration of his estate, reported to be about $15 million at the time, passed from receiver McBride to federal trustee Terry Smith (no relation to Stephen). The Florida comptroller's office protested this shift in control from receiver to bankruptcy trustee on grounds that it would jeopardize the compensation of losing investors. The attempt to block the transfer was unsuccessful, however, and estate trustee Terry Smith set out to liquidate the assets and pay the proceeds to the Internal Revenue Service (IRS), creditors, and investors. That task encountered legal obstacles and would consume much time (Cardinale, March 3, 1989; Sills, June 3, 1989).

Heather Smith drew early suspicion as a fellow conspirator in her husband's scandal because in the immediate aftermath of the shutdown, she sold a number of horses and deposited the proceeds into a bank account under her maiden name. Authorities targeted her as one of the "aiders and abettors" who "were touting the [SH Oil] projects to others." The guilt of anyone suspected of aiding and abetting, according to the deputy state comptroller, hinged upon "whether these people knew that Smith was operating a 'classic Ponzi scheme.'" The state specifically accused Heather Smith of aiding and abetting because she accompanied her husband during sales pitches to investors and negotiations with bankers (Cuthbertson and Sills, February 2, 1988, February 8, 1988; Cuthbertson and Keough 1988).

In 1990 a panel of judges "said there was insufficient evidence to declare that she played a part in the SH Oil and Gas Exploration scheme." At the same time when the state withdrew the accusation against her, Heather made a deal with the bankruptcy trustee for Steven's estate, giving up her claim on assets in return for over $700,000. One of the many investors who lost money in SH Oil remarked bitterly, "Look at what she got—$700,000. She came out smelling like a rose." Although $700,000 is indeed a soft cushion to fall back on, Heather Smith had reasons to be "drawn and nervous": Both the media and the IRS hounded her. Heather divorced Stephen in November 1991 (Sills, May 5, 1990; Cardinale, June 6, 1990; Loftus 1991).

The crash of SH Oil spawned allegations of ethical misconduct between Barnett Bank and certain investors. One disgruntled group made quick plans to sue Barnett in federal court because the bank approved of making investments in SH Oil and lent money to individuals so that they could do so. The plaintiffs reasoned, in their suit launched in March 1988, that "Barnett thus effectively financed and funded the fraud by becoming a primary source of funds for SH Oil." These investors and another group who filed a suit in county court also argued that Barnett should have known that SH Oil was fraudulent because investor Ed Rooney implied it was. When Rooney told Barnett's John Dunn that SH Oil apparently owned no wells in Pennsylvania, Dunn looked into the matter. But according to the plaintiffs, Dunn and other bank officials continued to endorse SH Oil and that made Barnett liable for their losses. Barnett retaliated with a countersuit, which alleged that Deane Briggs wanted to suppress the bad news about SH Oil and Rooney did not tell all he knew. Barnett accused Briggs and Rooney, who continued to invest in SH Oil until the shutdown, of withholding information so that they could make money as long as possible (Cuthbertson, March 9, 1988; Cuthbertson and Sills, March 12, 1988; Cardinale, June 6, 1989, December 22, 1990; Cardinale, 1989, $1 million; Calonius 1990).

None of the allegations, in either the investors' suits against Barnett or Barnett's countersuit against investors, held up in court. Soon after authorities clamped down on SH Oil in late 1987, Barnett Bank carried out an "internal investigation" in January 1988 and determined that two of its loan officers were innocent of "any wrongdoing or illegal acts" in connection with SH Oil. Although a corporation's decision that its employees did not violate its own ethical standards has no bearing on legal proceedings, it creates the impression that Barnett officials were victims, not perpetrators. The legal process made the same impression. Shortly thereafter, in February 1988, Judge Maloney decided that "SH Oil was a fraudulent business." Recall that Smith also pleaded guilty in 1989 to bank fraud. As for the investors' suit against Barnett, which concluded in 1990, a county judged ruled that "Rooney hadn't proven the bank engaged in fraud." The implication is that Smith defrauded Barnett; the bank did not defraud investors. It is perhaps interesting and amusing to note that in defense of itself against accusations that it was responsible for investors' losses, Barnett hired a "former Harvard University professor" to investigate the deep psychological underpinnings of why anyone would invest in SH Oil. According to the results of that scholar's research, "They invested to make lots of money." Having withstood these legal accusations of ethical misconduct and perhaps also putting the focus on Smith as the real perpetrator, Barnett withdrew its countersuit against investors in late 1990

(Cuthbertson and Sills, January 19, 1988; Sills, September 6, 1991, October 12, 1991; Cardinale, March 2, 1989, December 22, 1990).

Barnett was not done grappling in the legal arena, however. In April 1990 the bank sued the Stanley–Wines law firm on grounds of conflict of interest. Barnett alleged that Stanley–Wines organized disgruntled SH Oil investors for the previously mentioned lawsuit against it, which argued that bank officials endorsed SH Oil and were therefore liable for investors' losses. This amounted to a conflict of interest because at the same time Stanley–Wines "was representing Barnett on other matters." The bank described those "other matters" as "foreclosures, loan closings, and civil litigation." The law firm described them as "minimal legal services." Barnett also argued that one partner in the law firm, J. Mason Wines, was guilty of conflict of interest because he presided on the bank's board of directors during SH Oil's spree and then helped take action against the bank. According to James C. Rinamon, Jr., a past president of the Florida Bar, "Stanley–Wines could not have ethically represented those interests adverse to Barnett Bank." The parties to the suit agreed to mediation in 1992 (*Ledger,* December 22, 1990; Cardinale, January 28, 1991; Sills, June 25, 1992). The outcome of that mediation was either undisclosed or unknown.

The ethical case of "winning" investors continued to confound the interested parties after Smith went to prison. The court set out to decide whether winners would have to repay their ill-gotten profits in order to subsidize the losers. One's basic sense of fairness suggests that no one should benefit from a Ponzi scheme. Perhaps the winners should be required to return their profits in order to compensate the losers.

Reporter Art Sills explained: "The law describes these profits as 'fraudulent conveyances.'" "Even if investors didn't know that SH Oil was a fraud," according to Sills's understanding, "their profits were illegally made and can be seized for distribution among 'losing' investors and creditors." There were other views, however. A lawyer representing a winning investor illustrated his perspective with dollar amounts. Suppose, he said, someone initially invested $10,000 in SH Oil, earned a $5,000 profit, and recovered his principal. Sometime afterward the individual invested another $2,500 and lost it all. "The investor is entitled to file a claim against the estate to get his $2,500 back since the investment scheme was a fraud," according to that lawyer. A lawyer for the bankruptcy estate put forth an alternative interpretation: "When the transactions in the example are taken together the investor is a $2,500 net winner, not a loser," he said (Sills, June 30, 1991; Ward 1991).

Judge Alexander L. Paskay distinguished between investors who were naïve about the SH Oil fraud and those who were not. "Winners" among the former group could keep their profits, he ruled, but winners among the latter group could not. In September 1991 Judge Paskay decided that winners could submit claims on Smith's bankruptcy estate and SH Oil along with the IRS, creditors, and losing investors. Lawyers for the bankruptcy estate protested his decision. One claimed that Judge Paskay's decision "constitute[d] the first ruling ever to allow investors to actually profit from such a blatantly fraudulent operation." Lawyers for the estate trustee announced their intention to sue winners who, they planned to argue, knew SH Oil was a Ponzi scheme (Sills, August 25, 1991, September 6, 1991, September 13, 1991).

Some winners voluntarily returned most of their profits to the estate. Fourteen investors who took about $161,000 in profits paid back about $121,000 in March 1990. That was insignificant compared to the estimated 100 investors who accumulated $13 million in profits. In the meantime, trustee Smith auctioned off miscellaneous assets of the perpetrator Smith, including Rolex watches, guns, mink coats, a Japanese sword, and less exotic items such as furniture and office equipment (Cardinale, March 21, 1990; Cardinale, March 25, 1990).

The trustee for the bankruptcy estate adopted a more aggressive legal strategy to recover profits from winning investors who were reluctant to give them up and who also had some reason to believe SH Oil was based on fraud. Ed Rooney, alleged to have the Briggs family's report that Smith owned nothing in Texas and the recipient of nearly $180,000 in profits, eventually settled with the trustee and paid back $30,000 in October 1991. Mitchell Kalogridis "knew the SH Oil & Gas Exploration Company was fraudulent when he took nearly $400,000 in SH Oil profits," according to the trustee. However, as of March 1992, the trustee had abandoned his plan to recover those profits due to "legal costs and clogged court calendars." Legal pressure finally led Dr. Deane Briggs, who was accused of encouraging further investments in SH Oil even though he knew the company was a scam, to settle with the bankruptcy estate in June 1992 by repaying $95,000. The Briggs family was the last group of "winners" to settle with the estate trustee, which brought the trustee close to paying off investors (Cardinale, March 21, 1990; Sills, July 11, 1991, October 16, 1991, January 8, 1992, June 20, 1992).

Foreign Intrigue

Rumors swirled that Stephen Smith had hidden assets overseas. Officials considered the possibility as early as January 1988 that Smith's bank accounts "may include some in an unidentified European country." A local investment advisor and newspaper columnist, Thomas R. Oldt, wrote that "speculation about the missing $5 million has always centered on unnumbered accounts in offshore banks, or gold bars secretly stashed in safety deposit boxes" (1989). Smith himself introduced the character of John P. Curry, who would add the most foreign intrigue to the story. Smith first mentioned Curry shortly before entering prison in June 1989 at the meeting with creditors in bankruptcy court. According to the court reporter, Smith claimed to have employed Curry to obtain a multimillion dollar loan from a German bank, which he would then use to payoff SH Oil investors and then move on to other ventures (Cuthbertson, January 5, 1988; Sills, June 3, 1989).

The trustee for Stephen Smith's bankrupt estate, Terry Smith, became interested in Curry when he was searching for assets to augment the payouts to losing investors. T. Smith declared: "Curry was basically paid $750,000 during the last two years of SH Oil operation, and I can't see where he produced anything." Stephen Smith responded from prison. He claimed that Curry was negotiating the loan from the German bank. After paying off SH Oil investors, he planned to use $60 million to explore for oil and gas in Louisiana. And he expected a $4 billion profit (Sills, May 7, 1991, July 25, 1991).

Curry began talking in 1991. He fancied himself as a "consultant on an international level" and an "international financial strategist." There was a connection between SH Oil and the Middle East, he explained, whereby investors from Saudi Arabia and the United Arab Emirates wanted to put up $35 million toward Smith's prospecting for oil and gas in Louisiana. According to Curry's story, he relayed a payment by Smith to an Arab named Michael Askari, who negotiated directly with the Arab investors. Curry fueled the mystery by claiming that Askari "worked for the Mitchell Group," which he further claimed was "a clandestine operation based in Washington, D.C., which had its origins with the late U.S. Attorney General John Mitchell." The reporter noted that Curry's story about the so-called Mitchell Group "cannot be verified." "Perhaps the most bizarre assertions," wrote the reporter, "concern Smith's dealings with shadowy figures involved in U.S. covert operations, allegedly including the Central Intelligence Agency and the Drug Enforcement Agency." Curry did not explain why Smith would have anything to do with the CIA or the DEA (Sills, September 15, 1991, October 12, 1991, December 31, 1991).

Trustee Smith scrutinized the financial dealings between Stephen Smith and Curry in bankruptcy court during 1992. Judge Paskay denied the trustee's effort to regain $500,000, which Smith had paid Curry for "fees and expenses" in 1986 and 1987. The judge did, however, arrange a trial to determine whether Curry should repay another $250,000 Smith paid him near the end of 1987. According to Smith's story, the $250,000 was payment for the services of negotiating the loans to finance the payoff of SH Oil investors and the Louisiana venture. Curry said he transferred the money to Sheik Abullah Fahti Younis of Oman, on the Saudi Arabian peninsula. Sheik Younis then worked to procure a loan from the Saudi Arabian government. Before the trial over the $250,000, the FBI and IRS twisted the plot when agents took control of Curry's financial records. The FBI divulged very little about why it made the move. An agent of the Florida comptroller's office nevertheless speculated that the reason had something to do with the Pilot Company, headquartered in the Turks and Caicos Islands, led by Curry and Smith.

Curry claimed that yet another Middle Eastern government had loaned $25 million to the Pilot Company in 1987. This deal would raise the FBI's suspicion because it involved the government of Abu Dhabi, which also lent money to the notorious Bank of Credit and Commerce International (BCCI). BCCI engaged in a long list of illegal activities, such as money laundering and tax evasion. Government agencies of the United Kingdom and the United States investigated BCCI and closed the rogue bank in 1991. There was at least a weak connection between SH Oil and BCCI; court receiver McBride listed BCCI on a list of many banks he was examining for SH Oil deposits in his report to the court in February 1988. Nevertheless the government's taking of Curry's financial records effectively ended the trustee's pursuit of the $250,000 (Sills, July 23, 1992, August 14, 1992; *Wikipedia* 2006; *Winter Haven News Chief,* February 27, 1988).

Trustee Smith prepared the final stages of the distribution of perpetrator Smith's bankrupt estate among losing investors. The IRS settled for a $1.2 million hunk of the estate in 1992. A year later, Judge Paskay approved distributions to investors. Investors made claims against the bankrupt estate; trustee Terry Smith "allowed" claims no higher than these amounts claimed. There are two ways to view the distribution of assets to investors. The trustee paid approximately 19 percent of investors' original investments. Alternatively, he returned "about 24 percent of the claims he allowed." By this time, ironically, Stephen Smith had already left prison (Sills, June 20, 1992; Cardinale, May 18, 1993).

New Developments

The day before authorities set Smith free on parole, his mother told the media she wished people would forget the whole episode. She added that "the truth has never been printed." Smith's grandmother refused to say anything. Likewise, Peter Kalogridis, the lawyer for SH Oil, and William Stuart, whose family lost $10 million, opted not to talk. Smith served not quite four years of the 15-year state sentence and ten-year federal sentences he was able to serve simultaneously. One investor thought the perpetrator's time served was not harsh enough. Generally, though, former investors were putting the financial trauma behind them (Cardinale and Schottlekotte 1993; *Winter Haven News Chief,* May 4, 1993).

Smith departed prison on May 5, 1993, with $100 in his wallet. He was optimistic. "I'm just glad it's all over," he said, "and I look forward to the future with great anticipation." He expressed no remorse or any other comment over SH Oil. His father, who met him upon his release from prison, said, "We've just decided not to say anything about it." Smith planned to live in Pensacola, Florida. When Judge Strickland sentenced Smith back in 1989, he required Smith to repay $10 million plus 12 percent interest to investors in person with an apology within 18 months of his release. The judge also required Smith to do community service and deliver speeches on ethics in the state universities of Florida and the high schools of Polk County. (He later withdrew the requirement that Smith speak to high school students.) Among the financial restrictions, Smith could not earn more than $30,000 a year, possess more than $10,000 of assets, or run a business (Cardinale and Schottlekotte 1993; Sills, May 5, 1993).

Vaughn C. Brennan, a new lawyer for Smith, complained that the stipulations of Smith's parole were onerous. In 1995 he and Smith requested a private meeting with Judge Strickland to present a new business plan and ease the parole restrictions. Smith did release some details to the public, however. He intended to raise $500,000 from new investors and use that to purchase stock options. After exercising the options contracts and generating profits, he would reimburse SH Oil investors and then create a new business providing "commercial and technological services to foreign governments." The financial maven predicted that he could earn a return of ten percent a month. He dubbed it "the strategic plan." Judge Strickland refused to meet with Brennan and Smith in private and therefore rejected the proposal. The judge scolded Brennan for requesting to meet in private (Cardinale, January 29, 1995).

Over the next few years Smith made token contributions toward compensating SH Oil investors. By October 1999, when the Winter Haven public heard of him again, this amounted to just over $13,000 of the more than $10 million plus interest he owed according to Judge Strickland's orders. This time Judge J. Michael Hunter issued a warrant for Smith's arrest on grounds that he ran afoul of his parole. Altogether, Smith broke four terms of his parole, the most significant of which was the ban on his running a business. One of these businesses was Berndene Overseas Limited, headquartered in Pensacola, Florida. The other was Alcazar Trust in Louisiana. Residents of Louisiana and Texas who invested in Berndene and Alcazar accused Smith of swindling them out of around $1.5 million (Cardinale, October 2, 1999; Chambliss 2000).

Assistant State Attorney Wayne Durden, Smith, and his lawyers gathered in Judge Susan K. Roberts's Polk County courtroom in early September 2000. Prosecutor Durden argued for a 27-year prison sentence for the parole violations. Smith's lawyers asked for leniency. "Restitution for victims is paramount here," one argued, "and you can't do that in prison." On his own behalf, Smith uttered, "I pray the court will have mercy." Judge Roberts sentenced the Ponzi schemer and parole violator to 27 years. In a strange twist, the Department of Corrections set Smith free after spending only 42 days of the 27-year sentence in jail. The apparent confusion revolved around whether the four years Smith served from 1989 to 1993 applied to the original 15-year sentence and the new 27-year sentence. Judge Roberts made her ruling clear: Smith had to go back to prison (Davis 2002; *Winter Haven News Chief,* November 16, 2000).

Smith served another three years and re-emerged from prison in February 2004. The terms of his probation were similar to those set back in 1989. Judge Roberts had updated the limits on his income and assets for the effects of inflation. The parolee sought occupations "in marketing and fundraising," which his parole officer rejected (Kohn 2004). As of yet the general public has not heard a call for new investors.

References

Calonius, Erik. "The Great Florida Oil Scam," *Fortune,* July 16, 1990, 84–88.

Cardinale, Sam. "Guilty Plea Set Today by Smith of SH Oil," *Ledger* (Lakeland, FL), March 2, 1989, 1A, 12A.

_____. "Fate of Smith's $15 Million Worth of Assets Still Unclear," *Ledger* (Lakeland, FL), March 3, 1989, 13A.

_____. "Stephen Smith Pleads Guilty to 98 Charges in SH Oil Scam," *Ledger* (Lakeland, FL), March 3, 1989, 1A.

_____. "SH Oil's Smith to Be Sentenced for State Charges," *Ledger* (Lakeland, FL), May 30, 1989, 1B.

_____. "Smith Faces State Sentence," *Ledger* (Lakeland, FL), May 30, 1989, 1W, 10W.

_____. "SH Oil's Smith Gets Unusual Probation," *Ledger* (Lakeland, FL), June 1, 1989, 1A, 14A.

_____. "Smith Admits SH Oil Not on the Up and Up," *Ledger* (Lakeland, FL), June 3, 1989, 1A, 8A.

_____. "Barnett Countersues 16 SH Oil Investors," *Ledger* (Lakeland, FL), June 6, 1989, 2B.

_____. "Smith Begins His Prison Term Today," *Ledger* (Lakeland, FL), June 7, 1989, 1B, 2B.

_____. "SH Oil Investors to Pay $120,000," *Ledger* (Lakeland, FL), March 21, 1990, 1W, 6W.

_____. Gavel Comes Down," *Ledger* (Lakeland, FL), March 25, 1990, 1W, 10W.

_____. "SH Oil Auction a Hit in Haven," *Ledger* (Lakeland, FL), March 25, 1990, 1B, 2B.

_____. "Claims against Smith's Wife Dropped," *Ledger* (Lakeland, FL), June 6, 1990, 1W, 2W.

_____. "Barnett, Investors' Suit Ends," *Ledger* (Lakeland, FL), December 22, 1990, 1A, 12A.

_____. "Bank Accuses Law Firm of Unethical Conduct," *Ledger* (Lakeland, FL), January 28, 1991, 1B, 3B.

_____. "SH Oil Investor Refunds Are OK'd," *Ledger* (Lakeland, FL), May 18, 1993, 1B, 3B.

_____. "SH Oil Conman Asks for Another $500,000," *Ledger* (Lakeland, FL), January 29, 1995, 1A, 13A.

_____. "Ex-SH Oil Exec Faces New Charges," *Ledger* (Lakeland, FL), October 2, 1999, B1, B4.

Cardinale, Sam, and Suzie Schottlekotte. "SH Oil's Smith Set to Leave Prison Today," *Ledger* (Lakeland, FL), May 4, 1993, 1A, 5A.

Chambliss, John, Jr. "Conman Smith Surrenders in Escambia County," *Ledger* (Lakeland, FL), December 5, 2000, B1.

Cuthbertson, Cathy. "Millions Feared Lost in Alleged Swindle," *Winter Haven News Chief*, December 31, 1987, 1A, 5A.

_____. "State Investigates Oil Scheme," *Winter Haven News Chief*, January 1, 1988, 1A, 5A.

_____. "SH Oil Money Traced to Europe," *Winter Haven News Chief*, January 5, 1988, 1A, 7A.

_____. "Smith Vows 'Dollar-for-Dollar' Repayment," *Winter Haven News Chief*, February 10, 1988, 1A, 6A.

_____. "Court Battles Brewing over SH Oil Operation," *Winter Haven News Chief*, March 9, 1988, 1A, 8A.

Cuthbertson, Cathy, and William Bygrave. "Reaction to Fraud Allegation Ranges from Shock to Disbelief," *Winter Haven News Chief*, January 1, 1988, 1B.

Cuthbertson, Cathy, and Larry Keough. "Smith's Wife Implicated in 'Scheme,'" *Winter Haven News Chief*, February 5, 1988, 1A, 7A.

Cuthbertson, Cathy, and Art Sills. "SH Oil Probe Takes Officials to Texas, New Mexico," *Winter Haven News Chief*, January 6, 1988, 1A, 4A.

_____. "Judge Orders Banks to Turn Over SH Accounts," *Winter Haven News Chief*, January 7, 1988, 1A, 7A.

_____. "Smith's Death Threats Taken Seriously," *Winter Haven News Chief*, January 15, 1988, 1A, 5A.

_____. "Loan Officers Cleared in Smith Case," *Winter Haven News Chief*, January 19, 1988, 1A, 7A.

_____. "Smith Assets $100 Million Short of Liabilities—Report," *Winter Haven News Chief*, January 20, 1988, 1A, 5A.

_____. "$2.1 Million of Smith's Account 'Uncollectable,'" *Winter Haven News Chief*, February 2, 1988, 1A, 8A.

_____. "Officials Issue Warrant for Smith's Arrest," *Winter Haven News Chief*, February 3, 1988, A1.

_____. "Smith's 'Surrender' Awaited Today," *Winter Haven News Chief*, February 4, 1988, 1A, 8A.

_____. "Attorney: Smith Will Attend Hearing," *Winter Haven News Chief*, February 8, 1988, 1A, 8A.

_____. "Smith Attorneys to Demand Jury Trial, *Winter Haven News Chief*, February 27, 1988, 1A, 7A.

_____. "Barnett 'Aided' SH Oil 'Scheme,'" *Winter Haven News Chief*, March 8, 1988, 1A, 10A.

_____. "More SH Oil Investors Providing Information," *Winter Haven News Chief*, March 12, 1988, 1A, 4A.

_____. "State Gets Delay in Smith Case," *Winter Haven News Chief*, March 14, 1988, 1A, 7A.

Davis, John, Jr. "Prisoner!" *Winter Haven News Chief* (September 9, 2002), http://polkonline.com/stories/090900/loc_sentencing.shtml (accessed October 21, 2005).

Kohn, Keith W. "Swindler's Victims Try Their Best to Move On." *Naples Daily News* (March 14, 2004), http://www.naplesdailynews.com/npdn/cda/article_print/0,1983,NPDN_14910_27278 (accessed October 21, 2005).

Leach, Kimberly. "Fellow Classmates Recall Smith during High School," *Winter Haven News Chief,* January 1, 1988, A1, A5.

Ledger (Lakeland, FL). "Chronology of SH Oil Civil Complaint," December 22, 1990, 12A.

Loftus, Mary J. "Is Heather Smith Another Victim of SH Oil?" *Ledger* (Lakeland, FL), December 30, 1991, 1A, 5A.

Oldt, Thomas Roe. "Uncle Sam, Lawyers Stand to Gain with SH Oil Assets, Attorney Says," *Ledger* (Lakeland, FL), March 2, 1989, 3W.

Sills, Art. "Extravagant Life of Smith Is Detailed," *Winter Haven News Chief,* January 20, 1988, A1.

_____. "Smith Declares Bankruptcy," *Winter Haven News Chief,* February 25, 1989, 1A, 9A.

_____. "Smith Trial to Begin Thursday," *Winter Haven News Chief,* March 1, 1989, 1A, 7A.

_____. "Smith Pleads Guilty to 98 Felony Counts," *Winter Haven News Chief,* March 2, 1989, 1A, 7A.

_____. "Smith Adds Guilty Pleas to Federal Fraud Charges," *Winter Haven News Chief,* March 3, 1989, 1A, 7A.

_____. "Smith Assets up for Grab," *Winter Haven News Chief,* March 18, 1989, 1A, 9A.

_____. "Feds to Quiz Smith on Assets," *Winter Haven News Chief,* June 1, 1989, 1A, 7A.

_____. "Smith Reveals Former Plan to Close Firm," *Winter Haven News Chief,* June 3, 1989, 1A, 7A.

_____. "Attorney Asks State to Drop Case against Stephen Smith's Wife," *Winter Haven News Chief,* May 5, 1990, 1A, 7A.

_____. "SH Oil 'Mystery Man' Targeted," *Winter Haven News Chief,* May 7, 1991, 1A, 3A.

_____. "SH Oil Creditors Face Shallow Money Pool," *Winter Haven News Chief,* June 30, 1991, 1A, 5A.

_____. "Smith to Be Quizzed Again," *Winter Haven News Chief,* July 11, 1991, 1A, 7A.

_____. "Smith May Reveal $4 Billion Secret," *Winter Haven News Chief,* 299, July 25, 1991, 1A, 5A.

_____. "SH Oil 'Winners' Focus of Hearings," *Winter Haven News Chief,* August 25, 1991, 1A, 8A.

_____. "Prof Concludes People Invested in SH Oil Co. to Make Money," *Winter Haven News Chief,* September 6, 1991, 1A.

_____. "Winners to Share in SH Oil Leftovers," *Winter Haven News Chief,* September 6, 1991, 1A, 8A.

_____. "Legal Action May Put Smith on the Road to Washington," *Winter Haven News Chief,* September 13, 1991, 1A, 5A.

_____. "Consultant Describes SH Oil's Mideast Ties," *Winter Haven News Chief,* September 15, 1991, 1A, 9A.

_____. "Rise and Ruin: The SH Oil Story," *Winter Haven News Chief,* Special Report, Week of October 12, 1991, 1-3, 7-8.

_____. "Bankruptcy Court to Go after Local Doctor's SH Oil 'Winnings,'" *Winter Haven News Chief,* October 16, 1991, 1A, 7A.

_____. "Businessman: Smith Had Links to CIA," *Winter Haven News Chief,* December 31, 1991, 1A, 5A.

_____. "Trustee: Haven Businessman Knew SH Oil Was Fraudulent," *Winter Haven News Chief,* January 8, 1992, 1A.

_____. "Ex-Federal Agent to Unravel European Deal in Smith Scam," *Winter Haven News Chief,* March 13, 1992, 1B-2B.

_____. "Judge Approves $95,000 Deal with W. H. Doctor in SH Oil Case," *Winter Haven News Chief,* June 20, 1992, 1A, 6A.

_____. "Mediator Seeks to End Battle over SH Oil," *Winter Haven News Chief,* June 25, 1992, 1A, 5A.

_____. "Trial to Examine Smith's Alleged Payoff to Sheik," *Winter Haven News Chief,* July 23, 1992, 1A.

_____. "FBI, IRS Seize Documents of Smith Partner," *Winter Haven News Chief,* August 14, 1992, 1A, 5A.

_____. "Stephen Smith's Troubles 'May Be Long Way from Over,'" *Winter Haven News Chief,* May 5, 1993, 1B.

Winter Haven News Chief. "McBride Presents Summary of SH Oil Report," February 27, 1988, 2B.

_____. "More Banks Probed for Smith Assets," February 27, 1988, 1B.

_____. "SH Oil Profits," March 24, 1988, 1A, 7A.

_____. "Summary of Receiver's Report on SH Oil Investigation," January 20, 1988, 2B.

_____. "'We're All Working Together' on SH Case," January 9, 1988, B1.

_____. "Investigation of Smith, SH Oil," March 1, 1989, 7A.

_____. "SH Oil's Smith Leaving Prison," May 4, 1993, 1A.

_____. "Smith's Release Challenged" (November 16, 2000), http://www.polkon-line.com/cgi-bin/printme.pl (accessed October 22, 2005).

Ward, John. "SH Oil Investors Are Both Winners and Losers, Attorneys Say Thursday," *Winter Haven News Chief,* April 26, 1991, 4A.

Wikipedia. "Bank of Credit and Commerce International," http://en.wikipedia.org/wiki/Bank_of_Credit_and_Commerce_International (accessed June 24, 2006).

The Spanish Cooking Oil Scandal: Toxic Oil Syndrome or Cover-Up?

16

JAMES P. JOHNSON

Contents

In the summer of 1981, a sudden outbreak of flu-like symptoms, nausea, and vomiting in the working-class suburbs and dormitory towns around Madrid, Spain, left almost 400 people dead and 20,000 suffering from the lasting effects of what appeared to be toxic poisoning. It began on May 1 with 8-year-old Jaime Vaquero Garcia; when his condition suddenly deteriorated and he had severe difficulties in breathing, his mother rushed him to the La Paz Children's Hospital in Madrid, but, on the way there, he died in her arms. When the doctors learned that Jaime's five siblings had similar symptoms, they had them all brought into the hospital. One of the girls was immediately put into intensive care, while the other four were transferred to Hospital del Rey, Madrid's prestigious clinic for infectious diseases. There, the doctors treated them with antibiotics for "atypical pneumonia" (Woffinden 2001).

The following day, the director of the clinic, Dr. Antonio Muró Fernández Cavada, rejected the initial diagnosis of pneumonia; it was almost unheard of for six members of the same family to contract pneumonia simultaneously. Although the initial symptoms were similar to the flu and patients soon developed fluid buildup in the lungs, which was typical of pneumonia, it was followed by a skin rash and muscle pains, which were not usually associated with pneumonia. In the following days, more patients were hospitalized with the same baffling symptoms. Muró noted that the patients were coming in from the sprawling housing projects in the towns and villages around Madrid; none of them came from the city itself. The localization of the outbreak suggested that the cause might have been in the food chain, so Muró quizzed the relatives of the victims about what they had eaten recently. Almost immediately, the evidence appeared to indicate a commonality: All the patients had eaten salad—typically, lettuce/tomato/cucumber, dressed with olive oil (Woffinden 2001).

By now, the country had been alerted to the mysterious outbreak around Madrid. Some patients started to experience limb deformity, especially of the fingers and hands, as well as muscle weakness and hair loss. The outbreak had become headline news in the newspapers as well as on the radio and TV. There were demands for the government to take action, but government officials, too, were as much in the dark as the doctors and nurses who were trying to treat the symptoms. On May 12, Muró invited officials of the Health Ministry to his clinic, where he showed them maps of the local area indicating where the patients lived. He concluded that there was contamination somewhere in the food supply chain. Most local residents shopped in weekly street markets (*mercadillos*) that set up in a different location each day. Based on his research and careful mapping, Muró predicted where the next outbreak would occur: he was correct but, instead of being praised for his foresight, he was relieved of his duties as director of the clinic. Although no reason for this was made public, it is possible that government officials thought that Muró was too outspoken and that his pronouncements might cause public unrest.

At that time, Spain was just emerging from almost four decades of a totalitarian regime under General Francisco Franco, who had died in 1975. Franco had seized power after leading his forces to victory in the civil war that ravaged Spain from 1936 to 1939 and, with the support of the army and the police, he ruled with an iron fist. Opposition political parties and non-government trade unions were banned, the media were strictly censored, and dissent was dealt with harshly. At his death, Franco bequeathed a fascist-style, statist economy in which the government played a major role. Many important industries, such as transportation, telephones, oil, tobacco, and radio and TV, were government-owned monopolies. The government also controlled the price of staple goods such as gasoline, electricity, sugar, and bread, and tightly regulated the banking industry. The global oil crises of 1973 and 1979 hit the Spanish economy particularly hard since the country imported most of its oil from the Middle East. Apart from the booming tourist industry and agricultural exports, international trade was limited and the unemployment rate was high. Spain had hopes of joining the European Economic Community (EEC) and, by 1980, the EEC was the major export market for Spanish agricultural produce. Spanish farms were generally smaller and less efficient than those in the EEC, but efforts were taking place to consolidate small holdings and to introduce more intensive farming methods, such as drip irrigation and the widespread use of pesticides, in order to improve crop yields.

Upon Franco's death, the Spanish monarchy was restored and King Juan Carlos quickly appointed a centrist, Adolfo Suárez, as prime minister. Political parties were re-established, and democratic elections were held in 1977. However, during this period of transition to democracy, the government's focus was more on political reforms, including developing a new constitution, than on fixing the economy. In 1980, Catalonia in northeast Spain and the Basque country in the north were granted a measure of autonomy, following local referendums. To many of Franco's followers, it appeared that the government was intent on handing the country over to communists and socialists. In January 1981, Prime Minister Suárez resigned; several weeks later, just three months before the outbreak in Madrid, an attempted coup d'état aimed at restoring military rule was suppressed after King Juan Carlos personally intervened to express his support for the democratic reforms. Nevertheless, there were still rumors of unrest among senior military officers. A prolonged public health crisis might bring people onto the streets and provoke a right-wing backlash, so there was strong pressure for government ministers to be seen to be in control of the situation.

Whatever the reason for his dismissal, Muró now had the time to conduct his own investigation. In doing so, he stood on the shoulders of giants. In 1854, Dr. John Snow had founded the science of epidemiology in England when he observed the link between patients who had contracted cholera and the pump from which they drew water in London's Soho district. Previously, scientists had believed that cholera was contracted and spread through miasma—atmospheric vapors (LeFanu 1999). Snow identified the epicenter of the cholera outbreak as a water pump on Broad Street and was able to persuade the authorities to remove the pump handle in order to make it inoperable. Over the next several days, the number of new cases of cholera plummeted. Thus, following Snow's example, Muró went around the mercadillos in the suburbs, where he noticed large containers of cooking oil being sold cheaply. He gathered samples of cooking oil from the homes of patients, sent them off to the government research laboratory for analysis, and awaited the results.

Coincidentally, the very same day that Muró was relieved of his duties, the head of the endocrinology department at Madrid's La Paz hospital, Dr. Angel Peralta, claimed that the best explanation for the symptoms was "poisoning by organophosphates." Organophosphates are pesticides that affect the functioning of the central nervous system. They are the most commonly used pesticides since they can be used on a wide range of crops as well as on lawns and around buildings (U.S. Environmental Protection Agency 2006). The following day, Peralta was contacted by an official from the Ministry of Public Health and told not to say anything about the epidemic and not to mention organophosphorous poisoning.

Government officials were at a loss as to what to do. The outbreak reached epidemic proportions by late May (see fig. 16.1) with several hundred new cases per day being reported, but still no one knew what the cause was. The people were demanding answers and action. There was a fear that the government could fall.

New Cases of Epidemic Illness
x Axis Interval = 3 days

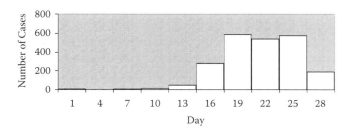

Fig. 16.1 New cases of epidemic illness in Madrid, 1981. (From Philan, R. and R. Dicker, *Case Studies in Applied Epidemiology*, No. 002-800. Atlanta, GA: Centers for Disease Control and Prevention, 2002.)

Then there was a sudden ray of hope: A doctor treating affected children discovered that they had all consumed cooking oil shortly before falling ill. The government seized on this news and issued an official announcement on June 10 stating that the epidemic was caused by contaminated cooking oil. Sales of cooking oil slumped. On June 30, officials announced that people could exchange suspect cooking oil for pure olive oil at government expense.

Meanwhile, Muró had received the results of the laboratory tests conducted on the cheap oil from the mercadillos; although none of the samples was the pure olive oil that the customer thought she was buying, there was such a range of oils in the samples that it was highly unlikely that contaminated oil was the source of the toxicity. Nevertheless, the official explanation seemed to be persuasive. The government hastily convened a board of inquiry, which concluded that the cause of the poisoning was industrial rapeseed oil that had been imported into Spain and illegally repackaged for sale as cooking oil. Rapeseed is a member of the Brassica family and is related to cabbage, broccoli, and cauliflower. The Brassica family of crops has been cultivated for thousands of years, and it is likely that the production of rapeseed oil began in Europe in the Middle Ages (Raymer 2002).

In order to protect its domestic olive oil industry, Spain allowed the import of substitute products such as rapeseed oil only if they were first denatured with aniline, a chemical compound that makes oil inedible. The government report concluded, therefore, that unscrupulous merchants had imported industrial rapeseed oil and failed to remove the aniline. Epidemiological studies appeared to support this conclusion and 13 oil merchants were subsequently convicted and sentenced to long terms in prison, although they were cleared of charges of murder. In 1983, the epidemic was officially blamed on "toxic oil syndrome" (TOS) and, over the next 20 years, funding became available from governmental and supragovernmental sources (such as the World Health Organization) for dozens of scientific studies on the physical and psychological effects of TOS on its victims (Gelpi et al. 2002).

Even today, victims who survived the outbreak live diminished lives; many suffer from chronic depression and from other physical and psychological disabilities that limit their daily activities and social roles. Yet after 25 years, the precise etiologic agent in TOS still has not been identified. Attempts to reproduce the condition in laboratory animals have been unsuccessful, and no condition similar to TOS has been reported in the scientific literature (Gelpi et al. 2002). Furthermore, a re-examination of the events that occurred in the summer of 1981 (Woffinden 2001) revealed anomalies and inconsistencies in the original reports, suggesting that the authorities either overlooked or ignored scientific evidence that did not support the TOS theory and suppressed evidence indicating that the true cause of the outbreak was not adulterated cooking oil imported from abroad. Spanish researchers who conducted postepidemic studies in the 1980s interviewed food distributors and retailers and thousands of victims' families and discovered that many of the victims had not consumed cooking oil at all, but had eaten tomatoes that originated in the same farming region of southeast Spain. They concluded that the poisoning was caused by organophosphate pesticide used on produce grown in Spain. Furthermore, in a review of toxicological databases, Hard (2000) found that the symptoms of TOS are not wholly consistent with the adverse toxic effects produced by more than 70 chemical entities and mixtures associated with mineral oils. In contrast, however, the symptoms of organophosphate poisoning are identical to the symptoms presented by the victims in Spain (Furtado and Chan 2001).

It is unlikely that the Spanish government will reconvene a committee of inquiry into the TOS incident and we may never know the real cause of the toxic poisoning. Nevertheless, subsequent investigators have raised important questions that have been left unanswered. Facing a public health crisis, what is the first duty of government leaders? Is it to prevent panic, to protect the public, or to seek the truth? Does the answer depend on whether the government is democratic or totalitarian? Did the Spanish government exhibit a failure of leadership by trying to silence Dr. Muró and Dr. Peralta? Did the two doctors behave ethically? Should they have been more outspoken? Given the precarious state of Spain's democracy; its rapidly increasing agricultural exports to the European Community (later the European Union), which it desired to join; and the urgent need to restore public calm, did the Spanish authorities make a scapegoat of mineral oil importers in order not to damage the nation's burgeoning agricultural interests?

References

Furtado, Marina C., and Lisa Chan. "Toxicity, Organophosphate," *Emergency Medicine,* http://www.emedicine.com/med/topic1677.htm, 2001.

Gelpi, Emilio, Manuel Posada de la Paz, Bendetto Terracini, Ignacio Abaitua, Agustín Gómez de la Camara, Edwin M. Kilbourne, Carlos Lahoz, et al. "The Spanish Toxic Oil Syndrome 20 Years after Its Onset: A Multidisciplinary Review of Scientific Knowledge," *Environmental Health Perspectives,* 110(5) (2002): 457–464.

Hard, Gordon C. "Short-Term Adverse Effects in Humans of Ingested Mineral Oils, Their Additives and Possible Contaminants—A Review," *Human Experimental Toxicolgy,* 19(3) (2000):158–172.

LeFanu, James. *The Rise and Fall of Modern Medicine.* London: Little Brown, 1999.

Philan, Rossanne, and Richard Dicker. "TOS (Toxic Oil Syndrome): An Epidemic of Mass Proportions in Spain, 1981," *Case Studies in Applied Epidemiology,* No. 002-800. Atlanta, GA: Centers for Disease Control and Prevention, 2002.

Raymer, Paul L. "Canola: An Emerging Oilseed Crop." In *Trends in New Crops and New Uses,* ed. J. Janick and A. Whipkey, 122–126. Alexandria, VA.: ASHS Press, 2002.

U.S. Environmental Protection Agency. *Organophosphate Pesticides in Food.* Washington, D.C.: U.S. Environmental Protection Agency, 2006, http:// www.epa. gov/pesticides/op/primer.htm.

Woffinden, Bob. "Cover Up," *Guardian,* August 21, 2001, magazine sec., http://www. guardian.co.uk/print/0,3858,4244093-103425,00.html.

Bibliography

Martin-Arribas, María Concepción. "Quality of Life, Disability and Handicap in Patients with Toxic Oil Syndrome," *Journal of Advanced Nursing,* 50(6) (2005): 595–604.

Fraud in the Corporate World V

Leaders are supposed to set a vision for an organization, then encourage and enable others to achieve the vision. Unfortunately, there is no guarantee that the leader's vision will be appropriate or that managers will respond appropriately even if the vision is for a valid purpose. These issues of strategy, measurement, and control are at the heart of the modern corporation.

The 1990s was a decade when many of these principles of organizational management were tested. While corporate fraud had occurred in the past, the excesses of the 90s seemed to indicate that corporate greed knew no bounds. Corporate executives around the world took advantage of their positions by leading their organizations in directions that were socially questionable, by trying to grow the organizations too rapidly, or by siphoning corporate resources for personal use.

This section contains stories of recent cases of business failures caused by greed, corruption, or fraud. Many Americans are familiar with failures such as those occurring at Adelphia Communications (chapter 17) or Enron—one of the more famous examples of corporate fraud in U.S. history (chapter 18). The owners of Adelphia Communications diverted corporate resources for their own use, blurring the distinction between what is good for the corporation and what is good for the individual.

But similar failures occurred in other countries. An Italian firm, Parmalat, is an example of fraudulent financial reporting (chapter 19). Royal Ahold, a Netherlands company, is an example of an organization that depended on growth, accompanied by higher levels of debt, if success was to continue (chapter 20). Chapter 21 discusses Vivendi, which became one of the world's entertainment conglomerates, with subsidiaries in Europe and the United States. When the company was unable to sustain success, managers manipulated accounting records to create fictitious results.

Adelphia Communications: The Public Company That Became a Private Piggy Bank: A Case of Fraud in the Rigas Family Firm

17

ROLAND E. KIDWELL

Contents

Introduction

John Rigas's rags-to-riches-to-rags story began more than 50 years ago when he invested in his first cable endeavor in a small town in Pennsylvania. Several years earlier, his immigrant family had started a hot dog restaurant in Wellsville, New York, and, at age nine, John developed his first business skills there, cleaning tables. After service in the U.S. Army, which opened the doors to college through the G.I. Bill, Rigas graduated from Rensselaer Polytechnic Institute and came back to Wellsville to work in the family restaurant.

A few months following his return from college, he scraped together several thousand dollars from his friends and bought a movie theater in nearby Coudersport, Pennsylvania, where he sold tickets and served as an usher. Said Rigas, "Initially, I could have made more money, gone into engineering the corporate way. But I decided to take a risk in the business world…I tell you, sometimes people have to make a career choice rather than a financial one" (Sullivan 1998, M6). Within a year, he had diversified into the cable television business, purchasing his first cable franchise for $100. Cable ventures at the time focused on bringing the relatively new phenomenon of television to mountainous areas and remote places where it was not possible to get a good signal over the air. John and his younger brother, Gus, founded their company with $300 from an overdrawn bank account and saw it take off from there.

The business expanded steadily, as did the Rigas family. John married Doris Nielsen in 1953, and the next year their eldest child, Michael, was born. Over the next six years, Timothy, James, and Ellen would follow. Eventually, the three sons would join John in the family business, as had Gus. Gus started Wellsville's cable system, and the brothers worked many long hours constructing cable operations in several other small Pennsylvania towns.

For John and Gus, development of the cable franchises was difficult physically, in terms of long hours worked, and financially, as local partners came and went. At one point, a partner went bust during the building of the Rigases' third cable network in Punxsutawney, Pennsylvania (home of Phil, the famous groundhog). As the authorities prepared to foreclose, Rigas said he believed he was at the end of his business adventures in cable because all of his holdings served to back the company's loan. But an employee provided the company with $50,000 of her own savings, which helped bring the business back from the brink.

Rigas's daughter Ellen told a Buffalo newspaper columnist that as a child she could tell that her father was in an industry with much risk and uncertainty: "It was scary. They [John and Gus] were Main Street guys trying to make a decent living and put meals on the table. He may not have known what it would come to. But I think this is what makes a great entrepreneur. Even if they don't know exactly what they're creating, they know they're on to something far more than what they imagined."

Family Business to Industry Giant

By 1972, the company provided service to more than 6,000 cable subscribers and was incorporated as Adelphia, from *adelphos,* the Greek word for brother. Ten years later, John Rigas bought his brother Gus's share of the business. In the mid-1980s, Adelphia was ready to go public although the family took steps to maintain control of the corporation's activities. Eventually, investors would own the majority of Adelphia's regular shares, but special "supervoting" stock was designed to allow the Rigas family to retain more than 80 percent of voting control (Williams, May 2, 1999). As Adelphia grew, the three Rigas sons joined their father in running the company, and they provided important assistance and support as the organization increased in size through expansion and acquisition of other cable companies across the nation.

What one industry publication described as a "shy, cable industry loner" became, in the late 1990s, an $8-billion concern with a stock share price that topped $86 at its peak (Colman 1999). By then, Adelphia boasted 500,000 cable customers in Western New York and had large numbers of customers in Florida and New England as well as its traditional base in Western Pennsylvania and New York. Through the 1990s, Adelphia incurred large amounts of debt as it aggressively acquired companies and built an empire that stretched from coast to coast.

The driving force in the growth of Adelphia seemed to be its second generation of ownership. Timothy Rigas, the middle son and an economics graduate of the Wharton School at the University of Pennsylvania, served as the company's chief financial officer. Michael Rigas, two years older than Tim and a graduate of both Harvard University and Harvard Law School, became executive vice president for operations. James, two years younger than Tim, graduated from Harvard, obtained a law degree and a master's in economics from Stanford University, and took on the role of vice president for strategic planning. All four of the Rigases served on the company's board of directors; John Rigas was the chairman of the 11-member board and Tim Rigas acted as head of the board's audit committee from 1992 to 2001. Nonfamily board members who became key players at Adelphia included Rensselaer graduate James Brown, who joined the company after graduating from college and rose to be its vice president of finance, and Michael C. Mulcahey, who became Adelphia's director of internal reporting and assistant treasurer.

In early 1999, Adelphia announced the purchases of FrontierVision Partners, Century Communications Inc., and Harron, quickly doubling the size of the company and expanding its operations into Philadelphia and Los Angeles. The company was now operating in 31 states and serving five million customers. "Yes, there are extreme risks," Rigas said during a speech celebrating a corporate leadership award bestowed on him by a Western New York university. "But we feel that the opportunities of video on demand, high-definition television, and high-speed [Internet access]...are exciting" (Williams, March 9, 1999, E3).

The acquisitions of other companies led to the need for Adelphia to issue additional shares to finance the rapid growth. John Rigas became concerned, noting at board meetings that family ownership would be diluted as more company shares were issued. Son Tim offered a strategy to deal with the problem: The family could buy more shares to maintain its level of ownership. However, unbeknownst to many of the board members and the shareholders, the Rigases set up a line of credit to borrow funds from Adelphia to buy the stock that allowed the family to retain its significant ownership share.

The nonfamily board members also seemed to be unaware that the Rigases were diverting Adelphia funds to build a multimillion dollar golf course near Coudersport or to buy timber rights for themselves. The family used Adelphia money for the purchase of private automobiles, to hire a personal trainer, to pay church dues, and to operate businesses that were solely owned by family partnerships. John Rigas was a particularly big spender, and at one point was put on a $1 million a month allowance by his son Tim.

Strong family connections within the business led none of the Rigas management team or their close associates to raise questions about these practices. Assistant treasurer Mulcahey later defended the family's billing of Adelphia for golf course investments and personal club memberships; it was a routine part of doing business. "The longer I worked there, the more I understood the importance of developing business relationships," Mulcahey said. These activities and purchases were "very important in maintaining and developing good relations with our vendors, lenders, and investment bankers....It wasn't uncommon for Adelphia to make investments in various things that weren't related to the cable business" (Zremski 2004, B1).

As Adelphia grew and its elderly founder faced health problems that involved visits to the Mayo Clinic, industry analysts fretted about succession issues in the publicly traded, family-run company. Illustrating the strong bonds that existed at Adelphia, the Rigas sons and their father viewed guidance of the operation as a family team effort with no one sibling designated heir apparent. Rigas told *Broadcasting & Cable* magazine, "Over the past few years, when I talk to investors or employees, I tell them that one of the strengths of Adelphia—and it's a big strength—is the passing of leadership from one generation to the second generation, which has in fact occurred. Now it's more of a partnership. Sometimes people ask me which son would take over. I would never want to make that decision" (Colman 1999, 24).

Stock analysts were not satisfied that the family connections were as strong as John Rigas stated and believed the leadership succession issue might ignite a family feud if it were not resolved. "This is like the Mafia—one of the sons has to rise," an analyst told *Broadcasting & Cable*. Family business experts agreed. "For a company like this, there is no other issue," said Leon Danco of the Center for Family Business in Cleveland. "You have the seeds for disaster at the time of the incumbent founder's disappearance from the scene." Stock analysts also did not like the fact that the new corporate giant did not relocate to a cosmopolitan city. Adelphia maintained its headquarters in tiny Coudersport, the site of John's first new venture and a place where the Rigases were viewed as key community supporters and philanthropists.

Community Leadership and Corporate Jets

In Adelphia's heyday, Coudersport was a two-stoplight town of about 3,000 in a rural Pennsylvania valley about 110 miles from Buffalo, New York. The hometown folks viewed the Rigas family as model corporate citizens whose philanthropic activities and contributions to needy individuals in the community were unparalleled. A cleaning lady at the company told *Wall Street Journal* reporter Robert Frank that Rigas had paid for her dying daughter to fly to Denver to see a faith healer. Coudersport local Shirlee Leete shared a story of how Rigas flew her son-in-law, an Adelphia employee, in the company jet to Cleveland for cancer treatment.

Corporate jets were employed for less noble purposes. Rigas, who had used Adelphia's undisclosed financial backing to take majority ownership control of the Buffalo Sabres hockey team in the late 1990s, frequently flew on a company plane from his Coudersport home to Buffalo so that he could watch the team play. The flights saved Rigas ten minutes a trip compared with driving, but they cost the company $1,400–$2,600 per hour. The company's three airplanes were also used by the family for excursions to Greece, to an African safari, and to furniture shows in North Carolina. Company funds totaling about $6,000 were spent to jet two Christmas trees to John's daughter in New York City, and more costs were incurred by Timothy Rigas, who used a corporate plane to ferry actress Peta Wilson (star of TV's *La Femme Nikita*) back from the Caribbean for a hockey game appearance and on multiple trips to Los Angeles and Jamaica. The trips may have been part of Adelphia's then-CFO's efforts to woo the Australian beauty, but she later described her relationship with Tim as "just friends" (Hays 2004; Gearty 2004).

In Coudersport, Adelphia and the Rigases not only contributed philanthropically to the community but the company also employed as many as 700 people at the corporate headquarters. The $30 million headquarters building, completed in early 2002, was located not far from the movie theatre where John Rigas began his business career. Just outside the town was the Rigas family estate, Wending Creek Farms. Despite stock analysts' pressure for the company to relocate its headquarters to a big city, the Rigases resisted. "As long as the Rigas family is involved with it, I think they'll stay here," Coudersport pharmacy owner Richard Buchanan had told the *Buffalo News* in 1999. "It's a real family business."

Western New York, anchored by the city of Buffalo, also received a large economic boost from Adelphia's presence. In addition to employing hundreds of workers in the region, the company was moving toward the construction of a 15-story, $125-million operations center as the signature building on the Buffalo Inner Harbor waterfront, which would bring another 1,000 high-paying jobs to the city. In exchange, state and city officials planned to offer the company tax breaks to make the project a reality. Rigas was also recognized as an important figure on the Western New York sports scene through his ownership of the Sabres. Rigas gained majority control of the hockey team a few years after Adelphia established the Empire Sports Network, a cable channel that offered a variety of events, including televising Sabres games.

Accompanying the corporate growth were kudos from the Buffalo community. In 1998, John Rigas was lauded by newspaper columnist Jerry Sullivan as the most popular person in Buffalo due to Rigas's civic work, his efforts in taking over the ailing Sabres hockey team, and Adelphia's role in strengthening the regional economy. In 2001, Rigas was identified as Western New York's most powerful and effective businessman in a survey of local leaders by the *Buffalo News*. The following year, Rigas was described as a "white-haired corporate knight who, with his ivy league-educated sons, promised to help pull Buffalo into the 21st century" (Williams 2002, B6).

In March 2002, Adelphia intended to hire 1,250 more workers in Buffalo to support its digital cable and high-speed Internet operations. The company planned to lease 50,000 square feet of temporary space, as its employees could no longer fit in Adelphia's complex near Lake Erie. Even as the company's financial challenges increased due to its acquisition binge, Buffalo economic development officials counted on Adelphia's operations there to continue to support 5.8 million cable customers. The hiring pace had been increasing when some bad news emerged.

Public Humiliation, Quick Family Exit

The purchase of three large cable systems in 1999—at a cost of $3,000 per new subscriber—ran Adelphia's debt obligations to $10 billion as industry journals and newspaper accounts documented its growth to become the fifth largest cable company in the country based on number of subscribers. Three years later, the debt had surpassed $12 billion, and rumors flew that the high level of borrowing and other factors would make Adelphia a prime takeover target in a merger–acquisition consolidation of the cable industry. Expansion had forced the company to look for new sources of revenue such as business telephone service and high-speed modems to service the debt. Adelphia's marketing campaign identified the company as "your link for everything" as it expanded into fast Internet service in residential markets and into the business telephone market through a subsidiary.

On March 27, 2002, CFO Tim Rigas conducted a conference call with Wall Street analysts to discuss the company's 2001 results. That day, several important revelations came to light: Adelphia had lost more money in the fourth quarter of 2001 than had been stated previously, and Adelphia Business Solutions, the company's telephone spin-off that was $500 million in debt, had filed for Chapter 11 bankruptcy protection. But the most interesting element of the conference call was the offhand disclosure that over the years Adelphia had cosigned $2.3 billion in loans for Rigas family members. The money had been used by partnerships that were controlled and run outside the corporation by the Rigases, and the loans did not appear on Adelphia's financial statements, according to newspaper accounts.

The disclosure occurred at a time when scandal after corporate scandal had been rocking the country; thus, reaction was swift and severe: Adelphia's stock price dropped sharply and federal securities regulators and law enforcement officials moved to begin civil and criminal investigations. "In the post-Enron world, they couldn't have picked a worse time to have such disclosures surface," Thomas Morabito, a telecommunications industry analyst, told a reporter.

Stockholders were not the only potential victims. Adelphia had thousands of employees, some of them new to the organization. A few days after the news surfaced, one employee told the *Buffalo News* that she had quit her job to become a tech support worker at Adelphia. "I thought it would be a better step, but now I don't know." The Buffalo-area woman gave up a $10/hour accounting job for the Adelphia position and had taken months of evening classes to qualify.

Adelphia stock had been slowly declining from its 1990s all-time high as the company incurred more debt and as the financial markets generally dropped from 2000 to 2002. The stock unraveled from $20.39 per share the day before the March conference call to 79 cents per share by the time it was removed from trading in June. The Department of Justice began a criminal investigation, the Securities and Exchange Commission started a civil inquiry, and in June the company declared its plans to reorganize in Chapter 11 bankruptcy proceedings. A new management group removed the Rigas-appointed board of directors and moved the headquarters from Coudersport to a town near Denver.

By then, John Rigas and his three sons had been forced to leave their family business. On May 15, 2002, John resigned as chairman, president, and CEO. He was replaced by an interim CEO, and the NASDAQ stock market ceased trading Adelphia stock. The next day, Adelphia announced Tim Rigas's resignation as CFO. This move was followed by the disclosure that the company missed $44.7 million in interest payments on its bonds and that federal grand juries were now investigating Adelphia's finances. The following week, on May 23, the Rigas family gave up control of the company when the patriarch and his three sons resigned as directors. As they left the company, the family agreed to turn over $567 million in future cash flow from other Rigas-owned cable ventures and to pledge all stock owned by the family as collateral. At this point, the family-accumulated debt owed by Adelphia topped $3.1 billion. As Adelphia attempted to deal with the financial shambles, the Rigas family awaited the outcome of the investigations, which seemed certain to result in indictments.

Rigas Family in the Dock

On July 24, 2002, federal authorities, who had refused the Rigases' request to surrender to them, conducted an early morning raid at a Manhattan condo owned by the family. In what one cable executive called "an outrageous piece of show business," U.S. postal inspectors handcuffed the 77-year-old Rigas and two of his sons and walked them past a battery of news media cameras, the classic "perp" walk straight out of a cable television police show. Also that day, John, Tim, and Mike Rigas, along with former vice president of finance Jim Brown and assistant treasurer Mike Mulcahey, were formally charged by the Department of Justice with nine criminal counts of conspiracy, wire fraud, and bank fraud (Farrell 2002, 1, 42).

In addition, the Securities and Exchange Commission brought civil allegations against John Rigas and all three of his sons. The SEC complaint alleged that the Rigas family

> (1) fraudulently excluded billions of dollars in liabilities from its consolidated financial statements by hiding them in off-balance sheet affiliates; (2) falsified operations statistics and inflated Adelphia's earnings to meet Wall Street's expectations; and (3) concealed rampant self-dealing by the Rigas Family, including the undisclosed use of corporate funds for Rigas Family stock purchases and the acquisition of luxury condominiums in New York and elsewhere. (Securities and Exchange Commission 2002)

The complaint charged that although the Rigases' private business interests—other cable systems, a furniture and interior design company, a car dealership, and the Buffalo hockey team—"were not Adelphia subsidiaries and were wholly owned by the Rigas family, they were treated, in effect, as if they were Adelphia entities, with little or no recognition of their divergent ownership or interests."

Criminal charges painted a similar picture, and although the Rigases were released on $10 million bond after the arrests, a multiple-count federal indictment on conspiracy, bank fraud, and wire fraud followed two months later. "The scheme charged in the indictment is one of the most elaborate and extensive corporate frauds in United States history," U.S. Attorney James Comey told the assembled media.

The government charged the Rigases with plotting to buy stock in Adelphia each time the company issued new shares so that the percentage of their own holdings would not be diluted. To make sure they had the money to buy the stock, they set up a credit line to borrow funds, with those loans being underwritten by Adelphia. The family drew down Adelphia's credit line by hundreds of millions of dollars to buy stock and thus raised the company's already massive debt load. They also accessed more than $250 million in Adelphia money so that they could meet requirements to repay loans when the value of their stock decreased, according to the indictment. In addition, John and his two sons were accused of taking more than $50 million for personal use, including company-paid travel and purchases of real estate and timber rights, and $13 million for the development of a golf course near Coudersport (Department of Justice 2002).

The scheme that resulted in the Rigases enriching themselves at the expense of shareholders and using company funds to back personal loans was less intricate than it might seem. Family members viewed the public company as their own "private piggy bank," as federal prosecutor Richard Owens termed it. The Rigases displayed an attitude of family entitlement toward the business and its financial resources, an attitude that may have seemed acceptable in the first 34 years of Adelphia's existence as a small family firm but one that is not applicable in a publicly traded corporation.

"In Enron you needed to be a financial engineer to figure out what people were trying to do. The reason why this case is so compelling is that there's nothing fancy about it. This is just $3 billion sucked out by insiders without disclosure by anybody, with the banks funding the illegal business," a bankruptcy specialist working on the Adelphia case told *Forbes* magazine as the family awaited a trial. The bottom line: "John Rigas stole tens of millions of dollars from Adelphia, and used tens of millions of dollars for his own personal purposes," prosecutor Owens told the jury when the trial began in the spring of 2004.

Shortly after the indictments, Jim Brown had pleaded guilty to conspiracy, wire fraud, and bank fraud in exchange for testifying against the other defendants. He became the government's star witness and spent almost two weeks on the witness stand relating how he and other company officials had falsified Adelphia's finances, its profits, and its number of cable subscribers so as to mask the company's fiscal woes.[1] At one point, Brown testified that the company had participated in "wash" transactions with vendors Motorola and Scientific-Atlanta, a supplier of cable converter boxes. Brown testified that Scientific-Atlanta inflated the price of each box sold to Adelphia above the price that appeared on financial statements, and then paid Adelphia an identical amount per box for fake marketing services; this transaction, which had no net financial effect, allowed Adelphia to understate operating expenses and overstate pretax earnings. "It was critical that we get the deals done with Scientific-Atlanta or we would miss the numbers we were reporting," he testified. The transactions helped Adelphia hide its true financial performance.

Earlier in his testimony, Brown recounted a litany of lies: "I lied about a lot of things. I lied about Adelphia's earnings. I lied about the strength of its balance sheet. I lied about its operating statistics. I lied in person to investors when I met with them. I lied in the company's filings. I lied in the company's press releases." Brown, the Rigases, and others at Adelphia exaggerated the company's cash flow numbers and then used the deals with its vendors to fool company auditors by inflating Adelphia's pretax earnings figures.

Federal prosecutors built their case of greed and lies by portraying the Rigases as individuals who could not distinguish between a private family business and a publicly traded company. In his four years as a board member from 1998 to 2002, former board director Dennis Coyle testified that he had never heard the term "fiduciary duty" mentioned at a board meeting. (Fiduciary duty requires company officers and directors, such as the Rigases, to act loyally to promote the best interests of the corporation rather than their private, personal interests.) Coyle identified CFO Tim Rigas as the person who came up with the co-borrowing agreements that allowed the Rigases to use Adelphia to back loans that were made to Rigas family members.

In addition, John Rigas's former accountant testified Adelphia had paid for Rigas's private purchase of other cable systems. Prosecutors said Adelphia would send funds to the cable system sellers and then book the money as a receivable owed by Rigas or one of his family members. The practice began in the early 1990s and continued until the end of the decade. In his testimony, accountant Christopher Thurner also punctured John Rigas's image as a kindly company patriarch by recounting how the Adelphia chief had threatened to fire him if he did not produce fake invoices to draw money for Rigas out of Adelphia's treasury. The invoices claimed nonexistent guests of Adelphia had stayed at Rigas-owned condominiums and time shares in Colorado and Mexico and resulted in payment to Rigas of about $2,500 for each phantom guest's stay. The accountant also related that Rigas, who was short on cash at one point in the mid-1990s, asked Thurner to borrow $20,000 for him through Empire Sports Network. Thurner got the loan and wrote a check to Rigas, who never paid him back.

Finally, Robert DiBella, an Adelphia consultant who analyzed 100,000 of the company's transactions from 1999 to 2002 testified about the money the Rigases had borrowed through Adelphia for their private business ventures. As of April 2002, the Rigas family owed Adelphia $2.85 billion in loans guaranteed by the company, according to the analysis. The testimony was designed to bolster the government's accusations that the Rigases hid billions in debt and took hundreds of millions for themselves before the company was forced into bankruptcy.

The Rigases' defense against the charges came on several fronts. Their lawyers claimed that everything the Rigases had done was approved by either company attorneys or the board of directors. The family viewed the co-borrowing arrangement with Adelphia merely as a joint checking account. Lawyers portrayed the Rigases as unaware of company finances and distracted by health matters, rapid growth, and day-to-day management chores.

Tim Rigas—"a hands-off manager"—was so busy performing as CEO in place of his ailing father that he had no time to perform financial duties, which were being taken over by Jim Brown. Michael Rigas—"a busy man"— was so focused on technology, programming, and customer service that he relied on accountants to take care of financial matters. John Rigas—"out of the loop"—did not steal up to $1 million a month from Adelphia; he borrowed that money and intended to pay it back. Codefendant Michael Mulcahey testified that the $1 million a month in company funds provided to John Rigas was considered a loan by Adelphia because most of his wealth was tied up in the company: "It seemed like a way for Mr. Rigas to enjoy his retirement years and not have to sell his stock in Adelphia."

The Jury Decides

Unfortunately for John Rigas, the Adelphia founder would not be able to enjoy those retirement years as planned. After a trial that lasted more than 126 days and accumulated 16,000 exhibits, the federal jury convicted Rigas on 18 of the 23 charges against him, including bank fraud and conspiracy. Tim Rigas was convicted of similar charges. Mike Rigas was acquitted on conspiracy and wire fraud charges, but the jury deadlocked on the securities and bank fraud charges against him. (To avoid a retrial, Mike pleaded guilty in 2005 to a greatly reduced charge: making a false entry in a company record.) The only nonfamily board member who went to trial with the Rigases, Michael Mulcahey, was found not guilty of all charges.

Sentencing of John and Tim Rigas took place almost a year after the jury found them guilty. John Rigas received 15 years in federal prison and Tim Rigas faced 20 years, but both skipped their initial prison report date of September 19, 2005; they were allowed to remain free while attorneys appealed their convictions to a higher court. The Rigases contended that the convictions should be overturned because the prosecution ought to have been required to call an expert witness to testify about the way accounting practices were handled within Adelphia. When John Rigas did report to prison, Judge Leonard Sand ruled that the Adelphia founder, who had battled heart disease and bladder cancer in the late 1990s, must serve at least two years and then could be released if it was determined he had less than three months to live.[2]

The Rigases' nightmare continued in October 2005 when John and Tim were indicted in a $300 million tax evasion scheme, "one of the largest personal income tax evasion cases in the history of federal tax law enforcement." The indictment charged the two with conspiracy to defraud the United States and separate counts of tax evasion from 1998–2000, alleging that the two failed to report almost $400 million in income they diverted from Adelphia (Department of Justice 2005).

By then, Adelphia's new management had agreed to settle claims that the SEC and the Justice Department had brought against the Rigas-led Adelphia. In 2005, the company, which employed 14,000 people, reached deals with Time Warner Inc. and Comcast Corporation, allowing those cable companies to acquire substantially all of Adelphia's U.S. assets on July 31, 2006. Shortly before the transaction, Adelphia stock had dipped to about 7 cents a share.

Rigas apologized to Adelphia shareholders who had lost their money when the stock collapsed, but he did not admit to any criminal wrongdoing either in court or outside to reporters at the sentencing hearing. Mistakes were made at Adelphia, he told Judge Sand, but, "in my heart and conscience, I'll go to my grave believing truly that I did nothing but try to improve conditions" for the company and its employees.

The judge had these words for John Rigas: "The man I have to sentence is the man reflected in the evidence, a man who long ago sent Adelphia on a track of lying and cheating and defrauding. Regretfully for everyone, this was not stopped over ten years ago but continued and got more brazen and culminated in one of the largest frauds in corporate history."

Notes

1. The testimony recounted in this case is taken from trial reporting provided by the *Buffalo News*, *Multichannel News*, *Bloomberg News*, the Associated Press, and other media outlets listed in the references and bibliography.
2. In August 2007, John and Tim Rigas reported to the federal correctional center in Butner, North Carolina, to begin serving their sentences after a federal appeals court in May upheld the securities fraud, bank fraud, and conspiracy convictions. Although the Rigases' court appeals continue, the judge rescinded an order allowing them to remain free during the appeals process (Neumeister 2007; Waggoner 2007).

References

Colman, Price. "Family Ties," *Broadcasting & Cable,* 125–129 (1999): 24, 34.
Department of Justice. *United States of America vs. John J. Rigas, Timothy J. Rigas, Michael J. Rigas, James R. Brown, and Michael C. Mulcahey,* defendants, Department of Justice, 2002, www.usdoj.gov/dag/cftf/chargingdocs/rigasindictscan.pdf (retrieved January 31, 2006).

_____. News release from Thomas A. Marino, United States Attorney, Middle District of Pennsylvania, Department of Justice, 2005, http://www.usdoj.gov/tax/usaopress/2005/txdv05100705.htm (retrieved January 31, 2006).

Farrell, Mike. "No Surrender: Rigases Arrested," *Multichannel News* 23-30, July 29, 2002, 1, 42 (retrieved August 12, 2003, from ProQuest).

Gearty, Robert. "Actress Peta Wilson Testifies in Adelphia Corporate-Greed Trial," *Daily News (NY), Ridder/Tribune Business News,* March 16, 2004 (retrieved October 5, 2005, from Lexis-Nexis database).

Hays, Tom. "Attorney: Adelphia Official Relied on Accountants," Associated Press, business news; state and regional, March 2, 2004 (retrieved October 4, 2005, from Lexis-Nexis database).

_____. "Adelphia Jurors Hear of Excess, Rigas Style," Associated Press, business news; state and regional, June 2, 2004 (retrieved October 4, 2005, from Lexis-Nexis database).

Neumeister, Larry. "Prosecutors Spruce Up Tempo of Trial with Talk of Christmas Trees and Golf Courses," Associated Press, state and local wire, March 16, 2004, BC cycle (retrieved October 4, 2005, from Lexis-Nexis database).

Neumeister, Larry. 2007. "Appeals Court Rejects Rigas Appeal," Associated Press, May 24, 2007 (retrieved June 28, 2007, from Yahoo! Finance).

Securities and Exchange Commission. Securities and Exchange Commission v. Adelphia Communications Corporation, John J. Rigas, Timothy J. Rigas, Michael J. Rigas, James P. Rigas, James R. Brown, and Michael C. Mulcahey, 02 Civ. 5776 (KW) (S.D.N.Y.), Securities and Exchange Commission, 2002, http://www.sec.gov/litigation/litreleases/lr17627.htm (retrieved January 30, 2006).

Sullivan, Jerry. 1998. "The Most Popular Person in Buffalo: With Courage and a Touch of Magic, Sabres Owner John Rigas Reminds Us How to Dream," *Buffalo News First Sunday Magazine,* November 1, 1998, M6 (retrieved October 22, 2003, from Lexis-Nexis database).

Waggoner, Martha. "Adelphia's Rigases Report to Prison," Forbes.com, August 13, 2007.

Williams, Fred O. "Adelphia Chief Says Acquisitions Risky but Rewarding," *Buffalo News,* March 9, 1999, E3 (retrieved October 22, 2003, from Lexis-Nexis database).

_____. "Small-Town Roots Anchor Ever-Widening Branches of Cable TV Empire," *Buffalo News,* May 2, 1999, A1 (retrieved October 22, 2003, from Lexis-Nexis database).

_____. "Rigas Has Some Explaining to Do: Wall Street Wants to Know the Precise Details of Adelphia Communication's Loans," Buffalo News, March 31, 2002, B6 (retrieved October 22, 2003, from Lexis-Nexis database).

Zremski, Jerry. "John Rigas Didn't Steal, He Borrowed, Jury Told/Co-defendant Calls Actions Proper," *Buffalo News,* June 9, 2004, B1 (retrieved October 4, 2005, from Lexis-Nexis database).

Bibliography

Bloomberg News. "Ex-Adelphia Executive Recalls Fake Payments," *New York Times,* May 25, 2004, C17 (retrieved October 4, 2005, from Lexis-Nexis database).

_____. "Rigas Family Debt to Adelphia Is Spelled Out," *New York Times,* May 27, 2004, C5 (retrieved October 4, 2005, from Lexis-Nexis database).

Donohue, Steve. "Jim Brown to Court: 'I Lied,' Former Aide to Rigases Testifies to Inflating Adelphia Finance Reports," *Multichannel News* 25-18, May 3, 2004, 8 (retrieved October 4, 2005, from Lexis-Nexis database).

Fabrikant, Geraldine. "Indictments for Founder of Adelphia and Two Sons," *New York Times,* September 24, 2002, C1 (retrieved August 12, 2003, from Lexis-Nexis database).

Farrell, Mike. "At Rigas Trial, Prosecution Keys on Greed," *Multichannel News* 25-13, March 29, 2004, 54 (retrieved October 4, 2005, from Lexis-Nexis database).

_____. "A Blow to Rigas' Paternal Image; Adelphia Jury Hears Testimony on a History of "Phony" Invoices," *Multichannel News* 25-14, April 5, 2004, 3, 36 (retrieved October 4, 2005, from Lexis-Nexis database).

Farrell, Mike, and Steve Donohue. 2004. Defense: Rigases Were "Clueless," *Multichannel News* 25-10, March 8, 2004, 1, 77 (retrieved October 4, 2005, from Lexis-Nexis database).

Frank, Robert. "In Coudersport, Pa., Adelphia Chief Is a Hometown Hero: Locals Stand by John Rigas as Inquiries Proliferate—A Line at the Coffee Shop," *Wall Street Journal,* May 28, 2002, A1 (retrieved August 12, 2003, from Lexis-Nexis database).

Gallagher, Leigh. "What Did They Know?" *Forbes,* May 26, 2003, 53–54.

Higgins, John M. "Like a Witch Hunt," *Broadcasting & Cable,* June 28, 2004, 12 (retrieved October 4, 2005, from Lexis-Nexis database).

Kidwell, Roland E. "Adelphia Communications and the Rigas Family." In *Managing Organizational Deviance,* ed. Roland E. Kidwell, and Christopher L. Martin, 301–308. Thousand Oaks, CA: Sage, 2005.

Linstedt, Sharon, and Fred O. Williams. "Adelphia Ready to Take Big Step: Amid Skepticism about Its Operations Center, the Company Has Brought Jobs to the Area and Is Hiring an Architect," *Buffalo News,* January 16, 2002, A1 (retrieved October 22, 2003, from Lexis-Nexis database).

Markon, Jerry, and Robert Frank. "Five Adelphia Officials Arrested on Fraud Charges," *Wall Street Journal,* July 25, 2002, A3 (retrieved January 29, 2006, from ProQuest).

Moss, Linda. "The Image That Shocked Cable," *Multichannel News* 23-30, July 29, 2002, 1, 46 (retrieved August 12, 2003, from ProQuest).

Moules, Jonathan, and Peter Thal Larsen. "Family's Private Affairs Hit Public Domain," *Financial Times,* U.S. edition, July 25, 2002, 2 (retrieved August 12, 2003, from ProQuest).

Nuzum, Christine. "Adelphia Paid for Rigas' Private Cable Buys," Associated Press, state and local wire, May 24, 2004, BC cycle (retrieved October 4, 2005 from Lexis-Nexis database).

Sorkin, Andrew Ross. "Fallen Founder of Adelphia Tries to Explain," *New York Times,* April 7, 2003, C1 (retrieved August 12, 2003, from Lexis-Nexis database).

Williams, Fred O. "Adelphia Reveals $2.3 Billion in Off-Books Debt," *Buffalo News,* March 28, 2002, F1 (retrieved October 22, 2003, from Lexis-Nexis database).

Zremski, Jerry. "Adelphia Trial Underway. Company Is Called Rigases' Private Piggy Bank," *Buffalo News,* March 2, 2004, A1 (retrieved October 4, 2005, from Lexis-Nexis database).

_____. "Jury Convicts John Rigas, Son Timothy; Second Son Acquitted of Some Counts; Others Pending/Panel Finds Mulcahey Not Guilty on All Charges," *Buffalo News,* July 9, 2004, A1 (retrieved July 21, 2004, from Lexis-Nexis database).

_____. "John Rigas Sentenced to 15 Years in Jail; Watches as Son Gets 20-Year Prison Term; Former Adelphia Owners Continue to Deny Fraud Charges," *Buffalo News,* June 21, 2005, A1 (retrieved October 4, 2005, from Lexis-Nexis database).

High Stakes and High Energy at Enron: The Meteoric Rise and Fall of the "Crooked E"

18

STEPHEN F. HALLAM
ROGER C. MAYER

Contents

Introduction

During the night of January 25, 2002, Cliff Baxter, the 43-year-old vice chairman of Enron, slipped carefully out of bed to keep from disturbing his sleeping wife. He climbed into his new black Mercedes-Benz S500 and drove to Palm Royale Boulevard, about a mile from his home. With the motor still running and the headlights burning, he lifted a silver .357 Magnum to his right temple and blew away most of his head. At the subsequent services were photos of Cliff with his loving family—sailing, playing the guitar. His wife Carol, his 16-year-old son, and his 11-year-old daughter were heartbroken (McLean and Elkind 2003, xxii).

According to the *Houston Chronicle,* Cliff's suicide note to his wife Carol read (Fusaro and Miller 2002, 206):

Carol,

I am so sorry for this. I feel I just can't go on. I have always tried to do the right thing but where there was once great pride now it's gone. I love you and the children so much. I just can't be any good to you or myself. The pain is overwhelming. Please try to forgive me.

Cliff

A Brief Timeline

The Enron story is a tale of human tragedy on multiple levels. It begins triumphantly in July 1985 with the merger of Houston Natural Gas with Inter-North. The $2.3 billion merger created the longest pipeline network in the United States, stretching 37,000 miles to join oil fields in Canada to markets in Florida. Kenneth L. Lay was the chairman and chief executive officer (CEO) of Houston Natural Gas, and after the merger he became chairman and CEO of Enron. Throughout 1985 and 1986 Enron's stock price hovered around $5 per share.

Ken Lay followed Jeff Skilling's advice and moved Enron's headquarters from Omaha to Houston. The new corporate symbol became the now infamous "crooked E," a large letter "E" tipped slightly backwards, that adorned the front of corporate headquarters in Houston and became the letterhead on all Enron correspondence.

A major milestone occurred in 1988 when Enron shifted its business strategy from being a natural gas supplier to becoming basically a "gas bank" offering financial and risk management services to the energy industry. The following year it officially launched GasBank, which allowed natural gas producers and wholesale buyers to purchase gas supplies at set prices, thereby protecting them from large price swings. Key executives soon realized there was more money to be made in processing the paperwork associated with gas than with drilling, piping, and processing it. Why bother to get your hands greasy when the real money is in the paperwork? This shift is what made Enron stand out from all the other oil and gas pipeline companies in America. As one Enron executive put it, "This is almost like printing money" (McLean and Elkind 2003, 320).

During the booming 1990s Ken Lay's reputation and Enron's stock flourished. Enron's reported earnings in 2000 were $101 billion, and the number of employees grew to 21,000. Many Enron employees had been among the top 1 percent academically; they were captains of athletic teams and generally considered among those most likely to succeed. They were achievement-oriented, hard chargers who did not like to lose.

For six consecutive years in the 1990s, *Fortune* magazine named Enron one of the world's leading electricity, natural gas, and communications companies, not to mention one of the one hundred best places to work. Enron reported that it owned approximately 30,000 miles of gas pipeline. One of its new ventures included ownership of or access to 15,000 miles of fiber optics. After hanging around $5 per share during much of the 1980s, on January 25, 2001, Enron's stock skyrocketed to $81.39.

Exactly one year later, on January 25, 2002, Enron's stock was worthless and Enron Vice Chairman Cliff Baxter, unable to stand the pain, shot himself in the head. Unfortunately, this was only the beginning of the pain. Soon over 20,000 Enron employees had lost their jobs and most of their life savings. Enron's auditing firm, Arthur Andersen, was accused of shredding tons of Enron documents and soon this giant accounting firm also folded. Some people were even beginning to question the overall integrity of the American stock market and the ethics of American business leaders. To better understand what went wrong, we have to get to know a few of the key architects of Enron's dramatic success and even more dramatic collapse.

The Key Players

Ken Lay

Ken Lay was born the son of a Baptist preacher in 1942. He earned his BA and MA degrees from the University of Missouri and received his doctorate in economics in 1970 from the University of Houston. Before becoming CEO of Houston Natural Gas in 1984, Lay served in various capacities at Exxon, Florida Gas, the Continental Group, and Transco. In 1992 he served as cochairman of the President George H. W. Bush Re-election Committee.

During Lay's tenure as CEO, Enron became known as a socially responsible corporate citizen. In Enron's home of Houston, Lay built a reputation for raising money for various charitable causes and for Republican candidates. He became a close personal friend of George W. Bush and was one of his top fundraisers. According to the Center for Public Integrity, Enron raised $550,025 for Bush by mid-1999. Lay's connections with the Bush family provided him with tremendous political clout as he lobbied for energy deregulation. When George W. Bush became president in 2001, many suggested Lay ("Kenny Boy," as he was affectionately called by President George W. Bush) would be the secretary of energy or perhaps secretary of commerce.

Lay's tenure as Enron's CEO lasted from 1986 until his resignation on January 23, 2002, except for the few months in 2001 when he stayed on as chairman of the board but turned over the job of CEO to Jeff Skilling. When Skilling resigned as CEO after only a few months in the top slot, Lay returned to the post of CEO, a move that drew applause from Enron employees. Unfortunately, the applause did not last for long. In 2001 and 2002 Lay had the "honor" of captaining the Enron ship to the bottom of the sea. Instead of making sure all his "passengers" were safe or else bravely going down with the ship himself, he managed to escape carrying away $101 million while most of the rest of the crew and passengers lost everything. Was Ken Lay the sole cause of this disaster that some have called the worst scandal in American business history?

Jeffrey Skilling

Jeffrey Skilling was Enron's chief operating officer (COO) from 1996 to February 2001, during which time he was instrumental in transforming the company from a natural gas pipeline company into a global marketer and trader of energy. This financial wizard was born to a working-class family in Pittsburg and earned his BS in applied science at Southern Methodist University and his MBA from Harvard. After Harvard he landed a choice position at the prestigious consulting firm of McKinsey & Company.

We can gain some insight into Skilling's ego and goals through the following story. When Skilling was being interviewed by one of Harvard's deans as part of the Harvard Business School admission process, he was asked, "Are you smart?"

"I'm [expletive deleted] smart," he shot back.
"Why do you want to go to Harvard?" the dean inquired.
"I want to be a businessman," Skilling replied. "I really want it bad" (Eichen-
    wald 2005, 28).

At first Skilling was intimidated by Harvard, but he soon found he could outscore most of his classmates on tests. He graduated in 1979 as a Baker Scholar, an honor bestowed only upon the top 5 percent of the class. As with many Baker Scholars, upon graduation a position awaited him at the prestigious consulting firm of McKinsey & Company.

Skilling met Lay when Enron hired McKinsey & Company to consider the firm's move from Omaha to Houston. Later Skilling was instrumental in recommending that Enron use long-term contracts with large energy users as a means of locking in a set price. Major energy consumers, such as large factories and producers of electricity from gas or oil, could lock in a price for 10–20 years and not have to be concerned about the sharp unexpected turns in the price of fuel. Basically this approach reduced risk to such huge consumers of gas and oil. Eventually those contracts became more valuable than the actual gas—at least on paper.

Skilling was also instrumental in building Enron into one of the world's largest energy, commodities, and services companies. At Skilling's urging, Enron began marketing contracts for electricity and natural gas and was actively moving into such diverse markets as the sale of Internet bandwidth capacity and even weather futures. Skilling was known for innovation and for believing that real value comes from human creativity and new ideas. He was not very interested in the physical aspects of drilling for gas or oil, pumping it through pipelines, refining, or in any of the other humdrum aspects of the energy business. He was more interested in new ways to trade on the stock market. It was the contract itself, rather than the actual product or service behind the contract, that most interested Skilling. By 2000 Enron was trading in more than 800 types of contracts, from advertising risk management to wind energy. Skilling seemed to have a magic skill in generating high stock prices. Was Skilling the cause of Enron's collapse?

Andrew Fastow

Andrew Fastow, born December 22, 1961, was chief financial officer (CFO) of Enron. He grew up in Washington, D.C., and graduated from Tufts University in 1983 with a BA in economics and Chinese. After earning his MBA from Northwestern University, he went to work for Continental Bank in Chicago. Fastow moved up quickly at Continental. In 1990 Jeff Skilling brought him to Enron because of his expertise in securitization, a technique banks use to pool similar loans and sell interests in them to outside investors—thereby raising additional funds for the bank.

At Continental, Fastow used securitization to group mortgages together and, in effect, turn them into tradable securities. It is common for banks to do this. Mortgages on homes, for example, are a debt owed to a bank. The bank looks at them as an asset, but home mortgages are also an exposure or risk for the bank. The homeowner might default on the mortgage, causing the bank to suffer a loss. Bank regulations therefore limit the amount of the bank's money that can be tied up in such mortgages. Selling the mortgages to other investors increases the amount of money the bank can lend to potentially more profitable and secure borrowers.

Fastow had exactly the expertise Skilling needed. Skilling was, in effect, using Fastow to transform Enron from an old-fashioned oil company into something much sexier to investors. Enron swiftly moved from delivering actual supplies of natural gas to brokering energy futures. Instead of dealing with the messy world of making holes in the ground for wells and pipelines, Fastow helped Enron begin dealing in the paperwork of long-term energy contracts.

Essentially, he showed Enron executives how it was more profitable to deal in the paperwork relating to the ownership of energy than in the energy itself. However, was there really anything substantial backing up the paperwork?

By the end of 2001 Fastow had created over 3,000 special purpose entities (SPEs), several naming his wife as their CEO and others named after his children and even characters from popular science fiction movies. Enron was not one entity, but rather a collection of thousands of SPEs, making it nearly impossible for even those highly trained in accounting to fully understand Enron's financial condition. In effect, Fastow sat at the controls, moving assets and liabilities around the vast network of accounting entities, and increasing or decreasing numbers on Enron's income statement and balance sheet as he saw fit. As long as Enron's stock prices continued to climb, no one dared to question Fastow's methods.

Throughout Fastow's tenure at Enron, Ken Lay and Jeff Skilling continued to express their complete confidence in his financial wizardry and personal integrity. A posting at www.time.com on February 10, 2002, describes a meeting on October 23 where energy trader Jim Schwieger asked Lay why CFO Andrew Fastow was still around, given that he had just blown half a billion dollars mismanaging several Enron partnerships while earning $30 million for himself doing it. Lay put his arm around Fastow and proclaimed his "unequivocal trust" in Andy. The next day, however, was Fastow's last at Enron.

Eventually Fastow and his wife entered into a plea-bargaining arrangement that provided the prosecution with important evidence against Lay and Skilling. Some want to blame Enron's failure on Fastow and suggest that he hid the true nature of his accounting tricks from Lay and Skilling. Then, in the ultimate act of deceit, he turned on Lay and Skilling to save his own skin. Was the disaster really Fastow's fault?

Sherron Watkins

Sherron Watkins worked several years as an accountant for Arthur Andersen and then moved to Enron, where she reported to Fastow and eventually reached the position of vice president. Her background at Arthur Andersen gave her confidence in her ability to understand complex financial matters. She became increasingly concerned about Enron's financial statements not properly reflecting Enron's true financial condition.

In mid-August 2001, Sherron Watkins wrote an anonymous letter to Ken Lay. The first two lines read, "Dear Mr. Lay, has Enron become a risky place to work? For those of us who didn't get rich over the last few years, can we afford to stay?" The letter outlined several concerns regarding off-the-books deals and continued, "I am incredibly nervous that we will implode in a wave of accounting scandals. My eight years of Enron work history will be worth nothing on my resume, the business world will consider the past successes as nothing but an elaborate accounting hoax." (The full text of that letter can be found at http://www.itmweb.com/f012002.htm.) Ultimately, Watkins became the whistleblower who broke the scandal.

Was Watkins merely a disgruntled employee violating a confidence, acting like a tattletale, and causing Enron's downfall? Was she trying to destroy Ken Lay's defense that he really was not aware of accounting irregularities by writing the letter and later leaking it to the press or was she a hero for finally exposing what so many were seeing but were too scared to speak up about?

The players in this story were not, as some believe, always nasty crooks. Instead they were people with sterling reputations, well known for raising money for various charities and very involved in political and socially responsible causes. The key player was Ken Lay, who later insisted at his trial that he did nothing wrong and that Enron's failure was caused by underlings such as CFO Andy Fastow, negative stories about Enron in the *Wall Street Journal,* and short sellers on Wall Street, who panicked over the bad news.

As the trial began in early 2006, the case against Lay and Skilling hinged on whether these executives committed fraud by lying or had themselves been the victims of the secret actions of Fastow and others. Did they knowingly deceive stockholders and others by telling outright lies about the financial condition of Enron or, as their defense attorneys claimed, did they merely make some business mistakes that, although unfortunate, were not criminal? According to the defense, Lay and Skilling were victims, not criminals.

What Was the "Accounting Hoax" That Alarmed Watkins?

The trial, much like the nearly 3,000 SPEs that made up Enron, was really a series of trials. However, this chapter focuses on the one that received the most media attention and primarily involved Ken Lay and Jeff Skilling. Several of the trials are likely to drag on for years, but this one ended on May 25, 2006, after nearly four months of testimony and six days of jury deliberation. There were also numerous accounting "irregularities," but we will focus only on two: securitization and mark-to-market accounting.

The trial revealed that Skilling and Fastow had hatched a plot to apply the technique of securitization to Enron's contracts. These contracts were much riskier than home mortgages. If a homebuyer fails to repay a home mortgage, the mortgage holder obtains title to the house and can then evict the homeowner and sell the house. In contrast, Enron was contracting with the builders of very risky power plants, pipelines, and oil wells. Skilling and Fastow applied to the risky oil business a process set up for relatively safe home mortgages. The history of oil has been one of boom and bust where millions have been made or lost overnight. Instead of being backed up with something as tangible as a house, these securities were backed up with Enron stock that, by the end of 2001, was worthless.

The U.S. Securities and Exchange Commission (SEC) was established by President Roosevelt following the Depression to "protect investors, maintain fair, orderly, and efficient markets, and facilitate capital formation" (see www.sec.gov). However, SEC rules regarding securitization only required the company purchasing the contracts to come up with 3 percent of the value of the contracts and to be independent of the company originating the contracts. Fastow set up SPEs with apparently no other purpose than to buy Enron contracts. This maneuver took the risky contracts off Enron's balance sheet and greatly improved its financial condition—at least this process made things *look* that way.

The Financial Accounting Standards Board (FASB) recommends an SPE only be allowed to take a contract off the original firm's balance sheet if the owners of the SPE have made a substantive capital investment in the SPE, are independent of the original company, and exercise control over the SPE. The SEC staff had taken the position that "substantive capital" is a remarkably low 3 percent . Furthermore, they considered the matter of the owners being independent and exercising control to be a subjective standard. However, when the SPE owner is the original company's CFO (Fastow) or members of his immediate family (e.g., Fastow's wife), it should certainly have raised questions about the owner's independence from Enron.

Such "owners" thought they were taking very little risk because Enron agreed to make up for any loss the SPE owners might have with Enron stock. This is somewhat like having your father cosign the loan you take out to buy your first car. With Enron, however, the amounts were obviously far more than the cost of a car, and "Father Enron" in the end did not really have the money to cover the contracts. At the time of its bankruptcy, Enron had over $2 billion hidden away in this manner.[1] Securitization was not the only questionable business practice. Enron was also playing tricks in how it did its accounting.

Shell Games in Accounting Using the Mark-to-Market Method

Tax law permits security traders to elect a method of accounting called the mark-to-market method. Security traders are in the business of buying and selling stocks all the time. But when does the trader consider a particular stock to be sold and thereby count it as either a gain or a loss for tax purposes? Stock traders can choose the mark-to-market method. Using this method, at the end of each year traders treat any stocks held on December 31 as if the stocks were sold on that day at the current market value. If the stock has gone down since the date of purchase, the trader reports a loss; if the stock has gone up, it is a gain.

In the long run this accounting method has little effect upon stock trading companies. There may be some benefit or negative consequence to the trading company in the first year this method is elected, but after that, it balances out over time. Furthermore, the stock markets, such as the New York Stock Exchange, provide a well-documented place where the market price for stocks can clearly be defined. What was different about Enron using the mark-to-market method beginning in 1992 was that Enron did not apply this concept to the regular daily trading of stocks. Instead, it applied it to long-term energy contracts where, unlike the stock market, no stable market exists.

In theory, Enron could determine the value of such contracts to sell energy over the next 20 years by also buying a contract to purchase the same amount of energy over the next 20 years. The difference between the market values of the two contracts, discounted for the present value of money, would set a market value for the event. These contracts typically involved Enron or one of its subsidiaries making a 20-year contract to sell energy to a factory or some organization that uses huge amounts of either natural gas or electricity. The *actual sale* of energy did not take place. The long-term contract merely established a set price for the energy for the period of the contract—often 20 years.

The organization buying the energy would only pay for it as the energy was actually used. Enron counted as revenue huge sums of money at the outset of the contract, but no money had actually been realized and would not be realized until the energy purchaser *actually used* the energy. With such long-term, risky contracts, the generally accepted accounting practice was to use the percentage of completion method. For example, if the energy customer during the year were to actually use 1/20 of the energy covered by the 20-year contract, then the energy supplier would count as income 1/20 of the amount of the total contract amount. No revenue would be recorded until the energy was actually used (i.e., bought). Using the percentage of completion method, the actual flow of money from the user of the energy to the seller of the energy coincides with the recording of profit on the energy seller's books. In contrast, the mark-to-market method, approved by the SEC and Arthur Andersen for use by Enron beginning in 1992, allowed Enron to count the total profit of a 20-year contract as income in the year the contract was initially signed. Thus, all 20 years of anticipated energy consumption would be counted as income for Enron even before, in some cases, the customer's factory was fully constructed and any energy had actually been consumed. Furthermore, since no official market for such energy contracts existed, Fastow was free to make the profit figure almost anything he wanted.

Skilling believed that the mark-to-market method actually resulted in a fairer evaluation of an asset. Instead of using the old-fashioned traditional method of carrying an asset on the books at the cost originally paid for the item minus some rather arbitrary depreciation amount, the mark-to-market method looks at the current market price. What could be fairer than to hearken back to the economist Adam Smith and the "invisible hand" of the marketplace? An asset is worth its market value in today's market. He argued that the SEC should not apply arbitrary regulation to these energy contracts but rather let the free market decide. Why should the government get in the center of this business decision? After all, was this not an era of government deregulation? The SEC chose not to object to the use of this accounting method (McLean and Elkind 2003, 40–43).

The immediate effect was a huge boost to Enron's revenue at the time of contract signing. The SEC allowed Enron to count the entire amount of such contracts, less costs, as revenue during the quarter in which the contract was signed. This enabled Enron to show quarterly earnings per share that were far in excess of what Wall Street analysts had forecasted. The ordinary investor had no idea of the details of this accounting method. The stock market responded with a flurry of buying, shooting the price of Enron stock through the roof. Enron executives were given huge bonuses based on the "revenue" generated and the increased "value" of Enron's stock (Eichenwald, 2005, 67).

To put it in more tangible terms, think of the electric meter for your house or apartment. When your meter is read, you are billed for the actual amount of energy consumed. If you go on vacation and turn off your furnace, lights, and all appliances, then your monthly bill would be much lower, reflecting your actual usage. If you move away and totally shut down your house, usage could drop to zero. In a like manner, if a factory shuts down, energy consumption can drop to zero—which makes trading in such anticipated future use of energy rather risky. Unfortunately for Enron, a business downturn in late 2000 caused several of their huge customers to put their plans for plant expansion on hold. As a consequence, the planned rate of energy use dropped rapidly. The house of cards was beginning to fall. To keep the investors happy, Fastow knew he had to report earnings per share at or above what the leading financial analysts were predicting. Eventually even the mark-to-market accounting procedure and the purchase of Enron's risky contracts by Fastow's vast network of SPEs was not enough. The separation was too great between the actual flow of cash and the recording of revenue on the accounting statements.

If All Else Fails, Just Make Up the Numbers

Paula Rieker, former secretary to Enron's board of directors, testified in court that she heard Jeff Skilling and Chief Accounting Officer Richard Causey discussing the need to "change the numbers" so that Enron would report quarterly earnings of 31 cents per share as expected by Wall Street analysts (*New York Times,* February 22, 2006, C4). Rieker testified that at another time the accounting reports indicated earnings per share would be 31 cents but that Skilling wanted to beat analysts' forecasts by 2 or 3 cents. Four days later the reports were simply changed to show earnings per share to be 34 cents.

At another time Rieker said she drafted a news release reporting that $150 million in Enron's broadband unit earnings were from the one-time sale of so-called "dark" or unused fiber. She told Skilling that the news release needed to reveal this fact because this one-time sale represented virtually all of the revenues for that unit. Nevertheless, the final news release claimed only a third of the revenues came from that source. In short, investors and the public were not told the truth. They were left to believe that Enron's income was coming from continuing operations instead of one-time events. Enron's true financial health was nothing like what official statements presented (*New York Times,* February 22, 2006, C4).

As the various trading schemes got more and more complicated, many bankers, auditors, and SEC officials who should have been providing checks and balances simply could not understand the financial complexities. Rather than showing their ignorance, some began to consider Enron a black box where investors simply put money in one end and much more money mysteriously came out the other end. To an outsider, everything appeared to be on the level at the "Crooked E." Its books were being audited by Arthur Andersen, one of the nation's largest and most respected public accounting firms. Andersen was, however, also making money providing consulting services to the energy behemoth. This provided Andersen with a potential conflict of interest: Bad marks on an audit might cost the firm lucrative consulting business with Enron (McLean and Elkind 2003, 144).

In March 2002, the once proud accounting firm of Arthur Andersen was charged with obstruction of justice after the disclosure that its employees shredded documents related to audits of Enron. Three months later, officials at Andersen were convicted. Hundreds of clients immediately dropped the company. In May 2005, the Supreme Court overturned the conviction, but it was too late. Most of the firm's clients were gone, as were almost all of its 25,000 employees. For all practical purposes, the Enron scandal killed Andersen. The "Big Five" accounting firms became the Big Four. Today, most of Andersen's former clients have chosen Ernst & Young, KPMG, Deloitte & Touche, or PricewaterhouseCoopers (*New York Times,* February 21, 2006, C4).

Would a Code of Ethics Have Helped?

Management textbooks often suggest organizations should have a code of ethics to guide their decision making. On July 1, 2000, Ken Lay sent a 64-page booklet to all employees entitled "Enron Code of Ethics." In his cover memorandum, Lay instructed all Enron employees to read the document carefully and to make certain that they "fully comply." In addition to the Enron Code of Ethics, the document included a statement of Principles of Human Rights. It spelled out Enron's vision to become the world's leading energy company and delineated its core values with regard to respect, integrity, communication, and excellence. The implication was that all Enron employees were to go far beyond the minimum expectations of obeying the law and abiding by ordinary standards. Instead, Enron was supposed to be an ethical leader.[2]

Jury Decides Lay and Skilling Are Guilty; Judge "Throws the Book" at Them

On May 25, 2006, a jury of eight women and four men convicted Lay and Skilling. The 108-day trial concluded that Enron's top executives deliberately hid the company's foundering finances from investors. Essentially, they were guilty of lying. The federal jury convicted Lay on all six counts of fraud and conspiracy and Skilling on nineteen counts of fraud and insider trading, bringing to a climax one of the most notorious corporate scandals in U.S. history.

From the verdict, it appeared that Lay and Skilling each would face prison terms that could be lifelong. "The jury has spoken and they have sent an unmistakable message to boardrooms across the country that you can't lie to shareholders, you can't put yourself in front of your employees' interests, and no matter how rich and powerful you are, you have to play by the rules," declared Sean M. Berkowitz, director of the Justice Department's Enron Task Force (*New York Times,* May 25, 2006).

Before the sentences for the two former Enron executives could be set, Ken Lay died on July 5, 2006, of an apparent heart attack. His death made it questionable whether any money could be recovered from his estate to offset the damage that had been done to others. But the human tragedy does not end with Lay and Skilling. Thousands of lives were badly damaged, some, such as Cliff Baxter's, irreparably so. Trust in the American stock market—which is at the very core of the U.S. economy—was severely damaged. How could this tragedy have been prevented? How can you avoid getting caught in such a tangled mess when you enter the high-pressure, fast-paced world of corporate management?

Notes

1. For a more extensive discussion of SPEs see http://files.findlaw.com/news.findlaw.com/hdocs/docs/enron/sicreport/chapter1.pdf.
2. Source: http://www.thesmokinggun.com/graphics/packageart/enron/enron.pdf (accessed February 22, 2006). For a series of articles on Enron and ethics, see http://www.businessethics.ca/enron/.

References

Eichenwald, Kurt. *Conspiracy of Fools.* New York: Broadway Books, 2005.

Fusaro, Peter, and Ross Miller. *What Went Wrong at Enron.* Hoboken, NJ: John Wiley & Sons, 2002.

McLean, Bethany, and Peter Elkind. *The Smartest Guys in the Room.* New York: Portfolio, 2003.

New York Times. February 21, 2006, C4.

_____. February 22, 2006, C4.

_____. May 25, 2006.

Bibliography

Fox, Loren. *Enron: the Rise and Fall.* Hoboken, NJ: John Wiley & Sons, 2003.

New York Times, *Enron Trial Stirs Memory of Andersen*, February 21, 2006, C4.

_____. February 22, *Executives Modified Enron Data, Jury Is Told*, 2006. C4.

_____. May 25, *Judge Approves 3 Enron Banks Civil Settlement*, 2006.

Swartz, Mimi, and Sherron Watkins. *Power Failure: The Inside Story of the Collapse of Enron.* New York: Doubleday, 2003.

The Inside Story of the Parmalat Scandal: Family Leadership Gone Wrong in a Multinational Group

19

BAHRAM SOLTANI
FLORA SOLTANI

Contents

Tanzi the Innovator

In 1961, Calisto Tanzi dropped out of university to concentrate on turning around the small family business, near Parma, Italy. Tanzi was 22 when he inherited the family business that was started by his grandfather. Tanzi Calisto e Figli—Salumi e Conserve (Tanzi Calisto & Sons—Cold Cuts and Preserves) produced processed foods like seasoned ham, cured meat, and tinned tomatoes. Tanzi, who had a strong entrepreneurial streak, was not satisfied with simply running the family business and decided to diversify. After noticing a carton in a supermarket in Switzerland, he decided that the route to success was through milk. Aged 23, he ventured into dairy products, building a milk pasteurizing plant in Colleccchio, near a railway station in Italy's gastronomic capital, Parma. The milk produced at the plant was supplied to Parma and surrounding towns, mainly through door-to-door sales.

In what could be described as a stroke of entrepreneurial genius, Tanzi applied new technologies and marketing strategies to the milk business. The firm and its product were named Parmalat (meaning milk from Parma) and Parmalat was the first branded milk in Italy. Dairy shops were set up in the provinces of Liguria and Tuscany.

Parmalat pioneered new disposable cartons developed in Sweden and a new process called "ultra-high temperature" (UHT), where milk was heated to 140° for a few seconds and then quickly cooled and packaged. It gave Tanzi's milk a longer shelf life when it was unopened—more than six months without refrigeration. Tanzi also started packaging the milk in a tetrahedron pack, which came to be known as Tetra Pak. The Tetra Pak was more hygienic than ordinary packaging and extended the life of the milk by three days once it was opened. Parmalat milk quickly became very popular and soon it had conquered other regions of Italy.

In structuring Parmalat, Tanzi was traditionally Italian. From the beginning, the firm was controlled by Tanzi surrounded by a small group of family members and friends. The company existed as an extension of the family, exclusively for the benefit of family members. Given that the family was the sole owner of the firm, no one would have then questioned such an arrangement.

The Boom Years

By the 1970s, Parmalat was producing cream, yogurt, butter, fruit juices, and chopped tomatoes. The firm expanded to Brazil, Argentina, Venezuela, Colombia, other European countries, China, Canada, and Australia. From 1975 to 1986 the Parmalat name became a household word in Italy, thanks to the company's sponsorship of sports heroes such as Gustavo Theoni, Niki Lauda, and Nelson Piquet. Business was booming. Revenue went from €23 million in 1975 to €460 million in 1986 (figures converted from lira).

During the 1980s, Parmalat diversified into biscuits and ready-made sauces. The company also rapidly expanded internationally and reinforced its position as a world leader in the dairy market and in foods such as bakery products. Tanzi also attempted to expand into television to rival former Italian Prime Minister and businessman Silvio Berlusconi. In 1987, Parmalat spent €130 million on a station called Odeon TV that he hoped to build into Italy's third major network. The acquisition of Odeon TV had nothing to do with the group's core activities or its strategy; it was one of Tanzi's expensive, personal whims.

By the end of 1990 Odeon TV had declared bankruptcy and Tanzi was obliged to sell it at a loss of about €45 million. Tanzi, who had guaranteed Odeon TV debts, had to pay out huge amounts of money. This was one of the first instances in which Parmalat money was used to cover Tanzi's debts in other business areas.

Notwithstanding the Odeon affair, Tanzi had created one of the giants of Italian industry. He became very well known for his Catholic fervor and his political connections with Christian Democrat leaders. In particular, he was considered to be a close friend of Ciriaco De Mita, the powerful leader of the ruling Christian Democrat party during the 1980s. He developed ties with Italy's great and good—especially in the Catholic Church in Parma. Bankrolled by the success of Parmalat, he became a major patron of the Church and was active in social issues, sports, and political parties. A pious Catholic, Tanzi was a generous benefactor who sponsored the restoration of Parma's 11th century basilica. The firm also diversified into professional sports through the sponsorship of a number of domestic Italian and foreign football teams. Tanzi's company began sponsoring Italian skiers, plastering the Parmalat logo all over their competition uniforms. Parmalat was billed as the "milk of champions."

The firm continued growing throughout the 1990s to become a food giant with interests in fruit juices, vegetable sauces, baking products, soups, yogurt, cream, and mineral water. The Parmalat Group expanded its international operations further, particularly with several major food industry acquisitions in South America. By this time, Parmalat was operating in 31 countries across six continents; the company was employing more than 36,000 people in more than 140 plants around the world, and 5,000 dairy farms in Italy depended on the company to purchase the bulk of their products.

Creation of Parmalat Finanziaria: A Family Affair

Through a complex financial transaction, Tanzi used the shares of his family's holding company[1] (Coloniale SpA) to raise capital for a publicly traded company, Finanziaria Centro Nord (FCN). In 1990, the Tanzi family had merged Parmalat with FCN, and FCN subsequently changed its name to Parmalat Finanziaria SpA and became the parent company of Parmalat SpA, the main operating company under Tanzi's control. Through the financial transaction, Coloniale kept a controlling stake of around 51 percent in Parmalat Finanziaria, which became the holding of a group formed by 58 companies, of which 33 were based outside Italy. This enabled Parmalat to raise money through a rights issue,[2] selling stock to repay reported debts of €268 million.

Parmalat had grown into a complex group but was still owned and controlled by the Tanzi family, which ran a large network of companies on a pyramidal structure. Pyramidal groups, which are very widespread in Italy, are organizations where the same entrepreneur controls legally independent firms or controls a group of selected executives through a chain of ownership.

The major change in the company's structure came in 1990 when the need to raise capital caused Parmalat to be listed on the Milan Stock Exchange. However, Tanzi and his family had no intention of letting go of the reins, and they retained 52 percent ownership. With the Tanzi family acting as a block, their control of the firm remained absolute. Tanzi served as chairman and managing director for the whole group and two of his sons, Giovanni and Stefano, were executive members of the board. These three also held high-ranking positions on the executive committee, which was composed of seven directors.

Diversification into Football and Tourism

Using the funds of Parmalat, Tanzi invested substantially in the football business in the 1990s by acquiring Parma Calcio (Parma's soccer club), the well-known Brazilian club Palmeiras, and a Chilean club named Audax Italiano (ECGI 2005, 7). Parma Calcio was handed to Tanzi's son Stefano, who became the club's president in 1996. Over the following decade, backed by Parmalat's cash, Tanzi's son turned Parma AC into one of the big names in European football, winning two UEFA Cups and one European Cup Winners' Cup.

Tanzi also entered the tourism market in the 1990s. Through many transactions and acquisitions, the Tanzis' tourism firm, HIT, reached a turnover of €550 million. Stefania, Calisto Tanzi's daughter, was in charge of the business. Parmalat's affiliates also included a tourism agency, Parmatour. Like the Odeon TV venture, all these operations lost money from the beginning and generated a mountain of losses and debt.

Parmalat and the Italian Code of Best Practice

In 1999, Italy introduced the voluntary Preda code of best corporate practice, which recommended that the appointment of the board members of public companies be a transparent procedure. The code required detailed information about the personal and professional attributes of the candidates to be deposited at the company's registered office at least ten days prior to the date of the general meeting during which the board members were selected. Because compliance with the code was voluntary, Parmalat simply ignored it.

The code also recommended that a board be balanced between executives who were employed at the firm and non-executive members to guard against an unhealthy concentration of power in a management clique. Before the Preda Code was enacted, Parmalat's board of directors was primarily controlled by the Tanzi family. To satisfy the code, Parmalat would have had to restructure its board of directors and disclose a lot of information about its board members, but the board of directors simply ignored the code or paid only lip service to it. For example, in 2001 only three out of thirteen members of the board were independent, but the company considered that "adequate."

It was the same story on the company's internal audit committee, which was responsible for assessing the adequacy of internal controls and reporting periodically to the board. Parmalat's committee was a toothless tiger. One of its two executive members was the firm's chief financial officer (CFO) and the one outside director was a close friend of the Tanzi family.

The minutes of one of the company's general meetings stated: "We believe that the Group's existing structure is already sufficiently well-organized to manage so-called internal audit procedures and that the existing internal procedures, are, in line with the needs of the Group, capable of guaranteeing healthy and sufficient management, adequate to identify, prevent, and manage risks of a financial and operational nature and fraudulent behavior that may damage the company" (Parmalat Company meeting minutes 2001).

International Expansion

At the end of the decade the Parmalat Group was still expanding. Between 1998 and 2000 it purchased around 25 companies. In 1999, Parmalat acquired the Italian milk-processing business Eurolat, with operations in Argentina and the United States, from Italian entrepreneur Sergio Cragnotti for €400 million. "Concerned by the possible effects of the acquisition on competition in the fresh milk market in Italy, the Italian Competition Authority authorized the acquisition only on the condition that Parmalat would dispose of a number of brands and production facilities" (Hamilton 2004, 2). The acquisitions opened new doors to the company's products, enabling the company to substantially increase its market share around the world. By the end of 2001, Parmalat's sales outside Europe accounted for 67 percent of its total sales. Only ten years previously, Parmalat operations were entirely dependent on the Italian market, where it was selling 83 percent of its products.

By 2002 Parmalat was at its peak. It was a corporate giant composed of more than 200 companies in 50 countries, employing 36,000 people. Parmalat was the eighth largest industrial group in Italy and a world leader in dairy, food products, and beverages. It was estimated that Parmalat purchased about 8 percent of all the milk produced in Italy and provided milk for about half the people in New York City. The firm had consolidated revenue of €7.6 billion and a good cash position, at least on paper.

The richest plum remained the United States and in 1997 Parmalat decided to harvest it. The Parmalat road show blazed a trail across the United States with a sales pitch that induced investors to purchase nearly $1.5 billion in notes and bonds. Tanzi, company CFO Fausto Tonna, and other executives crossed the Atlantic to add their weight to the effort. They also invited American investors to meetings at Parmalat headquarters near Parma.

Almost as fast as the money flowed into Parmalat, it flowed out again. Tanzi and his board members made many poor business decisions, particularly with their South American acquisitions. Of the €14 billion raised between 1990 and 2003, €3.8 billion was gobbled up by unproductive acquisitions.

An estimated €2.3 billion was used for unknown, unreported transactions. They were mostly undocumented expenses and in some cases without evidence of any service rendered. Tanzi used company money to indulge his personal whims, while other cash flowed into the pockets of family members. Parmalat reportedly funneled money through companies in Luxembourg to pay CFO Tonna a €3 million bonus. Another €500 million was injected by Parmalat top management into private companies solely owned by the Tanzi family, such as Parmatour, the tourism agency. An example of the schemes used to siphon off funds was the case of the private Tanzi companies that received €2 million after investing €30,000 in a company that belonged to Parmalat.

Milking the Banks, Offshore Tax Havens, and "Big Bath" Accounting Behavior

With full control and no outside scrutiny, this tightly knit group built the firm according to its own peculiar code of practice. The aggressive expansion that Parmalat experienced throughout the 1990s and until 2003 was fueled by enormous amounts of borrowed money. To finance its acquisitions, Parmalat also raised more than €8 billion in bonds, mainly by selling them to institutional investors. Over a ten-year period the company issued more than 30 bonds, increasingly using non-Italian banks as a source of financing. The Bank of America was among some 20 European and U.S. banks that sold Parmalat bonds between 1997 and 2002. It has also been reported that U.S. investors bought more than $1.5 billion of Parmalat bonds. Of the approximately €14.2 billion the group took in during that period, €13.2 billion was loans—80 percent of which came from foreign lenders—and only €1 billion came from internal operations. Parmalat was relying on other people's money and was not generating cash by selling milk or the firm's myriad other products. However, the outside world was largely ignorant of the firm's financial condition. According to one analyst, "Fausto Tonna, Parmalat's CFO for 16 years, had a fierce reputation within the financial community. He was prone to berating analysts who wrote critical reports on Parmalat and created tough competition among banks for Parmalat's business. But at the same time, Tonna and Parmalat were seen as a constant source of potential business for many banks" (Hamilton 2004, 2).

The group used fictitious financial transactions and trades to hide the losses of operating subsidiaries and to inflate assets and income. For example, Parmalat misused the "advances on active invoices" system, in which banks advance money on the expectation of imminent revenues. Parmalat would milk the banks by presenting the same invoice to several banks. Parmalat justified loans by inflating its revenues through fictitious sales to retailers. Then, in a scheme that authorities later charged was devised and executed by Tanzi and a small group of executives and lawyers working for him, the firm "cooked its books" to make debt simply vanish. Taking advantage of the complex network of companies, Parmalat would transfer debt to shell companies based in offshore tax havens such as the Cayman Islands, the Antilles, the British Virgin Islands, Malta, and Luxembourg, where the debt could be hidden. Citigroup, one of the world's largest financial services companies, created a Delaware-based entity called *Buconero*, the Italian word for "black hole," as part of a complex arrangement that allowed Parmalat to borrow about $140 million without recording it as debt on its balance sheet. Similarly, uncollectible accounts receivables were transferred from the operating companies to these nominee entities, where their real value was hidden.

Parmalat also used these countries as a means of raising extra funds. Parmalat borrowed money through credit institutions and merchant banks, taking advantage of the relaxed local legislation. With a little accounting magic, these loans were then treated as equity.

A Crude Forgery and the Black Hole "Buconero" at Parmalat

In reality, Parmalat was crumbling under the weight of its borrowings, and its executives were desperately trying to hide the cracks from the world. Eyebrows were raised when a company so apparently flush with cash embarked on yet another bond issue. In April 2003, Tanzi replaced CFO Tonna with a new man, Alberto Ferraris, who stated there would be no new bond issues and that the group would pay its debts in cash. Despite the promise, the company quietly issued a new bond.

The Italian newspaper *La Repubblica, Affaire e Finanza,* ran the story in July 2003, and the Italian securities market regulator Consob decided to act. Consob asked Parmalat to disclose all relevant information on this issue and asked the firm's external auditors, Deloitte, to examine its accounts. Deloitte said it was unable to certify the €497 million value of Parmalat's mutual fund Epicurum, which was backed by a complex currency transaction. Deloitte was also worried about an unreported complex contract between a Swiss subsidiary of Parmalat and Buconero.

Meanwhile, in America, Parmalat was raising funds as fast as it could. At the end of 2002, the group claimed that it was holding €3.95 billion (approximately $4.9 billion) in an account at the Bank of America in New York City in the name of Parmalat's Cayman Islands subsidiary, Bonlat Financing Corporation. Bonlat's auditors had certified its 2002 financial statements based on the confirmation of these assets at the Bank of America. The €3.95 billion was in turn included in Parmalat's 2002 and 2003 consolidated financial statements, which were presented to U.S. investors in August 2003 as proof of Parmalat's financial well-being. "Liquidity is high with significant cash and marketable securities balances," said a Parmalat memorandum (SEC 2003a). The problem was that there was no €3.95 billion. The Bank of America confirmation letter had been forged, apparently by a Parmalat executive using a scanner and a fax machine. Over the next three months Parmalat sold $100 million of unsecured notes[3] to U.S. investors in a last-ditch attempt to avert a looming cash shortage.

While accumulating losses and with debts to the banks, "Parmalat started to build a network of offshore mail-box companies, which were used to conceal losses, through a mirror-game which made them appear as assets or liquidity, while the company started to issue bonds in order to obtain money. The security for such bonds was provided by the alleged liquidity represented by the offshore schemes" (Celani 2004, 2). The largest bond placers were the Bank of America, Citicorp, and J. P. Morgan. These banks, like their European and Italian partners, rated Parmalat bonds as sound when they knew or should have known that they were worth nothing. One of the offshore mailbox firms used to channel the liquidity coming from the bond sales was Buconero.

Fraud Mechanisms, Cooking Books, and Auditors

The technical means used to conceive the fraud were extremely basic. Parmalat hid losses, overstated assets or recorded non-existent assets, understated its debt, and diverted company cash to Tanzi family members. To hide losses, Parmalat used various wholly owned entities, among which the most significant was Bonlat, the Cayman Islands waste basket of the group in its final five years and the holder of the false Bank of America account.

Through different fraudulent schemes, Parmalat also mischaracterized its debt or simply did not record it. However, it recorded non-existent repurchases of bonds. It also sold its accounts receivables,[4] which normally should have been collected by the company.

Funds were diverted to Tanzi family members and their private companies. A recurrent scheme was to record payments as receivables and then
move the false receivables through the web of the offshore entities to blur
their true nature. The Tanzi family also channeled annual repayments for
quantity discounts made by Tetra Pak into a bank account held by a company
wholly controlled by the family. The funds were used by the family as spending money. For the period from 1995 to 2003 the discount payments averaged
around $15 million per year.

Considering the scale of fraudulent accounting and financial reporting
at Parmalat, it is surprising how a string of reputable auditing firms was not
capable of detecting it. Italy was at that time one of the few countries to insist
on auditor rotation every nine years, a measure generally thought to mitigate
against complacency and to promote tighter scrutiny. Italian auditors Hodg-
son Landau Brands were responsible for auditing Parmalat in the 1980s and
then Grant Thornton from 1990 to 1998, followed by Deloitte & Touche as
principal auditor, supported by Grant Thornton, until 2002. No one knew or
no one blew the whistle.

Reality Bites: The €14 Billion Black Hole

The crunch came for Parmalat on December 8, 2003, when Parmalat defaulted
on a €150 million bond. The management claimed that this was because a
customer, a speculative fund named Epicurum, did not pay its bills. Parmalat
had allegedly won a derivative contract[5] with Epicurum, betting against the
dollar. But it was soon discovered that Epicurum was owned by firms whose
address was the same as some of Parmalat's own offshore entities. In other
words, the Epicurum Fund was owned by Parmalat. Pushed to respond to
Consob's questions about Epicurum, Parmalat admitted on December 8 that
the €497 million supposedly in the fund was in fact not there. At the same
time, the company found it could not make a bond payment amounting to
€150 million.

On December 9, 2003, Calisto Tanzi, then Parmalat's chairman and chief
executive officer, and his son, Stefano Tanzi, a senior Parmalat executive, met
with representatives from a New York City-based private equity and financial advisory firm to talk about a leveraged buyout of Parmalat. During that
meeting, as Parmalat's executives talked about the firm's liquidity problems,
one of the New York firm's representatives noted that Parmalat's financial
statements showed that the company had a huge amount of cash, nearly €4
billion. Stefano Tanzi admitted that the cash was not there and that Parmalat
really had only €500 million.

Then Parmalat's new CFO, Luciano Del Soldato, told the New Yorkers that
Parmalat's debt was actually €10 billion, much higher than the balance sheet

showed. Del Soldato said that the balance sheet was incorrect because the company had not repurchased €2.9 billion of Parmalat bonds, even though the balance sheet falsely reflected that the bonds had been repurchased.

The meeting continued the next day, this time with members of the New York firm's restructuring group. They explained to the Parmalat executives that there could be no secret rescue effort; Parmalat had to tell the truth publicly about its financial position. When it became clear that Parmalat's top executives were unwilling to do so, the New York firm's representatives left the meeting.

The next day, Parmalat's share price collapsed and Consob launched a detailed investigation of the groups' accounts. It was not long before news about the forgery of the Bank of America document came out, and Parmalat made front pages all over the world. Soon the U.S. Securities and Exchange Commission (SEC) began its own investigation.

Parmalat acknowledged in a press release on December 19, 2003, that the assets in its 2002 audited financial statements were overstated by at least €3.95 billion (approximately $4.9 billion at current exchange rates). The "excess cash balances," which actually did not exist, were supposed to repurchase €2.9 billion of corporate debt securities (approximately $3.6 billion), but in fact those debt obligations remained outstanding. It was a serious admission for a firm that had used these faked figures to lure U.S. investors just weeks before. Figures released by the company in January 2004 showed Parmalat's debt to be eight times the amount reported in its previous financial statements, placing the company's accounting discrepancy at more than €14 billion. Parmalat announced the findings of its new auditor, PricewaterhouseCoopers, in a statement released on January 27, 2004. The company said that its net debt minus liquid assets was €14.3 billion at the end of September—far more than the €1.8 billion reported earlier. The company's executives had also overstated earnings by 500 percent on five occasions and sales by 35 percent in the company's statement for the first nine months of 2003.

Tanzi Loses Power: Behind Bars

On December 27, 2003, Parmalat was declared insolvent by the court of Parma and placed into extraordinary administration by Italian legislative decree. That same day, Calisto Tanzi returned from vacation to Milan and found he had been toppled as head of the company by the Italian minister of productive activities, who appointed an extraordinary commissioner of Parmalat to manage the firm while it was in bankruptcy. Tanzi was arrested on charges of misappropriating the company's funds and jailed at Milan's San Vittore Prison. The investigation landed 11 people in jail, among them CFO Del Soldato, former CFO Tonna, and attorney Gian Paolo Zini. Also under arrest were two employees of the former Italian arm of Grant Thornton, the auditing firm. After a few months, Tanzi, Del Soldato, and Tonna were released under house arrest; however, Zini—described as the mastermind behind many of the scams—stayed behind bars. "The Parmalat fraud has been mainly implemented in New York, with the active role of the Zini legal firm and of Citibank" (Celani 2004, 2).

The New York-based Zini law firm had played a role that seems to have come out of the movie *The Godfather*. Through Zini, firms owned by Parmalat were sold to certain American citizens with Italian surnames, only to be purchased later by Parmalat. The money for the sale in the first place came from other entities owned by Parmalat, and it served only to create "liquidity" in the books. Thanks to that liquidity, Parmalat could keep issuing bonds. Zini also registered Parmalat's mutual fund Epicurum through Maples and Calder (the largest law firm in the Cayman Islands), but Epicurum acted only as an escrow[6] account through which Parmalat-related transactions moved; many of these were based on fake intercompany credits.

Because Parmalat was in reorganization under Italian jurisdiction and the Italian authorities were prosecuting its executives, the SEC and U.S. Department of Justice pursued Parmalat under Italian rather than U.S. law. The Americans focused particularly on Parmalat's last-ditch fund raising effort in the United States in the last months of 2003.

The SEC described the Parmalat affair as "one of the largest and most brazen corporate financial frauds in history" (SEC 2003b). According to the SEC, by overstating assets and understating liabilities by approximately €14.5 billion ($17.2 billion) from 1997 through 2003, Parmalat perpetrated a bigger fraud on investors than those of WorldCom and Enron combined. The Parmalat scandal was also described by the Tax Justice Network as the largest corporate fraud in Europe, representing nearly one percentage point of the Italian gross national product. The reorganization of the company by Enrico Bondi, a government-appointed trustee, called for the cutting of 15,000 of the 32,000 jobs at Parmalat and a rolling back of operations from 30 to ten countries.

The SEC put the blame squarely on Tanzi and Tonna, saying that Parmalat had concealed losses and overstated assets through related entities, including nominee companies. It used nominee companies, for example, to conceal uncollectible and impaired receivables,[7] extend loans to Parmalat subsidiaries[8] that those subsidiaries used to hide expenses, and serve as counterparties to transactions from which Parmalat subsidiaries recorded inflated or fictitious revenue.[9]

Second, said the SEC, Parmalat understated debt by approximately $9.16 billion. According to the SEC's complaint, Parmalat eliminated about $3.8 billion in debt through a fictitious transaction in which a nominee entity purportedly acquired that debt, and the company falsely portrayed another $1.16 billion in debt as equity.

Third, the SEC alleged that Parmalat unlawfully diverted about $400 million to members of the Tanzi family. The company concealed these payments by recording them as receivables to unrelated third parties.

Former CFO Tonna told prosecutors that he benefited personally from funds held by subsidiaries in Luxembourg, and he claimed that the company took kickbacks from TetraPak—an allegation that the Swedish company has denied. According to the SEC, U.S. investors, who bought over $1 billion in Parmalat bonds between 1997 and 2003 (*SEC v. Parmalat Finanziaria, SpA.*, July 28, 2004), suffered enormous losses because of Parmalat's dishonesty.

The U.S. District Court of New York held that Parmalat's executives acted knowingly or recklessly and that they were reckless in not knowing that the company's consolidated accounts for 2002 and for the first quarter 2003 through the third quarter 2003, inclusive, contained material misstatements and omissions.

In July 2004, the SEC announced that it had reached a settlement with Parmalat that brought the regulator's action to a close. The settlement, which was filed in the United States, is significant because Parmalat agreed to a variety of corporate governance reforms. As such, the Parmalat case marks the continuation of a trend in which corporate governance undertakings are becoming a common remedy in major SEC enforcement actions.

The auditors did not escape responsibility for their negligence. In August 2004, the commissioner in charge of the administration of Parmalat sued auditing firms Deloitte Touche Tohmatsu and Grant Thornton International and their Italian and U.S. affiliates. The commissioner held that both networks failed to properly audit Parmalat's companies and their related party transactions.

Despite the ongoing investigations and problems of untangling the complex web of intercompany relationships that was Parmalat, extraordinary commissioner Bondi quickly moved to keep the business trading, placate creditors, and safeguard jobs at Parmalat. Bondi also set about mapping out a restructuring plan, including businesses to be continued and those to be divested, unproductive assets to be offloaded, and ways of satisfying creditors and restoring the financial health of the group. The proposal of composition with creditors was signed on July 27, 2004, by Bondi and the *new* Parmalat—a different legal entity from the old firm. The old Parmalat was dead and buried.

Notes

1. A holding company or parent company is a company that owns enough voting stock in another firm to control management and operations by influencing or electing its board of directors.
2. A company's shares can be offered either to investors at large or directly to the firm's existing stockholders. The first method is called *a general*

cash offer; the second is called *a privileged subscription* or *rights issue.* When a company wants to increase its share capital, it must offer rights issue to its existing shareholders according to the proportion of their existing numbers of shares. If existing members do not accept this offer, company management issues such shares in a manner that it thinks fit.

3. Unsecured notes, in contrast to secured notes, are backed only by the promise of the issuer to pay interest and principal (the original borrowed money) on a timely basis. Secured notes are generally backed by a legal claim on some specified assets of the issuer in the case of default. In fact, Parmalat issued unsecured senior guaranteed notes, but the guarantee was mostly given by the general credit of the company and was not based on particular assets.

4. Accounts receivable financing and factoring are financial operations to improve the company's cash flow. Under these financing programs, the company can sell its accounts receivables to financial institutions such as banks. In many instances, the banks have financed the amount of the receivables and then assumed responsibility for collecting the accounts. Some accounts receivable programs are *recourse* in nature, meaning the company selling the receivables is contingently liable for accounts on which the purchaser cannot collect. In the case of a *no-recourse* feature, which was used by Parmalat, the bad debt accounts cannot be returned to the company.

5. Derivatives are financial instruments that have no intrinsic value, but derive their value from something else. They hedge the risk of owning things that are subject to unexpected price fluctuations (e.g., foreign currencies, bushels of wheat, stocks, and government bonds). There are two main types: futures, or contracts for future delivery at a specified price, and options that give one party the opportunity to buy from or sell to the other side at a prearranged price.

6. Very simply defined, an escrow is a deposit of funds, a deed, or other instrument by one party for the delivery to another party upon completion of a particular condition or event.

7. Parmalat Finanziaria transferred uncollectible and impaired receivables to "nominee" entities, where their diminished or non-existent value was hidden. As a result, Parmalat Finanziaria carried assets at inflated values and avoided the negative impact on its income statement that would have been associated with a proper reserve or write-off of bad debt.

8. Parmalat Finanziaria used the nominee entities to disguise intercompany loans from one subsidiary to another subsidiary that was experiencing operating losses. Specifically, a loan from one subsidiary would be made to another subsidiary operating at a loss. The recipient then improperly applied the loan proceeds to offset its expenses and thereby

increase the appearance of profitability. As a result, rather than having a neutral effect on the consolidated financial statements, the loan trans- action served to inflate both assets and net income, which ultimately affect stockholders' equity.

9. Parmalat Finanziaria recorded fictional revenue through sales by its subsidiaries to controlled nominee entities at inflated or entirely ficti- tious amounts. In order to avoid unwanted scrutiny due to the aging of the receivables associated with these fictitious or overstated sales, the related receivables would be transferred or sold to nominee entities.

References

Celani, C. "The Story behind Parmalat's Bankruptcy," *Executive Intelligence Review (EIR)*, January 19, 2004.

European Corporate Governance Institute (ECGI). "Financial Scandals and the Role of Private Enforcement: The Parmalat Case," law working paper no. 40, 2005. www.ecgi.or/wp, 57 pp.

Hamilton, S. "Case Study: How Going Global Compromised Parmalat," *European Business Forum (EBF)*, (2004): 9 pp.

Parmalat Finanziaria SpA. "Information Regarding Compliance with the Guide- lines Contained in the Voluntary Code of Best Practice for Listed Companies," Ordinary and Extraordinary General Meetings April 30 and May 2, 2001.

"Parmalat Finanziaria (under Extraordinary Administration)," Commissioner's Report on the Reasons of Insolvency of the Company and its Subsidiaries, 2004, pp. 7.

SEC (Securities and Exchange Commission). "SEC Charges Parmalat with Financial Fraud," Accounting and Auditing Enforcement Release No. 1936/December 30, 2003a. Litigation Release No. 18527.

_____. *Securities and Exchange Commission v. Parmalat Finanziaria SpA,* United States District Court for the Southern District of New York Complaint. Case No. 03 CV 10266 (PKC) (S.D.N.Y.), 2003b.

_____. *SEC v. Parmalat Finanziaria, SpA.,* Lit. Rel. No. 18803, 2004 SECLEXIS 1631, July 28, 2004.

Bibliography

Carpenter, G. "Casualty Specialty Update," September, 2006, www.guycarp.com.

Consob (Italian Securities Exchange Commission). "Official Prospectus Regarding the Restructuring Plan of the Parmalat Group of Companies under Extraordi- nary Administration 2005," (http://www.parmalat.net), 532 pp.

Fama. E. F. "Agency Problem and the Theory of the Firm," *Journal of Political Econ- omy,* 88 (1980): 288–307.

Fama, E. F., and M. C. Jensen. "Separation of Ownership and Control," *Journal of Law & Economics,* 26 (1983): 301–325.

McCahery J. A., and E. P. M. Vermeulen. *Corporate Governance Crises and Related Party Transactions: A Post-Parmalat Agenda* In K. J. Hopt et al, *Changes of Governance in Europe, Japan and U.S.* (pp. 215–245). Oxford, Oxford University Press, 2005.

Maddaloni, A., and D. Pain. 2004. "Corporate Excesses and Financial Market Dynamics," *European Central Bank, Occasional Paper Series,* no. 17, July, 2004.

Melis, A. "Corporate Governance Failures: To What Extent Is Parmalat a Particularly Italian Case? *Corporate Governance: An International Review,* 13(4) (2005).

———. "Critical Issues on the Enforcement of the True and Fair View Accounting Principle. Learning from Parmalat," *Corporate Ownership & Control,* 2(2) (2005).

Preda Code. "Code of Conduct for Listed Companies *Comitato per la Corporate Governance Delle Società Quotate,*" sponsored by the Italian Stock Exchange (*Borsa Italiana*), 1999, 2002.

PricewaterhouseCoopers. "2004 Foreign Securities Litigation Study," 2004, 28 pp.

———. "Commissioner's Report on the Reasons of the Insolvency of Parmalat Finanziaria SpA and Those of Its Subsidiaries Included in the Proposal of Composition with Creditors," June 21, 2004.

Shleifer, A., and R. W. Vishny. "A Survey of Corporate Governance," *Journal of Finance,* LII(2) (1997): 737–783.

Sverige, C. "The Parmalat Scandal and Globalization: Impact on the Italian Economy," April, 2004. World Socialist Web site, http://www.wsws.org/.

Tax Justice Network. "The Public Eye Awards 2006—Nomination Form A," http://www.evb.ch/cm_data/NOM-CITIGROUP.pdf.

Gumbel, P. "How It All Went So Sour," *Time Europe Magazine,* January 26, 2006.

Royal Ahold: Leadership Failure and "Big Bath" Accounting

20

BAHRAM SOLTANI
FLORA SOLTANI

Contents

Early Days

In 1887 in the Netherlands, Albert Heijn took over his father's store, selling a wide variety of products, from groceries to dredging nets and tar. The family business was then incorporated as a limited liability company under the laws of the Netherlands and grew steadily. Ten years later Heijn opened stores in Alkmaar, The Hague, and Amsterdam and soon the firm had 23 stores.

In 1911, the firm was making cookies and selling them under the Albert Heijn brand name. From these modest beginnings, the firm developed activities including the production of tea, coffee, and peanut butter, and the bottling of wine.

Heijn had serious financial difficulties in the 1940s, and in 1948 the Albert Heijn firm went public and was listed on the Amsterdam Stock Exchange. However, the Heijn family kept control of the company with Heijn's two sons, Gerrit Jan and Ab, holding 50 percent of the shares. To reinforce the power of the family in the company while taking advantage of public investment, the two sons received 50 percent of the outstanding shares. In the public offering, the two sons received "founder" shares, also referred to as "priority" shares. These entitled the Heijn family to effectively control the firm, having the right to nominate members of the management board and one member on the supervisory board. The family members also had a right to a higher dividend. In 1951, the firm acquired the Van Amerongen retail chain and then opened the first self-service supermarket, in Rotterdam, in 1955.

In 1973, further growth in the Netherlands and abroad was enabled by the founding of Ahold N.V, with the Albert Heijn firm as prime subsidiary. Throughout the 1970s and 1980s, the group continued its expansion in retailing. A liquor chain, Alberto, and health and beauty care chain, Etos, were Ahold's first specialty stores. In 1977, Ahold entered the U.S. market for the first time, acquiring the BI-LO supermarket chain in the Carolinas and Georgia. In 1981 and 1988, Ahold acquired its second and third U.S. supermarket companies, Pennsylvania-based Giant Food Stores and Finast in Ohio. Two decades of success were crowned in 1988 when Queen Beatrix of the Netherlands awarded Ahold the designation "royal" for its 100th anniversary.

Throughout this time, Ahold had never ceased to be a family company. The Ahold Group operated under a two-tier board structure; the management board was monitored by a supervisory board, and the Heijn family dominated both. Family members Jan Heijn, the founder of Ahold, and his two sons CEO Ab Heijn and Gerrit Jan Heijn,[1] were members of the management board and at the same time the family-controlled supervisory board.

A Bright New Dawn

In 1988, Royal Ahold seemed to be standing on the edge of a new era. The third-generation manager, Albert Heijn, retired after 27 years and was succeeded as president by Pierre Everaert, the first nonfamily member to hold the position. Five years later Royal Ahold—now the center of an expansive web of companies—was listed on the Amsterdam Stock Exchange. In theory, at least, this meant the weakening of the control of the Heijn family. In reality, Ahold employed a range of devices to preserve the power of the main shareholder block (the Heijn family) and deny influence to smaller shareholders. Ahold preferred to issue non-voting shares and its use of founder or priority shares, which gave the company founders the right to nominate board members, kept minor shareholders far from the decision making. Other mechanisms, such as using preferred shares,[2] were designed to defeat any hostile takeovers.

Given that the Dutch code of governance is relatively flexible and contains different alternatives, Royal Ahold management was able to run the company for the benefit of family ownership without being disturbed by dispersed shareholders. The company was using the two-tier system of management in which a supervisory board exists alongside the management board. Prior to 1987, the management board consisted primarily of Ab Heijn and Gerrit Jan Heijn. Although after 1987 the management board was expanded from two to seven members and included some outside professional management, several of them were selected by the Heijn family.

Buy! Buy! Buy!

With the full backing of the family, Everaert was set on transforming Royal Ahold into a corporate giant, comparable with Wal-Mart in the United States and Carrefour in France. He upped the already ambitious ten percent annual growth in earnings per share[3] to 15 percent. Of that, ten percent was to come from internal growth and 5 percent from external growth. To make good his promise, Everaert embarked on a massive campaign of acquisitions in the 1990s. The company's management wanted to use these acquisitions as the engine of growth by diversifying out of groceries into the food service business. The strategy was based on acquiring a large number of companies with high equity values and profit expectations. With the 15 percent growth target and the inherent risks associated with acquisitions, the pressure was on Ahold's management. That pressure continued in 1993 when Cees van der Hoeven—another Heijn family choice—took over as CEO.

In the 1990s, the fall of Communism in central Europe enabled Ahold to establish a holding company in Czechoslovakia. During the same period Royal Ahold flexed its muscle in the United States by several acquisitions, such as Tops Markets, Inc. in New York, Red Food Stores' 55 supermarkets in Tennessee and Georgia, Georgia Mayfair in the New York metropolitan area, Stop & Shop in New England, and Giant Food, with operations in Maryland, Virginia, West Virginia, and the District of Columbia. Ahold stock was traded for the first time on the New York Stock Exchange in 1993. In Europe, Ahold was listed on the Amsterdam, Zurich, and Brussels exchanges. Ahold and its Portuguese partner formed Jerónimo Martins Retail, and later Ahold acquired 150 supermarkets in Madrid, southern Spain, and Catalonia.

In South America, Ahold's Brazilian partner, Bompreço, acquired Super-Mar in 1997. In 1998, Ahold acquired Velox Retail Holdings and formed a partnership to acquire a majority stake in Disco, the Argentine supermarket chain, and Santa Isabel in Chile, Peru, and Paraguay. Etos, Ahold's chain of health and beauty care stores, acquired Le Drugstore. At the end of 1999, Ahold teamed up with La Fragua, Central America's leading food retailer, in Guatemala, El Salvador, and Honduras. Two years later, Ahold and La Fragua announced their intention to team up in a new joint venture with

Costa Rican market leader CSU, creating the largest food store network in the Central American region, with sales of $1.3 billion. Ahold also moved into Asia by developing food retail activities with local partners in Singapore, Thailand, Malaysia, and China.

Growing Out of Control

Early in the 1990s and towards the end of the decade, when acquisition activity became frenetic, management was apparently overwhelmed by the workload. Most of its time was devoted to investment decisions and worrying about the 15 percent projected earnings growth. Too little time was given to managing and monitoring a sprawling empire. Royal Ahold acquired these companies without adopting appropriate planning and control systems within the acquired companies. Ahold let the local operations run themselves. In contrast to the policies of Carrefour and Wal-Mart, whose acquired companies operate under one name, Ahold's leadership left the store chains under their own names, local management, and local identities. There was not even much communication or feedback between the different units of the group and, as a consequence, an "us and them" mentality developed between the head office and the subsidiaries.

Several members of the supervisory board were previous employees of Royal Ahold and had been nominated internally. They were also committed to several outside business activities and their overcommitment and close links to the controlling Heijn family prevented them from being as vigilant as they might have been.

The Heijn family was also interested in nominating some political personalities to the Ahold boards. Several members of Ahold's board of executives had strong political ties and high-ranking political responsibilities before joining the company. They included Dutch political personalities such as former members of parliament and ministers Roelof Nelissen, Rempt-Halmmans de Jongh, De Koning, and Jos A. van Kemenade, as well as a former U.S. ambassador to the Netherlands, Cynthia P. Schneider.

Royal Ahold also suffered from a 50 percent board member turnover between 1998 and 2002. Ahold did try to infuse itself with new blood by means of an option-based incentive scheme to attract some of the top executives of other companies. Company officers were given shares of stock to increase their loyalty to the company. However, this system did not serve to cement the loyalty of the executives because most of the shares obtained through this plan were rapidly sold by the executives.

The quest for more acquisitions continued into 2000. Etos, Ahold's health and beauty business, finalized its acquisition of British drugstore chain Boots Stores in the Netherlands, and Santa Isabel, Ahold's Chilean joint venture operation, agreed to acquire 100 percent of Chilean Supermercados Agas S.A. Ahold announced its intention to acquire U.S. Internet grocer Peapod, in Chicago, and the Golden Gallon convenience gas store chain in Tennessee. Ahold also helped found the Worldwide Retail Exchange, a Web-based business-to-business e-commerce initiative, with 17 U.S. and European retailers. It was another marvelous year for Ahold. The firm announced a net earnings surge of 48 percent to €1.1 billion. Operating results rose 61 percent to €2.3 billion, sales increased by 56 percent to €52.5 billion, and earnings per common share were up by 32 percent to €1.51.

The "Big Bath" at U.S. Foodservice

One of Ahold's acquisitions in 2000, U.S. Foodservice, was to have repercussions for the whole group. U.S. Foodservice was a food distributor with over 130,000 institutional customers, and it grew even bigger after its acquisition by Ahold. U.S. Foodservice then completed the acquisition of southeastern U.S. operator, PYA/Monarch, closely followed by Parkway Food Service, a broadline distributor in western Florida, and Mutual Distributors, Inc.

U.S. Foodservice, however, was a sick company. Even before the Ahold acquisition, its executives had fallen into the habit of artificially inflating the firm's revenue figures. In the absence of adequate oversight from the new Ahold parent company, these practices—known in the world of accounting as "big bath" behavior or "making the numbers"—spiraled out of control.

The scam at U.S. Foodservice related to promotional allowances—rebates that suppliers pay to client firms for committing to purchase a given volume. U.S. Foodservice colluded with its suppliers to pump up the amount of promotional allowances received from them. Its personnel would typically contact vendors and urge them to sign and return the false confirmation letters. Suppliers that had scruples about participating in the scheme were apparently put under considerable pressure by their important client. Sometimes, U.S. Foodservice executives provided side letters to the vendors assuring them that they did not in fact owe the company the amounts reflected as outstanding in the confirmation letters. The letters clearly stated that the confirmations were being used in connection with the annual audit and directed the suppliers to return the confirmations directly to U.S. Foodservice's auditors. The amounts overstated in the confirmations were often inflated by more than 100 percent, in amounts measured in millions of dollars. In this way, many suppliers were entangled in a web of illegal activity emanating from U.S. Foodservice.

The company's personnel also colluded among themselves to systematically hide the reality from the firm's auditors. The prevalence of this scheme can be appreciated by the degree of distortion it produced in the stated revenues of U.S. Foodservice. The overstated promotional allowances added up to at least $700 million for fiscal years 2001 and 2002. This sum was then included in Ahold's audited figures and caused the parent firm to report false income for those periods. Because the preparation of financial reports and the choice of accounting methods were the responsibilities of Royal Ahold's management, U.S. Foodservice's actions entangled the Heijn family and other members of the group's board of directors in fraudulent financial reporting.

Stretching the Truth in Amsterdam

Back in Amsterdam, the Dutch executives of Ahold were playing much the same game, but on a far bigger scale. Ahold's international expansion was largely based on joint ventures with local companies, which clearly provided for joint and equal control by Ahold and its partners. Ahold executives illegally consolidated these joint ventures, claiming that Ahold had something more than 50 percent ownership, in collusion with the joint venture partners. Ahold executives would ask the partners to sign letters stating that Ahold controlled the venture, and they would then sign secret, side letters with the partner reaffirming the joint control. The first letters were passed on to Ahold's auditors to help justify the firm's excellent revenue results. The side letters were hidden from the auditors. The top management of Ahold was implicated in the scam.

Chief Financial Officer (CFO) Michiel Meurs signed all but one of the control and rescinding letters on behalf of Ahold. He also knew that Ahold's auditors were relying on the control letters and were unaware of the existence of the rescinding letters. CEO Cees Van der Hoeven cosigned one of the rescinding letters; if he was not colluding in the scam, he was at least reckless in not knowing what was happening.

As a result of the fraud, Ahold wildly overstated net sales by approximately € 4.8 billion for fiscal year 1999, and then €12.2 billion for 2001. For the same period Ahold materially overstated operating income by approximately €222 million for 1999 to €485 million for 2001.

Pats on the Back

Publicly, the year 2001 was another triumph, with Ahold developing the Internet as a selling tool and buying up another leading foodservice operator, Alliant Exchange, the parent company of Alliant Foodservice, Inc., a U.S. business with net sales of approximately $6.6 billion in fiscal year 2000, as well as the Bruno's supermarkets chain, a prominent food retailer in the southeastern United States. Ahold also won the new Dutch Reputation Award. It picked up the Dutch Investor Relations Prize and was named

U.S. Retailer of the Year by prominent trade publication *MMR* (*Mass Market Retailers*). Ahold announced a 2001 sales surge: 27 percent to a record €66.6 billion with net earnings of €1.11 billion. In April 2002, Ahold opened a new financial center, Ahold Finance Group Suisse, in Geneva, Switzerland. CEO van der Hoeven especially was reaping the praise for transforming the once staid family firm into an aggressive global player in food.

The company appeared to be in good shape. Ahold was the world's third largest group in its sector, after Wal-Mart and Carrefour, with consolidated net sales of €62.7 billion from around 5,606 stores in 27 countries in the United States, Europe, Latin America, and the Asia Pacific region. There was to be no letup in the firm's expansion program. Van der Hoeven announced a "tough program for future growth and profitability" focused on portfolio rationalization and debt reduction.

Despite the confident talk, the company's strategy was running into serious trouble. The acquired companies were not generating the income that Ahold's executives had imagined, and now almost the entire acquisitions program was relying on borrowed money. For example, Ahold had raised €2.2 billion around the world to partially pay for the Alliant acquisitions. But with the borrowings based on falsely inflated revenue figures, time was running out for the Dutch giant.

Black Monday: Judgment Day

February 24, 2003, was a black day in the long history of Ahold. Apparently understanding the fraud, or at least that it could no longer continue like this, the firm came clean with the world about the accounting irregularities. Ahold announced that net earnings and earnings per share would be significantly lower than previously indicated for fiscal year 2002 and that the financial statements for fiscal years 2000 and 2001 would be restated. In fact, the 2002 results would be restated as a loss of €1.2 billion. Ahold revealed more than $880 million in accounting irregularities at U.S. Foodservice and a range of lesser legal problems at subsidiaries in Argentina and Scandinavia.

Following the announcement of the accounting irregularities, Ahold's share price plummeted. In New York, the company's shares closed at $10.69 on Friday, February 21. However, word about its accounting woes was on the street when U.S. markets opened on Monday, and Ahold's stock prices went into freefall, losing two thirds of their value almost immediately. The firm's credit rating[4] was reduced to junk and it was forced to rely on an expensive emergency credit to pay its bills. In terms of litigation risk, the Ahold group was rated *very aggressive* for the 19 consecutive quarters beginning in January 2000 and ending in mid 2004, placing it in the riskiest 1/10 of 1 percent

(0.1%) of all public companies in the United States according to the rating of consultancy firm Audit Integrity.

Heads rolled at Ahold. A string of top executives resigned, including CEO van der Hoeven[5] and CFO Meurs. Jim Miller, president and CEO of U.S. Foodservice and a member of the board of Ahold, resigned from these positions together with three of his management team members.

Road to Recovery Program and Forensic Accounting Investigation

To respond quickly to the financial disaster, which had caused a 60 percent plunge in the value of Ahold shares on the Amsterdam and New York stock markets, the group designed its "road to recovery program." This included a three-year financing plan and strategy to restore public confidence. Ahold also appointed a former CEO of IKEA, Aners Moberg, as its new CEO. Ahold accepted responsibility for past fraudulent accounting and reporting and promised the future would be different. The new Ahold would value transparent communication within the company and with the general public. To press the point, the promises were delivered in a leaflet to every household in the Netherlands. The new management team admitted that the high management turnover rate at Ahold and option-based incentive schemes, coupled with the strong influence and voting rights of the Heijn family, were considered as one of the major sources of management failure at Ahold.

However, Ahold's most immediate problem was cash. Facing a €12 billion mountain of debt and significant financial losses, the firm obtained a commitment for a new credit facility[6] totaling €2.65 billion. Ahold entered into a new revolving credit facility[7] with ABN AMRO, Goldman Sachs, ING, JP Morgan, and Rabobank.

Ahold's auditors (Deloitte & Touche) decided to suspend the 2002 fiscal year audit while Ahold itself was put under the microscope by PricewaterhouseCoopers (PWC), another Big Four auditing firm. When PWC released its report on the forensic investigation in July 2003, it had found hundreds of internal-control weaknesses and accounting irregularities. According to the Web site for senior finance executives, these included 470 accounting irregularities and 278 internal-control weaknesses. "Things were worse than anyone could have imagined," the accountancy firm said. At U.S. Foodservice, PricewaterhouseCoopers found an additional €73 million of intentional accounting irregularities. Ahold appointed Larry Benjamin as U.S. Foodservice CEO and he set about a thorough purge and reorganization of the firm. Ahold also said that certain joint ventures would be deconsolidated based on information that had not previously been made available to Ahold's auditors.

The Legal Fallout

Then the lawyers moved in. In July 2003, Dutch authorities conducted a search of Ahold headquarters as part of their investigation into the company. The Dutch authorities were particularly interested in the side letters that facilitated the wrongful consolidation of joint ventures. By September, it was all over. Ahold announced that it had reached a settlement with the Dutch public prosecutor and that the firm would pay €8 million. In turn, the Dutch public prosecutor would not institute proceedings against the company.

The American authorities' action wound up almost as quickly. The Security and Exchange Commission (SEC) alleged that, as a result of the fraudulent inflation of promotional allowances at U.S. Foodservice, the improper consolidation of joint ventures through fraudulent side letters, and other accounting errors and irregularities, Ahold's original SEC filings for 2000 through 2002 were false and misleading. For fiscal years 2000 through 2002, Ahold overstated net sales by approximately €33 billion ($30 billion). For fiscal years 2000 and 2001 and the first three quarters of 2002, Ahold overstated operating income by approximately €3.6 billion ($3.3 billion) and net income by approximately €900 million ($829 million).

Ahold admitted nothing, but in October 2004 agreed to settle the SEC action by promising to obey the securities laws in the future. Ahold's cooperation with the SEC and its willingness to clean its own house made the American regulator more lenient with the Dutch company.

"This case is also an example of the clear corporate advantage to conducting a comprehensive internal investigation and fully cooperating with the SEC," the SEC said. "Ahold promptly provided (SEC) staff with the internal investigative reports and the supporting information and waived the attorney–client privilege and work product protection with respect to its internal investigations. Ahold promptly took remedial actions including, but not limited to, revising its internal controls and terminating employees responsible for the wrongdoing."

The SEC left the individual Ahold executives to the Dutch authorities to avoid any problem of double jeopardy, and individuals such as former CEO van der Hoeven escaped relatively unscathed. Even their legal expenses were covered by Ahold. The fallout might have been greater for certain smaller fish. For example, the American regulator prosecuted those directly involved in the U.S. Foodservice affairs, including the suppliers who had colluded with company personnel.

Ahold's minority shareholders in the United States and the Netherlands were hurting badly. More than $30 billion had been wiped off the market capitalization of the firm since 2000, an equity decline of 75 percent. The shareholders—aided by the Association of Dutch Shareholders—brought a class action shareholder lawsuit against the company and filed a request with an Amsterdam court for an investigation into the affairs of Ahold between 1999 and December 18, 2003. The request for an investigation included Ahold's consolidation of joint ventures, U.S. Foodservice and certain other American subsidiaries, financial and accounting matters, and internal controls. Ahold settled the class action lawsuit of U.S. investors regarding its 1999–2003 accounting irregularities for $1.1 billion in a deal that covered the parent company, its subsidiaries, and present and former officers. Some officers and directors of Ahold were personally named in both criminal and civil cases. The investors also said they would push ahead with plans to sue Ahold's auditors during the period of the fraud, Deloitte & Touche, for $3 billion. The results of those legal actions are still pending. After the crash of Ahold, the firm tried to shore up its position by divesting certain assets and, perhaps ironically, this also embroiled the company in legal action.

Corporate Governance Practices at Ahold

The Ahold supervisory board unveiled changes to its composition: Chairman Henny de Ruiter was to resign at the following shareholders' meeting and Karel Vuursteen was to succeed De Ruiter. Shareholders approved the appointment of Anders Moberg as president and chief executive officer and Hannu Ryöppönen as chief financial officer at the general meeting of shareholders in July 2003. When Ryöppönen decided to join the firm, he said a friend warned him that it would be like "going into a sauna and staying there for a year." At the time, "I didn't understand how right he was," Ryöppönen said. The newly appointed CFO also stated that "the old structure was an 'us and them' situation between CFOs of the units and the centre." In response to public debate on executives' remuneration at Ahold, CEO Anders Moberg announced his agreement to adjust his remuneration package in September 2003.

On December 9, 2003, the Netherlands adopted a voluntary corporate governance code, which set out a set of "best practice" principles for corporations. Early the next year, Ahold Group announced it would comply with the code. At an extraordinary general meeting of shareholders in March 2004, shareholders gave their consent to all the proposed changes to the corporate governance structure. According to company reports, Ahold Group applies all of the relevant provisions of the Dutch corporate governance code with a couple of (perhaps minor) exceptions. For example, the code recommends board members must keep shares obtained under a long-term incentive plan for at least five years, but Ahold allows divestment after three years. Given that the Dutch code is not considered particularly severe by international standards and given Ahold's recent history, it is surprising that the firm could not manage total compliance with the code.

Although the scandal of 2003 hurt Ahold, it was far from fatal. Over the following two years the company was able to claw its way back to financial health and respectability. The annual report of 2005 showed Ahold with net sales of approximately €52 billion.

Notes

1. Gerrit Jan Heijn was kidnapped and murdered in 1987 (De Jong et al. 2005, 20).
2. Preferred share refers to capital stock that provides a specific dividend paid before any dividends are paid to common stock holders and takes precedence over common stock in the event of a liquidation. Preferred stock is classified as a fixed-income security because its yearly payment is stipulated as either a coupon (e.g., 5 percent of the face value) or a stated dollar amount (e.g., $5 preferred).
3. Net income attributed to each common stock.
4. A credit rating assesses the credit worthiness of an individual, corporation, or even a country. Credit ratings are calculated from financial history and current assets and liabilities. A credit rating tells a lender or investor the probability of the subject being able to pay back a loan. A poor credit rating indicates a high risk of defaulting on a loan and thus leads to high interest rates.
5. De Jong et al. reported that "in 2002, the management board held about 2 million options; Van der Hoeven (CEO) had about half of those options. However, some members of groups' management owned very few shares, 188,000, and van der Hoeven ranked a distant third among board with 34,000 shares" (2005, 24).
6. Financial institutions (mostly commercial banks) offer a credit facility that gives qualified borrowers fast, flexible, and affordable access to short- and long-term credit.
7. A revolving credit facility, also known as a "revolver," is designed to optimize the availability of working capital by enabling a firm to borrow up to a prespecified amount, usually over a 1- to 5-year period. As the borrower repays a portion of the loan, an amount equal to the repayment can be borrowed again under the terms of the agreement.

References

Ahold Group. "Annual Report" (2000, 2001, 2002, 2003, 2004, 2005, 2006). http://www.ahold.com.

_____. "Corporate Governance Report," November 2006, http://www.ahold.com.

_____. "Ahold Outlines 3-Year Financing Plan and Strategy to Restore Value."
     November 2003.
_____. "History of Ahold," November 2006, http://www.ahold.com.
Corporate Governance Committee. "The Dutch Corporate Governance Code: Prin-
     ciples of Good Corporate Governance and Best Practice Provisions," Decem-
     ber 2003, 71 pp.
De Jong, A., D. V. Dejong, G. Mertens, and P. Roosenboom. "Royal Ahold: A Failure
     of Corporate Governance and an Accounting Scandal," working paper, March
     2005, 56 pp.
Securities and Exchange Commission. "SEC Charges Royal Ahold and Three Former
     Top Executives with Fraud," http://www.sec.gov/news/press/2004-144.htm.
_____. "Nine Individuals Charged by the Securities and Exchange Commission
     with Aiding and Abetting Financial Fraud at Royal Ahold's U.S. Foodservice
     Subsidiary for Signing and Returning False Audit Confirmations," http://www.
     sec.gov/news/press/2005-7.htm.
Soltani, B. *Factors Affecting Corporate Governance and Audit Committees in Selected
     Countries (France, Germany, the Netherlands, the United Kingdom, and the
     United States)*, 200. Altamonte Springs, FL: The Institute of Internal Auditors
     Research Foundation, 2005.

Bibliography

Karaian. J. "Retail Therapy," Web site for senior finance executives, 2005, http://
     www.cfoeurope.com.
Tabaksblat Committee. The Dutch Corporate Governance Code, December 2003.
White G. I., A. C. Sondhi, and D. Fried. *The Analysis and Use of Financial State-
     ments*. New York: John Wiley & Sons, Inc., 1994.

The Vivendi Debacle: The Fallen Superstar

21

BAHRAM SOLTANI
FLORA SOLTANI

Contents

The Making of a French Corporate Name

In 1953, the French utilities firm Compagnie Générale des Eaux (CGE) could look back on 100 years of success. The drinking water distribution company had been founded by imperial decree and won its first contract to supply Lyon (France's second biggest city) in 1853. It went on to win similar contracts in other French cities. CGE began supplying drinking water to Venice, Italy, in 1880 and then moved into wastewater treatment. The company continued its steady if unspectacular progress, always staying close to its core activities. Just three years after the company's centenary, in 1956, the person who would take the venerable old firm on a roller coaster ride to disaster was born in Grenoble, a city in southern France near Switzerland.

An Ambitious Young Man

The son of an accountant, Jean-Marie Messier was a serious and hardworking student in his high school years. Although he failed on his first attempt to gain entry to the elite École Polytechnique (French engineering school), he retook the entrance examinations the following year and was admitted. He did well in his studies, graduating from the school with high marks in 1976. Messier then attended the École Nationale d'Administration (ENA, National School of Administration), the traditional educational route to a high position in the French government. ENA trains the elite of business, civil service, and politics in a nation where the three are intimately linked. ENA's list of alumni reads like a *Who's Who* of modern France and includes the former president Jacques Chirac and a clutch of past and present prime ministers, party leaders, and ministers. Critics of ENA say it operates as a sort of club whose members dominate the highest echelons of French society, sharing out the plum posts among themselves.

After graduating from ENA in 1982, Messier's ambition, reputation as a smart operator, and contacts propelled him up the career ladder. He first joined the French Ministry of Economy and Finance as an auditor of state-owned companies. Then he went to work for the minister of economy, finance, and privatization, Édouard Balladur, to help him privatize those companies. Balladur would go on to be prime minister.

Messier went to work for the Lazard Frères et Compagnie investment bank between 1988 and 1994, where he quickly became the youngest partner in the bank's history. During his years at Lazard, Messier gave advice to French companies about expanding their businesses in the United States. A French journalist said of him at the time: "He was someone who was having an exceptional career. He was growing in power very quickly. He got the reputation of someone who was a very quick thinker." Then he was recruited by the head of CGE in 1994 and just two years later, at the age of 40, Messier became chief executive of the company.

Water, Water Everywhere

CGE had grown a lot since the 1950s but, despite a diversification program during the 1980s, remained essentially a utilities company. Its acquisition of Compagnie Générale de Chauffe in 1980 transformed CGE into the largest private energy group in France. In the 1980s the company also acquired Omnium de Traitement et de Valorisation, a water management company, and Compagnie Générale d'Entreprise Automobiles, a transportation and waste management company. By the early 1990s, GCE was Europe's leading waste management operator. Throughout the 80s and 90s, the company continued its expansion in the United States, buying a wastewater treatment firm and becoming operator of the world's largest household waste incineration plant, in Miami. The company also became majority shareholder of AWT, which supplied drinking water to New York City. The firm acquired other more far-flung subsidiaries, in Australia, Argentina, Mexico, Venezuela, and Spain and, by the end of the 1980s, was making 20 percent of its sales outside France.

CGE also started straying from its original business. In 1983, CGE and the Agence Havas French media group established CANAL+, the first ever pay television channel in France. CGE held a 15 percent stake in the new company. CGE also co-founded mobile telephony provider SFR and even involved itself in the healthcare industry.

Messier Superstar

Messier caught the imagination of France when he arrived as the head of the company. His youth and obvious charisma made him the darling of the French media, and he in turn liked being on television. He looked good in photos and had a talent for the quotable phrase. *Forbes* and *Time* called him a "rock-star CEO." The company got an image makeover too. In 1998, the shareholders dumped the clumsy old Compagnie Générale des Eaux for the more upbeat Vivendi.

This flamboyance was considered more American than French and so too was Messier's management style. French business has traditionally operated on a collegial model of shared decision making, but Messier led from the front. According to Johnson and Orange (2003), Messier had two very different faces: "In public, Messier played the role of a modern, approachable chief executive who believed in collegial management. Inside the company, he could appear authoritarian, sometimes cutting."

According to the *International Directory of Business Biographies,* Messier also relied on his charm to sway board members. He displayed an uncanny ability to play down the downside and pump up the upside of almost any situation. Messier's early successes only added to his aura of invincibility as he set out on a course of corporate conquest on a Napoleonic scale. He aimed to propel the company to the heights of the global media industry and at the same time to consolidate its position as a major utilities firm.

The Man Who Tried to Buy the World

In 1998, the firm merged with Havas, the leading French publishing and multimedia company, and then embarked on a massive buyout of media companies. The company took over the American firm Cendant Software, one of the world's leading producers of PC educational and "how-to" software. It bought MediMedia, an international group specializing in medical information, and an educational publisher in Argentina. A leading American publisher, Houghton Mifflin, became another Vivendi property.

In new media, Vivendi bought MP3.com, the world leader in online music distribution; associated itself with Sony Music Entertainment to launch online music service; and invested $1.5 billion in EchoStar Communications Corporation. In 1999, the company employed 275,000 people around the world with consolidated net sales of €41.6 billion and €2.3 billion operating income.

The acquisitions made headlines and none more so than the 2000 Vivendi–CANAL+–Seagram (Canada) merger. It made Vivendi Universal a giant in media and communications with activities in music, television and film, publishing, telecommunications, and the Internet. The public relations coup for Messier was that now Vivendi controlled Universal studios, the American icon that gave the world movies such as *ET, Jaws,* and *Jurassic Park.* Vivendi Universal was now a media conglomerate second only to AOL Time Warner in size and income.

The Seagram Deal

France congratulated Messier on his North American conquest, but few understood that the merger was in fact a poisoned chalice. The European Commissioner for Competition, Mario Monti, had originally blocked the deal on the grounds that it would restrict free competition. There was a standoff between Messier and Monti during August–October of 2000, but finally the European Commissioner gave the go-ahead. However, the price of acceptance was high. Messier had to give up exclusivity of Universal Music content on the Vizzavi portal (mobile, PC, and interactive TV portal), and was forced to divest a 24 percent shareholding in Rupert Murdoch's BskyB television system. Another concession that saved the deal cut the deepest. Messier was obliged to give up on the exclusive right of French pay-television firm CANAL+ to broadcast all new-release movies and settle for only 50 percent of new releases. The other 50 percent went to CANAL+ rivals. It was a body blow to CANAL+'s profitability and to that of Vivendi. At the same time, the acquisition of Seagram cost around €30 billion. Of this, €29.5 billion was paid on a noncash basis, but making up the shortfall made the group even hungrier for cash.

While Vivendi's media acquisitions excited the public's imagination, the firm's expansion in utilities in the late 1990s and early 2000s was also startling. In Stockholm, the company won a ten-year contract to operate the metro and tramway network. In Melbourne, Australia, a Vivendi subsidiary started running almost half the commuter train network. In Germany, the largest roadwork company became a Vivendi company. By undertaking a diversification strategy, the company was involved in businesses such as water treatment, waste management, transport and train networks, energy services, roadwork, publishing, pay television, mobile telephony, multimedia, entertainment, Internet services, and telecommunications.

Messier rode high on the wave. In 2001 he received the insignia of *Chevalier de Légion d'honneur* (the Knight of the Legion of Honor), and moved with his family into a $17.5 million apartment on Park Avenue in New York. He served on the boards of prestigious companies such as Alcatel, BNP Paribas, Compagnie de Saint-Gobin, LVMH Moët Hennessy, Louis Vuitton, and USA Networks, Inc. He was also a member of the board of the New York Stock Exchange. It must have seemed like the heady days would last forever.

The Big Bluff

The cancer quietly eating away at Vivendi Universal was debt. The firm had grown almost entirely through buyouts. Messier spent more than €60 billion building his empire in 2000 and 2001, and he used different types of borrowings, including the issuance of bonds convertible into common shares, to raise funds. The danger of financing with debt is that the firm must repay the debt and pay interest while the debt is still outstanding. As long as business goes well, the company will be able to pay the interest and repay the capital by generating the cash flows out of its operations. If the company's operations are not profitable, it is difficult for the company to meet its obligations.

As the dot-com bubble burst, it was clear that the company had paid too much for some of its acquisitions. Messier had been paying for these acquisitions with stock prices high, but when prices began to fall toward the end of 2001, the company found itself stacking up huge losses and debt financing.

It is hard to imagine that Messier did not realize the company was sliding to disaster and harder to imagine why he did not act to head it off. Messier instead tried to cover up the truth. He was issuing press releases portraying Vivendi's cash flow (an indicator of its ability to service debt) as "excellent" or "strong" even as the end approached (Vivendi's earnings release dated March 5, 2002).

When Vivendi issued its earnings release for the 2001 fiscal year, the language was extravagant. Vivendi typically announced in press releases and other public statements its earnings before interest, taxes, depreciation, and amortization, which is commonly known as EBITDA and is a frequently used indicator of a firm's ability to pay interest. Vivendi announced that its media and communications business had produced €5.03 billion in EBITDA. In its press release, Vivendi stated that these results were better than projections and that cash flow was well ahead of the company's own internal targets. A press release (March 5, 2002) also emphasized "the excellent operating results that have been achieved" and stated that the results "confirm the strength of Vivendi Universal's businesses across the board despite a very difficult global economic environment." Further, the earnings release highlighted Vivendi's "fundamentally strong operating results" and claimed that Vivendi was "the only media and communications company not to change its numbers and targets." To cap it all, the firm announced it would pay a dividend in May 2002 of €1 per share (press release March 5, 2002).

In addition to its March 5, 2002, earnings release, Vivendi issued other press releases in the first, second, and third quarters of 2002. All were authorized by Messier and presented a materially misleading picture of the company's financial condition. For example, on May 30, 2002, Vivendi issued a press release stating that its "cash situation, which, the company believes, is comfortable—even assuming an extremely pessimistic market—will enable the company to continue its debt reduction program with confidence and with a view to creating the best possible value for its shareholders." This press release was false and misleading because Vivendi's cash situation was not "comfortable," and the company's management knew at this time, or were reckless in not knowing, that Vivendi's cash flow was "zero or negative." In fact, at year-end 2001 and during the first half of 2002, Vivendi produced negative cash flow from core holdings such as its entertainment businesses, indicating that it would not be able to meet its debt obligations.

This was barely offset by cash flow from minority interests such as Cegetel and Maroc Télécom. These factors hindered Vivendi's struggle to reduce its debt and meet its obligations, a condition that was in stark contrast to Vivendi's public statements. Vivendi's €1 per share dividend promise compounded the problems. Vivendi had to borrow to pay the dividend, which cost more than €1.3 billion after French corporate taxes on dividends.

Cooking the Books and "Big Bath" Behavior

The management of Vivendi was quick to embrace "aggressive," "creative" accounting methods that flattered earnings projections, concealed risks, and portrayed a smooth record of profit growth. During 2001 and 2002, Vivendi engaged in a variety of improper accounting practices, euphemistically called "stretching," to meet or exceed earnings targets and give investors a false impression of the firm's financial condition. For example, the firm announced its earnings before interest, taxes, depreciation, and amortization, which gave a rosier picture than the reality. Vivendi's top management, on Messier's orders, improperly adjusted certain reserve accounts of subsidiaries and made other accounting entries without supporting documentation and not in conformity with French and U.S. accounting standards. Certain inconvenient obligations and contingencies were simply left out of the accounts.

Central to public confidence in Vivendi was the company's debt evaluation by rating agencies such as Moody's Investors Services and Standard & Poor's, companies that publish independent credit opinions, research, and commentary to assist investors in analyzing the borrowing risks associated with fixed-income securities. Moody's and Standard & Poor's based their ratings of Vivendi's credit primarily on the company's debt-to-EBITDA ratio. In a series of critical meetings in December 2001, the firm's management was seeking "preclearance" from Moody's and Standard & Poor's that the firm's pending $12 billion acquisitions of parts of USA Networks and Echostar Communications would not lead to a downgrading of Vivendi's rating. Vivendi did not tell the rating agencies the whole truth about the firm's debts, but even then the analysts were skeptical that the coming acquisitions would not overload the firm with debt. However, both credit rating agencies told Vivendi that they would not downgrade its credit rating if Vivendi committed to taking certain debt reduction measures in 2002. Senior officers of Vivendi, particularly Messier, assured Moody's and Standard & Poor's that Vivendi would reduce its debt.

Inconvenient Facts

Economy with the truth was a habit at Vivendi, even in its dealings with regulators. Vivendi's management failed to disclose the full information concerning the firm's investment in a fund that purchased a 2 percent stake in Telco, a Polish telecommunications holding company. In June 2001, Vivendi, which owned 49 percent of Telco's equity, publicly announced its intention to purchase an additional 2 percent of Telco's shares from Vivendi's partner in the Telco joint venture. This purchase would have increased Vivendi's ownership of Telco equity from 49 to 51 percent. Vivendi anticipated that it would have to pay approximately €100 million for the additional Telco shares. After this announcement, Vivendi learned that Poland's antitrust authorities would have to approve the acquisition, a process that could have taken several months. Vivendi also learned that the securities market in general, and the credit rating agencies in particular, might react negatively to Vivendi's acquisition of additional Telco shares. As a result, rather than directly purchasing the 2 percent interest in Telco, Vivendi deposited $100 million into an investment fund administered by Société Générale Bank & Trust Luxembourg. That fund subsequently purchased a 2 percent stake in Telco in September 2001, but the purchase was not disclosed to investors or the rating agencies. Vivendi's Form 20-F submitted to the U.S. market regulator (SEC) for the fiscal year ended

December 31, 2001, and filed with the commission on May 28, 2002, reported only Vivendi's 49 percent interest.

Similarly, Vivendi's top management failed to disclose to the SEC commitments regarding Cegetel and Maroc Télécom that, had Vivendi made the required disclosures, would have revealed doubts about the company's ability to meet its cash needs.

Too Good to Be True

The board of Vivendi Universal included some of the big names of French business, including Bernard Arnault, who was ranked seventh among the world's richest people in 2006 with $21.5 billion, according to *Forbes*. It also included Marc Viénot, honorary chairman (chairman and executive director from 1973 to 1997) of Société Générale, a leading French bank. Marc Viénot acted as a chairman of the audit committee of Vivendi Universal during 2000–2004. He had prepared two French corporate governance codes in 1994 and 1999, entitled Viénot I and Viénot II French corporate governance codes, so he should have been an authority on corporate governance. Such boards are supposed to act in the general interests of the company and its shareholders, but no one raised the alarm. It seems that no one even questioned the CEO about his strategy or the information he was releasing. Nor did the French Financial Market Authority (AMF) or the SEC apparently have any inkling of the coming crash.

But some journalists were asking searching questions, and Messier responded with more and more bluff. On June 26, 2002, in response to media speculation regarding the company's liquidity, Vivendi claimed that it had "around €3.3 billion in unused credit lines to back up its outstanding commercial paper of nearly €1 billion. The cash situation has greatly improved since the beginning of the year" (press release Vivendi Universal, June 26, 2002). Vivendi also claimed that "owing to its strong free cash flow, combined with the execution of the disposals program and potential bond issues, Vivendi Universal is confident of its capacity to meet its anticipated obligations over the next 12 months." In reality, Vivendi's access to credit was much worse than this press release indicated. In fact, the day before Vivendi issued its June 26, 2002, press release, at least €900 million of the €3.3 billion in Vivendi credit lines expired. Further, by this date, Vivendi's cash situation had not improved since the beginning of the year, but rather had worsened as a result of a demand made weeks earlier by its Cegetel telecommunications subsidiary minority shareholders for the repayment of a loan Cegetel had made to Vivendi.

Messier proved that you can fool some of the people some of the time. One analyst even noted that Vivendi's results were a "pleasant surprise," while another news report specifically noted that the results of Cegetel and Vivendi's other telecommunications businesses "defied...the telecommunications meltdown" (SEC April 14, 2004, 4). Vivendi share prices increased by 5 and 5.5 percent in New York and Paris, respectively.

Golden Boy Turns Pariah

As the debt pressure mounted on Messier through 2001 and the first half of 2002, he also seemed to lose his magic ability to charm. Once admired, his arrogance and outspoken style now only caused irritation. His love of things American became a liability in France. In 2001, when he spoke out, saying that the French cultural exception was "dead," Messier caused outrage among many French people. Messier angered especially French politicians and filmmakers by scoffing at the belief in this idea that French culture is precious and needs to be protected against outside, particularly American, dangers. President Chirac said that Messier must have suffered a "mental aberration."

His expensive New York apartment, paid for by Vivendi Universal, became another target for criticism, as did his complaints that, although he was the best paid French executive, he was grossly underpaid by American standards. In 2001, Messier received a gross remuneration of €5.1 million and held around 600,000 shares in the company, but claimed that comparable executives in U.S. companies received double that. When Messier fired Pierre Lescure, the head of Vivendi's pay television company CANAL+, in April 2002, the company employees invaded the studios, stopped program transmission, and broadcast their protests live from the studios. *The Economist* (2002) commented: "In France, JM Messier is too American: an emblem of the 'hollywoodisation' of French culture. In America, he is too French. In Hollywood, he is simply an outsider." Messier was bitter. "The media burns what it yesterday adored," he wrote in his autobiography. His book was entitled "j6m.com"—Jean-Marie Messier, *Moi-Même Maître du Monde* (*Myself, Master of the World*).

The Crash

The end, when it came, was brutal. In late May 2002, the firm was talking about a "comfortable" cash situation, reducing debt, and making its shareholders still richer. In July, Vivendi admitted it was in a crisis situation. The company announced a loss of €13.6 billion for fiscal year 2001 and accumulated debts of €37 billion—most of which were due to the asset write-down of the companies. The next year, the loss was €23 billion and the debt €12.3 billion. Vivendi's colossal, €37 billion loss for 2002 was reportedly the biggest annual corporate loss posted in France's corporate history and surpassed the €20.7 billion loss posted by France Telecom just a day before. The value of the firm's shares fell by 70 percent and trading in them was suspended on the Paris Stock Exchange. The board of Vivendi Universal unanimously asked Messier to quit, and in July 2002 he stepped down. He did not go quietly.

Messier's Golden Parachute

A golden parachute is a clause in an executive's employment contract specifying that he or she will receive large benefits in the event that the company is acquired and the executive's employment is terminated. These benefits can take the form of severance pay, a bonus, stock options, or a combination thereof. Messier's golden parachute was remuneration to July 2002 of €5.6 million; however, he also claimed more than €21 million as a severance package, which included back pay and bonuses for the first half of 2002, under a U.S. contract (in 2003 valued at approximately $25 million, including interest). Jean-René Fourtou, the new Vivendi chairman and CEO, refused, but Messier took it to the arbitration tribunal and won. He would not win against the SEC. It brought a civil fraud action against Messier and former Vivendi CFO Guillaume Hannezo, which resulted in Messier agreeing to pay $1 million and surrender the €21 million severance package. "Messier and Hannezo, Vivendi's two most senior executives, failed in their responsibilities to Vivendi's shareholders. Vivendi and its senior officers participated in a year and a half long effort to avoid acknowledging the company's liquidity problems," said the SEC (SEC 2004b, 1).

The End of the Honeymoon

Messier was also prohibited from serving as an officer or director of a public company for ten years; however, a worse indignity awaited him in France, where he was arrested in June 2004 by the financial brigade on suspicion of disclosure of false financial information on Vivendi's earnings and cash flows, insider trading, improper manipulation of stock prices, misuse of company funds, holding private information, and what the French term "abuse of power." French police were investigating whether the company broke French stock trading rules by repurchasing some of its own shares in 2001. The 2-year investigation dealt especially with Vivendi's actions immediately after September 11, 2001, when financial markets began tumbling and Vivendi began an aggressive buyback of its shares to prop up the price. Vivendi purchased about 21 million of its shares in late September and October 2001, spending €1 billion on this financial operation. French regulations prohibit buybacks in the 15 days before the release of a company's financial results, and they strictly limit the number of its own shares that a company can repurchase. According to the prestigious French daily newspaper *Le Monde*, Deutsche Bank was enlisted to assist in the transaction but backed out because it doubted whether it was legal.

Messier also held in his personal account around 600,000 shares in Vivendi, which he sold before the company's collapse and on which he obtained a substantial capital gain. In fact, Messier had borrowed money from Vivendi to buy the shares and, although such a transaction must be stated in a company's annual report, this was not revealed to the shareholders at the time.

Messier spent only a short time behind bars. He was released on bail of €1.35 million in June 2004 and never went back to prison. In spite of having access to more information than the SEC and given that Vivendi was a French company, the French authorities (including market regulator AMF) acted slowly compared to the SEC. In December 2004, Vivendi and Messier were each fined €1 million, a penalty that was later halved on appeal, and the matter finished there. Messier might have gotten off lightly compared, for example, to the American executives embroiled in the Enron scandal. Nevertheless, he acidly described his former peers, the captains of corporate France, as the "papi flinguers"—the "granddaddy gunslingers."

The Vivendi corporate scandal has had a significant impact on the French financial market. However, this did not really create a panic among the professional bodies (accounting, auditing, financial analysts) or with AMF, the financial market regulator. This passive attitude did not relate to the lack of French public interest, for there was as much media coverage of the Vivendi debacle as of the American corporate scandals. In fact, the defense of the "French exception" in corporate management, similar to other areas, was a determining factor in the accounting profession taking the view that the scandal "does not concern us" or that "nothing like it could happen in France" (Stolowy 2005, 3).

The insufficiency of transparency, monitoring and accountability mechanisms at all institutional levels, along with the generally accepted doctrine of unique thinking (*pensée unique*), can be considered as major sources of social conflicts in French society that have caused serious economic and social damages. In spite of regular public debates in the media, a large number of questions regarding the social and economic issues remain unanswered. As stated by Seidel,

> The institutional framework in France has shown its incapacity to create specifically French concepts and tools in the realm of business ethics. This failure puts large French companies and especially multinationals in a very uncomfortable position. On the one hand it is getting more and more difficult for

them not to succumb to the urgent pressure to act morally in their markets as well as in their organizations as is demanded by many foreign stockholders and authorities supervising financial markets; on the other hand it proves equally difficult to devise and to implement ethical policies that would be easily acceptable in their homeland. (Seidel 2005, 15)

Picking up the Pieces

All that was left was for the new board of Vivendi Universal to pick up the pieces of the shattered company. The firm paid $50 million to settle an action with the SEC and then turned its attention to the debt problem. To cut their losses and increase the cash flows, the new board had to sell many subsidiaries and acquisitions made by Messier. First on the divestment list was CANAL+, a millstone around the firm's neck. The company divested subsidiaries in Italy, Hungary, Monaco, the United States, and France, but it still was not enough.

Vivendi Universal had no choice but to borrow more to pay debts and expenses and throughout 2002 its survival was in the hands of its banks. Without their support, the world's second largest media group would run out of cash within weeks. Vivendi negotiated €3 billion in refinancing with seven banks led by BNP Paribas, Deutsche Bank, and Société Générale. In 2003, Vivendi Universal issued a high-yield bond for a total amount of €1.2 billion to pay its bills.

Messier seemed unmoved by the chaos that his stewardship of the old water company had caused. "I tried to do too much too quickly" was his analysis.

References

Economist. "Messier Than Ever," April 20, 2002, http://www.economist.com/.
International Directory of Business Biographies. http://www. Referenceforbusiness. com.
Johnson, J., and M. Orange. *The Man Who Tried to Buy the World: Jean-Marie Messier and Vivendi Universal.* New York: Portfolio, 2003.
Securities and Exchange Commission. United States of America before the Securities and Exchange Commission. Securities Act of 1933 (release no. 8406) April 14, 2004, http://www.vivendi.com/corp/en/press_2002/20020626_Deleveraging_and_Liquidity_Details.php.
————. "Commission Settles Civil Fraud Action against Vivendi Universal, S.A., Its Former CEO, Jean-Marie Messier, and Its Former COF, Guillaume Hannezo," 2004b, http://www.sec.gov/news/press/2003-184.htm.
Seidel, F. "Institutional Change Needs Public Debate: Some Remarks on the French Failure to Define New Rules of the Game," School of Management of Lyon, working paper no. 2005/07 March 2005, 24 pp.

Stolowy, H. "Nothing like the Enron Affair Could Happen in France (!)," working
paper, HEC School of Management, Paris, France, 20005, 25 pp.

Vivendi Universal. Press release June 26, 2002, http://www.vivendi.com/corp/
en/press_2002/20020626.

_____. Earnings release, March 5, 2002, http://www.vivendi.com/corp/en/files/
cp050302_ang.pdf.

Bibliography

Becht, M., P. Betts, and R. Morck. "The Complex Evolution of Family Affairs,"
Financial Times, February 3, 2003.

Briançon, P. 2002, "The Making of a Mogul," *France Magazine,* 61 (2002), http://
www.francemagazine.org.

Business Strategy Case Studies Collection. "Vivendi Universal: In a Strategic
Flux," http://icmr.icfai.org/casestudies/catalogue/business/.

Khurana, R. "False Prophets, Lost Profits, the Globe and Mail Metro," Bell Globe-
media Publishing Inc. July 3, 2002, 3 pp. http://www.hbs.edu.

Mintzberg, H. "Engaging Leadership—The Thought Leadership Series," an interview, 6 pp, 2005.

Securities and Exchange Commission. *Securities and Exchange Commission v.
Vivendi Universal, S.A., Jean-Marie Messier, and Guillaume Hannezo,* United
States District Court, Southern District of New York, 2003. http://www.sec.
gov/litigation/compaints/.

Soltani, B. *Factors Affecting Corporate Governance and Audit Committees in Selected
Countries (France, Germany, the Netherlands, the United Kingdom, and the
United States).* Altamonte Springs, FL: The Institute of Internal Auditors
Research Foundation, 200 pp., 2005.

Teather, D., and Tran, P. "Another Fine Messier: French Giant in Freefall amid Whiff
of Scandal," *Guardian,* February 7, 2002.

Vivendi Universal. *Annual Report Summary,* 1999.

_____. *Annual Reports,* 2003, 2002, 2001, 2000, 1999 and Form-F.

Watchdogs Caught Napping VI

One feature that separates developed from developing countries is the degree of corruption. Most developed countries have institutional arrangements or government organizations designed to identify or control the amount of fraud. Guardians of the public trust include independent auditors, regulatory agencies, the news media, and the courts.

Even under good circumstances, it is not always possible to identify the occurrence of fraud. When the watchdogs do not act independently of the organizations they should be monitoring, fraud becomes even more prevalent.

This section features chapters relating to failures by the watchdogs. In the case of Arthur Andersen (chapter 22), the watchdog developed a too close relationship with the client that it should have been monitoring. In the case of San Diego's city government (chapter 23), public officials either did not understand or ignored the risks they were undertaking. At United Airlines (chapter 24), business leaders tried unsuccessfully to balance the goals of management, labor, shareholders, and creditors.

The Fall of a Giant: The Case of Arthur Andersen & Co.

22

BONITA K. PETERSON KRAMER
CHRISTIE W. JOHNSON

Contents

Introduction

Few people would have expected to witness the demise of one of the "Big 5" public accounting firms, let alone have imagined the velocity of events that brought Arthur Andersen LLP down. On June 15, 2002, the firm was convicted on charges of obstruction of justice due to the destruction of documents related to its audit of Enron, the Houston-based energy giant.[1] By September 2002, Arthur Andersen LLP essentially ceased to exist as a U.S. accounting firm, having surrendered all of its state licenses to practice. The collapse of the firm came just eleven months after in-house Andersen attorney Nancy Temple sent an email to Enron engagement partner David Duncan saying, "I suggested deleting some language that might suggest we have concluded the release is misleading."[2]

Temple's e-mail refers to the third-quarter press release and $1 billion write-down of investments, pivotal in bringing Enron's financial problems into public view. Some view this message (sent a few days after her e-mail reminding auditors of the firm's document retention policy) as encouraging document destruction, the infamous shredding to which Duncan pleaded guilty to a criminal charge of obstruction of justice (Bravin 2005). On May 31, 2005, the U.S. Supreme Court unanimously overturned the criminal conviction of the firm, ruling juror instructions were too vague for them to determine if Arthur Andersen LLP obstructed justice; the Department of Justice later decided against retrying the case. An anonymous official within the Justice Department commented, "Why would we charge a company that's already defunct?" Defiant to the bitter end, a statement issued by Andersen read, "This represents an important step in removing an unjustified cloud over the professionalism and integrity of the people of Arthur Andersen" (AccountingWEB.com 2005). Duncan was allowed to withdraw his plea and the criminal charge against him was dropped. But the overturned conviction came too late for the now defunct firm and its former 85,000 employees.

What could possibly have happened that led to the rapid demise of such a well-established and respected accounting firm? Some blame the firm as a whole, while others vehemently defend it and blame only the individuals involved. Still others blame the accounting profession and find fault with the audit process, or blame the accounting standard-setters. Many might say Arthur Andersen's demise was due to a failure of leadership and changes in the firm's internal culture. Those same people might go further and argue that perhaps the changes that occurred at Andersen had permeated the public accounting profession as a whole.

It has been widely publicized that Arthur E. Andersen, the firm's founder, was schooled by his mother in the Scandinavian axiom, "think straight, talk straight," a phrase that eventually became the firm's motto and appeared on many internal documents. What might Arthur Andersen think if he had lived to witness these events? Perhaps knowing more about the man and the firm he founded and reading a 1940 memo he wrote to his staff will provide some clues.

Arthur as a Young Man

Orphaned in 1901 at age 16, Arthur Andersen faced many life challenges that most young people do not. While his four younger siblings found homes with relatives, Arthur and his three older siblings were expected to make a living on their own. Arthur first landed a mailroom job with his father's former employer, Fraser & Chalmers Manufacturing Company, and his boss provided him with some financial help to complete his education. Arthur completed high school and then enrolled in evening college courses while working in the mailroom. He performed his duties well and within three years advanced from his entry-level position to that of assistant controller. In 1907, he accepted a position with the accounting firm of Price Waterhouse & Co. and at age 23 became the youngest certified public accountant (CPA) in Illinois. In 1908, he graduated with his degree in business administration from Northwestern University, and the following year he began to teach there in the evening. Two years later, in 1911, he was the controller for Schlitz, a Milwaukee, Wisconsin, beer-brewing company. His move to Milwaukee required that he commute 180 miles daily to continue teaching at Northwestern University in the evenings. He was appointed to the position of assistant professor and head of the Accounting Department in 1912 and was promoted to the highest rank, professor, in 1915. He taught for seven more years until the accounting firm he founded began to demand more of his time and attention.

The Beginning of the Firm

On December 1, 1913, Arthur E. Andersen opened his first accounting practice with Clarence M. DeLany in Chicago at 111 West Monroe Street by purchasing the Audit Company of Illinois for $4,000. They renamed the firm Andersen DeLany & Company. The practice was renamed Arthur Andersen & Co. after Clarence DeLany quit the partnership in 1918.

The firm grew slowly, according to Arthur's philosophy; he was concerned that rapid growth would be detrimental to the quality of service he could provide to clients. Arthur believed he could trust only the staff he himself had trained; new offices were opened only if he could staff them with individuals he had personally groomed. Each partner reported directly to Arthur and had been carefully handpicked and tutored in the firm's methods, a lesson learned by experience when he first opened his practice in 1913. He eventually terminated every member of the Audit Company of Illinois as none met his high expectations.

The partnership grew steadily; annual billings increased from $45,000 to $322,000 between 1913 and 1920, and the firm consisted of two partners with 54 employees in two offices. By 1930, the firm had grown to seven partners, over 400 employees in seven offices, and over $2 million in annual billings. Yet the partnership never grew larger than 26 partners and 16 offices during Arthur's lifetime. He wanted the partnership to remain small to maintain consistent high quality throughout the firm. His "one voice, one firm" philosophy was instilled in all those who worked for him and was part of the firm's culture for decades.

Arthur set high standards for himself and all who worked for him. Some considered him difficult and demanding, too stern and blunt; his brother Walter resigned from the firm in 1932 and they never spoke again. Leonard Spacek, Arthur Andersen's successor, recalled that the two brothers, both with strong personalities, one day got into a fight that ended with Arthur ordering his brother out of the office. "It was a clash of strong wills and bright minds that led to Walter Andersen's departure from the firm," said Spacek (Moore and Campton 2001, 78). Arthur's son, Arthur Arnold Andersen, joined the firm in 1940 but quit after only three years, finding his father unforgiving and overbearing in the workplace. Arthur E. Andersen died in 1947 at age 61. More than half a century later, stories are still told about how he took a hard stance with clients when he knew it was the right thing to do, even if it meant losing the client's business. His legend grew.

Legends of Arthur

One of the first stories to become part of Arthur's legend involved his firm's earliest and most profitable client. It was 1914 and Andersen DeLany & Company had existed for less than a year. Arthur found his client had inflated earnings by postponing significant maintenance expenses, rather than correctly recording them immediately. Arthur told the president of the company that he would describe the improper accounting treatment in his audit report if the company did not make the corrections. The president flew to Chicago, arrived at Arthur's office, and demanded he issue nothing other than the best audit opinion on his company's financial statements. Arthur replied, "There is not enough money in the city of Chicago to induce me to change the report!" (Squires et al. 2003, 32). Arthur stood his ground and lost the client, but his reputation for straight talk and not being bought was clearly established. Months later, his former client filed for bankruptcy, which underscored Arthur's integrity early in his firm's history.

Arthur's objections to misleading financial reporting arose again shortly afterward, also involving another lucrative client, a steamship company. The client was planning to raise money with a bond offering and needed to attract investors. The firm was engaged to audit the financial statements as of December 31, 1914, and to certify them as of that date. However, the company had suffered the loss of one of its new ships shortly after the year's end, in February 1915—an event that would have an adverse impact on the steamship company's future profitability. Once again, Arthur refused to acquiesce to his client's demands as he believed the loss needed to be disclosed in the financial statements to inform potential bond investors fully about the future prospects of the company. In little more than a year, Andersen's reputation for straight talk was growing; his firm's name on audited financial statements was becoming an increasingly sought-after commodity.

Arthur also believed that if his staff had made any errors during an audit, the firm should pay to correct their mistakes. When Arthur learned his firm failed to discover a $190,000 discrepancy between cash on hand and the recorded amount of cash, he immediately traveled to Ohio to visit with the president of the client company. When the meeting ended, Arthur wrote a check to reimburse his client saying that auditors "should save you money, not cost you money. I hope this will compensate you for our shortcomings" (Moore and Crampton 2001, 79).

Arthur's Heir

Toward the end of his life, Arthur Andersen struggled to find a suitable heir for his firm. His brother Walter had quit the firm in anger many years before and the two men had not spoken since; his son, Arthur, had left the firm within three years of joining it. While logical choices might have been other partners in the firm, each personally handpicked and groomed by Arthur himself, some say Arthur's ego eventually interfered with every choice of a potential successor. In fact, none of the partners he had considered even remained with the firm by the time Arthur died; most left years earlier when Arthur grew jealous of the increased attention and recognition a potential successor began to receive. John Jirgal, who had joined the firm in 1920, was one considered. However, according to another partner, "Arthur was not one to stand in the shade, and he was too obstinate to move...so what he did with Jirgal was move the tree. He banished John to New York, reduced his authority, wrote him off as a potential successor—and eventually cost the firm one of its very best partners. It was tragic all the way around" (Moore and Crampton 2001, 78).

At Arthur's death in 1947, no suitable heir had been selected. While the remaining partners feuded over how to continue the firm in the absence of its founder, Leonard Spacek eventually emerged as their new leader, after reconciling the warring factions. Spacek earned his own legend within the firm as the only person in the world who could fight with Arthur and remain unscathed. Spacek later reminisced, "I used to tell him, 'I'm from Iowa and I can always go back there and plow corn'" (Toffler 2003, 17).

Spacek carried on his mentor's values, upholding Arthur's philosophy of personal and professional integrity and honesty, beginning with acts of compassion immediately upon the founder's death. The night before Arthur's burial, Leonard arrived at the funeral home after midnight to pay his respects to his long-time partner and mentor. Secretly, he brought along Arthur's brother Walter, who had not spoken with Arthur since their argument 15 years earlier. Arthur's widow, Emma, was furious when she learned of this because she had never forgiven Walter. Nonetheless, Leonard believed he had done the right thing. Spacek also arranged for a $600,000 annuity to be paid to Emma, even though the partnership agreement did not provide any payment clause for a partner's widow.

While Andersen established the "think straight, talk straight" motto, Spacek was credited with developing the firm's logo in the 1950s: a pair of heavy, mahogany closed doors, with three indented panels on each and the firm's name printed in gold across both doors. The original set of doors was installed in the early 1940s in the firm's new Chicago office, the top two floors of 120 South LaSalle Street. When the partnership was later trying to choose a firm-wide symbol, Spacek found he disliked every idea presented to him; the use of the firm's initials, AA, invariably reminded him of Alcoholics Anonymous. While waiting for the elevator one day, Spacek glanced back at the Chicago office doors and suggested they be used as the symbol. Similar doors were installed in every Arthur Andersen office throughout the world and became the logo for business cards and internal documents. The symbolic doors came to represent integrity, confidentiality, privacy, and security; they announced to the world "trust us; what we do behind these doors is beyond reproach."

Spacek's stature within the accounting profession also grew over time. Some accountants considered him to be the conscience of the accounting profession, which was sorely in need of change. Leonard found many accounting pronouncements and regulatory guidelines outdated, coining the phrase "generally *antiquated* accounting principles," instead of the more familiar "generally accepted accounting principles" (Toffler 2003, 18). He believed railroads could overstate their earnings as much as 50 percent due to old accounting rules developed by the Interstate Commerce Commission, a regulatory body that did not require railroads to depreciate long-lived property (such as rails and ties). The firm dropped all of its railroad clients, except the two that agreed to change their accounting practices to conform to the firm's views. Spacek carried on Arthur Andersen's tough stance against client pressure to prepare misleading financial statements, which further underscored the firm's reputation as one that was not afraid to take a stand on principle, even if it meant losing a client.

Even after Leonard Spacek retired in 1973, this philosophy continued. When the savings and loan (S&L) crisis filled the front-page news in the early 1980s, nearly all of the then Big 8 public accounting firms were trapped, eventually settling lawsuits brought by the federal government for substandard audits of failed institutions.[3] However, Arthur Andersen & Co. was spared in most cases; the firm had earlier decided to resign from its S&L engagements, believing these clients were taking advantage of a loophole in accounting rules that allowed them to overstate earnings and produce misleading financial statements. Efforts to persuade its S&L clients to change their accounting treatment failed; when all of Andersen's clients refused, the firm followed what it considered to be its only option and resigned from these engagements rather than support what it considered to be incorrect and misleading accounting.

Although Arthur Andersen & Co. did not come through the S&L crisis completely unscathed, in 1985 it resigned from Lincoln Savings and Loan Association, which was subsequently seized by the federal government in 1989. Lincoln was the most egregious and fraudulent of the S&L failures, and successor auditing firms paid millions of dollars to settle with the federal government and state boards of accountancy.

The Arthur Andersen Culture

Arthur Andersen's values permeated his namesake firm as it continued to grow, providing an invisible framework for uniformity. Integrity and honesty were core values of the firm; new hires were carefully screened to ensure they shared these values. The first campus interview helped determine a student's personality type and later developed into "critical behavior interviewing," a technique used by every Arthur Andersen recruiter by the mid-1980s. The recruiter would ask the student to describe a situation where his or her integrity had been questioned or to explain how he or she had handled a recent ethical dilemma. A candidate lacking a strong response did not gain a job offer.

Arthur's "one voice, one firm" philosophy meant that even a decentralized local office system could function effectively because all members had been trained in the firm's methods and standards. In fact, some staff joked that there was a method for everything and since employees were so accustomed to doing everything as it should be done, they even took restroom breaks at the same time. Even decades after Arthur's death, the culture of the firm discouraged and did not tolerate independent decision making on important matters by individuals in local offices, in order to prevent an individual's decision from jeopardizing the reputation of the entire firm. Partners and employees were to follow the rules established by the leaders of the firm, a cornerstone philosophy that was key to maintaining the firm's highly respected reputation, premised upon the honesty and integrity among its leaders and established firm rules.[4]

"One voice, one firm" extended further and included Arthur's strong belief that staff training must be uniform and consistent and that only by doing so could the firm trust its employees to make the right decisions. In 1970, Arthur Andersen & Co. purchased the campus of the old St. Dominic's College, a small 150-acre women's college in St. Charles, Illinois, and renamed it the "Center for Professional Education." Commonly referred to as "St. Charles," it was considered a crown jewel, cradling the firm's culture by supporting in-house staff training. Every member of the firm, from partners down to new entry-level staff, spent time each year attending professional development courses at St. Charles.

Andersen's methods of selecting and training staff produced a fairly homogenous workforce that some began to refer to as "Arthurs" or "Arthur androids" (Toffler 2003, 20). Such unflattering terms signified what many viewed as a complete lack of individuality in firm members. An "android" was the perceived stereotype of an Arthur Andersen employee, one with a bland personality, hired straight out of an undergraduate business program not for individual creativity, but for the ability to conform to and follow rules set long ago; an android did not rock the boat. For example, the firm even had strict dress code expectations; until the 1960s, all men were expected to wear a hat—a felt hat from Labor Day until Memorial Day and a straw hat during the summer. Even into the 1990s, men were required to wear dark suits with a white, neatly pressed shirt and a power tie. Women wore skirts of a respectable length, closed-toe shoes, and a conservative blouse with a jacket or blazer. Clients would often joke with the Andersen staff that they could not understand how they ever found their own coats at the end of the day because they all looked identical.

The Beginning of the End

By 2001, the firm boasted of an 89-year history with 85,000 employees and 350 offices in 84 countries serving 100,000 clients. The firm still enjoyed the exceptional reputation associated with its prestigious name, but its culture began to change in the late 1980s and early 1990s, as perhaps did its sterling reputation for honesty and dependability. It is important to place this cultural shift in context; change permeated the entire accounting profession at this time. The hallmark independence began to give way as firms increasingly became business advisors and advocates representing their audit client interests, sometimes overshadowing their duty as advocates for maintaining public trust and confidence. Throughout his 1993–2000 term as Securities and Exchange Commission (SEC) chairman, Arthur Levitt aggressively pursued his agenda of cracking down on accounting abuses and strengthening auditor independence.[5]

Consulting or nonaudit services were offered by Arthur Andersen & Co. almost from its inception, in addition to auditing services. Arthur Andersen advertised "investigations for special purposes, such as to determine the advisability of investment in a new enterprise or the extension of an old business" and "the designing and installing of new systems of financial and cost accounting and organization, or the modernizing of existing systems" (Arthur Andersen & Co. 1974, 3). After World War II, Leonard Spacek hired two men to design payroll systems, one of whom studied the first computer developed at the University of Pennsylvania, and convinced the partners to allocate resources to learn more about this invention in 1951. Within two years, the firm provided consulting services to General Electric (GE), first

Table 22.1   Arthur Andersen & Co. Revenue

Year	Firm revenue (in thousands)	Percent of revenue from audit and tax	Percent of revenue from consulting
1984	$1,387,947	72	28
1985	$1,573,883	70	30
1986	$1,924,006	67	33
1987	$2,315,769	64	36
1988	$2,820,412	60	40
1989	$3,381,900	57	43

performing a feasibility study about which type of computer to install and then helping GE install its computers.

However, the consulting division remained a relatively small part of the entire firm until the mid- to late- 1980s, when consulting services and revenues grew at a phenomenal rate (see table 22.1). Similar growth in consulting was also taking place in most of the Big 8 firms, not just at Arthur Andersen, though Andersen's early entry and consulting prosperity set it apart from other firms.

Although the audit and tax division revenues grew during this period, consulting revenues grew at a significantly faster rate. By 1989, the consulting division generated 43 percent of the firm's total revenue, despite the fact that only 586 (or 27%) of the firm's 2,134 partners were consulting partners. The consulting partners, on average, were bringing in considerably more revenue than the partners providing auditing and tax services.

While auditors and consultants are both in the business of providing client service, there are critical differences in the purpose and perspective of these engagements. Consulting services are voluntary purchases of professional services and are designed to meet the specific needs of each particular client. The consultant maintains a focus on the company, rather than on protecting the interests of outside parties. "Keeping the client happy" is simply providing quality service that fulfills a specific need and meets the client's expectations. A job well done might be rewarded with future consulting engagements.

Auditing services, by contrast, have a single, primary purpose: to provide an independent and unbiased opinion on information made available to outside parties that rely upon this information when making decisions. The Securities and Exchange Commission (SEC), a federal regulatory agency, requires an annual audit of the financial statements of all publicly traded companies. Other companies may be required to have an audit while in negotiations with a prospective buyer or to obtain a bank loan or construction contract bond, etc. The independent auditor provides a professional opinion stating that the financial statements are fairly presented, based on generally accepted accounting principles (GAAP), and free of material (significant) misstatements.

Although the audit report does not draw conclusions about whether the company is a good or bad investment, the outside parties are more confident in relying upon this information when making their own decisions about the company. The audit report is signed by a Certified Public Accountant (CPA) who is licensed by the state and is subject to the code of professional conduct. Although the company hires and must pay the CPA for audit services, the auditor has a duty to the "public," the "P" in CPA. There is an inherent conflict between "keeping the client happy" and serving as the "watchdog" to protect the public interest, particularly when controversial accounting issues are at stake.

As consulting grew to be such a big part of the firm, acrimony developed between the more traditional accounting (audit and tax) partners and the consulting partners. In 1989, the consulting division eventually split and became a separate business unit named "Andersen Consulting" (renamed "Accenture" in 2001). As a result, the consulting partners and staff were no longer under the control of any accounting partner and had much greater freedom to conduct business as they chose.

One of Andersen Consulting's first orders of business was to develop its own brand and separate identity in the marketplace. The staid, conforming "Arthur androids" were not the ideal consulting staff. Instead, Andersen Consulting hired innovative, creative, freethinking employees who were not accountants and had little or no accounting educational background. They neither understood nor shared the values and standards of the accounting profession, and they were not subject to the professional code of conduct for auditors.

Consulting services were still offered by Arthur Andersen & Co. after 1989, even without its sister branch of Andersen Consulting. The accounting partners had grown accustomed to enjoying the profits generated by successful consulting engagements, while revenues from auditing and tax services had reached a plateau. Pressures to cut costs and increase profits led to a dramatic decision to remove many partners in 1992; only the most performance-driven partners, as measured by the number of billable hours in a year, were to be retained. A disproportionate number of old-style audit partners were removed, many of whom were more conservative and believed in upholding the firm's historical values, by focusing on quality and protecting the public interest. Losing these senior partners made it easier for the culture to shift from quality client service to an increased emphasis on generating fees, which invariably meant more consulting.

In many cases, the firm provided both auditing *and* consulting services for some clients, raising questions of independence and conflicts of interest. Revenues generated from the consulting side of an engagement sometimes exceeded the audit fees, and consulting engagements were typically much more profitable than audits. For example, in the Enron engagement, the firm generated $27 million annually in consulting fees and $25 million in audit fees. If auditors questioned a client's method of accounting, the firm risked losing not only the audit fees if the client dropped them, but also significant consulting fees. Worse yet, clients understood this game and used it to their advantage. Gone were the days when an auditor told the client what to do and not vice versa. And gone were the days when a client refusing to acquiesce to auditor demands would be dropped by the firm without hesitation, a consequence clients dreaded, as news of such action usually translated into a stock price decline. But clients now held much more power as the firm focused on generating revenues and profits.

Consulting staff increasingly challenged the firm's traditional values. Auditing was about conforming to procedures and guidelines and doing things correctly, as had always been done; consulting was about making new rules for the game and thinking independently and creatively. Auditors focused on their core responsibility to the public, while consultants focused on making clients happy and winning additional engagements. The focus on making money caused a shift from the firm's traditional values and its public stewardship role. As professional standards were relaxed and competitive bidding for audit services emerged, audits were often viewed as loss leaders to gain lucrative consulting engagement business. During this era, the accounting profession was increasingly referred to as the accounting "industry" and the American Institute of Certified Public Accountants (AICPA) as a "trade association."

Even symbolic changes signaled the decay of the long-standing culture of Arthur Andersen. One Midwestern office finally broke the tradition of the famous heavy, mahogany doors. Instead, the consulting staff had glass doors installed, overriding considerable resistance from the audit and tax partners. This story was often told with a great sense of shock and dismay by those who still held onto the firm's traditional values and viewed this as symbolic of the widening gap between auditing and consulting. Yet another change occurred in 2000, when the firm renamed itself "Andersen" and changed its well-known, traditional logo representing the mahogany double doors to that of a small orange-red circle that appeared meaningless, an action one insider referred to as "a desperate attempt to grab some New Economy buzz" (Toffler 2003, 37).

A Fast Crash and Burn

Many people, including Andersen employees throughout the world, were stunned by the speed with which one of the five largest international public accounting firms dissolved. Most thought only the few individuals involved with Enron and the related document shredding would be affected. But less than one year after news of Enron first hit the front page of the newspapers,

Andersen as a firm essentially ceased to exist. Although the U.S. Supreme Court later overturned the conviction, it could not bring the firm back to life.

What could have happened? There were many changes in the accounting and business environment that helped set the stage. Once held in high regard for their objectivity and independence, and respected for their role in protecting the public interest, the profession moved more toward roles as business advisors and representing the interests of their clients. Companies used existing accounting standards to their advantage to manage earnings, structured transactions to circumvent unfavorable rules, and formed powerful lobbies to derail new accounting standards that might portray economic reality.

The big accounting firms now generated half of their revenue from consulting engagements, often providing both auditing and consulting services for the same client. Gaining the audit also meant gaining the more lucrative consulting business. Taking a tough stance with an audit client might lead to losing the client or having to resign from the engagement, with the risk of losing the consulting engagement as well. Providing consulting services with the notion of client satisfaction is in direct conflict with the objective and unbiased perspective demanded of an independent auditor.

Could what happened to Arthur Andersen have happened to another firm instead? Many believe so. Did the government move too quickly in its attempt to restore investor confidence? Perhaps. But most clear is that Arthur Andersen LLP lost sight of the values of its founder and the importance he placed on his firm's reputation for honesty and integrity.

What might Arthur E. Andersen think if he had lived to see what the firm bearing his name experienced during the past few years? One can only imagine. Arthur Andersen's death in 1947 spared him from witnessing his firm's rapid fall from grace and ultimate demise. Yet his values might still be known today, several decades after writing a memo from his Chicago office reminding his partners of the importance of the "enhanced reputation of the firm." Figure 22.1 contains Arthur Andersen's 1940 office memo. His words resonate and serve as a simple, yet poignant reminder of values that remain relevant to this day.

Epilogue

A quick visit to Andersen's Web page (http://www.andersen.com) reveals the collapse of the firm. Nothing is shown other than the firm's Chicago address, phone number, and fax number. No links exist on the Web site. If there is such a thing as a ghost town on the Web, this is it. The page is virtually blank, giving no evidence of the vibrant worldwide company that had existed not long ago. As of 2006, approximately 200 employees were still employed by Andersen, performing primarily administrative duties related to shareholder lawsuits resulting from the firm's earlier work for Enron, Global Crossing,

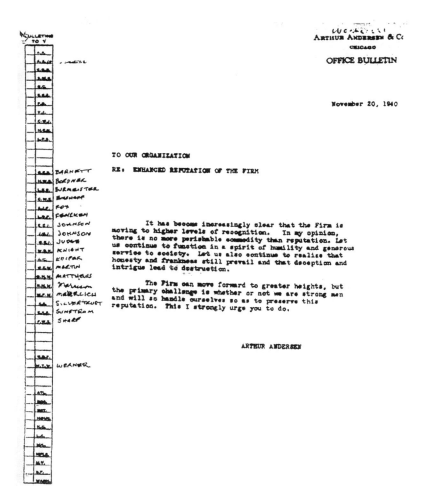

Fig. 22.1 Arthur Andersen's 1940 memo.

WorldCom, and other clients that had been allegedly involved in fraudulent financial reporting.

Former Andersen consultant Jonathan Goldsmith launched a Web site in 2002 to help former Andersen employees reconnect and provide useful resources. Other former employees of Andersen maintain their own Web sites of support. For example, see http://www.andersenalumni.net/ or http://domino-20.prominic.com/A55916/AlumniAndersen.nsf/index?OpenForm.

Acknowledgments

The authors gratefully acknowledge and thank Rebecca Homola, one of our former students who is now an auditor with Clark Nuber & Associates in

Bellevue, Washington, and her grandfather, Norman Tucker of Barrington, Illinois, a retired partner with Arthur Andersen & Co. Mr. Tucker found the Arthur Andersen memo in his files and shared it with Rebecca and with us so that others might read what Andersen had to say.

Notes

1. Enron, the Houston-based energy giant that filed for Chapter 11 bankruptcy in December 2001, was created from the 1985 merger of two natural gas pipeline companies; Kenneth Lay was its CEO for most of its 15-year existence. Energy deregulation presented an opportunity for Lay to transform his company from the mundane operations of transporting natural gas into a sophisticated energy contract trading company, with 90 percent of its profits coming from trading operations at its peak. Financial wizards Jeffrey Skilling and Andrew Fastow, along with MBAs and engineers from prestigious colleges, created complex business structures and developed sophisticated models to predict demand and natural gas costs.

   Initial successes led Enron to expand trading operations to electricity, bandwidth, water, and other ventures. Enron grew rapidly, and by 2000 it had a market capitalization of $70 billion, revenues of $100 billion, 21,000 employees, and a peak stock price of $90. However, in less than a year, its stock price plummeted to 26 cents a share, just prior to filing for Chapter 11 bankruptcy protection on December 2, 2001—the largest in U.S. history at that time (WSJ.com 2006b). Enron was the first in a wave of many business scandals that were revealed in subsequent months.

   Central to Enron's phenomenal growth and one major factor leading to its ultimate and rapid decline was its creative ability to generate financing. Enron set up "separate" entities to finance growth and report profits, without reporting the debt on its own balance sheet. "Special purpose entities" (SPEs), a term once used only in sophisticated accounting and business circles, later became a household word. For years, the Financial Accounting Standards Board (FASB) encountered resistance and roadblocks in its efforts to revise accounting standards to prevent the type of abuse Enron used to its advantage. Once the Enron scandal broke, the FASB was urged by Congress and the SEC to adopt "quick-fix" standards to curb future abuse.

Pushing "substance versus form" boundaries under accounting standards existing at the time, Enron could create separate entities or enter into agreements for its own benefit (often via complex limited partnership structures), finance such arrangements with as much as 97 percent from borrowings (mostly from banks) and as little as 3 percent from "outside investors," and yet omit the associated debt/obligations from its own balance sheet. Enron could eliminate unprofitable assets and operations from its own financial statements, report profits from selling assets to a separate entity, and/or report income from a separate entity long before it generated profitable operations. In some cases, it was later learned that the requisite outside investor financing actually came from within: from Enron, its board members, and/or its executives, including Enron CFO Andrew Fastow, who received substantial compensation and personally profited from such investments. It also came to light that Enron had guaranteed some of the separate entity debt, backed by shares of Enron stock or guaranteed via other obligations.

Declining energy prices, coupled with such off-the-books arrangements, contributed to Enron's accelerated tailspin and ultimate demise. A partnership debt default triggered an Enron share guarantee (the price of which had fallen from $90 to $34 a share); in the third quarter of 2001, it disclosed a $1.2 billion reduction of shareholders' equity and a $638 million loss. Restatements for the previous five years reduced prior reported earnings by 20 percent or $586 million, and Enron's debt was downgraded below investment grade (WSJ.com 2002). Enron lost credibility and its financing dried up.

SEC and Department of Justice investigations ultimately led to guilty pleas and convictions of top executives, including treasurer Ben Gilsan, the first in 2003; CFO Andrew Fastow and his wife, Lea, in 2004 (Fastow eventually received a reduced sentence of six years in prison due to his cooperation in the case); and chief accountant Richard Causey in 2005 (WSJ.com 2006a; Johnson, October 18, 2006).

Finally, on May 25, 2006, Chairman and CEO Kenneth Lay and President Jeffrey Skilling were convicted. Lay was convicted on ten criminal charges, including all six counts of fraud and conspiracy. Skilling was convicted on 19 of 28 counts (though only 1 of 10 counts of insider trading); both were to be sentenced in October 2006.

In an ironic twist of events, just six weeks after his conviction and only a few weeks before he was to be sentenced, Kenneth Lay passed away near the resort town of Aspen, Colorado. On October 17, 2006, a federal judge dismissed Lay's indictment, applying the legal doctrine of "abatement" regarding defendants who die prior to exercising their rights to appeal a conviction. In effect, the ruling erased Lay's criminal convictions on ten criminal charges. On October 23, 2006, former Enron president Jeffrey Skilling was sentenced to 24 years in prison and was to turn over the majority of his assets to help compensate former Enron employees for their losses (Johnson, October 18, 2006, October 24, 2006).

2. Nancy Templeton, email message to David Duncan, October 16, 2001, http://news.findlaw.com/wp/docs/enron/tmpl2dunc101601eml.pdf (accessed June 10, 2007).

3. The S&L crisis of the 1980s led to the failure and ultimately to the regulatory closure of over 1,000 (nearly half) of federally insured institutions, which held over $500 billion in assets. These failures cost taxpayers an estimated $124 billion (via federally insured deposits) and the S&L industry another $29 billion (Curry and Shibut 1991, 26).

Although S&L failures occurred all over the country, the southwest region of the United States was particularly affected. Every sector of the oil-patch economy had been booming; wages and employment rates were high, as were real estate values, and speculative acquisition and development ventures were very attractive. Then oil prices declined, and the resulting domino effect was devastating, particularly in the southwest region. Unemployment rates soared, real estate prices fell, and there were massive defaults on consumer loans and losses on passive real estate investments no longer subject to favorable income tax treatment.

S&Ls were originally chartered to support family home ownership by providing mortgage loans in their communities. The money customers deposited into savings accounts was loaned to others making home purchases. Interest rates were regulated; thus, the S&Ls were almost guaranteed to earn a profit as the rate they were permitted to pay on savings was less than the rate charged on mortgage loans. In the years leading up to the crisis, the government first deregulated S&L interest rates.

An interest rate squeeze occurred when S&Ls were suddenly forced to compete with banks and others that were permitted to pay higher rates on customer deposits; the S&Ls paid depositors higher short-term interest rates than they were earning on their fixed rate, long-term mortgage loans. To alleviate this problem, further deregulation permitted S&Ls also to compete with banks and others by making types of loans and other investments inherently much riskier than the community-based mortgage loans.

The most egregious of these failures was Lincoln Savings & Loan and its notorious executive, Charles Keating, Jr. The fraudulent activities at Lincoln led to congressional hearings, convictions, and jail time; several of the Big 8 firms settled with federal government agencies and state boards of accountancy for millions of dollars, avoiding uncertain outcomes and costs of legal defense for alleged audit failures and fraud. Fingers of blame were pointed in many directions; not even Congress or government regulators were spared from criticism. Public confidence was eroded, the reputation of the accounting profession severely tarnished and its ability to self-regulate questioned, and employees lost their jobs and retirement nest eggs—not unlike the impact produced by Enron and the subsequent wave of business scandals.

Many S&Ls and their management teams were ill-prepared for the transition from making relatively safe mortgage loans to the much riskier investment and lending environment permitted under deregulation, but this was clearly more apparent in hindsight when economic boom turned into bust. It was argued that accounting standards were outdated, regulatory oversight was inadequate, and even the warning signs raised by the auditors were ignored. The auditing profession was accustomed to the relatively safe S&L environment of the past and had not yet developed the expertise or the degree of skepticism needed to evaluate these more sophisticated and risky loan portfolios and investments. Concerned about their constituencies, congressmen avoided taking a hard stance; perhaps they thought the S&L industry might ride out the bad times and thus did not want to cause widespread alarm that might further damage the already fragile S&Ls. Interestingly, Keating was implicated in influence peddling and was accused of receiving favorable treatment for his troublesome Lincoln S&L; he had contributed heavily to the election campaigns of five prominent senators who later became known as the "Keating Five."

4. Ironically, when the Enron situation was unraveling, Arthur Andersen & Co. was the only one of the Big 5 firms where a local partner could overrule an executive office decision. Andersen had established an internal professional standards group (PSG), a group of experts at Andersen headquarters who tackled difficult accounting issues and oversaw accounting decisions on complicated issues facing local offices. Carl Bass was a member of the PSG; he documented problems with Enron as early as 1999. At Enron's request, Bass was removed from its account, a highly unusual move. Furthermore, apparently without informing the PSG, the Enron audit partner chose to ignore its advice (Squires et al. 2003, 126).

5. It is important to place the cultural shift at Arthur Andersen & Co. in the context of changes permeating the entire accounting profession during this time. For decades, the accounting profession took its exclusive franchise for auditing services and duty to the public seriously. The hallmark was "independence"—the unbiased and neutral perspective accountants offered and outside parties relied upon. But over time, firms gradually became advocates for their clients, perhaps overshadowing their role in maintaining the public's trust. After all, it was the client that paid for their services, not the public.

A profession once active in establishing accounting standards and vocal in promoting needed changes later became their lobbyists, objecting to proposals that might adversely impact a client and providing advice on how to structure transactions to get around the substance of an accounting rule while still complying with its form. Companies, powerful professional organizations, such as the Financial Executives Institute (now Financial Executives International), and even the accounting firms lobbied members of Congress.

Historically, during the course of an audit, ways to improve the client's accounting/control systems or business operations were noted and recommendations were provided at the end of the engagement via the management letter. Some consulting engagements resulted from these recommendations. As professional standards were relaxed and competitive bidding for audit services emerged, audits were often viewed as loss leaders to gain more lucrative consulting engagement business. Over time, accounting firms increasingly became business advisors, providing information technology (IT) and other nonaudit services; consulting eventually generated nearly half of the big firms' total revenues.

The Private Securities Litigation Reform Act of 1995 also changed the legal climate. Firms faced the continuing threat of litigation for company and audit failures and could be subject to joint and several liability in their existing partnership structures. The new legislation made it much more difficult to impose several liability; many firms formed limited liability partnerships (LLPs) during this time, and some contend the firms were more willing to accept their clients' aggressive accounting as a result.

For years, many public interest advocates expressed concern about changes in the profession, including accounting abuses and independence issues. Arthur Levitt, SEC chairman from 1993 to 2000, had a very aggressive agenda. In a 1996 speech he said, "I'm deeply concerned that 'independence' and 'objectivity' are increasingly regarded by some [in the accounting profession] as quaint notions...I caution the [accounting] industry, if I may borrow a Biblical phrase, not to 'gain the whole world, and lose [its] own soul'" (Zeff 2003, 278). In his legendary 1998 "Numbers Game" speech, Levitt pointed an accusing finger at many financial market participants, including auditors and their clients, for their roles in accounting abuses and managed earnings (Levitt 1998).

In a March 12, 2002, PBS *Frontline* television interview, former chairman Levitt reflected on his three big accounting battles of the 1990s. He took on independence and conflict of interest issues and proposed SEC rules prohibiting firms from providing certain nonaudit services for their own audit clients. When he approached leaders of the Big 5 accounting firms in a private meeting, only two firms agreed to try to work with the SEC, while three said they would go to war with the SEC and would fight in Congress and in the courts (*Frontline* 2002).

The firms' lobbying efforts were powerful and effective; Levitt received a letter threatening a rider to the appropriations bill if the SEC did not back off from its rulemaking. Eventually the opposing firms and Levitt reached a compromise: The firms would not be prohibited from providing IT services to audit clients as the SEC originally had proposed. Corporate audit committees were to be informed of these additional services, and financial statement disclosures would include a breakdown of fees paid for audit and nonaudit services. Near the end of his 2002 PBS interview (which occurred not long after the Enron saga unfolded), Levitt said he would not have compromised had he not been aggressively threatened by congressional action, and it was a compromise he would not make today (*Frontline* 2002).

References

AccountingWEB.com. "Andersen Prosecution Abandoned: Enron's Final Chapter?" (November 28, 2005) http://www.accountingweb.com/cgi-bin/item.cgi?id=101513 (accessed June 10, 2007).

Arthur Andersen & Co. *The First Sixty Years: 1913–1973*. Chicago: Arthur Andersen & Co., 1974.

Bravin, J. "Justices Overturn Criminal Verdict in Andersen Case," *Wall Street Journal,* June 1, 2005, A1, A6.

Curry, T., and L. Shibut. "The Cost of the Savings and Loan Crisis: Truth and Consequences," *FDIC Banking Review* (1991): 26–35, http://www.fdic.gov/bank/analytical/banking/2000dec/brv13n2_2.pdf (accessed June 10, 2007).

Frontline. "Bigger Than Enron—Interview: Arthur Levitt" (a transcript of a television interview conducted by Hedrick Smith on March 12, 2002), http://www.pbs.org/wgbh/pages/frontline/shows/regulation/interviews/levitt.html (accessed June 10, 2007).

Johnson, C. "Judge Revokes Lay's Conviction," washingtonpost.com, October 18, 2006, http://www.washingtonpost.com/wp-dyn/content/article/2006/10/17/AR2006101700808.html (accessed July 31, 2007).

_____. "Skilling Gets 24 Years for Fraud at Enron," washingtonpost.com, October 24, 2006, http://www.washingtonpost.com/wp-dyn/content/article/2006/10/23/AR2006102300287.html (accessed July 31, 2007).

Levitt, A. "The Numbers Game" (a transcript of a speech given at the NYU Center for Law and Business on September 28, 1998), http://www.sec.gov/news/speecharchive/1998/spch220.txt (accessed May 25, 2006).

Moore, M., and J. Crampton. "Arthur Andersen: Challenging the Status Quo," *Journal of Business Leadership* (2000–2001): 71–89.

Squires, S. E., C. J. Smith, L. McDougall, and W. R. Yeack. *Inside Arthur Andersen: Shifting Values, Unexpected Consequences.* Upper Saddle River, NJ: Prentice Hall, 2003.

Toffler, B. L., with J. Reingold. *Final Accounting: Ambition, Greed, and the Fall of Arthur Andersen.* New York: Broadway Books, 2003.

WSJ.com. "A Chronology of Enron's Recent Woes," February 27, 2002, http://online.wsj.com/article/0,,SB101171396110000000.djm,00.html (accessed February 27, 2002).

_____. "Executives on Trial—In Trouble at Enron," May 25, 2006a, http://online.wsj.com/documents/info-enrontrials06.html (accessed May 31, 2006).

_____. "Market Cap to Maximum Sentence: Booking Enron by the Numbers," (May 25, 2006b, http://online.wsj.com/article/SB114780226218554397.html (accessed May 31, 2006).

Zeff, S. A. "How the Accounting Profession Got Where It Is Today: Part II," *Accounting Horizons,* 17 (December 2003): 267–286.

Bibliography

Primoff, W. M. "The S&L Crisis—Putting Things in Perspective," *CPA Journal Online* (December 1989), http://www.nysscpa.org/cpajournal/old/08033828.htm (accessed June 10, 2007).

The Fall of San Diego

23

DWIGHT V. DENISON
JONICA L. BURKE

Contents

With its moderate climate, seaside location, and an array of amenities, the city of San Diego is a desirable place to live and work. In addition to its traditional defense-based economy, San Diego benefits from thriving biotech, telecom, and tourism industries. The city's unemployment rates over the past decade have been consistently below the California and national averages. San Diego ranked number one on the 2002 *Forbes*/Milken Institute's "Best Places for Business and Careers" list because of its strong economic outlook and the attractive incentives it offered to local businesses (Badenhausen 2002). Despite desirable amenities and a strong economy, the city of San Diego now confronts a serious financial crisis. This crisis did not occur overnight. In fact, the seeds of the crisis were planted nearly three decades ago.

In 1978, the citizens of California approved a ballot initiative, Proposition 13, which amended the state constitution to restrict the amount that property taxes can increase on a parcel of property from year to year. Under Proposition 13, the assessed value of a property can increase by no more than 2 percent per year, unless the owner of the property changes. Property taxes traditionally have been a primary source of revenue for local governments, and with California's real estate market booming, this puts a substantial constraint on California city governments, forcing difficult trade-offs at budget time. While existing homeowners benefit from maintaining artificially low property taxes, cities like San Diego are forced to find alternative sources of revenue to fund public services, even as demand for them continually increases.

The exceptionally high inflation rates that led to the Proposition 13 property tax revolt in the late 1970s also made life difficult for retired city of San Diego workers. City retirees found it difficult to survive on their monthly pension checks from the San Diego City Employees' Retirement System

(SDCERS) and rallied union officials to seek higher benefits. The high inflation rate also led to higher than expected earnings by the investments in
the city's pension fund, so it appeared that the pension system had plenty of
resources to cover the pension benefits it was currently paying as well as the
estimated benefits for future retirees. Though investment returns are difficult
to predict, actuaries are hired to calculate the expected rate of return on fund
investments based, in part, on the past performance of similar investments.
Though SDCERS investments were earning well above the 8 percent rate of
return estimated by system actuaries, under normal conditions investment
surpluses are required to make up for below-average returns in other years to
achieve the average rate of return. Therefore, unless the actuaries' estimates
are grossly incorrect, in the long run true "surplus earnings" are impossible.
The use of surplus earnings for purposes other than maintaining the pension
system, such as to expand existing benefits, should be viewed as a loan from
the system that will require repayment in the future.

The concept of surplus earnings is easily misunderstood, so sometimes
these earnings are used inappropriately. The San Diego city council decided
in 1980 to grant 50 percent of that year's surplus earnings to current retirees
as an extra payment referred to as a "13th check." Though the 13th check was
intended to help retirees temporarily during the 1980 recession, this payment was provided again in 1981. In 1982, the city of San Diego decided to
withdraw from participation in the Social Security system, which required
the city to enhance the benefits offered by SDCERS. The city chose to finance
these benefit increases using the remaining 50 percent of surplus earnings,
leaving the pension fund without a cushion to cover periods when investments earned less than the 8 percent rate of return. For a third year, the
city paid the 13th check and retirees came to expect it as an entitlement,
regardless of economic conditions. In 1983, the SDCERS board of trustees
attempted to limit the spending of surplus earnings by capping the amount
distributed through the 13th check. Feeling shortchanged, SDCERS members sued for continuation of the customary 50 percent of surplus earnings
the following year. They accepted a cash settlement, along with enhanced
benefits, in return for allowing the city to set a limit on the annual 13th check
payments. Over the next decade, the practice of using surplus earnings to
fund the 13th check and other pension benefits became entrenched.

As with most pension systems, the San Diego pension system has three
sources of funding: employer (city) contributions, employee contributions,
and earnings on the investment of those contributions. An actuary calculates
how much money will be required to fund the pension plan in the future
and determines the city's required contribution each year. The city of San
Diego met its required contribution without difficulty until the early 1990s,
when the city experienced severe budget pressures. San Diego sought relief
by decreasing its required contributions to the pension fund. In 1991, at the

city's request, the SDCERS board of trustees approved the use of an alternative actuarial method that tends to estimate lower operating costs for the system, reducing the employer's required contributions. Actuaries for SDCERS continued to use this alternate methodology throughout the following decade.

The city of San Diego was plagued with budget problems again in 1996, but still ceded to unions an increase in pension and health care benefits—concessions made more expensive by the city's aging workforce. These benefit enhancements included increases to the formula for calculating basic pension benefits and the creation of a deferred retirement option program (DROP). The DROP program allowed employees to retire but continue working, drawing both a full salary and pension benefits. Under the DROP, pension payments were deposited into an account with SDCERS guaranteeing an 8 percent rate of return, plus a 2 percent annual cost-of-living adjustment, both backed by SDCERS assets. Financing these additional benefits should have increased the city's required contribution to the retirement system. However, the city manager made the additional benefits contingent on the SDCERS board's acceptance of city contributions that were well below the actuarially required rate to fully fund promised benefits. Under this agreement, the city's contributions would not return to the full actuarial rate until 2009.

This proposed trade-off of benefit increases in return for reduced city contributions was referred to as manager's proposal 1 (MP1). The proposal contained a safeguard, in that if the funded ratio of the pension system dropped below 82.3 percent, the city must immediately increase its contributions. The funded ratio compares the value of a pension fund's existing assets to the amount that would be required to meet the fund's projected obligations. If a fund presently controls sufficient assets to pay all promised present and future benefits, its funded ratio is 100 percent. By postponing a portion of the city's pension contributions into the future, this arrangement served as a kind of loan from the pension system to the city in its time of financial need.

There was some resistance to MP1 when it was presented to the board. Voting to allow reduced city contributions to SDCERS with full knowledge that the city would grant higher retirement benefits in the future created a potential conflict of interest for the members of the SDCERS board who were participants in SDCERS. One board member, John Casey, voiced concern about this possible conflict of interest in voting on the proposal. The board's attorney dismissed the concern, noting that the authors of the city charter knowingly included members of SDCERS on the board of trustees and that those members would inevitably have a financial interest in some board decisions. Still, this legal opinion ignored the fact that the board's decisions had previously been limited to investment strategies or approval of actuarial assumptions, not linked to the approval of new benefits.[1]

In November of the same year, voters approved the transfer of the full cost of postretirement health care benefits from the city to SDCERS, making it responsible for not only pension benefits but also retiree health care benefits. The result was to further expand the gap between the system's assets and its benefit obligations. With the costs of medical care escalating rapidly, this decision significantly increased the financial obligations of the pension system, though the city retained responsibility should any shortfalls occur in the future. This transfer occurred without any actuarial evaluation of the costs of providing retiree health benefits. In fact, the city had not examined its health care benefit obligations since 1989.

In 1997, the SDCERS board took a step further toward permanency for the 13th check benefit. Recognizing that surplus earnings might not always be so high, board members voted to set aside a portion of the current surplus earnings in a separate account to fund the 13th check in years when earnings were not sufficient to pay one. This decision marked the first time that board members acknowledged that lower investment returns could become an issue in the future. In 1998, the board created two additional reserve accounts from surplus earnings. The first was used to cover the increase in employees' contribution rates that resulted from the benefit enhancements under MP1. The second was used to guarantee future cost-of-living increases for retirees. Flush from the unusual and astonishingly high returns to its investments, the board established these three reserve accounts from surplus earnings to enhance benefits for its retirees. However, in creating these separate accounts, SDCERS diverted earnings above the predicted 8 percent rate of return to enhance benefits without planning for the return of those funds to the system to provide a safety net for leaner times. Both the city of San Diego and SDCERS officials behaved as though the bull market would continue indefinitely.

In 1997, the California Supreme Court ruled that overtime pay, accrued leave, and other forms of compensation must be included in calculating "final compensation" for pension benefits (*Ventura County Deputy Sheriffs' Association v. Board of Retirement of Ventura County Employees' Retirement System* 1997). This ruling led to a 1998 class action suit against SDCERS claiming miscalculation of retiree benefits. A settlement was reached in March 2000, requiring a large cash payment and a significant increase in the formula used to calculate benefits for retirees. The increased benefit was to be paid out of surplus earnings, but if surplus earnings were not enough to cover it in a given year, the obligation would carry over to future years. This legal settlement hinged on maintaining a 90 percent funded ratio for the pension system, but not all of the settlement requirements were included when the funded ratio was checked. The city council was notified about this omission but approved the settlement anyway, and the SDCERS board and members followed suit. Fortunately for the city, the settlement applied only to retirees who were active at the time of the settlement, so this obligation would decline over time.

These generous benefit increases appeared affordable given the strong investment returns occurring during the dot-com boom of the late 1990s, especially if one remained optimistic that the high investment returns would continue in the long run. Then the stock market began to decline in 2001, drastically reducing the return on the system's investments. In 2001, the mayor of San Diego appointed a blue ribbon committee to examine the city's financial status. The committee concluded that the city's contributions were insufficient to fund promised future pension benefits for current workers and pointed out the rapid rise in health care costs. Despite this warning, no policy changes resulted from the report. Later that year, there was growing concern that the SDCERS-funded ratio would drop below 82.3 percent and trigger a mandatory increase in city contributions under the MP1 agreement. Controversy arose over the city's required response if that minimum were reached. If it returned immediately to contributing at the actuarial rate, the city would be required to pay $25 million into the pension fund the following year. If it were required to restore SDCERS to at least an 82.3 percent funded ratio immediately, the city's contribution would be many times higher. In truth, the city could not afford either scenario.

The public remained largely unaware of San Diego's precarious financial condition. The city was noted for its low level of debt and apparently sound financial operations. San Diego was in compliance with all financial reporting laws and accounting regulations. In fact, the city was awarded a certificate of excellence from the Government Financial Officers Association for its comprehensive financial reports in 2001 and 2002. In May 2002, the city's financial position appeared to be rock solid when it was the only large city in California to achieve the highest possible credit rating for a city government. To outsiders, San Diego's economic future looked bright.

In an effort to prevent a large, sudden increase in the city's required contributions, in June 2002, the city manager offered another round of benefit increases if the SDCERS board would make additional concessions to the city. The terms included allowing the funded ratio minimum to drop to 75 percent of actuarially required assets. The SDCERS actuary, Rick Roeder, had supported the MP1 agreement as reasonable, but had serious reservations about early versions of the new offer, referred to as manager's proposal 2 (MP2). In a presentation to the SDCERS board of trustees, Roeder presented a slide asking the board, "Which Way Ya Goin'?" He pointed out that the "enhanced benefits" that had already been approved required larger contributions from the city, but instead the city had been granted "contribution relief," creating the growing funding gap. He also voiced concerns about inappropriate use of the concept of surplus earnings.[2]

Faced with objections from the SDCERS attorney as well, the city modified the MP2 proposal several times. On November 15, 2002, the board approved a watered down MP2, on the condition that the city council indemnify board members so that they would not be personally responsible for legal fees in the event of a lawsuit. The approved proposal maintained the minimum funded ratio at 82.3 percent. It also doubled the required annual increases to the city's contribution rates, but allowed a more gradual increase in contributions, rather than a balloon payment, if the minimum funded ratio was reached. Structured this way, MP2 would generate higher contributions from the city only until the minimum funded ratio was reached, which the SDCERS actuary predicted would occur by June 2003. Because there is always a delay in accurately estimating the funded ratio, it was not yet known that the minimum level had already been reached 5 months earlier, at the end of June 2002. When the board voted on MP2, its members probably assumed that the benefit increases offered by the city were still contingent on approval of the proposal, but the city council had already voted to provide them anyway. The changes increased the benefits of each board member belonging to SDCERS, but the deal included enhancements favoring two board members in particular: the president of the local firefighters union and an acting city auditor.

Only two SDCERS board members voted against the proposal. One of them, Diann Shipione, believed that the agreement violated the board members' role as trustees of the pension fund. In December, she shared her concerns about the underfunding of SDCERS in a letter to the assistant city manager. She also went public with her observations, generating the first widespread concern over the soundness of the system. Accounting standards at the time did not explicitly require the disclosure of pension fund details. Therefore, the city's published financial statements for 2002 did not discuss MP2, the new benefit increases, or the funding status of the retirement system. The statements also contained multiple clerical errors that were misleading about the city's liabilities related to its retirement system.

In January 2003, the city and SDCERS were named in a class action lawsuit for failure to fund the pension system at actuarially required levels. Additional suits followed. In March 2003, Public Financial Management, an external financial advisor hired by the city, made it clear that the system faced huge shortfalls in the coming years, but the city continued to underfund it by following the MP2 timetable. The Public Financial Management projections were kept confidential to prevent their use in the class action proceedings. In June 2003, the credit rating agencies investigated the city's pension liabilities for the first time. As the rating agencies probed the matter and the city revealed errors in earlier financial statements, concern grew about the city's financial position. The city had issued bonds in early 2003, but the documentation for that bond deal contained financial data current only through June 30, 2001, and the SDCERS funded ratio had subsequently dropped by 20 percent.

In September 2003, board member Diann Shipione wrote another letter, this time detailing her concerns about the accuracy and completeness of the disclosure documents prepared to support a new bond issue for the

wastewater district. Her letter was forwarded to Paul Webber, partner at a
law firm that had served as counsel for multiple city bond issues. Webber's
firm encouraged city officials to examine the issues raised by Shipione. The
city's accounting and auditing departments and outside auditors each found
multiple, significant errors in the footnotes of the 2002 financial statements
that were misleading to both investors and the rating agencies. The extent
to which the errors were simply oversights or typographical errors is a point
of contention. All may be attributable to uncorrected data entry problems,
failure to update data each year, or omissions in the data reported to the
city auditor's office. At one point during the investigation, however, Webber
accused the city auditor of attempting to "pull the wool over the eyes" of city
council by chalking all the problems up to typos.[3]

On January 27, 2004, at the insistence of bond counsel, the city issued
a Voluntary Disclosure to correct its 2002 financial statements. Though the
Securities and Exchange Commission did not yet have guidelines in place
requiring disclosure of public pension matters, Webber believed that the city
had a responsibility to disclose a complete picture of its financial liabilities to
the public. Though they were not included in the city's documents, most of
the decisions related to the city's SDCERS contributions had been available
to the public all along in the SDCERS financial statements. Still, within a
month of the Voluntary Disclosure, each of the rating agencies had down-
graded the city's credit rating, and repeated downgrades followed well into
2005. By downgrading the city's credit rating, the agencies indicated that
they considered the city's financial condition to be riskier, so the city would
have to pay higher interest rates when it borrowed money. In August 2004,
the class action lawsuit was settled, requiring a $130 million contribution to
SDCERS from the city in fiscal year 2005 and actuarial contributions from
then on. The city was also required to provide $500 million in real estate to
secure its contributions for the first four years. By this point, both local and
national media were following the story.[4]

The city of San Diego is still reeling from the public outcry and legal
investigations into the propriety of SDCERS management. In April 2005,
the city's mayor was dubbed one of the three worst big-city mayors in the
country by *Time* magazine for not handling the crisis well (McCarthy and
Underwood 2005). He resigned shortly thereafter. On May 17, 2005, six current or former members of the board of trustees for SDCERS were indicted
for felony violations of the state of California's conflict of interest law for
receiving personal benefits as a result of the MP2 vote. The city of San Diego
is also facing investigations by the U.S. Attorney's Office, the Securities and
Exchange Commission, and the Federal Bureau of Investigation for public
corruption and securities violations. The city's bond rating had dropped to
borderline "junk" status by 2005, and it became excessively expensive to
finance major projects through bond issues. More significantly, its low credit

rating prevents the city from borrowing funds to dig itself out of the pension fund deficit. San Diego has been forced to cut its operating budget and decrease basic services as it struggles to make its required contributions to cover the promised retirement benefits.

As of March 2006, three former board members and two pension fund employees were facing federal criminal charges, while the six board members indicted by the state were preparing for trial in San Diego Superior Court. A suit between SDCERS and the city attorney was headed for court in October 2006 to determine whether the increased benefits granted between 1996 and 2002 were legal. A rollback of the benefit increases would result in significant savings for the city. Though the city was facing higher contributions to SDCERS each year, its new mayor's chief financial officer claimed in March 2006 that the city was not close to filing for bankruptcy. The city paid $163 million into the pension fund during fiscal year 2006, the first year since 1996 in which city contributions met actuarial recommendations. This payment, however, did not make a dent in the unfunded liability. SDCERS faced a pension deficit estimated at an astounding $1.43 billion and its long-term health care liability totaled nearly $1 billion more.

Because of the city council's 2002 vote to indemnify members of the SDCERS board, the city was responsible for paying the legal expenses of the former board members charged with misconduct in the performance of their duties. The city council revisited this decision in March 2006, but fell one vote short of overturning the measure. The city had already spent $25 million on legal fees and internal investigations. The city attorney also sued Rick Roeder's actuarial firm for malpractice. In November 2006, the Securities and Exchange Commission found that San Diego had committed securities fraud in 2002 and 2003 by not disclosing its pension fund deficit to investors. Legal battles continued into 2007.

Though the stock market decline affected pension systems across the country, the combination of increased benefits and reduced city contributions exacerbated the shortfall in San Diego. Between 1996 and 2002, both the city and the labor unions used SDCERS as a bargaining chip in their negotiations. Members of the SDCERS board, anxious to serve their constituents directly and to keep the city viable as an employer, were complicit with each agreement. This series of decisions has jeopardized the soundness of both the pension system and the city itself. Stock values have largely recovered during the last few years, so the stock market decline was clearly not the only reason for San Diego's plight. At the heart of this crisis is 25 years of increasing retirement benefits and over a decade of reduced or delayed contributions by the employer, the city of San Diego.

Timeline of Significant Events

1980s

1980 San Diego city council begins paying 13th check to retirees.

1982 City drops out of Social Security system and must boost some benefits.

1983 SDCERS board of trustees places a cap on the 13th check benefit.

1984 SDCERS members sue over the new 13th check cap.

1990s

1991 SDCERS adopts alternative actuarial approach that estimates lower annual costs for the system and decreases the city's required contribution.

1996 MP1 agreement between the city and SDCERS board increases benefits while required city contributions are reduced.

1996 DROP program allow retirees to work, receiving a salary while their retirement benefit earns guaranteed 8 percent interest.

1996 Voters approve plan to transfer the cost of postretirement health care benefits from the city to SDCERS.

1997 Reserve is created from surplus earnings to fund 13th check when current year earnings are insufficient to cover it.

1998 Reserve is created to cover the increase in employee contribution rates caused by the 1996 benefit enhancements.

1998 Reserve is created to cover future cost-of-living increases for retirees.

2000s

2000 Lawsuit claiming SDCERS had miscalculated retiree benefits is settled, requiring a 7 percent increase in benefits for current retirees out of surplus earnings.

2001 Mayor's blue ribbon committee finds that city contributions will be insufficient to fund promised benefits.

2001 Fear is that the minimum funded ratio minimum required by MP1 would be reached; the city could not afford a large increase in its contributions.

2002 MP2 proposal approved by board, requiring city's contribution to increase annually, but allowing for a gradual increase in city payments if the minimum level was reached; another round of benefit increases is granted.

2003 Class action lawsuit is filed against city and SDCERS for failing to fund the system at actuarially required levels.

2004 Lawsuit is settled; city is required to pay $130 million to SDCERS in 2005 and make actuarial contributions from then on, with $500 million in real estate guaranteeing these payments for the first 4 years.

2005 Six board members are indicted on felony conflict of interest charges.

2005 City's bond rating falls to borderline "junk" status.

2005 City faces investigations by U.S. Attorney's Office, Securities and Exchange Commission, and the Federal Bureau of Investigation.

2005 Mayor resigns.

2006 City contributions to SDCERS meet actuarial recommendations for the first time since 1996.

2006 City council fails to overturn its vote to indemnify SDCERS board members and remains responsible for millions in legal bills.

2006 Securities and Exchange Commission finds that San Diego committed securities fraud in 2002 and 2003 by not disclosing its pension fund deficit to investors.

Notes

1. For a summary and analysis of the legal advice the SDCERS board received while considering MP1, see Maco and Sauer (2004, 48–52).
2. For a summary of the specific concerns Roeder voiced at this time, see Maco and Sauer (2004, 86–87).
3. For the text of Webber's e-mail, see Maco and Sauer (2004, 118).
4. See, for example, Broder (2004) and LaVelle (2004).

References

Badenhausen, Kurt. "Postcard Perfect: Despite the High-Tech Slowdown, Business Prospects in the West Continue to Shine," *Forbes,* May 27, 2002.

Broder, John M. "Sunny San Diego Finds Itself Being Viewed as a Kind of Enron-by-the-Sea," *New York Times,* September 7, 2004, sec. A-1.

LaVelle, Philip J. "Calculated Risk Runs into Harsh Reality: Pension 'Safety Net' Didn't Work as Planned," *San Diego Union-Tribune,* June 21, 2004, sec. A.

Maco, Paul S., and Richard C. Sauer. *Report on Investigation: The City of San Diego, California's Disclosures of Obligation to Fund the San Diego City Employees' Retirement System and Related Disclosure Practices 1996–2004 with Recommended Procedures and Changes to the Municipal Code.* Washington, D.C.: Vinson & Elkins, L.L.P., 2004.

McCarthy, Terry, and Jill Underwood. "The Worst Mayors in America: Dick Murphy/San Diego," *Time,* April 25, 2005.

Ventura County Deputy Sheriffs' Association v. Board of Retirement of Ventura County Employees' Retirement System, 16 Cal. 4th 483 (1997).

United Airlines: Pensions, Profits, and Ethics

24

RICHARD H. FERN
JUDITH W. SPAIN

Contents

Introduction

"Give me a fair wage. Keep your promises. I will give you 100 percent" (Hall 2006). This had been Gordon Hall's view of the relationship between management and labor at United Airlines during his 34 years of service. He wondered, on his last day of work in 2002, if the firm had ever shared the same opinion.

Gordon worked loading baggage, pumping jet fuel, and de-icing planes for United Airlines. During his career, he had asked for and received transfers to National, Dulles, and Denver airports. Throughout these transfers, he had kept his company and union seniority, which is a significant benefit and inducement to continue working for the firm.

At age 56, Gordon decided it was time to retire. He no longer enjoyed coming to work and was looking forward to retirement financed primarily by his United Airlines pension. In the fall of 2002, Gordon retired with a pension of approximately $3,000 per month. With the lure of a larger front-end pension (accompanied by reduced benefits at age 66 when social security would begin), Gordon thought that this would be the best time for him to retire. He had other savings and investments, including shares of stock in UAL (United's parent company) acquired as part of the company's reorganization in 1994. Part of his retirement benefits included health coverage. All things considered, the financial aspects of his retirement were looking promising.

However, by late 2004 his dream of financial stability during retirement was quickly fading. In December 2002, United Airlines filed for Chapter 11 bankruptcy. As part of the bankruptcy process, companies can sometimes transfer underfunded pension plans to a U.S. government pension agency, which has the ability to limit benefits. If United transferred the pension plans to the government, Gordon's pension benefits would likely decrease by about 30 percent, since some benefits stemming from recent labor agreements and from his choice of larger, early payments would be eliminated.

Gordon's problems were far from over. In 2004, he received a letter from United informing him that his company-sponsored health care benefits were being substantially cut. In addition, just before his retirement, Gordon Hall sold his UAL shares for $1,300. These shares, part of his retirement savings, had been worth as much as $120,000 in the late 1990s (Kesmodel 2004).

Gordon's dreams for his retirement had been shattered. Years after his retirement, he wondered, "These people like me came to work every day... and we're the ones paying the consequences of their mistakes and a government that has let them under fund these pension plans" (Kesmodel 2004). As Gordon said, "Things you worked for and negotiated for were taken away" (Hall 2006).

What happened to Gordon Hall was the result of several decades of mistrust between unions and management and questionable decisions by the top management of United Airlines in the face of rapidly changing marketplaces. Could this outcome have been avoided? Who bears the largest share of responsibility for this unfortunate outcome? Think about these questions as you learn about United Airline's slide into bankruptcy and its effect on longtime employees like Gordon Hall. What might have been done differently?

The Early Days

In April 1926, Walter Varney launched an air mail service between Pasco, Washington, and Elko, Nevada. This service, a predecessor of United Airlines, marked the beginning of commercial air travel in the United States. In May 1930, the airline offered the world's first stewardess service. As *Fortune* magazine noted, "Few airline executives came near guessing correctly the depth of the packed-down public demand for air travel" (United Airlines, March 1, 2006). In the 1940s, United solidified its base of operations around the Denver hub and expanded its service to Hawaii. In 1968, about the time that Gordon Hall began work at United, it became a wholly owned subsidiary of UAL, Inc.

After making record profits in the 1960s, the airline suffered substantial losses in the 1970s. The 1978 deregulation of the U.S. airline industry caught management by surprise and sent United into a tailspin. Scrambling to find a new identity in the late 1970s and early 1980s, the company went through six presidents, unsuccessfully expanded into nonairline businesses, and changed its name twice. United's history of contentious labor relations continued with a 58-day mechanics strike in 1979 and a 6-week walkout by pilots and flight attendants in 1985. Following the 1985 strike, pilots continued to show their disgust with management by deliberately burning extra fuel and harassing replacement pilots (Burns et al., July 13, 2003). As it entered the 1990s, United's top management faced major internal and external challenges.

A New Beginning

Early in the 1990s, United divested itself of all nonairline subsidiaries and substantially expanded its international routes. This turned out to be a costly strategy as fuel prices spiked due to continuing conflicts in the Middle East and low-fare discount airlines made major inroads into the traditional markets. Nevertheless, United CEO Stephen Wolf continued to believe that the company's competitive advantage lay in remaining a premium carrier catering to the high-end business traveler (Burns et al., July 13, 2003). While business travelers generated substantial revenue for United, they only made up a small fraction of total passengers. Despite management's optimism, this business model faced a dim future unless more global routes were added and the company's outsized labor costs and low employee productivity problems were addressed.

Following previous wage conflicts with management in the 1980s, the Airline Pilot's Association (ALPA) began investigating an employee buyout of the company. In 1993, CEO Wolf and the largest employee unions, ALPA and the International Association of Machinists and Aerospace Workers (IAM), negotiated an employee buyout. Unlike a majority of ALPA members who supported the deal, many members of the IAM only reluctantly went along with the buyout because of pressure from union leaders. Company management threatened job losses if the deal was not approved and reinforced its threats by firing janitors, outsourcing flight kitchen services, and threatening more layoffs (Burns et al., July 14, 2003).

In exchange for a 55 percent ownership interest in UAL, employees agreed to substantial cuts in wages (ground workers—15 percent; pilots—25 percent; nonunion employees, including top executives—8 percent), a 25 percent contribution to medical costs, and a two-tiered wage plan for new hires

(Kochan 2005). As part of the recapitalization plan, employees would be awarded shares of stock through an employee stock ownership plan (ESOP), a tax-advantaged strategy that gives employees a voice in governance issues. ESOPs had previously succeeded at many smaller companies, but this was the first time one had been tried on such a large scale. In fact, United's ESOP remains the largest on record.

The AFL-CIO, America's largest association of unions, termed this ESOP arrangement a "model of workers ownership." The new ownership structure worked extraordinarily well in the beginning. Employee productivity increased through work-rule changes, cross-functional cooperation, and creation of best of business (BOB) employee teams. Mechanics were able to inspect and sign off on their own repair work (Donkin 2005). Employees changed the way they acted toward each other and management (Mackin and Rodgers 2003). Employees and management seemed to have truly found a better way to run the airline. Union grievances and sickness absences dropped dramatically, per-employee revenue increased 10 percent, and shareholder value surged during the first year (Donkin 2005).

In addition to receiving shares of stock, employees received three seats on UAL's board of directors and veto power over key decisions such as selecting the CEO. The employees used this power to immediately force the resignation of CEO Steven Wolf. The employees had deeply resented him since he had practically forced their acceptance of the ESOP agreement through strong-arm tactics such as actual and threatened layoffs. In addition, he had made few management decisions that directly confronted United's market disadvantages: outsized labor costs and an increasingly noncompetitive routing system. Wolf left the company with almost $30 million, including stock options. The union-influenced board quickly replaced Wolf with Gerald Greenwald, who had a long history of union involvement and sympathy with their concerns.

For three years, United generated record profits. In 1996, management cheered its newfound success by saying: "We used our strong cash flow to repay debt...and to bring our U.S. pension plans to a fully funded level" (United Airlines 1996). Management strongly complimented the improvements made from the teamwork and admitted that, despite remaining workplace issues, employee ownership was working very well.

The Honeymoon Ends

Gerald Greenwald faced two substantial challenges when he became United's chief executive in 1994: internal labor friction and market competition from discount airlines. The ESOP arrangement had temporarily solved or covered up some of the long-standing labor problems. United's start-up airline, Shuttle by United, initially fared well against Southwest Airlines and other discounters due to its low-cost, point-to-point focus derived from a new business model and wage concessions by labor (Burns et al., July 14, 2003). For several years, revenue increased, costs dropped, and customers expressed increased satisfaction with United's employees and service. The stock market reflected these improvements by pushing the UAL stock price from $22 in late 1994 to $87 in late 1997.

In spite of these indicators of success, within several years some of the old labor–management problems began to return as Greenwald's idealism collided with reality (Burns et al., July 14, 2003). The CEO continually fought an uphill battle against old-guard board members and executives who wanted to return to the old days. In addition, Greenwald said from the beginning he would only serve five years as CEO. As the 5-year limit drew nearer, many of United's managers that did not share his manager–worker philosophy began to adopt their previous antagonistic relationship with workers.

Neither management nor labor was willing to make the sacrifices necessary for continued success under the new business model (Burns et al., July 14, 2003). Managers expected employee loyalty since they were now owners. However, many employees did not feel like owners since their wages had been reduced and they still had bills to pay but could not cash in their stock until retirement. Many employees did not fully understand their dual roles as workers and owners and day-to-day concerns outweighed any long-term potential owner benefits. Some employees resented management telling them to make decisions but then later criticizing those decisions. Team cooperation, which was supposed to put pressure on slackers to do better, often actually had the opposite effect of silencing the achievers out of fear of colleague resentment. Greenwald later admitted that his message to employees was misinterpreted and he did not adequately convey both the responsibility and accountability components of shared governance (Burns et al., July 14, 2003).

In the early 1990s, newly elected union leaders who favored the employee buyout were able to get it accepted by the membership. However, more traditional and combative union leaders who had resisted the plan soon regained control by exploiting continuing union resentment of management's previous intimidation tactics. Employees such as Gordon Hall felt that they were induced by the union and management to be enthusiastic about the employee buyout. But, as a result of receiving overvalued stocks instead of raises for six years, employee enthusiasm soon began to wane. Hall and his fellow co-workers began more and more to distrust the union leadership (Hall 2006). ALPA lost its biggest ESOP proponent when the leader of the pilots union was forced out over questionable financial arrangements between the union and attorneys during the ESOP negotiations. Other divisive employee–management issues included a lack of ESOP shares for new hires and the concerns of many employees (e.g., flight attendants) who had not participated in the buyout at all (Rosen, Case, and Staubus 2005). Many employees were frustrated that their wage sacrifices came immediately but their promised rewards would only come later, if at all. These and other factors soon destroyed the company's brief flirtation with shared governance.

Wage givebacks by employees in 1994 were partly rescinded in 1996–1999 after contentious negotiations with the pilots' and mechanics' unions. Employees began to eye United's substantial profits and demanded large wage increases, especially after the top 600 executives split a $14 million bonus in 1994. Management offered profit sharing; employees demanded wage increases. During negotiations over new wage deals in 1997 and 2000, pilots (who had a 25 percent ownership stake in the company) deliberately flew at low altitudes to burn more fuel and disrupted schedules by refusing to work overtime (Donkin 2005). During this period, while their competitors were setting records for numbers of passengers and profits, employee disruptions at United caused passenger traffic to decline dramatically. To buy labor peace, Greenwald continued his practice of guaranteeing back pay during labor negotiations, which only encouraged union intransigence. He also agreed to restore pre-1994 wages by the end of 2000 (the year he expected to step down as CEO). This wage "snap back" would once again give United the highest wage structure in the industry.

As goodwill from the ESOP partnership disappeared, unionized employees pushed to rescind previous work-rule concessions and BOB teams were disbanded. The spirit of employee cooperation evaporated. Costs rose and revenue, profits, and the stock price all declined. As one IAM leader recalls, "Things were going along pretty well in those years [1994–1996]. I don't know if anyone had a crystal ball to see what was coming" (Burns et al., July 14, 2003).

CEO Greenwald came from a union background and was sympathetic to labor's workplace and wage issues. He spent most of his five years at the top trying to win labor's support. However, his handpicked successor for CEO was rejected by the ALPA and IAM members of the board, partly to demonstrate to their members the power they had at United (Burns et al., July 14, 2003). The return to pre-ESOP days at United Airlines was almost fully completed as Greenwald's successor as CEO, James Goodwin, came on board in 1999.

Major Challenges in the Year 2000

The parade of CEOs and their multimillion dollar compensation, retirement, and stock option packages antagonized many union members. During his last three years, CEO Greenwald averaged about $1.4 million in annual salary and bonus and left the company with about $47 million in stock options. While new CEO James Goodwin brought some personal trust to the position through his 30-year career at United Airlines, his million-dollars-plus compensation continued to remind rank and file employees of their wage concessions five years before. This pattern continued into 2002 when Goodwin's successor, Glenn Tilton, got a $3 million signing bonus.

The booming economy in 1999–2000 generated record airline traffic and the industry was at its peak. However, at United Airlines, the summer of 2000 was the "summer from hell." The pilots engaged in a "work by the book" slowdown that caused havoc with the schedule, dropped on-time arrivals to less than 50 percent, and infuriated passengers who departed in droves to the competition (Burns et al., July 15, 2003). The company continued to route passengers into several major hubs, which kept it dependent on just keeping planes in the air to feed the hubs. This also made the airline especially susceptible to employee slowdown tactics. Although CEO Goodwin was a company insider, he irritated the members of ALPA in 1999 by entering negotiations to buy USAirways. United's pilots did not want the postmerger competition for routes and pay with USAirways' pilots.

United's pilots also demanded substantial pay raises in 2000. The ESOP stock distribution was to end in April 2000 and pilots were determined to return their pay to pre-1994 levels. Based on three years of record profits in the airline industry, ALPA felt that United was able to meet its demands and competitors would quickly follow its lead (Burns et al., July 15, 2003). To buy labor peace, regain public trust, and stop schedule disruptions, Goodwin's management team agreed to immediate 25 percent pay raises for pilots along with another 4 percent per year for four years (Burns et al., July 15, 2003). For equity, he also gave double-digit pay raises to nonunion salaried employees.

Seeing the pattern, mechanics and other IAM ground workers also demanded substantial pay raises. To avoid pending work slowdowns, United's managers threatened loss of jobs for those mechanics who engaged in such activities. Only a few mechanics were actually fired, but management–labor relations continued to sour. Despite the few firings, mechanics continued to hinder maintenance operations with slowdown tactics that resulted in United suing the IAM for $66 million in damages. Unable to agree on a new wage contract, the National Mediation Board called both sides to Washington, D.C., for mediation. They were still negotiating on September 11, 2001, when wage negotiations suddenly became a secondary concern to other, more critical issues.

A "New" Business Plan

During the "dot-com" boom of the late 1990s, United generated about 40 percent of revenue from its California hubs and Silicon Valley connections (Burns et al., July 15, 2003). While showing record profits, management ignored the evolving airline marketplace and the changes to which other carriers were already responding. Instead of trying to compete with the discount carriers by expanding its Shuttle by United subsidiary, CEO Goodwin folded it back into United's major business line.

Not fully understanding United's overdependence on a narrowly defined market with limited passengers and the inherent weakness of its hub-and-spoke route model, he pursued a merger with USAirways, which was also struggling with high costs and low productivity. Goodwin thought that USAir's extensive East Coast routes were a good complement to United's mid-western and western routes and he also wanted to keep Delta and American from acquiring them. While Goodwin was popular with United's employees, his top associates feared that he was too easy-going to make the tough decisions needed as CEO. For example, some insiders at United felt that his $11.8 billion negotiated price for USAirways was excessive. Also, the proposed merger continued the pattern of "corporate whiplash" for United by initiating the third, almost incompatible business plan for United within a 10-year period (Burns et al., July 15, 2003).

The proposed USAirways merger was not popular with United's pilots. During wage negotiations in mid-2000, the leader of ALPA demanded a 21 percent wage increase, which Goodwin rejected. Since United's routing schedule depended on timely arrivals of connecting flights, the pilots had enormous leverage to disrupt one of the busiest summer travel seasons in many years. Their work-by-the-book tactics caused substantial turmoil in United's schedule. The militant head of ALPA described his long-term plan for wage negotiations with United: "We don't want to kill the golden goose; we just want to choke it by the neck until it gives us every last egg" (Burns et al., July 15, 2003).

The resulting turmoil in United's schedules in the summer of 2000 further reduced the number of friends that United had in the marketplace and, more importantly, in Washington, D.C. In early 2001, the U.S. Justice Department stopped the merger by finding that a United–USAir merger would reduce competition, raise fares, and hurt consumers. Not only had the proposed merger further antagonized the employees, but the airline had also incurred costs of $116 million (including a $50 million breakup fee paid to USAirways) related to the failed merger (United Airlines 2003).

In mid-2001, United was mainly operating under the same business model as it had in 1994 but in a dramatically changing market. The hub-and-spoke routing arrangement that was dependent on substantial revenue from a limited market segment was becoming untenable. United had not begun to address seriously the operational and organizational problems that hindered the company in competing in a discount-fare environment. American Airlines had recently surpassed United as the world's largest carrier by acquiring TWA. United had also returned to its status of having the highest labor costs in the industry.

When the bottom dropped out of the airline industry in late 2001, only one airline made any profit, and it was not United Airlines. Because of their higher costs and narrower revenue margins, carriers like United, American, and Delta were hit the hardest. Not only was the total number of airline passengers down dramatically, but the accompanying economic recession also hit United's high-end business base particularly hard. All airlines suffered in 2001 and 2002, but none more so than United.

Employee and Retiree Benefits

All unionized employees at United were covered by a pension plan funded by contributions from the company. Employees earned retirement benefits based on their pay scale and years of service. The funding burden for pension plans is on the employer to assure that there are enough funds (from contributions and investment earnings) to pay the guaranteed retirement benefits to employees.

Only someone familiar with the arcane terminology of actuarial science will fully understand the accounting and funding requirements for pensions. Primarily, however, the contributions and related expenses are based on broad averages that do not fully reflect the true over- or underfunding status of a company's pension plan related to its benefit obligations. To illustrate, in 1997, United expensed $215 million for pensions and contributed $173 million in cash to the pension fund. The airline ended the year with unfunded benefits of $400 million (pension obligations of $7.3 billion compared to pension assets of $6.9 billion).

United's pension plans fluctuated between adequate and inadequate funding during the 1990s as the stock market rose and fell. For example, as the market soared in 1997 the airline's pension fund earned investment returns of $1.1 billion. In 1999, the plans were actually overfunded by $1.3 billion! Yet, by the end of 2001, the funds were in the red by $2.5 billion as the stock market collapsed during the economic downturn.

Pension plans are regulated by the federal government through the Department of Labor and the Economic Retirement Income Security Act (ERISA) law. The Financial Accounting Standards Board (FASB), an accounting oversight group, controls the accounting and public reporting of pensions under the watchful eye of the Securities and Exchange Commission (SEC). United Airlines complied with all legal, accounting, and disclosure rules for pension plans over the ten years preceding its bankruptcy filing. Management's discretionary pension assumptions mirrored those used in airline and other large industries. A study of other companies' pension assumptions over this same time period shows that United's assumptions were not far out of line. In fact, they were actually a bit more conservative than those of some other firms (George 2003).

Besides the pension plans, one of the attractive employee benefits at United Airlines was employer-paid health insurance for workers and retirees.

Unlike pension plans that are federally regulated, health care plans are not subject to ERISA rules and do not have to be fully funded. Unlike pensions, employers can unilaterally rescind previously earned health-care benefits even after an employee retires. United routinely contributed substantially less money than was required to fully fund promised health care benefits.

Bankruptcy

In December 2002, United Airlines joined its rival USAirways in Chapter 11 bankruptcy. Since September 2001, the airline had limped along trying to find some way to recover its lost glory but the management team at United decided that it was not strong enough to do so without court protection. Like many legacy carriers, it faced rising fuel costs and stiff competition from low-cost carriers. The company was floundering under the highest paid, least productive workforce in the industry; too many planes; antiquated business methods; and a weak corporate sales force (Carey, January 13, 2006). In the year prior to bankruptcy, United had losses of $3 billion.

Many companies seek bankruptcy protection to get time to reorganize, reduce costs, and try to regain their competitiveness by not being "encumbered by high-legacy issues and burdensome restrictions under current labor agreements" (*Lexington Herald Leader,* October 9, 2005). Bankruptcy courts have the ability to rescind labor, lease, and other contracts and transfer underfunded pension obligations to the federal government.

A federal agency, the Pension Benefit Guaranty Corporation (PBGC), was created by Congress to promote and oversee the soundness of defined benefit pension plans. Corporations report their pension information annually to the PBGC and pay premiums ($19 per employee per year) into an insurance fund designed to provide benefits to employees if the parent company is unable to pay its pension commitments. When underfunded pension plans are terminated through bankruptcy, the PBGC takes over the plan and pays previously earned benefits up to about $45,000 per year (in 2005).

In May 2005, the bankruptcy court approved United Airlines' request to terminate the pension plans for 120,000 current and retired employees and transfer $6.6 billion of the unfunded pension obligations to the PBGC (Reed 2005). While this saved United Airlines about $645 million a year in pension costs, about one third of promised benefits disappeared since the PBGC only guarantees annual pensions up to about $45,000 per year. Some higher paid employees, such as pilots, lost up to 75 percent of their expected retirement benefits (Reed 2005). More traditional employees, like Gordon Hall, lost as well. Gordon's pension was reduced to $2,100 per month, since the PBGC can ignore increased pension benefits from recent labor contracts and increased benefits chosen in an employee's early retirement years.

In 2004, while still in bankruptcy, United's management made the decision to cut health care benefits for current workers and retirees. Former workers like Gordon Hall had retired from United under the assumption that their health care insurance costs would be fully paid in the future. Now, the company was reneging on that promise.

The Continuing Story

By 2005, after three years in bankruptcy, United Airlines had eliminated 20,000 jobs, downsized its fleet by 18 percent, and reduced its debt by $10 billion. The airline had raised per-seat revenue by 12 percent, reduced per-seat costs by 7 percent, and increased operating performance dramatically (Adams 2006). Pilots, mechanics, and other union employees either took negotiated wage cuts or had them imposed, since United's management team had convinced the bankruptcy court that costs had to be reduced for the airline to survive. The ESOP plan was terminated and the unions lost their votes and seats on the board.

During the bankruptcy process, the company's potential demise changed the tone of wage negotiations and brought management and workers together in a combined effort to survive (Burns et al., July 16, 2003). Many in the unions realized that the negotiated or court-imposed wage reductions were not temporary. This newfound sense of cooperation and commitment helped lead United to its first-ever top ranking in on-time performance in 2002. For some long-timers, however, it was also reminiscent of a similar feeling they had in 1994 when the ESOP employee buyout was finalized.

Many long-term employees, like Gordon Hall, still feel betrayed by their many years of loyalty during periods of benefit cuts, uncertainty caused by job reductions, and substantial decline in value of their UAL stock holdings. Those employees that survived the bankruptcy process emerged with a job but with less pay, fewer benefits, and less in pension guarantees. Current retirees still get some health care benefits and pensions, but not what was originally promised.

On the other hand, if United does not successfully exit the bankruptcy process, the company will be liquidated and the remaining 62,000 active employees will lose their jobs and all pay and benefits. Retirement benefits already earned, including those of current retirees, would be covered by the PBGC up to a certain amount. But all future benefits will be lost, including retirement, health care, life insurance, etc. As the bankruptcy judge put it, "The least bad of the available choices here has got to be the one that keeps an airline functioning; that keeps employees being paid" (United Airlines 2005).

Who Is to Blame?

Society must determine its proper role in guaranteeing employee benefits as major U.S. industries mature and face start-up and foreign competition. The U.S. airline industry is following the pattern of the steel industry of 20 years ago and, in turn, is being followed by the U.S. automotive industry today. Should the burden be borne by society, the industry, or the individual firms?

Did the leaders of the major employee unions appropriately represent their members during negotiations with United's management? An increasingly bitter employer–union relationship during the 1990s forced United to promise benefits that it could not afford in order to keep peace with labor and try to maintain its customer base. Why did union leaders take such a hard line and deliberately disrupt airline business, thus hastening United's decline?

In the wake of the September 11, 2001 tragedy, CEO Goodwin stated in an open letter to the employees that "we are in nothing less than a fight for our lives" (*Summers, Jerry, George Lenormand, and Wood Eppelsheimer et al. v. USAL Corporation Stock Ownership Plan* 2006). However, United's troubles did not begin on September 11, 2001. In a class action suit against the UAL ESOP Committee, some United employees alleged that Committee inaction during 2001 and 2002 caused substantial losses by not managing "ESOP investments prudently and solely in the best interests of the ESOP participants" as required by law. Even as late as October 2001, the stock was still selling at around $13 per share. The ESOP Committee (all employees of United) had first-hand knowledge of the financial risks to the ESOP over these two years. Yet, they did not sell any of the stock or try to diversify the ESOP investment portfolio until August 2002, when the price was around $2 per share. Why not? Was this a lack of strong leadership or did their years of "induced" company loyalty by employees overwhelm their better judgment? Whatever the reason, by holding on to the declining UAL stock the employees saw their long-awaited ESOP stock values decline even more.

How committed was United Airlines' top management to its corporation's responsibility to employees and society at large during the ten years prior to bankruptcy? Gordon Hall and many current and former employees wonder. Under the overall umbrella of its corporate governance policy adopted in 2003, United also adopted a code of conduct that states: "Managers (defined as employees who supervise others) are expected to exemplify the highest standards of ethical business conduct" (United Airlines 2006). Did this express a long-held commitment to employees, shareholders, and the larger society or was this just public relations spin? Which supersedes: pensions, profits, or ethics?

Epilogue

In February 2006, UAL emerged from bankruptcy by issuing 125 million new shares of stock (all prebankruptcy shares were cancelled). Twenty percent of shares went to the PBGC to cover underfunded pension plans. Over objections of unions and retirees, another 8 percent of shares were awarded to the top 400 managers of United. Most of the remaining shares went to United's unsecured creditors. Based on an expected market value of $15 per share, this gave the creditors about four to eight cents for each dollar of prebankruptcy claims (Carey, January 19, 2006). In mid-2006, UAL's stock was trading around $34 a share. In July 2006, United announced that it would have positive earnings for the second quarter, its first profit since 2000 (Carey, July 25, 2006).

As the company exited bankruptcy, management proposed a new business orientation. United would now devote considerable effort to attracting more casual flyers paying lower fares in an effort to diversify and combat discount airlines. Many traditional routes would still have full service, while some heavily traveled routes would now only offer economy seating (Burns et al., July 16, 2003). A new low-fare subsidiary would be started to compete head on with the discounters.

All remaining employees are working for smaller wages with no "snap-back" agreements in place. There are now performance-based bonuses and profit-sharing amounts available for all employees. The company has much more flexibility to outsource labor, including heavy maintenance work. However, if management pursues substantial outsourcing it risks antagonizing union mechanics and reigniting United's subdued, but still simmering, union–management tensions (Burns et al., July 16, 2003). In 2003, union mechanics voted to change their membership from the IAM to the more combative Aircraft Mechanics Fraternal Association.

Even CEO Tilton took a 36 percent pay cut over three years, beginning in 2002. However, he still has a buyout clause that pays at least three years of salary and bonus if he is terminated and he received a $3 million signing bonus in 2002. A fully funded retirement trust of $4.5 million has been established to guarantee his retirement income (United Airlines 2006).

Gordon Hall still lives in Denver on his reduced pension income. Luckily, his investments were not limited solely to UAL stock and he has some other, limited resources available to supplement his pension. His standard of living is significantly different from what he expected it to be 37 years ago when he loaded his first plane for United Airlines. "The bottom line is United wanted to make money. The government let them get into this situation. There was a lot of 'hocus pocus' going on and the American worker is now paying for it" (Hall 2006).

References

Adams, Marilyn. "Agreement Puts United's Exit from Chapter 11 Nearer," *USA Today,* January 12, 2006, C1.

Burns, Greg, Susan Chandler, Flynn McRoberts, and Andrew Zajac. "United's Undoing: A War Within. United's Rhapsody of Blues," *Chicago Tribune,* July 13, 2003.

_____. "ESOP's Fables Forces Airline to the Brink. United's Rhapsody of Blues," *Chicago Tribune,* July 14, 2003.

_____. "Summer of Hell Exacts Heavy Toll. United's Rhapsody of Blues," *Chicago Tribune,* July 15, 2003.

_____. "Bankruptcy Provided Time, No Guarantees. United's Rhapsody of Blues," *Chicago Tribune,* July 16, 2003.

Carey, Susan. "As Airlines Pull Out of Dive, United Charts Its Own Course," *Wall Street Journal,* January 13, 2006, A1.

_____. "Judge Approves UAL's Managers' Incentive Plan," *Wall Street Journal,* January 19, 2006, A2.

_____. "UAL Expects Earnings above Wall Street Views," *Wall Street Journal,* July 25, 2006, A2.

Donkin, Richard. www.richarddonkin.com/x_employee_share_ownership_royal_mail.htm, 2005 (accessed January 30, 2006).

George, Nashwa. "The Impact of Pension Accounting on Companies' Financial Statements," *Journal of the Academy of Business and Economics,* February (2003).

Hall, Gordon. Telephone conversation, February, 2006.

Kesmodel, David. "Cuts Mean Return to Work, Retirement Dreams on Hold," *Rocky Mountain News* (Denver, CO), December 25, 2004. http://www.rockymountainnews.com/drmn/other_business/article/0,2777,DRMN_23916_3424301,00.html (accessed November 14, 2005).

Kochan, Thomas A. *Corporate Governance and Accountability—United Airlines.* www.caseplace.org/cases/cases_show.htm?doc_id=82030 (accessed November 11, 2005).

Lexington (Kentucky) *Herald Leader.* "Main U.S. Maker of Auto Parts Files for Bankruptcy," October 9, 2005, A1, A11.

Mackin, Christopher and Loren Rodgers. "But What About United Airlines? Answering Tough Questions." http://www.ownershipassociates.com/united_questions.shtm (accessed May 11, 2005).

Reed, Dan. "Airlines Lobby for Relief on Pensions," *USA Today,* May 12, 2005, B3.

Rosen, Corey, John Case, and Martin Staubus. *Equity: Why Employee Ownership Is Good for Business.* Cambridge, MA: Harvard Business School Press, 2005.

Summers, Jerry, George Lenormand, and Wood Eppelsheimer et al. v. USAL Corporation Stock Ownership Plan. United States District Court for the North District of Illinois, Eastern Division. Count 35 of Complaint, http://www.hagens-berman.com/files/UAL%20ESOP%20Complaint1046475420825.pdf (accessed June 15, 2006).

United Airlines. "1996 Annual Report," http://media.corporate-ir.net/media_files/NYS/UAL/reports/UAL_AR_96Low.pdf (accessed February 16, 2006).

United Gets OK to Ditch Pensions. www.cbsnews.com/stories/2005/05/10/national/main694358.shtml (accessed May 11, 2005).

United Airlines. http://www.united.com/page/middlepage/0,6823,2286,00.html (accessed March 1, 2006).

Bibliography

CBS News. "United Gets OK to Ditch Pensions," www.cbsnews.com/stories/2005/05/10/national/main694358.shtml, May 10, 2005 (accessed November 11, 2005).

Holme, Richard. "Corporate Social Responsibility: Making Good Business Sense," World Business Council for Sustainable Development, January, 2000.

Schroeder, Michael. "House Clears Bill to Bolster Pensions," *Wall Street Journal*, December 16, 2005, A2.

United Airlines. http://www.united.com/page/middlepage/0,6823,2286,00.html (accessed March 3, 2006).

United Airlines. Form 10-K, December 31, 2003, http://media.corporate-ir.net/media_files/NYS/UAL/reports/UAL10K2003.pdf (accessed May 10, 2006).

United Airlines. http://phx.corporate-ir.net/phoenix.zhtml?c=83680&p=irol-IRHome (accessed February 14, 2006).

White, Allen. "Fade, Integrate, or Transform?" *Business for Social Responsibility*, 2005, http://www.bsr.org/CSRResources/ResourcesDocs/BSR_200508_Allen-White_Fade-Transform.pdf (accessed February 2, 2006).

Unhealthy Developments VII

In this part of the book we focus on a single case from three different points of view: the individual, the organization, and the watchdog. The HealthSouth Corporation fraud ranks among the largest in U.S. history. "King of Health Care" looks at the main protagonist in this tale, Richard Scrushy, who was involved in every aspect of operation but claimed that he had no knowledge of the creative accounting that existed in the company. "The HealthSouth Family" examines this fraud from the point of view of the company and the philosophy that Scrushy promulgated among its employees. Finally, "See No Evil; Hear No Evil; Speak No Evil" takes the auditor's side of the story and examines the leadership issues in the accounting firm responsible for certifying the company's cooked books.

The HealthSouth "Family"

25

FANNIE L. MALONE
RICHARD PITRE

Contents

Introduction

We are family. HealthSouth's former CEO (chief executive officer) Richard Scrushy's band might even know the words to the song "We Are Family," but that is another story.

In the Beginning

All organizations start with an idea and HealthSouth was no different. It started with an idea, $70,000, a small office, a table, four chairs, and one telephone. Anthony Tanner, one of the original founders, described Richard Scrushy, a former physical therapist, as the ideas man who led HealthSouth from its humble beginnings in Little Rock, Arkansas, to one of the nation's largest health care service providers of outpatient surgery, diagnostic imaging, and rehabilitation services (Castellano and Lightle 2005). After Medicare began in 1965 and paid generously for rehabilitation services, money poured into the health-care system and HealthSouth capitalized on these generous

315

payments. Within two years of its 1984 founding, HealthSouth had proven to be a successful business model.

From HealthSouth's inception in 1984 as Amcare, Inc., Scrushy served as CEO and chairman of the board of directors. As CEO, he managed every aspect of the company personally and became known for his short temper and relentlessness (Wikipedia, June 30, 2006). Scrushy got into the rehabilitation industry at a good time (HealthSouth Corporation 2007). It was during this period that rehabilitation was viewed as a means of reducing medical expenses. Specifically, rehabilitation could be used to minimize unnecessary, expensive surgeries. It also helped injured employees get back to work more quickly, thus eliminating expensive worker's compensation and disability costs. As health and insurance professionals began to recognize these benefits, the use of rehabilitation services soared (HealthSouth Corporation 2007). In 1985, the company moved to Birmingham, Alabama, and expanded to a chain of clinics with revenues of $20 million. In 1986, Scrushy sold shares of stock to the public. HealthSouth grew from one hospital in Arkansas in 1984 to an industry giant with facilities in all 50 states by the late 1990s and revenues of over $181 million. Its rapid growth sprang from buying and building rehabilitation hospitals, outpatient rehabilitation clinics, outpatient surgery centers, and diagnostic services centers (HealthSouth, July 14, 2007).

The appearance of an ethical organization was established early in the life of the organization when senior management created a corporate compliance department at the company before any law required one. There was a toll-free hot line for employees to call with concerns and anonymous tips (Wynne 2007). In a speech before his managers in 1988, Scrushy talked about finances in depth and threatened to fire anyone who ever hired a convicted felon. HealthSouth seemed poised for greatness.

However, all was not well in 1989 at HealthSouth. A former internal auditor stated that there was pressure to meet specific earnings targets and that he was fired for questioning accounting problems at the company. As evidence, in 1991, Medicare alleged that HealthSouth fraudulently included unallowable costs in its Bakersfield Rehabilitation Hospital cost reports involving outpatient physical therapy services and inpatient rehabilitation admissions (Department of Justice 2004). This allegation was just the beginning of Medicare fraud allegations against HealthSouth. Years later, HealthSouth would agree to pay the United States $325 million to resolve allegations of Medicare fraud (Department of Justice 2004).

The allegations of Medicare fraud did not put a damper on HealthSouth's innovative services. In 1993, it became a leading provider of gamma knife services with programs in six states. The gamma knife, a precision device that uses gamma rays without any incision, illustrated why HealthSouth showed great promise as a provider of rehabilitation services.

In 1994, Scrushy went on an acquisitions binge. In that year, he doubled HealthSouth's size and raised it from the number three company in comprehensive rehabilitation services to number one, with 250 locations in the United States. HealthSouth became a $1 billion company and could do no wrong. For nearly all of Scrushy's tenure, press reports about the company were almost universally positive (Ackman 2003). At the beginning of 1995, HealthSouth had no surgical facilities. After four acquisitions totaling $1.3 billion, it was by year's end the country's biggest surgical-center operator. The employees managing these acquired companies were run ragged and Scrushy was irked by employees who could not match his drive. In 1995, during one of a series of HealthSouth merger offers, Bloomberg News reported that then-U.S. House Speaker Newt Gingrich (R-Ga.) wanted Scrushy in Congress, and Alabama businessmen wanted him to run for governor (Ackman 2003). William Harnish, president of Forstmann Leff Associates, a money management firm, said, "There may not be another person who has come so far and accomplished so much in corporate America" (Ackman 2003). HealthSouth involved itself in more than mergers. It built facilities such as the $4 million Richard M. Scrushy/HealthSouth Sports Medicine Center at the Colorado Springs Olympic Complex that was started during 1995 (*Modern Healthcare* 2003). Assisting in that success story was Aaron Beam, known as the numbers man. He became the first CFO (chief financial officer).

1996 to Mid-2002

The family at HealthSouth had long used aggressive accounting interpretations to meet Wall Street expectations. In 1996, even with aggressive accounting, the company would not meet those expectations. Says Livesay: "In 1996, we crossed the line. Those aggressive methods were no longer enough so we crossed the line from gray to black" (*Accounting Department Management Report* 2005). According to Livesay, the family was to continue in the fraud until a series of acquisitions, just over the horizon, bailed them out. HealthSouth's expansion accelerated in 1997 (*Accounting Department Management Report* 2005). Scrushy indicated his interest in expanding into the United Kingdom and Australia, and HealthSouth made initial purchases in both countries. HealthSouth used stock to acquire Health Images for $270 million and ReadiCare for $70 million. But here is a key point: With these acquisitions, earnings grew from $70 million in 1996 to $600 million in 1998 (*Accounting Department Management Report* 2005).

HealthSouth moved to new headquarters at 1 HealthSouth Parkway, located south of downtown Birmingham, Alabama. In 1997, Scrushy, then 45, earned a total of $106 million in compensation, mostly from the sale of $93 million in stock options, including a $10 million cash bonus (Ackman 2003).

The compensation made him America's third highest paid CEO. Although things seemed good on the surface, there were big problems below the surface. Medicare funding arrangements along with pressure to meet the expectations of Wall Street were just around the horizon. At the end of 1997, Michael D. Martin, who had been treasurer, replaced Aaron Beam, who had been CFO since 1984. A change in the CFO position hinted at problems ahead. Employee turnover is often a warning sign for difficulties in the road ahead.

More than a third of HealthSouth's revenues came from Medicare. In mid-1998, new Medicare funding arrangements designed to prevent exploitation of the system commenced (HealthSouth, July 14, 2007). HealthSouth maintained firmly that its profits would not suffer as a result of the Medicare-overhaul bill that aimed to cut payments from that program by $100 billion. By the end of the year, profits dropped 93 percent at HealthSouth and Scrushy blamed managed care contracts for the drop (HealthSouth, July 14, 2007). Meanwhile, Scrushy sold shares of his stock in HealthSouth. A Medicare-authorized investigation by Alabama Blue Cross discovered that HealthSouth improperly billed Medicare for therapy by students, interns, athletic trainers, and other unlicensed aides. Also, a suit in Texas accused HealthSouth of widespread abuse of Medicare. The company faced accusations of billing for services it never provided, delivering poor care, treating patients without a formal plan of care, and using unlicensed therapists (HealthSouth, July 14, 2007). The suit in Texas alleged that HealthSouth routinely billed Medicare for individual therapy when patients were being treated in groups (Wynne 2003). Scrushy went to great lengths to defend the latter practice.

In 1998, home care was no longer profitable under the new Medicare payment system, so HealthSouth, like other companies, closed its home care unit (HealthSouth, July 14, 2007). HealthSouth claimed that it made other arrangements for the displaced patients (HealthSouth, July 14, 2007). Many patients that were once cared for at home ended up in nursing homes. Decisions affecting the care of the patients were not made at their bedsides or based on need, but rather in boardrooms on the basis of profits. The home care decision signaled that HealthSouth might be skimping on patient care. Generally, patients who are cared for at home receive a higher quality of care than those living in nursing homes.

Plans to split HealthSouth into inpatient and outpatient companies were announced in 1999 after earnings remained flat. Inpatient hospital services are ordinarily furnished by a hospital for the care and treatment of inpatients and are provided under the direction of a physician or a primary care practitioner. Outpatient health services are ordinarily provided in hospitals, clinics, offices, and other health care facilities by licensed health care providers and include services provided by or under the direction of a physician or a primary care practitioner. HealthSouth's outpatient services were more profitable than its inpatient services. As a result, the company planned to divide its inpatient and outpatient operations by spinning off the inpatient services into a new company, to be called HealthSouth Hospital Corporation (HealthSouth Corporation 2007). The plan would have enabled HealthSouth to focus on its more profitable outpatient operations. However, the plan to split HealthSouth was not implemented.

By 2000, HealthSouth dominated the rehabilitation services market and employed more than 50,000 people at 2,000 clinics in every state of the United States and also in the United Kingdom. A survey by *Modern Healthcare* examined the widespread failures and losses in large health care groups and found that HealthSouth was one of a few exceptions to the general trend. HealthSouth seemed to be beating the odds against companies in the health care industry (HealthSouth, July 14, 2007).

Ernst & Young was paid $1.16 million in audit fees and $2.39 million in audit-related fees in 2001 (*Ziff Davis CIO Insight*, 2005). The audit-related fees covered payments for so-called "pristine audits," which included checking magazines in waiting rooms and making sure bathrooms were clean. By 2001, the government restored some of the Medicare funding that had been removed earlier. This action may have been more hurtful than beneficial to HealthSouth because, in 2002, the Justice Department accused HealthSouth of seeking individual payment for services given to groups and payments for services provided by unlicensed employees. As these events were unfolding, Scrushy continued to exercise his stock options.

Mid-2002 to 2003

During this time, the band continued to play. In 2002, the HealthSouth band "Proxy" performed at the *Fortune* Battle of the Corporate Bands, an annual national music competition, started in 2001, for amateur company bands and musicians. Members of Proxy included CEO Richard Scrushy on guitar, CIO Ken Livesay on guitar, and CFO Bill Owens on drums (*Wikipedia* 2006). It was not too long before the music stopped.

The first signs of trouble emerged in October 2002 when Scrushy temporarily stepped down as CEO and HealthSouth lowered earnings estimates by $175 million due to changes in Medicare reimbursements. HealthSouth's stock prices plunged as a result of the announcement about Medicare reimbursements. Before the stock prices decreased, Scrushy sold $74 million of his stock. He claimed that he did not know about the Medicare issue until well after selling his stock.

In March 2003, Bill Owens turned informant for the FBI. Owens taped incriminating conversations with Scrushy. Under pressure, the last CFO standing, Weston Smith (the main whistleblower), cracked and agreed to wear a wire for the FBI. Smith went to federal prosecutors and told them about the creative accounting at HealthSouth and agreed to tape his colleagues. According to the civil suit filed in March 2003 against HealthSouth and Scrushy by the SEC, the fraud began in 1996. It was between that time and mid-2002 that the family members faked at least $2.7 billion in profits at one of the nation's largest providers of outpatient surgery, diagnostic imaging, and rehabilitation services (Castellano and Lightle 2005). Top officials would review quarterly unreported actual results and compare the results to Wall Street expectations. If the variance was unfavorable, managers were ordered to fix the problem. Family meetings were held by accounting staffers to manipulate earnings, which they called "filling the gap." To conceal their fraud, accounting staffers booked the false entries below the threshold at which outside auditors would question the entries. During the process, they created false documents such as invoices to hide their work. By mid-2002, HealthSouth had overstated its property, plant, and equipment account by $1 billion; cash by $300 million; and total assets by more than $1.5 billion. The overstatement of income dating back to 1999 was approximately 119 percent at the low end and 4,722 percent at the high end of actual earnings.

According to the SEC civil suit, HealthSouth used its auditing firm's own processes against it to perpetrate financial statement fraud (*SAS 99 & Confirmation Fraud Risk* 2004). HealthSouth executives knew that the auditing firm did not question fixed-asset additions below a certain dollar threshold, so they made random entries to balance-sheet accounts for fictitious assets worth less than the amount that the auditors would consider material. This is a classic example of the auditing firm not exercising professional judgment. Although auditors use sampling to draw a conclusion about the population, the sampling could have been improved by using all dollar amounts rather than those above a certain dollar threshold. Before all the blame is placed on the auditing firm, the relationship between HealthSouth accountants and CFOs and the Ernst & Young auditors may explain why the auditors did not discover the false entries. Many of the accountants and CFOs hired by HealthSouth were former employees of Ernst & Young. The family members were very much aware of the amounts considered material for auditing since they were former employees of the auditing firm.

HealthSouth fired Scrushy in March 2003 and in November 2003 Scrushy was criminally charged in the HealthSouth fraud. He pled innocent to all 85 counts, which included fraud, money laundering, conspiracy, and making false statements. The number of counts would be reduced to 36 later.

Cooking with HealthSouth

Feast or famine is the choice. What would management do? If you are the HealthSouth family, you gather up your ingredients and start cooking. Now it is time for the cooking lesson. Assume that the pot needs more earnings. What revenues can be added? Alternatively, maybe the earnings would be better off with lower expenses. The following recipe has not been tested in the kitchen, so beware that the dish may leave a bad taste in your mouth and cause some sleepless nights; do not count on this being a favorite family recipe. Here is HealthSouth's recipe for cooking its books.

First, the CFO delivers the amount of unreported actual earnings to the CEO (Scrushy). During the period of the fraudulent accounting, five CFOs prepared the amounts of unreported earnings. The kitchen is already getting crowded with Beam, Martin, McVay, Owens, and Smith working as CFOs during the cooking time period.

Second, the CEO (Scrushy) compares actual unreported earnings to estimates from the Wall Street analysts. If unreported earnings fall short of expectations, the CEO orders managers to fix them by recording false earnings. Now the cooking begins, with the senior accountants holding "family meetings" to manipulate the financial reports. Managers and senior accountants included Botts, Brown, Crumpler, Fowler, Harris, Hicks, and Livesay. Each employee had his or her own spice to add to the recipe. It is time to turn up the heat in the kitchen.

Third, one way to manipulate the reports is by reducing the contractual adjustment account, which estimates the difference between the amount billed to the patient and the amount insurance will pay. Harris added the spice to this portion of the recipe. This estimate helps determine net revenues and is difficult to verify.

The balance sheet has to be doctored because increases in revenue or decreases in expenses have to match with increases in assets or decreases in liabilities. The expertise of Botts, Fowler, Hicks, and Livesay proved invaluable in spicing up the assets.

To match the fictitious adjustments to the income statement, officials falsify fixed-asset accounts. To artificially inflate assets, the property, plant, and equipment (PP&E) account is used. Thousands of phony asset entries are made in the PP&E accounts of facilities. This is where Crumpler demonstrated his flair for spreading ingredients. Accountants must take steps to conceal their fraud. Because auditors question large additions to the PP&E accounts, HealthSouth's accountants had to keep the bogus additions below a certain threshold. Accountants must also create fake documents such as invoices to conceal the fraud. If accountants decide to increase inventories, they boost inventory accounts at facilities by different amounts so auditors will not question the figures. There were many cooks adding the ingredients for this step, including Ayers, Edwards, Morgan, and Valentine. Although they had fancy titles such as vice president, in many instances, they "cooked" like data entry clerks.

Table 25.1   Recipe for Cooking HealthSouth's Books

Preparation time: varies
Ease of preparation: average
Cook time: until desired bottom line is achieved

Ingredients

1. Essential HealthSouth personnel: head of the family, CEO; and family of CFOs and accountants
2. Analysis of HealthSouth's actual unreported earnings
3. Wall Street analysts' estimates for HealthSouth
4. Blank documents

Directions

1. CEO compares actual unreported earnings to Wall Street analysts' estimates.

2. If earnings fall short of expectations, the CEO orders managers to "fix it" by recording false earnings.

3. "Family meetings" are held by senior accountants to manipulate the financial reports.

4. One way to manipulate the reports is by reducing the "contractual adjustment account," which estimates the difference between the amount billed to the patient and the amount insurance will pay. This estimate helps determine net revenues and is difficult to verify.

5. The balance sheet has to be doctored because increases in revenue or decreases in expenses have to match with increases in assets or decreases in liabilities.

6. To match the fictitious adjustments to the income statement, officials falsify fixed-asset accounts.

7. To artificially inflate assets, use the property, plant, and equipment (PP&E) account. Make thousands of phony asset entries in the PP&E accounts of facilities.

8. Accountants must take steps to conceal their fraud. Know that auditors question large additions to the PP&E accounts, so keep the bogus additions below a certain threshold.

9. Accountants must also create fake documents such as invoices to conceal the fraud.

10. If accountants decide to increase inventories, they boost inventory accounts at facilities by different amounts so that auditors will not question the figures.

11. Bottom line: overstated PP&E account, cash, and total assets.

Tip: These steps must be repeated quarterly.

Source: Birmingham News, http://www.al.com/specialreport/birminghamnews/healthsouth/cook.jpg.

Fourth, when the books were done, the bottom line consisted of overstated PP&E account, cash, and total assets. An important recipe tip is that HealthSouth needed to repeat these steps quarterly (see table 25.1 for the recipe in tabular form).

The result of the recipe was a failure. Why? It failed because there were too many cooks at HealthSouth (table 25.2 displays the HealthSouth family). Scrushy claimed that he did not know how to cook, since he had neither experience nor training. Without corporate leadership, the CFOs and accountants had their way with the recipe, so it eventually failed.

Table 25.2 The HealthSouth "Family" (or the "Pack of Rodents")

Name	Position(s)	Comments
Ayers, Angela C.	Vice president and various accounting positions, 1994–2003	She made false entries into PP&E, cash, inventory, and goodwill accounts at various times from 1999 to 2002 and created false documents to support the entries.
Beam, Aaron Jr.	Cofounder and CFO, 1984–1997	His property has a regulation-size football field. During cross-examination he admitted to adultery.
Botts, Richard	Senior vice president for taxes, May 1998–July 2003	Members of the HealthSouth accounting staff provided him with false depreciation schedules, which were tied to and included fictitious assets on the company's general ledger. Botts filed the false depreciation schedules with tax officials.
Brown, Jason	Vice president of finance, May 2000–July 2003	He created documents to show HealthSouth selling $27 million worth of stock in another company in 2002 rather than in 2001. He also altered same-facility volume numbers (for Q3 2002) to understate decline in volume.
Crumpler, Hannibal "Sonny"	Former executive of HealthSouth; CFO of Source Medical Solutions	He was charged with conspiracy and lying to the auditors. His homework was to spread fraud across the country by using thousands of facilities.
Edwards, Cathy	Vice president and various accounting positions, 1993–2003	She made false entries into PP&E, cash, inventory, and goodwill accounts at various times from 1999 to 2002 and created false documents to support the entries.
Fowler, Catherine	Treasury, vice president, and cash manager, May 1994–March 2003	She was charged with creating a paper trail to falsify date of stock sale.

Continued

Table 25.2 The HealthSouth "Family" (or the "Pack of Rodents") (Continued)

Name	Position(s)	Comments
Harris, Emery	Various positions, including assistant controller, 1992–2003	He was charged with making and causing others to make false entries for the purpose of artificially inflating HealthSouth's earnings, and designing the fictitious accounting entries to avoid detection through methods such as manipulation of the "contractual adjustment" or other expense accounts to inflate revenue on the income statement and false entries on the balance sheet concerning PP&E.
Hicks, Will	Vice president of investments, March 1999–July 2003	He caused investment-portfolio summaries of assets to be provided to the auditors that contained false information and omitted material facts concerning HealthSouth's investment in a company that owned assisted-living facilities.
Livesay, Kenneth	Assistant controller, 1989–1999; chief information officer, 1999–2003	He directed staff members to commit fraud. Methods included overbooking reserve accounts, which could later flow out into revenue; creating fictitious entries to fixed-asset system; and overstating intangible-assets accounts.
Martin, Michael D.	Treasurer from October 1989; senior vice president, finance, and treasurer from February 1994; executive vice president, finance, and treasurer from May 1996; CFO, October 1997–February 2000, EVP investments, director from 1998–2000	In 2002, he won outstanding alumni award from UAB business school. He likened HealthSouth to the firm in John Grisham's novel The Firm.

Name	Position	Description
McVay, Malcolm "Tadd"	Vice president of finance from September 1999; senior vice president of finance and treasurer from February 2000; CFO, August 2002–January 2003; treasurer January–March 2003	He filed false financial reports. On the witness stand, he accused prosecution of making him look like "the scum of the Earth."
Morgan, Rebecca Kay	Group vice president and various accounting positions, 1987–2003	She made false entries into PP&E, cash, inventory, and goodwill accounts at various times from 1999 to 2002, and created false documents to support the entries.
Owens, William T.	Controller from March 1986; group SVP and controller from March 1998; CFO, February 2000–August 2002 and January–March 2003; president and chief operating officer, August 2001–2002; CEO, August 2002–January 2003; director, March 2001–2003	He certified false financial statements. He is the godfather to one of Weston Smith's children. He has never had a passport.
Smith, Weston	Direct of reimbursement from February 1987; senior vice president of finance and controller from March 2000; CFO, August 2001–2002; executive vice president of inpatient operations, 2002–2003	He certified false financial statements. There is speculation that he was trying to protect his wife, Susan Jones-Smith, who was also a finance executive at the company and appeared before Congress, but has not been criminally charged.
Valentine, Virginia B.	Assistant vice president and various accounting positions, 1995–2003	She made false entries into PP&E, cash, inventory, and goodwill accounts at various times from 1999 to 2002, and created false documents to support the entries.

Scrushy described his HealthSouth "family" as a pack of rodents, at the same time asserting that he knew nothing about the workings of the family. What do rodents know about cooking? Many of them were later convicted for their role of providing phony ingredients for the recipe (for complete details of the rodents' "ingredients" see table 25.2).

After the Whistle

In 2003, after Weston Smith blew the whistle that signaled it was time to stop cooking, the music of the Proxy band also stopped playing. Proxy band members Scrushy, Livesay, and Owens were indicted on federal charges of wire and securities fraud related to the scandal at HealthSouth. Livesay and Owens pled guilty and later testified against Scrushy. The band members hit a few wrong notes and were no longer on beat. Scrushy was always irked when the band did not play on beat.

The company was on the verge of bankruptcy. A key bondholder threatened to push HealthSouth into bankruptcy (Foust 2005). HealthSouth had been charged with Medicare fraud, investigated by the Securities and Exchange Commission, and sued by its investors (Foust 2005). On top of all that, HealthSouth paid so much in taxes on bogus income it had to borrow money to make ends meet.

Guilty pleas have been secured from 15 former HealthSouth executives. Smith's taping of his colleagues may be the key to the guilty pleas obtained. Two former HealthSouth executives, Scrushy and Crumpler, did not plead guilty and chose trial by jury.

How Scrushy Got Off

Former CEO Richard Scrushy, who did not have an accounting degree, CPA, or MBA, declared that he did not play a role in the family's creative accounting. A jury of Scrushy's peers found him not guilty of a crime (Steffy 2005). He faced 36 counts, including conspiracy, two counts of securities fraud, 13 counts of wire fraud, seven counts of mail fraud, two counts of false statements, false certification, and ten counts of money laundering (see the Scrushy scorecard in table 25.3). The jury found Scrushy not guilty for his role in the $2.7 billion accounting fraud at HealthSouth. In the end, ignorance of accounting proved to be a valid defense.

In his testimony about the early days of HealthSouth, Tanner, one of the five founders of HealthSouth and now suffering from multiple sclerosis, said that he could not recall many details about the compliance program that he started. Multiple sclerosis impairs memory, so Tanner did not remember

Table 25.3   Scrushy Scorecard

	Guilty	Not guilty
Conspiracy	0	1
Securities fraud	0	2
Wire fraud	0	13
Mail fraud	0	7
False statements	0	2
False certification	0	1
Money laundering	0	10

much from the late 1990s, including an occasion on which a staffer reported suspicions of fraud to the compliance department. He acknowledged that Scrushy had an active business mind, helped approve the company's early business plan, and then pitched it to venture capital firms and others. He stated that Scrushy knew about the company's finances.

Diane Henze, an accounting vice president, testified during the trial that an investigation of her complaint was dropped without action. She was transferred to another department after she filed her complaint. Former finance chief Michael Martin, a confessed conspirator, testified that he was worried that the Henze complaint would expose fraud, and that he informed Tanner to sit on it and not publicize it. Martin also indicated that he warned Scrushy about the Henze complaint and was told to keep the fraud hidden.

Daryl Brown, former HealthSouth vice president, supervised all U.S. physical therapy clinics while at the company. He stated that he knew nothing about illegal activity while at HealthSouth. He explained that billing and collections are difficult tasks in health care because of complicated agreements that cover patient expenses. He described how estimates of how much money HealthSouth would eventually collect from an insurance company were hard to nail down and the estimates varied at the company. Prosecutors contend that manipulating the estimates of eventual payment was one method conspirators used to perpetrate fraud.

During testimony against Scrushy, Martin, a former CFO at HealthSouth, said he and Scrushy first discussed falsifying numbers in 1993 (HealthSouth, July 14, 2007). HealthSouth was going to miss the earnings expectations and had to make an acquisition to close the gap (HealthSouth, July 14, 2007). Martin stated that Scrushy told him to "fix" the earnings shortfalls virtually every month during that time (HealthSouth, July 14, 2007). If the numbers were not meeting the expectations, Martin had to go figure it out.

According to Ken Livesay, a former assistant controller at HealthSouth, the metamorphosis from aggressive accounting practices to fraudulent develops from several factors. During his testimony against Scrushy, Livesay said fraud emerges from three factors: (1) external pressures, (2) gullibility, and (3) incentives (*Accounting Department Management Report* 2005). HealthSouth faced external pressures from Wall Street to meet earnings. They accomplished this by their long-standing practice of aggressive accounting interpretations. The gullibility factor, according to Livesay, was that a series of acquisitions would bail them out after a short period of time and the family would be able to stop the fraud. Finally, there is the factor of incentives. Livesay said, "I made money as a result of my actions" (*Accounting Department Management Report* 2005). He had amassed $1.1 million in mutual funds and a $300,000 house by 1999, after receiving bonuses and stock options from the company.

The evidence indicated that fraud may have existed with Scrushy's knowledge. However, the jurors believed there was not sufficient evidence to link Scrushy to the fraud since a review of the testimony indicated that, depending on which employee the prosecutor questioned, there may have been fraud at HealthSouth. Most of the witnesses agreed that Scrushy was an astute businessman.

How the Family Did Not Get Off

Looks like attendance at the family reunion may be down, due to some members paying their debts to society. However, the family leader, Scrushy, will probably be grilling the hot dogs and making lemonade and wondering what went wrong with his so-called family. How could they have misled him? He placed his trust in the accountants and CFOs. He paid them very well and gave them big titles. One finds it hard to ignore the differences between the family update table and Scrushy's scorecard (see table 25.4 for the family update).

Family members received punishments ranging from probation to eight years in prison. Six of the fifteen family members who pled guilty received prison sentences ranging from one week to five years. The remaining nine executives who pled guilty received probation ranging from six months to five years. The latter may be changing. McVay, who served as CFO for only four months and received a sentence of five years' probation, faces a review of his sentence. Also, Martin, who served as CFO and received a 1-week prison sentence, had his sentence overturned and faces a review of his sentence.

Hannibal Crumpler, who holds the dubious distinction of the only executive, other than Scrushy, who did not plead guilty, received the most severe sentence handed down in the case. He received eight years in prison after conviction by a jury in a trial where he was charged with conspiracy and lying to auditors. While working for HealthSouth, his homework assignment was to spread fraud across the country by using thousands of facilities.

The family members who pled guilty described how they were pulled into the fraud, often unaware of what they were doing or the extent until they were trapped by their own guilt (HealthSouth, July 14, 2007). They lived in fear.

Table 25.4 Family Update

Name	Scorecard
Ayers, Angela C.	Sentenced to four years of probation with six months of unsupervised home confinement; also required to pay a $2,000 fine
Beam, Aaron Jr.	Sentenced to three months' imprisonment
Botts, Richard	Sentenced to six months of home detention, five years of probation, fined $10,000, and required to forfeit $265,000
Brown, Jason	Sentenced to one year and one day in prison and two years' probation
Crumpler, Hannibal "Sonny"	On June 15, 2006, sentenced to eight years in prison; received the most severe sentence handed down in the HealthSouth case; the only HealthSouth person convicted by a jury in a trial; all others, except for Scrushy and Crumpler, pled guilty
Edwards, Cathy	Sentenced to four years of probation with six months of unsupervised home confinement; also required to pay a $2,000 fine
Fowler, Catherine	Sentenced to two years' probation and fined $5,000
Harris, Emery	Sentenced to five months' imprisonment
Hicks, Will	Sentenced to two years of probation, three months of house arrest, and $52,600 in forfeitures, fines, and court assessments
Livesay, Kenneth	Sentenced to pay $760,000 in restitution and fines ($750,000 restitution and $10,000 fines), but received no jail time; also, five years' probation, and six months of home detention
Martin, Michael D.	Sentenced to one week in prison; review of his sentence may send him to prison
McVay, Malcolm "Tadd"	Initially, received five years' probation with six months of home detention; fined $10,000 and ordered to forfeit $50,000; in May 2006, a federal appeals court's ruling for a review of his sentence may send him to prison after all
Morgan, Rebecca Kay	Sentenced to four years of probation with six months of unsupervised home confinement; also required to pay a $2,000 fine
Owens, William T.	Sentenced to five years in prison
Smith, Weston	Sentenced to 27 months in prison, $1.5 million in forfeited assets, and 1 year on probation after his release
Valentine, Virginia B.	Sentenced to four years of probation with six months of unsupervised home confinement; also required to pay a $2,000 fine

They feared losing their jobs and intimidation by Scrushy. In many instances, their sentences reflect their helplessness. In other cases, they have the time in prison to reflect on how their jobs may have been done differently.

The Tone at the Top

The failures at HealthSouth reveal moral and ethical shortcomings of its leaders. Other factors may have contributed to the failure, such as the economy, financial risks, poor organizational strategy, excessive growth, and aggressive accounting practices. However, to truly understand, it is necessary to examine the character of the leadership.

The tone at the top or the corporate culture set by Scrushy and his CFOs may have played a major role in HealthSouth's cooking of the books. In many cases, the tone set by top management, especially the CEO and the CFO, plays a crucial role in fraud and misrepresentation (Castellano and Lightle 2005, 6). The effects of Scrushy's tone on HealthSouth's culture and reporting environment cannot be overlooked. During Scrushy's trial, his lawyer described HealthSouth's CFOs as being of questionable moral character. The impact of the CFOs, referred to by Scrushy's lawyer as a "pack of rodents," also contributed to the culture and reporting environment of HealthSouth (Steffy 2005). According to Geoffrey Colvin of *Fortune,* companies like Health South have difficulty shedding the culture of their founders in spite of massive growth. He says that they also suffer from the personal greed of the founder and from being a slave to Wall Street.

The majority of the executives at Health South fit that pattern. They were underqualified and overpaid for the positions they held. Greed also played a role in their fraudulent behavior. In addition, many reached the top at an early age (Stuart 2005). Scrushy liked to hire and advance up from nowhere Alabamians like himself. All five CFOs in the company's history have admitted to cooking the books. At first glance, the CFOs who worked for HealthSouth seemed more "down home" than dastardly. A closer look, however, reveals an intricate web of personal and business relations going back decades. HealthSouth's first CFO, Beam, is described as a very nice guy, a give-you-the-shirt-off-his-back kind of guy (Stuart 2005). After Beam, Martin, who came from a working-class family in Birmingham and paid his way through school by working and attending classes part-time, took his place (Stuart 2005). Upon Martin's departure, Owens became the third CFO. He was also a local boy who did not even have a passport. After the departure of Owens, Smith, a close friend of Owens, became the fourth CFO. Smith married another HealthSouth employee and then vacated the position after the passage of Sarbanes-Oxley, which assessed stiff penalties for false corporate reporting. McVay was the fifth CFO. He is described as a devoted father and a very bright guy (Stuart 2005). After it was discovered how widespread the fraud was, McVay, who was CFO for only four months, was demoted to treasurer and Owens was back in the CFO seat (Stuart 2005).

Scrushy clearly fits the profile of the overbearing CEO who sets the wrong tone at the top (Stuart 2005). His powerful personality was a major factor in keeping the scheme a secret for so long. (Having installed security cameras throughout headquarters to keep watch on his employees, he generally allowed the rank and file into his executive suite only to berate them.) Scrushy was known to humiliate those who challenged him in public. He was often referred to as "the king." He was quoted as saying "Hey, I'm setting a tone for the company" (Tomberlin 2006). It is alleged that he knew what was going on and told the employees to not worry about it and keep doing their jobs.

Scrushy's management style is best described as based on fear and intimidation. Many decisions were elevated to the executive level, which limited checks and balances along the way (Stuart 2005). No matter what happened at HealthSouth, the CFOs will remain the bad guys in Birmingham (Stuart 2005). Scrushy is a local hero, with supporters in all corners (Stuart 2005). He is a lavish donor to local colleges, libraries, and medical centers as well as a regular preacher at area churches. He had even aired his own TV talk show each day before court (Stuart 2005). Scrushy could be seen cooking grits for his children while the lawyers subjected the CFOs to ridicule.

Scrushy seemed to be motivated simply by greed. He directed a $2.7 billion fraud designed to boost the company's stock price and to bankroll an extravagant lifestyle that included a Lamborghini, a 92-foot yacht, and paintings by Picasso and Renoir (Johnson 2003). Scrushy blamed the fraud on his family, saying they hid accurate financial information from him (Hubbard and Tomberlin 2005). However, in a taped conversation, Scrushy is quoted as saying, "I am convinced that there are 8,000 companies out there with __ on their balance sheet" (*Chief Executive* 2003). Guess what might be used to fill in the blank? Here is a clue. What is a four-letter word for waste product?

Epilogue

In many instances people like Scrushy turn to Jesus; Scrushy is now an ordained minister. He says that he has left the corporate world behind and works only for the "Supreme Being." However, the corporate world will follow him as he faces pending litigation regarding his past corporate dealings.

In June 2006, Scrushy was convicted in a state bribery scheme linked to his days as CEO of HealthSouth (Reeves, June 29, 2006). In this scheme, Scrushy was accused of arranging $500,000 in donations to former governor Don Siegelman's campaign for a state lottery in exchange for a seat on a state hospital regulatory board (Reeves, June 29, 2006). The verdict came a year and a day after jurors acquitted Scrushy on 36 criminal charges linked to the fraud at HealthSouth, but his legal troubles are not over (Reeves, June 29, 2006). Scrushy has stated that he plans to appeal the verdict, which could send him to jail for up to 30 years. In April 2007, Scrushy was scheduled to be back in court for the civil lawsuit filed by the SEC. The suit sought $786 million in penalties and restitution and would not allow Scrushy to serve as an officer or director at any public company for at least five years if he were to be found guilty (WebCPA 2006). Scrushy reached a settlement agreeing to pay more than $81 million. The settlement is not the largest the SEC has reached with an executive but it is probably in the top five (Whitmire 2007).

In 2006, a judge ordered Scrushy to repay $47.8 million in bonuses he received from 1997 to 2002 while running HealthSouth. While the company reported profits during the period, HealthSouth really lost money, making Scrushy ineligible for any bonuses (*Medical Device Week* 2006). Whether Scrushy knew about the fraud did not matter.

Combined with as much as $265 million in tax refunds that it paid on overstated income during the fraud, the court-ordered repayment could improve the financial condition of HealthSouth, which suffered a major financial setback due to Medicare fraud and the accounting fraud (*Medical Device Week* 2006). On December 30, 2004, the company agreed to pay the United States $325 million to settle allegations that it defrauded Medicare and other federal health care programs (Department of Justice 2004). The payment will resolve a range of allegations involving outpatient physical therapy services and inpatient rehabilitation admissions. As a part of this agreement, HealthSouth entered into a corporate integrity agreement (CIA) with the U.S. Department of Health and Human Services, Office of Inspector General, requiring the company to implement significant compliance efforts from 2005 to 2009 (Department of Justice 2004). HealthSouth believes a name change may be necessary to erase the stigma of the fraud.

References

Accounting Department Management Report. "How Fraud Snowballs," www.ioma, May (2005): 9.

Ackman, D. "For Years, HealthSouth Could Do No Wrong," Forbes.com, March, 31, 2003, http://www.forbes.com/2003/03/31/cx_da_0331topnews_print.html.

Birmingham News. "How HealthSouth Cooked the Books," http://www.al.com/specialreport/birminghamnews/healthsouth/cook.jpg.

Castellano, J., and S. Lightle "Using Cultural Audits to Assess Tone at the Top," *CPA Journal,* February (2005): 6–11.

Chief Executive. "The Man Who Destroyed HealthSouth Says in a Taped Conversation—Darts—Richard Scrushy," June, 2003, http://findarticles.com/p/articles/mi_m4070/is_2003_June/ai_103192708/print.

Department of Justice. "HealthSouth to Pay United States $325 Million to Resolve Medicare Fraud Allegations," www.usdoj.gov, December 30, 2004. http://usdoj.gov/opa/pr/2004/December/04_civ_807.htm.

Foust, D. "Breathing Life into HealthSouth," *BusinessWeek,* February 7, 2005. http://www.businessweek.com/print/magazine/content/05_06/b3919114.htm?chan=gl.

HealthSouth: Chronology. July 14, 2007. http://www.uow.edu.au/arts/sts/bmartin/dissent/documents/health/healthsouth_flowch.html.

HealthSouth Corporation. "Company Profile, Information, Business Description, History, Background Information on HealthSouth Corporation," 2007. http://www.washingtonpost.com/wp-dyn/content/article/2006/06/29/AR2006062901505.html.

Hubbard, R., and M. Tomberlin. "Auditor Relied on Conspirators," *Birmingham News,* April 29, 2005, http://www.al.com/printer/printer.ssf?/base/business/1114766811317980.xml&coll=2.

Johnson, C. "HealthSouth Founder Is Charged with Fraud," *Washington Post,* 2003, http://www.washingtonpost.com/wp-dyn/articles/A695-2003Nov4.html.

Medical Device Week. "Court Report," January 6, 2006.

Modern Healthcare. "The Rise and Fall of HealthSouth," March 24, 2003.

Reeves, J. "Scrushy Facing More HealthSouth Trials," Journal-News.com, June 29, 2006. http://www.journal-news.com/biz/content/shared-gen/ap/Finance_General/Scrushy_Convict.

SAS 99 & Confirmation Fraud Risk, industry white paper. Brentwood, TN: Capital Confirmation Inc., 2004.

Steffy, L. "Scrushy's Worst Crime Was Business Ineptitude," *Houston Chronicle,* June 30, 2005, http://www.chron.com/cs/CDA/printstory.mpl/business/steffy/3248558.

Stuart, A. "Keeping Secrets: How Five CFOs Cooked the Books at HealthSouth," CFO.com, June 1, 2005, http://www.cfo.com/printable/article.cfm/4007474?f=options.

Tomberlin, M. "Whistleblower: Scrushy Knew of Fraud in 1996," *Birmingham News,* March 22, 2005, http://www.al.com/printer/printer.ssf?/base/news/111148661776210.xml&coll=2&thispage=2.

WebCPA. "Feds Get Scrushy on Bribery Charges," July 8, 2006. http://www.webcpa.com/article.cfm?articleid=20780&searchTerm=Scrushy&print=yes.

Whitmire, K. "Scrushy to Pay $81 Million to Settle S.E.C. Lawsuit." *New York Times,* April 24, 2007.

Wikipedia. "*Fortune* Battle of the Corporate Bands," http://en.wikipedia.org/wik/Fortune_Battle_of_the_Corporate_Bands, 2006.

Wikipedia. "Richard M. Scrushy," June 30, 2006, http://en.wikipedia.org/w/index.php?title=Richard_M_Scrushy&printable=yes.

Wynne, M. "HealthSouth: Medicare Fraud," July 2003. http://www.uow.edu.au/arts/sts/bmartin/dissent/documents/healthsouth_medfrd.html.

———. HealthSouth: Overview and Entry Web Page. January 13, 2007. http://www.uow.edu.au/arts/sts/bmartin/dissent/documents/health/submission.html.

Ziff Davis CIO Insight. "First Sarbanes-Oxley Prosecution Under Way," May 2005, http://findarticles.com/p/articles/mi_zdc:s_200505ai_n13637916/print.

Bibliography

Abelson, R. "4 of 5 HealthSouth Executives Spared Prison Terms," *New York Times,* December 11, 2003.

Accounting Department Management Report. www.ioma.com, March 2004, 11–14.

Anthes, G. "Sarbanes-Oxley Requirements Put Legal Onus on CIOs," *ComputerWorld,* April 14, 2003, http://www.computerworld.com/governmenttopics/government/policy/story/0,10801,80291,00.html.

Birmingham News. "Scandal Scorecard," March 2, 2008, http://www.al.com/special-report/birminghamnews/healthsouth/scandal.jpg.

CFO. "CFOs Talk, CEO Walks," August 2005, 68.

Crawford, K. "Ex-HealthSouth CEO Scrushy Walks," CNN/Money, June 28, 2005, http://money.cnn.com/2005/06/28/news/newsmakers/scrushy_outcome/index.htm.

Donlon, J. "Scrushy 1, SOX 0," *Directorship,* July/August (2005): 3.

Economist. "With God on His Side," July 2, 2005, http://web26.epnet.com/DeliveryPrintSave.asp?tb=1&_ua=shn+29+0EA6&_ug=sid+35A6F.

Farrell, G. "Scrushy Acquitted of All 36 Charges," *USA Today,* http://usatoday.print-this.clickability.com/pt/cpt?action=cpt&title=USATODAY.com+-+Sc.

——. "Was CEO 'Very Cunning' or "Lied to'?" *USA Today,* http://usatoday.print-this.clickability.com/pt/cpt?action=cpt&title=USATODAY.com+-+Wa.

Financial Reporting News. July 4, 2003, http://www.pwcglobal.com/servlet/printFormat?url=http://www.pwcglobal.com/extweb/pw.

Fowler, T., and J. Roper. "Ex-HealthSouth CEO Drops by," *Houston Chronicle,* March 9, 2006, A15.

Freudenheim, M. "HealthSouth Linked to Major Fraud," *Milwaukee Journal Sentinel,* March 20, 2003, http://findarticles.com/p/articles/mi_qn4196/is_20030320/ai_n1086594/print.

Frieswick, K. "How Much Is Not Enough? Will Weston Smith and William T. Owens, Who Admitted They Helped Commit Massive Accounting Fraud at HealthSouth Corp," *CFO Magazine,* May (2003), http://findarticles.com/p/articles/mi_m3870/is_6_19/ai_101531501/print.

——. "How Audits Must Change: Auditors Face More Pressure to Find Fraud," *CFO Magazine,* July 1, 2003, http://www.som.yale.edu/faculty/Sunder/FinancialFraud/How%20Audits%20Must%20Cha.

Grow, B. "All Scrushy, All the Time," *Business Week,* April 12, 2004, 86–87.

HealthSouth Statement Regarding Scrushy Press Conference. http://www.healthsouth.com/medinfo/home/app/frame?2=article.jsp,0,091505_Scrushy_Pr.

HealthSouth Stock Ticker Symbol: HLSH 7 OTC Pink Sheets. http://www.healthsouth.com/medinfo/home/app/frame?cntx=01abouths&1=leftnav.jsp,abo.

Helyar, J. "Scrushy's Greatest Hits," *Fortune,* June 13, 2005, http://web26.epnet.com/DeliveryPrintSave.asp?tb=1&_ua=shn+29+0EA6&_ug=sid+35A6F.

Helyar, J., B. Cherry, and P. Neering. "The Insatiable King Richard," *Fortune* (Europe), July 7, 2003, http://web26.epnet.com/DeliveryPrintSave.asp?tb=1&_ua=shn+29+0EA6&_ug=sid+35A6F.

HLSH.PK. "Competitors for HealthSouth CP," http://finance.yahoo.com/q/co?s=HLSH.PK.

Jennings, M. "The Critical Role of Ethics: Recent History Has Shown That When Individual Ethics Are Compromised, Corporate Ethics Fail and Financial Disaster Is Not Far Behind," *Internal Auditor,* December (2003), http://www.findarticles.com/p/articles/mi_m4153/is_6_60/ai_1111737942/print.

Joseph, L. "How He Got Off," *Time,* July 11, 2005, http://web26.epnet.com/DeliveryPrintSave.asp?tb=1&_ua=shn+7+D084&_ug=sid+35A6F.

"Judge Lets SEC File New Suit over HealthSouth Fraud," http://www.al.com/printer/printer.ssf?/base/news-15/1124446503197480.xml@storylist=scr.

Mintz, S. "Virtue Ethics and Accounting Education," *Issues in Accounting Education,* Fall (1995): 247–267.

Mulford, C., and E. Comiskey. *The Financial Numbers Game: Detecting Creative Accounting Practices.* New York: John Wiley & Sons, 2002.

Peterson, B. "Education as a New Approach to Fighting Financial Crime in the USA," *Journal of Financial Crime,* February (2004): 262–267.

Peterson, B., and P. Zikmund. "10 Truths You Need to Know about Fraud," *Strategic Finance,* May (2004): 29–34.

Reeves. J. "Former CFO: Sarbanes-Oxley Pressure Began End of HealthSouth Fraud," *Detroit News,* February 5, 2005, http://www.detnews.com/2005/business/0502/05business-80305.htm.

———. "Former HealthSouth CFO Beam Sentenced," 2005, http://www.al.com/printer/printer.ssf?/base/business-47/1125024844110171.xml@storylist=.

———. "Former HealthSouth CFO Beam Sentenced in Fraud," 2005. http://www.al.com/printer/printer.ssf?/base/business-1/1124996944162741.xml@storylist=s.

———. "Judge Orders Scrushy to Repay $47.8 Million in HealthSouth Bonuses," SignOnSanDiego.com, January 4, 2006, http://signonsandiego.printthis.clickability.com/pt/cpt?action=cpt&title=SignOnSanDiego.c.

———. "Court Nixes Term for Ex-HealthSouth CFO," HoustonChronicle.com, July 12, 2006, http://www.chron.com/cs/CDA/printstory.mpl/ap/fn/4042541.

Romney, M., and P. Steinbart. *Accounting Information Systems,* 9th ed. Upper Saddle River, NJ: Prentice Hall, 2003.

SAS 99 White Paper: Audit Confirmation Fraud Risk, April 15, 2005, Alachua, Fl: CPA Mutual Insurance Company of America Risk Retention Group.

Taub, S. "Ex-CFO of HealthSouth Faces Resentencing," CFO.com, May 6, 2006, http://www.cfo.com/printable/article.cfm/6906724?f=options.

Tomberlin, M. "HealthSouth Former VP Gets Term of 1 Year, 1 Day," *Birmingham News,* December 22, 2005. http://www.al.com/printer/printer.ssf?/base/business/1135246857162390.xml&coll=2.

Vaughan-Adams, L. "HealthSouth Paid Ernst & Young More to Check Its Toilets Than to Audit Financial Results," *Independent* (London), June 12, 2003, http://findarticles.com/p/articles/mi_qn4158/is_20030612/ai_n12690905/print.

Vorhies, J. "The New Importance of Materiality," *Journal of Accountancy,* May 2005, http://www.aicpa.org/pubs/jofa/may2005/vorhies.htm.

Walsh, F. "A Family Resilience Framework: Innovative Practice Applications," *Family Relations,* April 2002, http://ddl.uwinnipeg.ca/conf_fam/files/articles/resilience_framework.pdf.

Walton, V., and R. Hubbard. "All Companies Fudge Numbers," *Birmingham News,* March 17, 2005, http://www.al.com/printer/printer.ssf?/base/news/1111054988212441.xml&coll=2.

Weld, L., P. Bergevin, and L. Magrath. "Anatomy of a Financial Fraud," *CPA Journal,* October (2004): 44–49.

Whitmire, K. "Scrushy Sues HealthSouth over Dismissal," *New York Times,* December 17, 2005, http://galenet.galegroup.com/servlet/BCRC?vrsn=149&locID=txshracd2575&srchtp=art.

Wikipedia. "Benevolence," July 20, 2007, http://en.wikipedia.org/wiki/Benevolence.

_____. "HealthSouth," June 25, 2006. http://en.wikipedia.org/w/index. php?title=HealthSouth&printable=yes.

_____. Richard M. Scrushy, June 30, 2006, http://en.wikipedia.org/w/index. php?title=Richard_M_Scrushy&printable=yes.

_____. "Talk: Richard M. Scrushy," June 30, 2006, http://en.wikipedia.org/w/index. php?title=Talk:Richard_M_Scrushy&printable=yes.

Richard Scrushy: The Rise and Fall of the "King of Health Care"

26

STEVEN A. SOLIERI
ANDREW J. FELO
JOAN HODOWANITZ

Contents

Richard Scrushy: A Self-Made Man

On his official Web site (www.richardmscrushy.com), Richard Marin Scrushy presents a self-aggrandizing account of his rags-to-riches life as the erstwhile king of health care. He was born into a middle-class family in the economically depressed city of Selma, Alabama, in 1952. The son of a cash register repairman and a nurse/respiratory therapist, Scrushy was an unusually precocious child who began teaching himself to play the piano and the guitar when he was only eight years old. When he was 12, he was already earning pocket money by mowing lawns, flipping hamburgers, and working as a bellhop at a local hotel. Despite the promise of his early childhood, Scrushy dropped out of school to get married at the tender age of 17. Lacking a high school diploma, he lived in a Selma trailer park and took menial jobs to support his family. But Scrushy soon realized that manual labor and trailer parks were not for him. One day when he was struggling to carry cement up a ladder, his boss chided him for his slowness. He quit that job on the spot and vowed to go back to school (Heylar 2003, 80).

With his mother's encouragement, Scrushy finished high school and earned his bachelor's degree in respiratory therapy from the University of Alabama at Birmingham (UAB) in 1974. He spent the next few years working as a UAB instructor and the director of a respiratory therapy program at a local community college. He got his first major career break in 1978 when he landed a position with Lifemark, a promising health care company in Houston, Texas. Scrushy's ambitious nature and persistent work ethic helped him race up the corporate ladder, and by 1980 he was in charge of operations valued at approximately $100 million.

Scrushy as Visionary Leader: Opportunity Knocks

Scrushy's experiences at Lifemark convinced him that government-funded programs like Medicare and Medicaid offered unlimited opportunities for an ambitious entrepreneur (Heylar 2003, 80). The government was committed to underwriting the health care costs of the poor, the elderly, and the disabled at a time when demographic and lifestyle changes were increasing the number of patients requiring such care. There was certainly no shortage of poor people, and the number of elderly patients was rising steadily thanks to recent advances in health care. In addition, many young, health-conscious Americans were constantly seeking medical help for injuries sustained during exercise and sports activities. Fortunately, Medicare and Medicaid provided a guaranteed revenue stream for businesses specializing in health care services for these market segments. Health care, once the domain of not-for-profit hospitals and insurance companies, was rapidly being transformed into a highly profitable growth industry of the future.

The profit potential of the health care industry was not lost on the charismatic Richard Scrushy. Working with Aaron Beam, the man who later became his first chief financial officer (CFO), and a handful of other Lifemark employees, Scrushy devised a new business model for a chain of health clinics specializing in outpatient diagnostic and rehabilitative services. Unlike traditional hospitals that incurred significant costs to provide 24-hour care, these clinics would function as low-cost providers of health care services, imitating as much as possible Wal-Mart's business model in the retail industry (Thomas 2003).

Scrushy shared his concept with Lifemark's management, hoping it would fund the first such clinics. Unfortunately, Lifemark was preparing to merge with another company and decided not to get involved (Mollenkamp and Moore 2003). Undaunted, Scrushy and his supporters left Lifemark to pursue their entrepreneurial vision. Investing $55,000 of their own money (Abelson and Freudenheim 2003), they started a business named AmCare Inc. in a one-room office in Birmingham, Alabama, in January 1984 (Ward, 2005). The company (renamed HealthSouth in May 1985) prospered virtually overnight. In September 1986, with $20 million in annual revenues, Health-South became a publicly traded company (Heylar 2003, 81).

HealthSouth's rise to the top of the health care industry was nothing less than meteoric, at least until 1997 (see table 26.1). Between 1987 and 1997, the company's stock price soared an average of 31 percent per year. In 1989, HealthSouth began acquiring potential competitors, and over the next decade, it grew at a fast and furious pace. HealthSouth's revenues finally topped $1 billion in 1994, making it the nation's undisputed leader in the rehabilitative services sector of the health care industry (Heylar 2003, 84). In 1995 alone, the company's share price, the basis for Scrushy's compensation as chief executive officer (CEO), jumped 60 percent. Three years later, having met or exceeded Wall Street's expectations for 48 consecutive quarters, HealthSouth became a Fortune 500 company, meaning it ranked among the 500 largest firms in the United States based on annual sales revenue. Almost everyone agreed that Scrushy had the Midas touch in an industry where most businesses struggled just to show a profit. The occasional critic who tried to question HealthSouth's record-breaking growth and profitability was drowned out by the many voices praising the company and its talented founder. Scrushy was the "fair-haired" entrepreneur who could do no wrong even though many people regarded him as a colorful, if somewhat condescending, personality:

> Flamboyant, natty, carefully tanned, Scrushy is almost a caricature of the modern swashbuckling CEO. He often pilots his company jet, he has cut a CD with his own honky-tonk band, and he promotes HealthSouth by hobnobbing with celebrity ex-jocks like Bo Jackson. In 1997, his pay, including cashed-in options, totaled $106.8 million. When Scrushy married his third wife in 1997, he chartered a plane to fly 150 guests to Jamaica and hired Bob Marley's widow to perform. (In a letter accompanying the invitation, he cast the occasion as a lesson in social consciousness, writing: "The poverty of this Third World country allows us to realize how blessed we are...") In Birmingham, where he is often referred to as King Richard, Scrushy doomed his own scheme to build a big-league sports stadium by telling a journalist he had the backing of "the little people" (Elkind 1999, 133).

Many of HealthSouth's employees regarded Scrushy as a "hands-on" type of leader. Theresa Sanders, former head of the company's Internal Audit Department, testified before Congress how Scrushy had directed her to develop a "pristine audit" checklist to ensure that every clinic in the

Table 26.1 HealthSouth Timeline

Date	Event
01/1984	HealthSouth begins operations in a one-room office in Birmingham, Alabama.
02/1984	HealthSouth incorporates in Delaware.
09/1986	HealthSouth completes its first public offering.
08/1997	President Clinton signs the Balanced Budget Act.
09/1998	HealthSouth issues its first profit warning.
05/14/2002	Scrushy sells personal stock for $74 million.
05/17/2002	The Center for Medicare and Medicare Services (CMS) issues a clarification on existing billing procedures for health care providers.
07/31/2002	Scrushy sells personal stock for $25 million.
08/14/2002	Scrushy and his CFO recertify HealthSouth's 2001 financial statements.
08/27/2002	HealthSouth issues its second profit warning based on its analysis of the CMS's change in billing procedures.
09/17/2002	The SEC announces an investigation of allegations of insider trading by Richard Scrushy.
10/01/2002	HealthSouth's institutional investors meet to discuss the company's bad corporate governance practices.
10/30/2002	HealthSouth issues a press release saying that the law firm of Fulbright & Jaworski LLP cleared Scrushy of all allegations of wrongdoing.
03/14/2003	Fulbright & Jaworski issues its final investigation report to HealthSouth's Board.
03/19/2003	HealthSouth fires Scrushy as CEO and chairman of the board of directors.
03/21/2003	Fulbright & Jaworski retracts its investigation report.
10/12/2003	Mike Wallace's interview with Richard Scrushy airs on 60 Minutes.
10/16/2003	Congress holds public hearings on the HealthSouth scandal.
11/04/2003	Scrushy is indicted on 85 criminal counts relating to the HealthSouth fraud.
11/05/2003	Congress concludes public hearing on the HealthSouth scandal.
06/28/2005	Scrushy is acquitted of all criminal charges related to the HealthSouth scandal.
09/15/2005	Scrushy claims he has the "clean numbers" (accurate financial information) for HealthSouth since the day he walked out of HealthSouth.
10/26/2005	Scrushy is indicted in federal court for paying former Alabama governor Dan Siegelman $500,000 for a seat on the state's regulatory board for hospitals.
12/05/2005	Scrushy resigns his position as a HealthSouth director.
12/15/2005	Scrushy sues HealthSouth for more than $70 million for breach of contract as CEO.
12/29/2005	HealthSouth countersues Scrushy for $76 million.
01/03/2006	The courts order Scrushy to repay HealthSouth $48 million in bonuses he had received as CEO. The bonuses were based on the fraudulent profit figures.
04/23/2006	Scrushy settles SEC civil suit by agreeing to pay $81 million.

Table 26.1   HealthSouth Timeline (Continued)

Date	Event
06/29/2006	Scrushy is convicted of bribery and mail fraud for paying former Alabama governor Don Siegelman $500,000 for a seat on the Alabama agency that regulates hospitals and other health facilities. He is sentenced to prison for 6 years and 10 months.

chain maintained the same high standards of cleanliness, maintenance, and customer service. She complied, but she thought the project was a waste of money. Scrushy paid Ernst & Young LLP, HealthSouth's independent auditor, to perform these pristine audits even though his own employees could have done the job at far less cost (U.S. House of Representatives 2003, part 1, 32). According to HealthSouth's 2000 and 2001 proxy statements, the company paid Ernst & Young more money for the pristine audits than it did for government-mandated financial audits. Whether the pristine audits reflected Scrushy's pursuit of excellence, his obsession with controlling every aspect of HealthSouth's operations, or some other agenda is a matter open for debate. At the end of the day, however, Ernst & Young must have been quite pleased with the additional revenue Scrushy sent its way.

Trouble in Paradise: The First Signs of Trouble

For HealthSouth, 1997 was a bittersweet year. Although the company recorded more than $3 billion in sales revenues, it saw its future profits put in jeopardy when Congress passed the Balanced Budget Act (Haddad, Weintraub, and Grow 2003, 71). Among other provisions, the act called for a $115 billion reduction in Medicare payments to health care providers over a 5-year period. This was certainly bad news for Scrushy since Medicare accounted for 37 percent of HealthSouth's revenues in 1997. If future revenues decreased significantly, so would Scrushy's compensation as CEO.

Scrushy became increasingly paranoid after the Balanced Budget Act became law. He surrounded himself with security guards and installed cameras and electronic surveillance devices throughout HealthSouth's Birmingham headquarters. According to one former employee, "the e-mail correspondence of employees suspected of being disloyal was routinely monitored. The company's surveillance methods were so thorough, he said, that he and other officers would go to restrooms at the corporate headquarters to have confidential conversations" (Romero and Abelson 2003). Scrushy even told his managers how "he received detailed financial reports every Friday and studied them at home to monitor the performance of individual facilities" (Shmukler and Morse 2005). Every Monday morning he grilled his division chiefs on the profits in their areas of responsibility and publicly berated any subordinate who failed to meet his expectations (Abelson and Freudenheim 2003). Shakespeare could have had Scrushy in mind when he penned the line: "Uneasy lies the head that wears a crown."

Even though many HealthSouth investors expressed concern that the Balanced Budget Act would limit future profits, Scrushy initially reassured them that the legislation would not hurt the company's bottom line. In September 1998, however, HealthSouth issued a profit warning informing investors that earnings for 1998 and 1999 would probably fall short of Wall Street's earlier estimates (Abelson and Freudenheim 2002). On October 7, 1998, the company's stock price fell to $8.31 from its record high of $30.56 less than six months earlier (U.S. District Court 2004, 6, 8), and earnings plummeted a whopping 86.5 percent from $343 million in 1997 to $46 million in 1998. Despite the drop in HealthSouth's profits, Scrushy managed to become the third highest paid CEO in the nation in 1998 (Liu 2003).

Scrushy's Long Reach

Also in 1998, many of HealthSouth's institutional investors (e.g., mutual funds, pension funds, and insurance companies) expressed concern over potential conflicts of interest between Scrushy and several directors on HealthSouth's board. According to HealthSouth's 1998 proxy statement, a shareholders' proposal submitted by the Iron Workers' Local No. 25 Pension Fund recommended that the company adopt the Council of Institutional Investors' (CII) criteria for director independence. The Iron Workers wanted to ensure that directors on HealthSouth's audit and compensation committee, the body responsible for overseeing financial reporting and recommending executive compensation, had no conflicts of interest with the company's senior management. These directors had to be completely independent of management to protect the shareholders' interests. But HealthSouth's board of directors, under Scrushy's leadership as chairman, opposed the Iron Workers' proposal because the directors already met the New York Stock Exchange (NYSE) and Internal Revenue Service (IRS) criteria for independence. The board also argued that the Iron Workers' proposal would reduce future profits by preventing HealthSouth from appointing the most qualified business leaders as directors. According to the company's second quarter report for 1998, the proposal was soundly defeated; it received less than 20 percent of voting shares during the annual shareholders' meeting.

HealthSouth's 1999 proxy statement contained a similar shareholder proposal by the Longview Collective Investment Fund, another institutional investor. Longview wanted at least 75 percent of HealthSouth's board members to be independent of HealthSouth's management as defined by the CII criteria. It argued that six of the twelve directors on the current board lacked independence. Five were company insiders (current or former HealthSouth executives), and the sixth was part of an interlocking directorate (a situation in which two boards of directors have at least one director in common). Longview also suggested that the board's overall lack of independence was responsible for the recent decline in HealthSouth's stock price and Scrushy's overly generous compensation package. In fact, Scrushy earned far more than most CEOs:

> Our CEO was recently named as one of ten "executive pay anti-heroes" by Graef Crystal, an expert on executive pay, in a report prepared by the Council of Institutional Investors. Crystal's conclusion was based in part on Mr. Scrushy's drawing a base salary 350 percent above the market; a salary and bonus 592 percent above the market; and a total direct compensation that is 225 percent above the market. (HealthSouth Corporation 1999, 10)

Once again, HealthSouth's board of directors (led by Scrushy) opposed the proposal, citing the same arguments used in 1998. The board also blamed the recent drop in the company's stock price on an industry-wide decline in earnings and dismissed complaints about Scrushy's compensation as "a gratuitous attack" on HealthSouth's founder. This time only 15 percent of the voting shares supported the Longview proposal.

Scrushy was clearly the dominant personality on HealthSouth's board, and his influence extended well beyond the boardroom. His ties with UBS Warburg, HealthSouth's banker, were so strong that UBS let him choose the person who would write future investment reports on his company, a practice unheard of in the investment banking business (Abelson 2004). Scrushy chose Howard Capek, an analyst who had always written glowing reports on HealthSouth. Capek continued to recommend HealthSouth's stock even after the government accused Scrushy of orchestrating a massive accounting fraud. In his private e-mails, however, Capek told his friends that the stock was really a pig.

When the auditors at Ernst & Young evaluated the risk of fraud at Health-South at the end of 2002, they concluded that Scrushy had "an overwhelming amount of control over the Company" (U.S. House of Representatives 2003, part 2, 490). Auditors regard such a concentration of power to be a potential red flag because of the increased risk of financial fraud. It seems, however, that Ernst & Young assumed that HealthSouth's board of directors could control its strong-willed chairman and CEO. In November 2003, the audit firm testified before Congress that its decision not to modify HealthSouth's financial audit to reflect an increased risk of fraud had nothing to do with the fact that the health care company was its highest paying client in the state of

Alabama (U.S. House of Representatives 2003, part 2, 123). How much cre-
dence Congress gave to Ernst & Young's testimony is a matter of conjecture.

Weathering the Storm?

Unlike most of its business competitors, HealthSouth eventually reversed
the financial losses it suffered in the late 90s following passage of the Balanced Budget Act (Haddad et al. 2003, 71–72). According to HealthSouth's
2000 Annual Report, net income rebounded to a respectable $278 million,
a feat the company attributed to cost reductions and an increased patient
load. By 2001, Scrushy's cash compensation ($3.96 million in salary plus a
$6.5 million bonus) was ten times the average compensation for health care
CEOs (Abelson and Freudenheim 2002). Scrushy, however, was not content
with his millions; he wanted to be highest paid CEO in the world (Hubbard 2003). According to Tom Winters, a Florida physician who knew him
well, the self-proclaimed king of health care simply "didn't know how much
money was enough" (Abelson and Freudenheim 2003).

Although HealthSouth eventually reduced the number of company
insiders on its board of directors in response to investor pressure, it never
completely eliminated the close financial ties between its directors and Health-
South or Scrushy (Lublin and Carrns 2003). For example, the company paid
Director Joel Gordon $250,000 a year for his services as a health consultant.
Phillip Watkins, a director on HealthSouth's compensation committee, not
only bought property in Florida with Scrushy, he invested in MedCenter-
Direct, one of HealthSouth's many corporate ventures. Charles Newhall III
served as a director at MedCenterDirect and HealthSouth at the same time.
The company even awarded a $5 million contract to Larry Striplin, a direc-
tor on HealthSouth's compensation and audit committee, to install glass at
one of the company's Birmingham facilities. This contract accounted for 77
percent of the revenues at Striplin's company in 2001. Several media analysts
questioned the independence of these directors because they profited from
their association with HealthSouth or Scrushy.

Another Profit Warning

During the 90s, HealthSouth attributed its leadership position in the health
care industry to cost controls and its acquisition of potential competitors. By
2002, however, there were no more costs to cut or rivals to acquire. Health-
South reluctantly changed it business strategy and started divesting itself of
facilities that were unable to meet profit goals. As it turned out, this was just
the beginning of the biggest crisis in the company's history.

On May 17, 2002, the Center for Medicare and Medicaid Services (CMS) issued a statement clarifying existing billing procedures for health care providers. HealthSouth, however, insisted that the CMS had issued a major policy change. Although the CMS and HealthSouth argued about the significance of this statement, everyone agreed that Scrushy sold a portion of his personal holdings of HealthSouth stock in May and July 2002 for a total of $99 million (Freudenheim, August 28, 2002).

On July 30, 2002, President George W. Bush signed the Sarbanes-Oxley (SOX) Act into law to protect the investing public's interests and hold corporate executives and directors accountable for their actions. A direct response to the accounting frauds at Enron, WorldCom, Tyco, and other corporations, this landmark legislation functioned as a wakeup call to the CEOs and CFOs of publicly traded companies. The Act requires these officers to certify the accuracy of their companies' annual financial statements, thereby holding them personally responsible for the actions of their subordinates. CEOs and CFOs can no longer shift responsibility for corporate fraud to subordinates who actually crunch the numbers on which financial statements are based. In addition, any person convicted of making a false certification under the provisions of the SOX Act can be sentenced up to 20 years in prison, fined $5 million, or both.

On August 7, 2002, Scrushy held a conference call with investors and market analysts, but he never mentioned a potential problem with future earnings. One week later, he and his CFO, Weston Smith, recertified the company's 2001 annual financial statements as required by the SOX Act. On August 27, however, HealthSouth issued a press statement claiming that the CMS's recent billing guidance would reduce the company's pretax earnings by $175 million per year. The company also announced that Smith was resigning as CFO and Scrushy was resigning as CEO, but not as chairman of the board. One Credit Suisse analyst, John Hindelong, described the company's profit warning as "discouraging, given the fact that management reiterated its confidence in guidance for analysts just a few weeks ago" (Freudenheim, September 6, 2002). Naturally, people began asking why future profits should drop so dramatically if the CMS had merely clarified existing billing procedures. More importantly, how reliable were Health-South's 2001 financial statements if the company had not used the correct billing procedures? At the same time, the Securities and Exchange Commission (SEC) expressed interest in the fortuitous timing of Scrushy's 2002 stock sales. Fearing future shareholder lawsuits, Scrushy's lawyers advised him not to answer any questions about HealthSouth's reduced earnings forecast or his stock trades.

While HealthSouth's August profit warning was, by itself, no proof of wrongdoing, the SEC and several angry investors demanded an explanation from Scrushy and HealthSouth's board of directors, especially its audit committee. In August 2002, HealthSouth's audit committee consisted of three directors: Chairman George Strong, Larry Striplin, and C. Sage Givens. Only Strong was truly independent of Scrushy and HealthSouth. As mentioned earlier, Striplin's glass company reaped 77 percent of its revenues in 2001 from a HealthSouth contract. Givens owed her success as a venture capitalist to Scrushy. Under his leadership, HealthSouth invested $3.5 million in her company. In addition, she invested heavily in MedCenterDirect, one of HealthSouth's many corporate ventures (Thomas 2003). The audit committee's apparent lack of independence fed the public perception that Scrushy influenced the very people who were supposed to oversee his actions as CEO.

The media, eager to exploit another juicy corporate scandal, released several titillating stories about Scrushy's extravagant lifestyle, his flawed leadership style and abuses of power, and the Federal Bureau of Investigation's (FBI) secret recordings of his private conversations. Meanwhile investors, dissatisfied with the CEO's constant reassurances that everything was fine, began filing lawsuits against Scrushy and the company he founded.

The Board's Special Litigation Committee

In September 2002, the SEC notified HealthSouth that it was investigating allegations of insider trading by Richard Scrushy and other unspecified problems. At the same time, HealthSouth's board appointed Directors Jon Hanson, Larry Striplin, and Robert May to a Special Litigation Committee to look into the SEC's allegations (Roth and Michaels, March 29, 2003). The company also engaged the law firm of Fulbright & Jaworski LLP to conduct an "impartial investigation" (Terhune and Mollenkamp 2003).

The independence of the Special Litigation Committee came under fire almost immediately. One member, Jon Hanson, joined HealthSouth's board in September 2002 at Scrushy's personal request. He and Scrushy were both directors on the boards of the National Football Foundation and the College Football Hall of Fame. A few months before Hanson became a HealthSouth director, HealthSouth donated $425,000 to the foundation to endow a trophy and scholarship. Another member, Larry Striplin, resigned from the committee within 1 month even though he insisted that his glass company's $5 million contract with HealthSouth would not impair his objectivity. The third member, Robert May, had "'publicly and prematurely' exonerated Mr. Scrushy while his own committee's investigation had just started" according to Judge Strine of the Delaware Court of Chancery. If the Special Litigation Committee were to later clear Scrushy, "there will always linger a reasonable doubt that its investigation was designed to paper a decision that had already been made." Strine also believed it was unlikely the committee could be impartial if its members had "compromising ties to the key officials who are suspected of malfeasance" (Roth and Michaels, March 29, 2003).

Scrushy Goes on the Offense

By October 2002, Scrushy had launched a major public relations campaign to defend himself against the government's allegations of misconduct. He reinvented himself as a born-again Christian who was being unfairly persecuted by an out-of-control judicial system (Grow 2004, 87). In addition to setting up his own Web site to publicize his version of events, Scrushy and his wife hosted *Viewpoint,* a religious television show that gave him much needed positive publicity in the Birmingham area (Terhune and Shmukler 2005). Meanwhile, approximately 160 institutional investors angrily confronted him about HealthSouth's lapses in corporate governance, specifically the board of directors' apparent lack of independence and financial conflicts of interest. They were also disturbed by Scrushy's apparent greed as demonstrated by the timing of his 2002 stock trades (Roth and Michaels, April 15, 2003). Instead of addressing their specific concerns, Scrushy reassured them that HealthSouth was taking the initiative to improve its corporate governance. This approach, however, failed to convince a growing number of skeptics inside and outside the company.

On October 30, 2002, before the investigation was complete, HealthSouth issued a statement claiming that Fulbright & Jaworski had "cleared" Scrushy of all allegations of wrongdoing (Terhune and Mollenkamp 2003). Given Scrushy's controlling nature, it is highly unlikely that this information would have been released to the press without his personal approval as chairman of the board. Unfortunately for HealthSouth and Scrushy, the statement did not have the intended effect of restoring investor confidence. Fulbright & Jaworski immediately challenged HealthSouth's characterization of its preliminary findings. HealthSouth was forced to issue a second statement explaining that the investigation failed to uncover any evidence of wrongdoing by Scrushy. In other words, the investigation failed to find evidence of guilt; it did not exonerate Scrushy.

The SEC Files Suit

Scrushy resumed his position as CEO in January 2003, but events quickly spun out of control. Former CFO William Owens became an informant for the FBI and wore a hidden wire to record his conversations with Scrushy. During one conversation, Scrushy discussed the importance of keeping the HealthSouth family together, a reference to senior management including all five CFOs in the company's 19-year history. Scrushy also reminded Owens that if the CFO chose to expose the fraud, Scrushy would blame him and the rest of the "family" (Shaw and Cook 2005).

In March 2003, the SEC filed a civil suit against HealthSouth and Scrushy in which it accused the CEO of directing his staff to overstate the company's earnings by at least $1.4 billion since 1999 (Terhune, Mollenkamp, and Carrns 2003). On March 14, 2003, Fulbright & Jaworski issued its final report to HealthSouth's board of directors and the SEC. Seven days later, however, the law firm notified the board that it should not rely on the report's findings because, as the firm later learned, HealthSouth had withheld information during the investigation (Terhune and Mollenkamp 2003). Unfortunately, it was a little too late for Scrushy to put a positive spin on this latest development. The SEC had already filed suit against him, and HealthSouth quickly followed up by firing him as CEO and chairman of the board of directors. Scrushy, however, retained his seat as a director. His contract as CEO ensured that only the company's stockholders could vote him out as a director.

The American Dream?

Scrushy not only lacked a sense of humility about his success, he had his own version of the American dream. In October 2003, Mike Wallace interviewed him for the CBS show *60 Minutes*. When Wallace brought up the subject of the 2002 stock sales that led to the SEC's allegations of insider trading, Scrushy explained that he was forced to exercise his stock options because they were about to expire. Not content to leave the matter alone, he went on to say, "When you build something from nothing, you should have the right at some point to have some liquidity. That's what every young MBA in America is working toward. So what I did was, you know, the American dream" (CBSNews.com 2004). But for Scrushy, the American dream went far beyond mere financial security for himself and his family. It meant making more money than anyone else and enjoying perks that were reserved for only the richest men.

Criminal Charges Are Filed

In November 2003, the U.S. Department of Justice (DOJ) indicted Scrushy on 85 criminal counts for allegedly orchestrating a $2.7 billion accounting fraud between 1996 and 2003 (U.S. Department of Justice 2003). The DOJ was convinced that the HealthSouth fraud started long before 1996, but it could not prove such a charge. The most serious charges in the indictment involved allegations of conspiracy, securities fraud (based on Scrushy's 2002 stock sales), wire fraud, mail fraud, money laundering, and violation of the SOX Act's certification provisions. Thus, Scrushy made corporate history by becoming the first CEO to be charged under the provisions of the SOX Act.

According to the DOJ's indictment, Scrushy and his alleged partners in crime had developed a special vocabulary to help carry out the fraud. For example, a "hole" was defined as the difference between HealthSouth's earnings estimates (usually inflated) and actual earning. If Scrushy detected a hole in HealthSouth's earnings, he would order his subordinates ("the family") to fill it with "dirt" (fictitious sales revenue). The family hid the bogus sales from public view by improperly adjusting the balances in accounts such as estimated insurance reimbursements and fixed assets (i.e., buildings and equipment). The perpetrators of the fraud were quite familiar with Ernst & Young's financial audit procedures (two of HealthSouth's CFOs had worked as auditors in Ernst & Young's Birmingham office). They knew several tricks to prevent the auditors from detecting the fraud. For example, they knew that Ernst & Young's auditors ignored most transactions below $5,000 (Mollenkamp 2003). As it turned out, most of the $1 billion in fictitious assets recorded on HealthSouth's balance sheet were based on bogus accounting entries that fell below the magic $5,000 threshold.

The Criminal Trial

Scrushy's criminal trial began on January 25, 2005, in Birmingham, Alabama, the city where HealthSouth's corporate headquarters were located. The presiding judge dismissed all but 58 counts of the original 85 counts, but she refused to throw out 3 counts accusing Scrushy of violating the certification provisions of the SOX Act (MSNBC.com 2005).

Scrushy's penchant for controlling people and organizations continued during his trial. Shortly after his indictment by the DOJ, Scrushy left his affluent Birmingham church and joined an African-American congregation on the other side of town. His son-in-law's local television station began broadcasting *The Scrushy Trial with Nikki Preede* twice a day. Donald Watkins, Scrushy's lead attorney, used the show to give the defense team's spin on each day's testimony. Herman Henderson, a local black pastor, claimed that Scrushy paid him to encourage other pastors, many of whom were also black, to attend the trial as part of "Scrushy's Amen Corner" (Grow 2006). Henderson also alleged that Scrushy paid his assistant, Audrey Lewis, to write a series of prodefense articles that ran on page 1 of the *Birmingham Times,* a newspaper targeting the local black community.

The prosecution called an impressive list of witnesses including all five men who had at one time served as Scrushy's CFO. In addition to admitting their roles in the fraud, all five testified that Scrushy directed them to make, or knew they were making, improper accounting entries to cover up the fraud. Scrushy's lawyers argued that he was unaware that the numbers presented in HealthSouth's annual financial reports were fraudulent. (This is known as the "Sergeant Schultz" defense, after the character in the television show *Hogan's Heroes*.) Scrushy's lawyers also portrayed the five CFOs as criminals hoping to lighten their own sentences by testifying for the prosecution. By the time the case went to the jury on May 19, 2005, the presiding judge had dismissed all but 36 counts of the original 85 counts (Morse and Terhune 2005).

On June 28, 2005, after 21 days of deliberations, the jury acquitted Richard Scrushy on all 36 counts. Several media pundits accused him of playing the religion and race cards, but the jurors insisted that he was acquitted because the prosecution failed to present a "smoking gun" linking him to the fraud (Farrell 2005). Some legal analysts, however, concluded that Scrushy was only acquitted because the prosecution's case was just too complicated for the jury to understand (Squeo 2005).

According to his official Web site, Scrushy resigned his position as a HealthSouth director in December 2005 and then sued his former company for more than $70 million. He argued that HealthSouth breached his contract as CEO because he was fired even though he was never convicted of wrongdoing in a court of law. Not surprisingly, HealthSouth filed a $76 million countersuit blaming Scrushy for the fraud (FOXNews.com 2005b). In January 2006, a court ordered Scrushy to pay HealthSouth approximately $48 million for bonuses he received based on fraudulent profit figures (Dade 2006).

Other Legal Issues

In April 2006, Scrushy settled the SEC's civil suit by agreeing to pay $81 million (Reeves 2007). This figure was divided into $77.5 million of ill-gotten gains and $3.5 million in civil penalties as required under the provisions of the SOX Act. HealthSouth's founder was also barred from serving as an officer or director of a public company anytime in the future. Despite the multimillion dollar settlement, Scrushy dodged yet another bullet. If the SEC had won in court, Scrushy could have been fined as much as $786 million (plus interest) (Taub 2005). Having received credit for $71.5 million paid in other HealthSouth cases, Scrushy may not even pay the remaining $9.5 million if the court accepts his claim of poverty.

On June 29, 2006, Scrushy was found guilty of bribery and mail fraud. He was accused of paying former Alabama governor Don Siegelman $500,000 for a seat on the state board that licenses hospitals and other medical facilities (FOXNews.com 2005a). Scrushy's position on the board enabled him to influence state approval of HealthSouth's facilities throughout Alabama. Despite his felony conviction, Scrushy's luck seems to have held. He was sentenced to only six years and ten months in prison, not the 30 years recommended by prosecutors (Lattman 2007). Perhaps he will use his time in prison to prepare for the pending class action suits by HealthSouth's investors and bondholders.

Conclusion

Even though Scrushy was not found criminally liable for the HealthSouth fraud, some critics have convicted him of serious ethical lapses as the leader of a multinational corporation (Steffy 2006). As HealthSouth's founder and CEO for nearly two decades, he created a culture that valued profits over ethical business conduct and entitlement over corporate responsibility. He undermined HealthSouth's internal corporate governance safeguards against fraud and used his connections as a business mogul to further his personal ambitions and greed. Having founded a Fortune 500 company, he was unwilling to relinquish even a small part of his control to internal or external parties. If he was not a participant in the fraud, he should have been aware of it since he controlled everything that happened at HealthSouth. He was a slave to Wall Street's earnings estimates and a hands-on CEO who micromanaged his company's financial performance at every level. Scrushy's word was law, but there were no effective checks and balances on his actions as HealthSouth's CEO.

Aaron Beam, one of the Lifemark employees who helped Scrushy start HealthSouth, recalled his impression of Scrushy after meeting him for the first time in the early 80s: "I told my wife that I just interviewed either the biggest con artist I ever met or the most brilliant young man" (Roth, Liu, and Michaels 2003). What Beam did not realize at that time was that Scrushy was both. He led the company he founded to the pinnacle of success, but he was also responsible for the corporate culture that nurtured one of the worst accounting frauds in American history. Scrushy's acquittal in the HealthSouth trial and his settlement with the SEC have angered critics who are convinced he masterminded a multibillion dollar fraud. But he lost more than his bank account. Richard Scrushy's reputation is largely in tatters, and he can look forward to several years in prison reminiscing about the good old days when he really was the king of health care.

References

Abelson, Reed. "Who Picks the Critic?" *New York Times,* January 11, 2004, business/financial desk.

Abelson, Reed, and Milt Freudenheim. "Will an Imperial Boss Bend with the Times?" *New York Times,* October 6, 2002, business/financial desk.

_____. "The Scrushy Mix: So Strict and So Lenient," *NewYork Times,* April 20, 2003, business/financial desk.

CBSNews.com. "Cooking the Books," http://www.cbsnews.com/stories/2003/10/08/60minutes/main577217.shtml (accessed December 21, 2004).

Dade, Corey. "Executives on Trial: Scrushy Is Told to Repay Bonuses," *Wall Street Journal,* January 5, 2006, eastern edition.

Elkind, Peter. "Vulgarians at the Gate: How Ego, Greed, and Envy Turned MedPartners from a Hot Stock into a Wall Street Fiasco," *Fortune,* June 21, 1999.

Farrell, Greg. "Against the Odds, Scrushy Walks Out of Court Free Man," *USA Today,* June 29, 2005.

FOXNews.com. 2005a. "Fmr. Ala. Governor Don Siegelman Indicted for Racketeering, Conspiracy," 2005a, http://www.foxnews.com/story/0,2933,173633,00.html (accessed February 6, 2006).

_____. "HealthSouth Sues Scrushy for $76 Million," 2005b, http://www.foxnews.com/story/0,2933,180070,00.html (accessed January 5, 2006).

Freudenheim, Milt. "HealthSouth Pulls Back Its Forecast, but Wall St. Questions Explanation," *New York Times,* August 28, 2002, business/financial desk.

_____. "HealthSouth's Chief Made Timely Sale," *New York Times,* September 6, 2002, business/financial desk.

Grow, Brian. "All Scrushy, All the Time: HealthSouth's Embattled Ex-CEO Takes His Defense Directly to the People," *Business Week,* April 12, 2004.

_____. "Richard Scrushy's 'Amen Corner,'" BusinessWeek Only, January 20, 2006, http://www.businessweek.com/bwdaily/dnflash/han2006/nf20060120_4440_db016.htm (accessed January 23, 2006).

Haddad, Charles, Arlene Weintraub, and Brian Grow. "Too Good to Be True: Why HealthSouth Began Deep-Frying the Chain's Books," *Business Week,* April 14, 2003.

HealthSouth Corporation. Proxy statement, 1999, http://www.sec.gov/Archives/edgar/data/785161/0001005150-99-000323.txt (accessed May 30, 2005).

Heylar, John. "The Insatiable King Richard," *Fortune,* July 7, 2003.

Hubbard, Russell. "Rocket-Like Ascent Tumbles Back with Crushed Investors," *Birmingham News,* April 13, 2003.

Lattman, Peter. "HealthSouth's Richard Scrushy Is behind Bars," *Wall Street Journal Online,* June 29, 2007, http://www.blogs.wsj.com/law/2007/06/29/healthsouths-richard-scrushy-is-behind-bars (accessed July 21, 2007).

Liu, Betty. "Southern Success Story Still a Big Hit in Alabama: Fraud Case Fails to Take Shine Off 'Generous' Founder at HealthSouth, *Financial Times,* March 22, 2003.

Lublin, Joann S., and Ann Carrns. "Directors Had Lucrative Links at HealthSouth," *Wall Street Journal,* April 11, 2003, eastern edition.

Mollenkamp, Carrick. "Missed Signal: Accountant Tried in Vain to Expose HealthSouth Fraud; Ex-Employee Took His Case to Auditors, Then Web—but Convinced No One; What about the Others?" *Wall Street Journal,* May 20, 2003, eastern edition.

Mollenkamp, Carrick, and Dan Moore. "Legal Woes Don't Crush Scrushy—Laws Passed in 2002, Witnesses Will Be Tested by Expected Trial of HealthSouth's Former Chief," *Wall Street Journal,* June 27, 2003, eastern edition.

Morse, Dan, and Chad Terhune. 2005. "Clean Sweep: HealthSouth's Scrushy Is Acquitted; Verdict Shows Challenges for Sarbanes-Oxley Act; SEC Suit Still Ahead," *Wall Street Journal*, June 29, 2005, eastern edition.

MSNBC.com. 2005. "Mostly Black Jury Chosen in Scrushy Trial," http://msnbc.com.id/6863221 (accessed January 25, 2005).

Reeves, Jay. "Scrushy Settles SEC Lawsuit for $81 Million," *USA Today*, April 23, 2007.

Romero, Simon, and Reed Abelson. "HealthSouth Officials Seek to Cut Deals with the U.S.," *New York Times*, March 24, 2003, business/financial desk.

Roth, Lisa Fingeret, Betty Liu, and Adrian Michaels. "Diagnosis of Fraud," *Financial Times*, April 15, 2003.

Roth, Lisa Fingeret, and Adrian Michaels. "Judge Questioned Links of HealthSouth Figures," *Financial Times*, March 29, 2003.

———. "Investors Worried about HealthSouth Last Year—Corporate Governance Shareholders Were Questioning Scrushy 7 Months Before Chairman Was Accused of 1.4 Billion Accounting Fraud," *Financial Times*, April 15, 2003.

Shaw, Helen, and Dave Cook. "Scrushy Acquitted on All Counts," CFO.com, June 28, 2005, http://www.cfo.com/article.cfm/4076776?f=related (accessed November 1, 2005).

Shmukler, Evelina, and Dan Morse. 2005. "HealthSouth's Scrushy Is Painted as Micromanager," *Wall Street Journal*, February 4, 2005, eastern edition.

Squeo, Ann Marie. "Acquittal Casts Cloud over Sarbanes-Oxley Law," *Wall Street Journal*, June 29, 2005, eastern edition.

Steffy, Loren. "Scrushy's Worst Crime Was Business Ineptitude," *Houston Chronicle*, July 1, 2005.

Taub, Stephen. "SEC Pursues Civil Case against Scrushy," CFO.com, July 8, 2005, http://www.cfo.com/article.cfm/4168705?f=search (accessed February 2, 2006).

Terhune, Chad, and Carrick Mollenkamp. "HealthSouth Independent Probe Had Gaps," *Wall Street Journal*, June 9, 2003, eastern edition.

Terhune, Chad, Carrick Mollenkamp, and Ann Carrns. "Close Relations: Inside Alleged Fraud at HealthSouth, a "Family" Plot—CEO Scrushy Cultivated Loyalties as Staffers Fixed Books, Played in His Band—'a Magical, Magical World,'" *Wall Street Journal*, April 3, 2003, eastern edition.

Terhune, Chad, and Evelina Shmukler. "'Scrushy Trial' on Local TV Is Family Affair," *Wall Street Journal*, February 15, 2005, eastern edition.

Thomas, Landon, Jr. "Questions about Investor on Board of HealthSouth," *New York Times*, April 17, 2003, business/financial desk.

U.S. Department of Justice. "HealthSouth Founder and Former CEO Richard Scrushy Charged in $2.7 Billion Accounting Fraud Conspiracy," 2003, http://www.usdoj.gov/opa/pr/2003/November/03_crm_603.htm (accessed May 26, 2004).

U.S. District Court. Northern District of Alabama, Southern Division. HealthSouth Corporation Securities Litigation; Exhibit A: HealthSouth's Daily Stock Prices, 2004, http://www.blbglaw.com/complaints/HealthSouthFactualBasis-CpltEXH.pdf (accessed February 21, 2006).

U.S. House of Representatives. Committee on Energy and Commerce. "The Financial Collapse of HealthSouth, Part 1," 2003, 108th Congress, first session. http://frwebgate.access.gpo.gov/cgi-bin/getdoc.cgi?dbname=108_house_hearings&docid=f:89963.pdf (accessed June 17, 2004).

———. "The Financial Collapse of HealthSouth, Part 2," 2003, 108th Congress, first session. http://a257.g.akamaitech.net/7/257/2422/19mar20041100/www.access.gpo.gov/congress/house/pdf/108hrg/91232.pdf (accessed June 20, 2004).

Ward, Andrew. "Black Appeal Is Scrushy's Guiding Light: The HealthSouth Boss's Fraud Indictment Prompted a Radical Change in His Lifestyle and Image," *Financial Times,* June 29, 2005.

See No Evil; Hear No Evil; Speak No Evil: Ernst & Young's Ethical Responsibility for the HealthSouth Fraud

27

STEVEN A. SOLIERI
ANDREW J. FELO
JOAN HODOWANITZ

Contents

Ernst & Young Meets "The King of Health Care"

Richard Scrushy, the reputed "king of health care" in the late 1990s, used money invested by business associates and a venture capital firm to found HealthSouth Corporation in Birmingham, Alabama, in 1984. Thanks to guaranteed payments from Medicare and Medicaid, HealthSouth was able to report a respectable $20 million in revenues by 1986. Scrushy knew he had created a highly profitable business model for outpatient health care services, but he needed to make HealthSouth a publicly traded company to finance its future growth. In accordance with Securities and Exchange Commission (SEC) regulations, he hired the accounting firm of Ernst & Young LLP to audit the company's financial statements and supporting records in preparation for the initial public offering (IPO) of HealthSouth's stock. Among other tasks, Ernst & Young investigated HealthSouth's senior managers to ensure their assertions concerning the company's financial condition could be trusted. Thus began a 17-year relationship between Ernst & Young and "the king of health care."

Ernst & Young Ignores Early Signs of Trouble

HealthSouth's profits increased steadily over the next ten years. By 1994, the company's revenues had topped the billion-dollar mark, and HealthSouth was the acknowledged industry leader for rehabilitative health care services. (Heylar 2003, 83–84) As HealthSouth's independent auditor throughout this period, Ernst & Young always gave the company a clean bill of financial health. Despite the audit firm's vote of confidence in its client's financial statements, documents exist that prove the health care giant was committing fraud as early as 1993. Many critics argue that Ernst & Young's failure to act on early signs of trouble enabled the HealthSouth accounting fraud to continue for years, eventually costing investors at least $2.7 billion.

According to a lawsuit filed by the Retirement System of Alabama (RSA), G. Marcus Neas, Ernst & Young's partner in charge of HealthSouth's 1993 financial audit, knew that the company had overstated its earnings by $27 million. Neas used his knowledge to force a HealthSouth executive to accept his guidance on how to account for a $3 million investment banking fee. Neas allegedly told the executive: "Don't question me on this; I turned my head on the $27 million" (U.S. District Court, Northern District of Alabama, Southern Division 2004a, 5–6, 191). If the allegation is true, it means that Ernst & Young knew HealthSouth was committing fraud as early as 1993 but did nothing to stop it.

Like all accounting firms, Ernst & Young reviewed its relationship with its audit clients on an annual basis to determine whether it should retain those clients for another year. Such reviews are designed to reduce the likelihood of retaining high-risk, fraud-prone clients that may expose the audit firm to costly lawsuits. As part of the client retention process, Ernst & Young hired the Center for Financial Research & Analysis (CFRA), a Maryland-based company, to assess the quality of HealthSouth's earnings in 1993 and 1994. The CFRA report was initially sent to James Conley, Ernst & Young's professional practice director, at the firm's national headquarters in New

York City. After reading the report's disturbing findings, Conley forwarded the document to Neas with the following note: "*Please do not copy or send the report to the client*. Please review the comments in this report, investigate them as you deem appropriate, and prepare a written report to me by April 19" (Center for Financial Research and Analysis 1995, 1). No one at Ernst & Young knows what actions Neas took, if any (U.S. House of Representatives 2003, part II, 104). He may have done nothing at all.

Perhaps the most prescient, and damning, part of the report was the CFRA assessment of HealthSouth's weak control environment (i.e., its operating philosophy, policies, and standards of conduct that set the ethical tone for the entire organization). Often referred to as "the tone at the top," the control environment reflects management's attitudes and core values. According to the CFRA, the weaknesses in HealthSouth's control environment were rooted in systemic problems with the board of directors, a critical corporate governance safeguard against fraud:

> In general, we feel that the outside members of a public company's Board of Directors should lack any significant affiliation with either [sic] the company, its executive officers, or the other Board members outside of their service as directors and their ownership stake in the Company. We also advocate that the Board should be comprised of individuals with a diverse set of experiences and perspectives. Furthermore, we feel that a public company should avoid engaging in any significant related-party transactions with either its directors or officers, or with any relatives of such directors or officers...*HEALTHSOUTH's Board appears lacking with regard to such criteria*. (Center for Financial and Research Analysis 1995, 6; emphasis added)

The CFRA report criticized HealthSouth for maintaining a combined audit and compensation committee at a time when most public companies separated these functions to avoid potential conflicts of interest. Not surprisingly, HealthSouth's audit and compensation committee met just once in 1993, even though similar committees in other public corporations usually met several times per year. The report also expressed concern over Richard Scrushy's extraordinarily generous compensation package as chief executive officer (CEO) and noted the growing shareholder unrest at the board's willingness to increase his stock options:

> It also deserves noting that HEALTHSOUTH had planned last year to implement a new, more generous executive stock option plan—but suffered the indignity of seeing the proposal voted down at a shareholder meeting in December 1994. While we consider it encouraging that the stockholders took this bold step in preventing what they considered an unwarranted transfer of investors' future wealth into certain executive officer pockets, *we are nevertheless troubled by HEALTHSOUTH's attempt to implement a plan that institutional*

investors (who reportedly led the charge against the stock option plan) would consider out of bounds. (Center for Financial and Research Analysis 1995, 7; emphasis added)

When Ernst & Young's representatives were questioned about this report during congressional hearings in November 2003, they could not explain why no one objected to retaining HealthSouth as an audit client (U.S. House of Representative 2003, part II, 104). Neas, the partner who handled the Health-South audit in 1993, was long retired.

More Red Flags

From 1995 to 1997, Cahaba Government Benefits Administration, a division of Blue Cross Blue Shield of Alabama, served as HealthSouth's fiscal intermediary. While processing HealthSouth's Medicare claims in 1996 and 1997, Cahaba noticed certain irregularities and started an investigation (U.S. District Court, Northern District of Alabama, Southern Division 2004a, 109). Cahaba determined that HealthSouth had violated Medicare regulations by submitting claims for services provided by unqualified personnel (i.e., support staff) and billing at an individual rate rather than the lower group rate. Ernst & Young should have been suspicious of HealthSouth's billing policies and the management team that put those policies in place, but it was not.

Like many public corporations, HealthSouth has been the subject of several lawsuits over the years. One such suit filed by Dewayne Manning, a former employee, accused the company of improper billing practices and other illegal acts dating back to 1996. In April 1998, a former HealthSouth patient named James Devage sued HealthSouth for overbilling Medicare. Mark Mandel and John Darling, two other patients, filed similar suits, and the federal government eventually joined both of these suits (U.S. District Court, Northern District of Alabama, Southern Division 2004a, 108, 111–112). Even though these suits and the government's participation were a matter of public record, Ernst & Young never considered dropping HealthSouth as a high-risk audit client.

Regulatory Changes Affecting HealthSouth and the Health Care Industry

In addition to ignoring the significance of multiple lawsuits against its audit client, Ernst & Young failed to consider how regulatory changes in the health care industry increased HealthSouth's risk of fraud. In 1997, President Clinton signed the Balanced Budget Act (BBA), a landmark piece of legislation that cut back Medicare payments to companies like Health-South by \$115 billion over a 5-year period (Haddad, Weintraub, and Grow 2003, 71). This bill triggered a dramatic decrease in revenues throughout the health care industry.

At first, Richard Scrushy, HealthSouth's CEO, insisted that the BBA would have no effect on his company's bottom line. But in September 1998, he suddenly issued a profit warning to HealthSouth's investors and Wall Street analysts (Abelson and Freudenheim 2002). The company's net income plunged 86 percent, from \$330 million in 1997 to \$46 million in 1998, and its stock price fell from its previous high of \$30.56 on April 20, 1998, to \$8.31 on October 7, 1998 (U.S. District Court, Northern District of Alabama, Southern Division 2004b, 6, 8). Many analysts suspect that this setback forced the HealthSouth fraud into high gear. By 2000, the company reported net income of \$278 million (HealthSouth Corporation 2001, 26) when, in fact, it should have reported a net loss of \$364 million (HealthSouth Corporation 2005, 66).

In 2000, *Modern Healthcare,* a major health care industry journal, surveyed 105 post acute-care providers, including HealthSouth, to determine how these companies were doing financially three years after implementation of the BBA (*Modern Healthcare* 2000, 20). The journal found that, except for HealthSouth, the largest health care companies tended to have the worst outcomes. HealthSouth's remarkable profitability at a time when its major competitors were struggling to recover from record losses should have triggered alarm bells at Ernst & Young, but the audit firm made no effort to conduct more extensive audit procedures to determine whether its client was committing fraud.

Whistleblowers on the Internet

HealthSouth's financial reports and industry journals were not the only sources of red flags with regard to HealthSouth's extraordinary profitability. The anonymity of the Internet offered disgruntled HealthSouth employees a relatively safe outlet for their concerns. Between July and October 1998, Peter Krum, a former HealthSouth food service manager, posted a number of defamatory messages on Yahoo! concerning the company, CEO Richard Scrushy, and Scrushy's wife, Leslie (Gibb 1998). Using the screen name, "I Am Dirk Diggler," a not so subtle reference to a porn-star character in the 1997 movie *Boogie Nights,* Krum accused Scrushy of "bilking taxpayers by sapping Medicare reimbursement." He also described the company's managers as "egotistical yahoos" and warned readers that "this house of cards was starting to collapse." Krum, however, proved to be his own worst enemy. In addition to accusing Scrushy of Medicare fraud, Krum claimed that he and Scrushy's wife had an extramarital relationship. HealthSouth's legal department promptly sued Krum for libel and forced him to post an Internet message retracting his claims. Krum's references to Scrushy's wife destroyed his credibility, but it seemed that he knew more about HealthSouth's accounting gimmicks than Ernst & Young knew or admitted knowing.

Another HealthSouth employee, Kimberly Landry, also posted messages about HealthSouth on a Yahoo! bulletin board in the late 1990s (Moss 1999). She changed the spelling of Richard Scrushy's surname to "Screwshe," labeled him a "crook" and a "megalomaniac," and warned readers that HealthSouth's stock was about to fall because the company paid too much money to acquire some of its facilities. In an interview with the *New York Times,* she accused HealthSouth of "keeping the numbers up" by accepting certain Medicare-eligible patients even though it could not provide adequate care for them (Abelson and Freudenheim 2003). HealthSouth initially responded by suing Landry for defamation, but it later dropped the suit citing "an inappropriate use of its resources." No one knows if Ernst & Young read the Internet messages posted by Peter Krum and Kimberly Landry. If the audit firm had read them, it chose not to investigate them.

Notes from a Knowledgeable Shareholder: Smoke and Mirrors

In November 1998, two months after HealthSouth warned investors that it would miss the earnings targets that management had earlier projected, an anonymous individual identified only as "Fleeced Shareholder" sent a rather remarkable memo to the following recipients: Ernst & Young's chairman, the American Institute of Certified Public Accountants (AICPA), the Health Care Financing Administration (HCFA), *Business Week,* Morgan Stanley (a nationally known investment bank), Milberg Weiss (a law firm specializing in securities fraud and investor rights), and the SEC's Division of Enforcement.

Unlike the average investor, Fleeced Shareholder obviously knew a great deal about accounting and the "smoke and mirror" gimmicks that accountants sometimes use to cook their books. He began, quite appropriately: "You bring the smoke, I'll bring the mirrors. At least the market has shown the wisdom to devalue HS [HealthSouth] stock. Wish I got out in time." The writer then challenged the propriety of some of HealthSouth's accounting practices. Although the memo contained multiple addressees, Fleeced Shareholder's anger was directed primarily at Ernst & Young:

> How can the HS outpatient clinics treat patients without pre-certification, book the revenue, and carry it after being denied payment?
> How can the company carry tens of millions of dollars in accounts receivable that are well over 360 days?

How did the E&Y [Ernst & Young] auditors in Alabama miss this stuff?

Are these clever tricks to pump up the numbers, or something that a novice accountant could catch?

How is it that a year ago Vencor [a HealthSouth competitor] announced that the BBA [Balanced Budget Act] would have a major impact on its Tefra [Tax Equity and Fiscal Responsibility Act of 1982] reimbursement, but HS management, similarly affected by BBA cutbacks in all divisions, was mute? They were busy though, cashing out before the big hit.

Does anyone really believe that nonsense about managed care pressure? It's the Medicare, stupid.

If the accounting is slick, what do the cost reports look like?"

You people and I have been hoodwinked. This note is all that I can do about it. You all can do much more, if all you do is look into it to see if what I say is true. (Fleeced Shareholder Memo 1998)

Ironically, Fleeced Shareholder alerted several corporate governance watchdogs to HealthSouth's fraud almost five years before the fraud was exposed. Unfortunately, none of these watchdogs, not even Ernst & Young, bothered to connect the dots. Ernst & Young did assign two auditors who were not involved with HealthSouth's financial audits to investigate the allegations, but they concluded, quite erroneously, that the problems described by Fleeced Shareholder "had no impact on [HealthSouth's] financial statements." Based on those findings, the audit firm decided not to inform HealthSouth's audit committee or its board of directors about Fleeced Shareholder's allegations. Five years later, however, Fleeced Shareholder was fully vindicated.

Shareholder Proposals: Calls to Reform HealthSouth's Board of Directors

For most public companies, the board of directors is the first line of defense against frauds perpetrated by management and other employees. If the directors are not completely independent of management, the board may not be able to protect the shareholders' financial interests. Since institutional investors (e.g., pension funds and mutual funds) have more money at risk than the majority of individual investors, they are not shy about calling for corporate governance reforms. HealthSouth's institutional investors were rattled by the dramatic drop in the company's earnings in 1998 and placed much of the blame on a board that was not independent of management.

In 1998, the Iron Workers' Local No. 25 Pension Fund proposed that HealthSouth adopt the Council of Institutional Investors' (CII) criteria for director independence (HealthSouth Corporation 1998a, 10–12). The Iron Workers wanted to prevent the directors on HealthSouth's audit and compensation committee from having any "personal, financial, and/or professional relationships with the CEO or other executive officer." Not surprisingly, the board opposed the Iron Workers' proposal, arguing that HealthSouth's directors already met the New York Stock Exchange (NYSE) criteria for independence. The board also pointed out that adopting the CII criteria for independence would only serve to reduce corporate profits by preventing HealthSouth from appointing the most qualified business leaders as directors.

The Iron Workers' proposal was soundly defeated during the annual shareholders' meeting, receiving less than 20 percent of HealthSouth's voting shares (HealthSouth Corporation 1998b, 15). In 1999, however, the Longview Collective Investment Fund, another institutional investor, reintroduced the Iron Workers' proposal in a somewhat watered-down form (Health-South Corporation 1999a, 11–14). Longview proposed a board in which at least three quarters of the directors would be independent of management. It argued that six of the twelve directors on the then current board lacked independence because they were company insiders or part of an interlocking directorate (a situation in which two boards of directors have at least one director in common). Longview also suggested that the board's lack of independence was responsible for the recent decline in HealthSouth's stock price and Richard Scrushy's overly generous compensation package as CEO:

> Our CEO was recently named as one of ten "executive pay anti-heroes" by Graef Crystal, an expert on executive pay, in a report prepared by the Council of Institutional Investors. Crystal's conclusion was based in part on Mr. Scrushy's drawing a base salary 350 percent above the market; a salary and bonus 592 percent above the market; and a total direct compensation that is 225 percent above the market (HealthSouth Corporation 1999a, 14).

Once again, HealthSouth's board of directors opposed the proposal, citing the same arguments used in 1998. It also blamed the recent drop in its stock price on an industry-wide decline in earnings and dismissed complaints about Scrushy's compensation as "a gratuitous attack" on HealthSouth's CEO and chairman of the board. Although only 15 percent of voting shares supported the proposal (HealthSouth Corporation 1999b, 21), the number of company insiders on the board dropped from five to two in 2000. Unfortunately, the problem of close financial ties between certain directors and management remained.

Like other independent audit firms, Ernst & Young was required to read its clients' annual reports, proxy statements, and related reports to ensure such documents did not include misleading or fraudulent financial information. There is no way the audit firm can claim it did not know about the shareholders' concerns. By themselves, these proposals may not have justified conducting a more extensive financial audit at HealthSouth. But when the proposals are considered in conjunction with so many other red flags, a far more intensive audit would have made sense.

HealthSouth's Pristine Audits: Got Toilet Paper?

Even though Ernst & Young was not paying close attention to the cumulative effect of multiple red flags in HealthSouth's finance and accounting departments, it apparently did a very thorough job when performing what was known as "pristine audits." Teresa Sanders, HealthSouth's former chief accounting officer (CAO), testified before Congress that Richard Scrushy ordered her to develop a 50-point checklist known as a "pristine audit" (U.S. House of Representatives 2003, part II, 25, 38). The word "audit," however, is clearly a misnomer because the checklist focused on cleanliness of facilities, maintenance standards for equipment, and similar issues, rather than on the accuracy of financial statements and properly maintained accounting records. Despite Sanders's objections, Scrushy tasked Ernst & Young, rather than HealthSouth personnel, to conduct these pseudo-audits. Ironically, HealthSouth paid Ernst & Young a total of $4 million for pristine audits between 2000 and 2002, but only $3.22 million for SEC-mandated financial audits during the same period (Weil 2003). During the 2003 public hearings on the HealthSouth fraud, Congressman James Greenwood (R-Pennsylvania) suggested the following scenario to explain why Ernst & Young never reported its client's illegal activities:

> And in retrospect, and I am not casting the tiniest dispersion [sic] on Ernst & Young when I say this, in retrospect when you see an indictment that says that the fraud began in 1996, *do you wonder whether Mr. Scrushy said to himself: I am about to start cooking some serious books here and I have an auditing company that might find out about this, let me invent a lovely sweetener of the pot?* Has that thought occurred to you? (U.S. House of Representatives 2003, part II, 120; emphasis added)

Richard Dandurand, an Ernst & Young partner, objected strongly to Greenwood's suggestion and insisted that HealthSouth was just one of thousands of his firm's audit clients. Nevertheless, there is no denying the fact that HealthSouth was also Ernst & Young's highest paying client in the state of Alabama.

The Michael Vines e-Mail: Spitting in the Wind

Michael Vines, a former HealthSouth bookkeeper, suspected that his company was committing fraud and tried, albeit unsuccessfully, to expose it (Mollenkamp 2003). Although he lacked a college degree in accounting, Vines worked in HealthSouth's Fixed Asset Management Department from April 1997 until he quit his job in May 2002 (U.S. House of Representatives

2003, part I, 27). He was responsible for processing transactions involving the purchase of major pieces of equipment.

By late 2001, Vines began to suspect that HealthSouth was overstating its reported earnings by transferring income statement expenses to fictitious balance sheet asset accounts in violation of generally accepted accounting principles. When a purchase is recorded as an expense, it is reported on the income statement, and it reduces the company's net income by the entire amount immediately. When, however, it is recorded as an asset, it is reported on the balance sheet (a process called "capitalization") and has no effect on income. The asset's cost is amortized over a period of several years and recorded as an expense each year (a process called "depreciation"). According to Vines, HealthSouth's accountants recorded expenses as assets only if the cost was under $5,000. The accountants, some of whom were former Ernst & Young employees, knew that the audit firm ignored individual expenses below this threshold.

Vines told his boss, Cathy Edwards, that he would not transfer expenses to the balance sheet unless she personally signed off on the accounting entries. (Edwards was one of the many HealthSouth employees who later pleaded guilty to the fraud.) In December 2001, Ernst & Young, as part of its annual financial audit, conducted a routine review of HealthSouth's procedures for depreciating certain balance sheet assets. The review posed a serious problem for Edwards because many assets on HealthSouth's balance sheet were nothing more than expenses that should have been reported on past income statements and that would have reduced net income. The assets did not exist. Because there were no invoices or other documents proving the existence of these assets, Edwards used a computer and scanner to alter the invoices of actual assets, thereby creating the missing documentation. Ernst & Young never realized that at least $1 billion of the assets recorded on the company's balance sheet existed only in Cathy Edwards's fertile imagination.

Aware of the growing public furor over the Enron fraud and the government's plan to increase criminal penalties for corporate fraud, Vines started having second thoughts about working for a Fortune 500 company that was obviously cooking its books. In June 2002, 1 month after he quit his job, he sent an e-mail to Ernst & Young urging the audit firm to review the accounting transactions in three specific accounts: minor equipment, repairs and maintenance, and public information. Unfortunately, Vines never told the auditors to look for transactions below the $5,000 threshold or to verify the existence of certain balance sheet assets. He assumed, incorrectly, that the auditors would examine all transactions in those accounts regardless of the dollar amount. By February 2003, he realized that Ernst & Young had done nothing to stop the HealthSouth fraud. Using the alias "Junior," he posted the following message on Yahoo's bulletin board: "What I know about the accounting at HRC [HealthSouth] will be the blow that will bring HRC to its knees" (Mollenkamp 2003). Unfortunately, no one at Ernst & Young took his allegations seriously until after the SEC charged HealthSouth and its CEO with defrauding investors of billions of dollars. Vines was simply written off as "a disgruntled employee" who was fired for fraternizing with women (U.S. House of Representatives 2003, part II, 96).

Assessing the Likelihood of Fraud at HealthSouth: Ernst & Young's Checklist Mentality

In preparation for public hearings on the HealthSouth fraud, Congress subpoenaed several documents from Ernst & Young's confidential work-ing papers. Congress later posted these documents on the Internet, thereby giving investors and other corporate stakeholders a rare glimpse into the secret world of financial audits. One of the most interesting of the subpoe-naed documents was a 2002 checklist entitled "Internal Control and Fraud Considerations." Ernst & Young used it to decide whether or not to retain HealthSouth as a financial audit client.

Ernst & Young was hardly unique in its use of checklists; most audit firms depend on them to document various audit functions. A checklist, however, is a double-edged sword that can cause major problems if it is not used prop-erly. On the one hand, it is a valuable mnemonic aid that ensures the auditor does not skip important steps in the audit process or ignore important infor-mation. On the other hand, its overuse can result in a checklist mentality—a form of "tunnel vision" in which the auditor misses the big picture while mindlessly checking off a series of seemingly unrelated items. Unfortunately, Ernst & Young seems to have developed a checklist mentality during its 2002 assessment of HealthSouth's internal controls and risk of fraud.

Dated December 31, 2002, the checklist was completed three months after the SEC first announced its investigation into allegations of insider trading by HealthSouth CEO Richard Scrushy. Even though the completed checklist raised several red flags with regard to HealthSouth's management, finance, and accounting functions, the audit firm concluded that its client's internal controls reduced the risk of fraud to an acceptable level. These red flags included, but were not limited to, "management's excessive inter-est in maintaining or increasing the client's stock price or trend earnings," Scrushy's domineering personality as a CEO "without effective oversight by the board of directors or audit committee," an increase in "public criticism or litigation," and an SEC investigation (Ernst & Young 2002, 5, 10, 12). Ernst & Young erroneously credited HealthSouth's management with creating an effective system of internal controls to prevent and detect fraud:

Overall, we believe that management has designed an environment for success. As a result of this environment, management has designed sufficient controls and oversight functions in order to prevent instances of material misstatement of financial statements. We believe that management is ethical, competent, and fully aware of all potential business developments. The oversight function of the Company has also been designed to prevent material misstatement of the financial statements. We believe the board of directors and audit committee oversight provides adequate control of management as well as provides adequate direction of the Company. (Ernst & Young 2002, 10)

The audit firm did note certain problems with HealthSouth's Internal Audit Department but, once again, it downplayed the significance of those problems (Ernst & Young 2002, 18). In addition to being poorly trained and severely understaffed (no more than 10 internal auditors to handle up to 2,000 clinics), HealthSouth's internal auditors were denied access to corporate-level accounting data (U.S. House of Representatives 2003, part I, 40–42, 49, 60–62). Scrushy personally tasked his internal auditors to perform operational audits, not financial audits, at various health clinics. Operational audits focused on how personnel performed their duties, whether procedures were followed, and similar matters. They did not include examination of accounting records, the proper recording of cash receipts or disbursement, and other aspects of financial operations. Scrushy did not allow the internal auditors to track the accounting data that the clinics forwarded to corporate headquarters in Birmingham for inclusion in the company's consolidated financial statements. That task he reserved for Ernst & Young. James Lamphron, the Ernst & Young partner who supervised HealthSouth's financial audits in 2000 and 2001, testified before Congress that the audit firm did not care that Scrushy's internal auditors played no role in auditing the company's consolidated financial statements:

[W]e were not in our audit process going to place much reliance on the work that internal audit did. I mean, let me say that prior to today [November 5, 2003], there was no requirement. Until yesterday, as a matter of fact, that a company has to have an internal audit department...And companies can choose to employ them several ways. They can direct them toward operational auditing or exclusively in operational areas, which we knew that it was they did. And that meant to us that we are not going to place much reliance on their work....So we put in thousands of hours doing the kind of work that internal audit might do. (U.S. House of Representatives 2003, part II, 106–107)

Lamphron ignored the fact that the head of HealthSouth's Internal Audit Department reported directly to the CEO rather than to the audit committee. According to the Institute of Internal Auditors (IIA), the organization that certifies internal auditors, internal auditors should report a CEO who abuses his or her corporate power to the audit committee. This was not an option at HealthSouth. In addition, Richard Scrushy had personally recruited many of HealthSouth's internal auditors from local colleges, and some lacked the professional training and experience to function effectively as accounting watchdogs. Many of these recruits were extremely loyal to "King Richard," the man who gave them jobs at a Fortune 500 company (Terhune, Mollenkamp, and Carrns 2003). Clearly, Ernst & Young should have asked why HealthSouth was not using its internal auditors to prevent corporate fraud. Considering the prevalence of Medicare and Medicaid fraud in recent years, a prudent company would take advantage of every possible safeguard.

Ernst & Young's checklist also contained a summary of the audit firm's discussions with selected members of HealthSouth's management team. Based on interviews with six senior managers, the audit firm concluded that management had not identified "significant instances of fraud. There have been [a] few isolated issues reported through the Corporate Compliance Hotline, but upon follow-up by management, the issues were determined to be minor or not systemic" (Ernst & Young 2002, 21). Ironically, three of the six managers who were interviewed—William Owens, Tadd McVay, and Emery Harris—played key roles in the fraud and lied when interviewed. Unfortunately, Ernst & Young lost its professional skepticism and accepted management's assertions at face value. If the audit firm had pursued even a handful of the red flags it uncovered during its 17-year relationship with HealthSouth, it probably would have uncovered the fraud and saved investors millions, if not billions, of dollars.

Ernst & Young's Victim Mentality

When Lamphron, an Ernst & Young partner, testified before Congress in November 2003, he tried to paint a picture of his firm as just another victim of the HealthSouth fraud:

> [W]e sat down and met with [the Corporate Compliance Department] face-to-face. There were two Ernst & Young partners and another person there. We asked them, tell us about activities in the compliance department. Tell us about everything that has come to your attention, whether resolved or whatever the status. Tell us anything that might have any effect on the financial statements. And they looked us in the eye and lied to us. (U.S. House of Representatives 2003, part II, 117)

Lamphron's version of events at HealthSouth did not mesh with the account given by at least one key witness during CEO Richard Scrushy's criminal trial in 2005. Emery Harris, HealthSouth's vice president of finance, was 1 of 15 employees who pled guilty to participating in the fraud. During his trial, Harris testified that Ernst & Young "had regularly turned a blind eye to material issues during the course of its audits" (U.S. District Court, Northern District of Alabama, Southern District 2004a, 7). He also accused Ernst & Young of giving HealthSouth a clean bill of health on its financial statements even though the auditor "had open audit questions on those financial statements and concerns about the accounting practices being utilized by the company." According to Harris, Ernst & Young was motivated by its desire to continue "its lucrative relationship with a long-standing client." But that relationship ended in March 2003 when HealthSouth fired Ernst & Young as its independent auditor. If the audit firm did, indeed, put profit ahead of its duty to protect the investing public, it was guilty of the most serious ethical lapses of all: greed.

Marshalling the Troops: Ernst & Young Gets Back to the Basics

Unlike HealthSouth and its CEO, Ernst & Young avoided indictment by the SEC or the Department of Justice (DOJ) for its role in a $2.7 billion accounting fraud. But the fraud and its aftermath proved to be a major wake-up call for the audit firm's leadership. On December 1, 2005, James Turley, Ernst & Young's chairman, gave a landmark speech to the U.S. Chamber of Commerce in Washington, D.C. Although Turley never mentioned HealthSouth by name, he made it clear that the audit firm had learned a number of important lessons since Enron's fall and the subsequent wave of accounting frauds. He admitted that his firm "has taken some shots from regulators and others over the last several years, and I'm here to tell you that we deserved some of those shots....The times have taught us the dangers of being arrogant...of not listening." He also acknowledged the accounting profession's role as a public servant and financial watchdog: "While the public may not fully know what we do or how we do it, they count on us to help keep the playing field fair and balanced." But he was probably thinking of HealthSouth and its autocratic CEO Richard Scrushy when he told his audience:

> Let's stop and remember. It wasn't long ago that public company auditors were being criticized for being too cozy with clients, for underpricing audit work to sell other services, or simply for not auditing enough....The public has seen imperial CEOs, since collared and cuffed, acting as if they, and not shareholders, owned the company. Such examples—while clearly exceptions—have broad-brushed the reputations of every corporate leader, myself included. (Turley 2005)

Turley also acknowledged that "[good] auditing is too often not a sufficient defense against the filing of legal claims." When a public corporation is convicted of fraud, its independent auditor is almost always the target of very costly lawsuits.

Hopefully, the lessons of the HealthSouth fraud have not been lost on Ernst & Young. Perhaps those lessons prompted Turley to reassure his audience that, after much "soul-searching," his firm decided to return to its roots: "We and others got caught up in a '90s-era rush to become one-stop global shops, hoping to provide not only our core services, but also hoping to be the biggest technology consulting firms and even the biggest law firms. Those days are over." Turley even chose an appropriate quote from President Harry Truman to end his speech: "Always do right, it will gratify some people, and astonish the rest."

Epilogue: Ernst & Young and the Courts

The SEC never filed suit against Ernst & Young for its role in the HealthSouth fraud, but it did publicly reprimand the audit firm for giving HealthSouth bad advice on how to classify pristine audit fees in its proxy statement. Based on that advice, HealthSouth included the fees paid for pristine audits in its "audit-related fees." Walter Schuetze, a former SEC chief accountant, explained the problem this way: "Calling [pristine audit fees] audit-related is false and misleading. It suggests that Ernst & Young was covering up the facts...When Ernst & Young deliberately misclassifies something that is clearly on its face wrong, that undermines everything that Ernst & Young says and does" (Weil 2003). The audit firm, for its part, rationalized its actions by insisting that "at the time of HealthSouth's disclosures, there were no SEC rules that defined audit-related services." Apparently, a legal loophole is better than no loophole at all.

Another legal loophole was probably the reason Ernst & Young never faced a criminal indictment for the HealthSouth fraud. Section 804 of the Sarbanes-Oxley (SOX) Act of 2002 sets the statute of limitation for securities fraud at "the *earlier* of (1) two years after the discovery of the facts constituting the violation; or (2) five years after such violation" (emphasis added). As a result, the DOJ was unable to file criminal charges against the audit firm based on allegations that its former partner, G. Marcus Neas, was aware of the fraud in 1993. The SEC did file a civil suit against Ernst & Young in May 2003 to prevent the audit firm from accepting new audit clients for a 6-month period, but that action was the result of an investigation into the firm's relationship with PeopleSoft, Inc. (Bryan-Low and Weil 2003). The SEC "attacked the firm's internal checks as inadequate" and accused it of "violating auditor-independence rules." Although HealthSouth was not mentioned in the suit, it appears that many of the problems plaguing Ernst & Young's relationship with People-Soft also played a role in the firm's relationship with HealthSouth.

Ernst & Young may have dodged a bullet with regard to disciplinary action by the DOJ and the SEC, but its legal problems from the HealthSouth fraud are far from over. On March 18, 2005, the firm filed a civil suit against HealthSouth in which it alleged that its former client deliberately concealed evidence of the accounting fraud from its auditor and, as a result, damaged the audit firm's reputation (HealthSouth Corporation 2005, 47). HealthSouth immediately returned the favor by countersuing Ernst & Young for gross negligence in the conduct of its financial audits from 1996 through 2002. Both suits are still pending.

The HealthSouth fraud notwithstanding, Ernst & Young is certainly no stranger to malpractice lawsuits. In 2003, it had the dubious honor of having "paid five of the 13 largest accounting malpractice settlements in history, more than any other firm, according to statistics compiled by Mark Cheffers, CEO of AccountingMalpractice.com" (Kahn 2003, 77). The audit firm must still deal with a major lawsuit filed by the RSA, one of HealthSouth's largest institutional investors.

Conclusion

Ernst & Young survived the HealthSouth fraud, although not without some permanent scars. The firm avoided criminal liability for failing to detect a major accounting fraud, but it will probably spend several years and large sums of money defending itself against civil suits and working to restore the public's trust. Ernst & Young forgot, at least temporarily, what the noted accounting ethicist, Abraham Briloff, calls its unwritten "covenant with society" to protect the financial interests of the investing public (Briloff 2002). The audit firm broke that covenant by failing to investigate thoroughly the many red flags involving fraud in the health care industry and HealthSouth's corrupt corporate governance structure and accounting practices.

Ernst & Young's behavior as HealthSouth's independent auditor calls to mind the old aphorism of the three monkeys: see no evil; hear no evil; speak no evil. Perhaps the audit firm did not want to look too closely for evidence of fraud or material misstatements in HealthSouth's financial statements. If Ernst & Young gave its client an unfavorable audit opinion, it would have risked losing its highest paying client in the state of Alabama. Whether or not the audit firm had a profit motive to overlook so many indicators of fraud, it is guilty of a lack of due diligence in the conduct of HealthSouth's annual financial audits. Ernst & Young was, at a minimum, an enabler of Health-South's $2.7 billion fraud. It committed a serious ethical lapse by neglecting its responsibilities as a public watchdog, thus putting the public's financial interests at great risk.

Ernst & Young steadfastly maintained that it was just another victim of HealthSouth's corrupt management. Certainly, only a court of law can convict the audit firm of misconduct. It may be some time before the public accepts the audit firm's opinions on financial statements at face value. Hopefully, as Chairman Turley told his audience, Ernst & Young has learned its lesson and is committed to doing the right thing. Only time will tell. If, however, Turley was merely telling his audience what it wanted to hear, Ernst & Young may yet meet the fate of its former (and now defunct) rival, Arthur Andersen LLP. Doing the right thing may bring in less revenue in the short term, but it is the only sure way to stay in the game for the long haul.

References

Abelson, Reed, and Milt Freudenheim. "Will an Imperial Boss Bend with the Times?" *New York Times,* October 6, 2002, business/financial desk.

_____. "The Scrushy Mix: So Strict and So Lenient," *NewYork Times,* April 20, 2003, business/financial desk.

Briloff, Abraham. "Accountancy and Society: A Covenant Desecrated," *CPA Journal,* December (2002), http://www.nysscpa.org/cpajournal/2002/1202/nv/nv3.htm (accessed February 7, 2004).

Bryan-Low, Cassell, and Jonathan Weil. "SEC Calls Ernst & Young's Internal Controls Inadequate," *Wall Street Journal,* May 30, 2003, eastern edition.

Center for Financial Research and Analysis, 1995, http://republicans.energycommerce.house.gov/108/Hearings/11052003hearing1123/69.pdf (accessed May28, 2004).

Ernst & Young LLP. "Internal Control and Fraud Considerations," 2002, http://republicans.energycommerce.house.gov/108/Hearings/11052003hearing1123/82.pdf (accessed May 24, 2004).

Fleeced Shareholder Memo, 1998, http://republicans.energycommerce.house.gov/108/Hearings/10162003hearing1110/hearing.14pdf (accessed May 28 2004).

Gibb, Tom. "Internet Attacks Bring Man Charges, Suit, Suspension," *Pittsburgh Post-Gazette,* November 8, 1998, http://www.post-gazette.com/regionstate/19981108cyber5.asp (accessed January 9, 2005).

Haddad, Charles, Arlene Weintraub, and Brian Grow. "Too Good to Be True: Why HealthSouth Began Deep-Frying the Chain's Books," *Business Week,* April 14, 2003.

HealthSouth Corporation. Proxy Statement, 1998a, http://www.sec.gov/Archives/edgar/data/785161/ 0001005150-98-000378.txt (accessed May 30, 2005).

_____. Second Quarter, Fiscal Year 1998 Form 10-Q, 1998b, http://www.sec.gov/Archives/edgar/data/785616/0001005150-98-000815.txt (accessed May 30, 2005).

_____. Proxy Statement, 1999a, http://www.sec.gov/Archives/edgar/data/785161/0001005150-99-000323.txt (accessed May 30, 2005).

_____. Second Quarter, Fiscal Year 1999 Form 10-Q, 1999b, http://www.sec.gov/Archives/edgar/data/785161/0001005150-99-000703.txt (accessed May 30, 2005).

_____. Form 10-K, 2001, http://www.sec.gov/Archives/edgar/data/785161/000100515001000286/0001005150-01-000286-0001.txt (accessed February 25, 2006).

_____. Restated Form 10-K, 2005, http://www.sec.gov/Archives/edgar/data/785161/000119312505131361/d10k.htm (accessed June 27, 2005).

Heylar, John. "The Insatiable King Richard," *Fortune,* July 7, 2003.

Kahn, Jeremy. "Angst & Young," *Fortune,* May 26, 2003.

Modern HealthCare. "Bigger Isn't Better; Our First Post-Acute-Care Survey Finds That Larger Firms Are Faring Worst in Turbulent Industry," July 24, 2000.

Mollenkamp, Carrick. "Missed Signal: Accountant Tried in Vain to Expose Health-South Fraud; Ex-Employee Took His Case to Auditors, Then Web—but Convinced No One; What about the Others?" *Wall Street Journal,* May 20, 2003, eastern edition.

Moss, Michael. "HealthSouth's CEO Exposes, Sues Anonymous Online Critics," *Wall Street Journal,* July 7, 1999, eastern edition.

Terhune, Chad, Carrick Mollenkamp, and Ann Carrns. "Close Relations: Inside Alleged Fraud at HealthSouth, a "Family" Plot—CEO Scrushy Cultivated Loyalties as Staffers Fixed Books, Played in His Band—'a Magical, Magical World,'" *Wall Street Journal,* April 3, 2003, eastern edition.

Turley, James. "Our Role in the Capital Markets…and Our Purpose as Professionals," 2005, http://www.ey.com/global/download.nsf/US/Turley_Speech_to_US_COC_12_01_05?$file/JST_COC_Speech_120105.pdf (accessed February 15, 2006).

U.S. District Court, Northern District of Alabama, Southern Division. 2004. HealthSouth Corporation Securities Litigation, 2004a, http://www.blbglaw.com/complaints/HealthSouthFactualBasisCplt8.2.04.pdf (accessed February 21, 2006).

_____. HealthSouth Corporation Securities Litigation; Exhibit A: HealthSouth's Daily Stock Prices, 2004b, http://www.blbglaw.com/complaints/HealthSouth-FactualBasisCpltEXH.pdf (accessed February 21, 2006).

U.S. House of Representatives. Committee on Energy and Commerce. "The Financial Collapse of HealthSouth, Part 1," 2003, 108th Congress, first session. http://frwebgate.access.gpo.gov/cgi-bin/getdoc.cgi?dbname=108_house_hearings&docid=f:89963.pdf (accessed June 17, 2004).

_____. "The Financial Collapse of HealthSouth, Part 2," 2003, 108th Congress, first session. http://a257.g.akamaitech.net/7/257/2422/19mar20041100/www.access.gpo.gov/congress/house/pdf/108hrg/91232.pdf (accessed June 20, 2004).

Weil, Jonathan. "What Ernst Did for HealthSouth," *Wall Street Journal,* June 11, 2003, eastern edition.

Index